Teach Yourself®
Microsoft®
Windows® 98

Teach Yourself®
Microsoft® Windows® 98

Al Stevens

with Brian Underdahl

IDG Books Worldwide, Inc.
An International Data Group Company

Foster City, CA • Chicago, IL • Indianapolis, IN • New York, NY

Teach Yourself® Microsoft® Windows® 98

Published by
IDG Books Worldwide, Inc.
An International Data Group Company
919 E. Hillsdale Blvd., Suite 400
Foster City, CA 94404
`www.idgbooks.com` (IDG Books Worldwide Web site)

Library of Congress Catalog Card Number: 98-88717

ISBN: 1-55828-594-6

Printed in the United States of America

10 9 8 7 6 5 4 3 2

1B/RU/RS/ZY/IN

Distributed in the United States by IDG Books Worldwide, Inc.

Distributed by Macmillan Canada for Canada; by Transworld Publishers Limited in the United Kingdom; by IDG Norge Books for Norway; by IDG Sweden Books for Sweden; by Woodslane Pty. Ltd. for Australia; by Woodslane (NZ) Ltd. for New Zealand; by Addison Wesley Longman Singapore Pte Ltd. for Singapore, Malaysia, Thailand, and Indonesia; by Norma Comunicaciones S.A. for Colombia; by Intersoft for South Africa; by International Thomson Publishing for Germany, Austria and Switzerland; by Distribuidora Cuspide for Argentina; by Livraria Cultura for Brazil; by Ediciencia S.A. for Ecuador; by Ediciones ZETA S.C.R. Ltda. for Peru; by WS Computer Publishing Corporation, Inc., for the Philippines; by Contemporanea de Ediciones for Venezuela; by Express Computer Distributors for the Caribbean and West Indies; by Micronesia Media Distributor, Inc. for Micronesia; by Grupo Editorial Norma S.A. for Guatemala; by Chips Computadoras S.A. de C.V. for Mexico; by Editorial Norma de Panama S.A. for Panama; by Wouters Import for Belgium; by American Bookshops for Finland. Authorized Sales Agent: Anthony Rudkin Associates for the Middle East and North Africa.

For general information on IDG Books Worldwide's books in the U.S., please call our Consumer Customer Service department at 800-762-2974. For reseller information, including discounts and premium sales, please call our Reseller Customer Service department at 800-434-3422.

For information on where to purchase IDG Books Worldwide's books outside the U.S., please contact our International Sales department at 317-596-5530 or fax 317-596-5692.

For consumer information on foreign language translations, please contact our Customer Service department at 800-434-3422, fax 317-596-5692, or e-mail rights@idgbooks.com.

For information on licensing foreign or domestic rights, please phone +1-650-655-3109.

For sales inquiries and special prices for bulk quantities, please contact our Sales department at 650-655-3200 or write to the address above.

For information on using IDG Books Worldwide's books in the classroom or for ordering examination copies, please contact our Educational Sales department at 800-434-2086 or fax 317-596-5499.

For press review copies, author interviews, or other publicity information, please contact our Public Relations department at 650-655-3000 or fax 650-655-3299.

For authorization to photocopy items for corporate, personal, or educational use, please contact Copyright Clearance Center, 222 Rosewood Drive, Danvers, MA 01923, or fax 978-750-4470.

is a trademark under exclusive license to IDG Books Worldwide, Inc., from International Data Group, Inc.

ABOUT IDG BOOKS WORLDWIDE

Welcome to the world of IDG Books Worldwide.

IDG Books Worldwide, Inc., is a subsidiary of International Data Group, the world's largest publisher of computer-related information and the leading global provider of information services on information technology. IDG was founded more than 30 years ago by Patrick J. McGovern and now employs more than 9,000 people worldwide. IDG publishes more than 290 computer publications in over 75 countries. More than 90 million people read one or more IDG publications each month.

Launched in 1990, IDG Books Worldwide is today the #1 publisher of best-selling computer books in the United States. We are proud to have received eight awards from the Computer Press Association in recognition of editorial excellence and three from Computer Currents' First Annual Readers' Choice Awards. Our best-selling ...For Dummies® series has more than 50 million copies in print with translations in 31 languages. IDG Books Worldwide, through a joint venture with IDG's Hi-Tech Beijing, became the first U.S. publisher to publish a computer book in the People's Republic of China. In record time, IDG Books Worldwide has become the first choice for millions of readers around the world who want to learn how to better manage their businesses.

Our mission is simple: Every one of our books is designed to bring extra value and skill-building instructions to the reader. Our books are written by experts who understand and care about our readers. The knowledge base of our editorial staff comes from years of experience in publishing, education, and journalism — experience we use to produce books to carry us into the new millennium. In short, we care about books, so we attract the best people. We devote special attention to details such as audience, interior design, use of icons, and illustrations. And because we use an efficient process of authoring, editing, and desktop publishing our books electronically, we can spend more time ensuring superior content and less time on the technicalities of making books.

You can count on our commitment to deliver high-quality books at competitive prices on topics you want to read about. At IDG Books Worldwide, we continue in the IDG tradition of delivering quality for more than 30 years. You'll find no better book on a subject than one from IDG Books Worldwide.

John Kilcullen
Chairman and CEO
IDG Books Worldwide, Inc.

Steven Berkowitz
President and Publisher
IDG Books Worldwide, Inc.

IDG is the world's leading IT media, research and exposition company. Founded, in 1964, IDG had 1997 revenues of $2.05 billion and has more than 9,000 employees worldwide. IDG offers the widest range of media options that reach IT buyers in 75 countries representing 95% of worldwide IT spending. IDG's diverse product and services portfolio spans six key areas including print publishing, online publishing, expositions and conferences, market research, education and training, and global marketing services. More than 90 million people read one or more of IDG's 290 magazines and newspapers, including IDG's leading global brands — Computerworld, PC World, Network World, Macworld and the Channel World family of publications. IDG Books Worldwide is one of the fastest-growing computer book publishers in the world, with more than 700 titles in 36 languages. The "...For Dummies®" series alone has more than 50 million copies in print. IDG offers online users the largest network of technology-specific Web sites around the world through IDG.net (http://www.idg.net), which comprises more than 225 targeted Web sites in 55 countries worldwide. International Data Corporation (IDC) is the world's largest provider of information technology data, analysis and consulting, with research centers in over 41 countries and more than 400 research analysts worldwide. IDG World Expo is a leading producer of more than 168 globally branded conferences and expositions in 35 countries including E3 (Electronic Entertainment Expo), Macworld Expo, ComNet, Windows World Expo, ICE (Internet Commerce Expo), Agenda, DEMO, and Spotlight. IDG's training subsidiary, ExecuTrain, is the world's largest computer training company, with more than 230 locations worldwide and 785 training courses. IDG Marketing Services helps industry-leading IT companies build international brand recognition by developing global integrated marketing programs via IDG's print, online and exposition products worldwide. Further information about the company can be found at www.idg.com.   10/8/98

Credits

Acquisitions Editor
Debra Williams Cauley

Development Editor
Ellen L. Dendy

Technical Editor
Art Brieva

Copy Editor
Ami Knox

Project Coordinator
Valery Bourke

Book Designers
Daniel Ziegler Design
Cátálin Dulfu
Kurt Krames

Layout and Graphics
Lou Boudreau
Linda M. Boyer
Angela F. Hunckler
Brent Savage
Kate Snell

Proofreaders
Christine Berman
Kelli Botta
Laura L. Bowman
Michelle Croninger
Nancy Price
Ethel M. Winslow
Janet M. Withers

Indexer
York Graphics Services

About the Authors

Al Stevens is a long-time columnist for *Dr. Dobbs Journal*, the leading programming magazine. He is a best-selling author for MIS:Press whose books include *Teach Yourself Windows 95*; *Teach Yourself C++, Fifth Edition*; *Windows 95 Games Programming*; and *C++ Database Development*, Second Edition.

Brian Underdahl has authored over 30 computer-related titles on a broad range of topics, including Windows 95, Microsoft Office, and the Internet. His recent efforts from IDG Books include *Presenting Windows 98 One Step at a Time*, *Windows 98 One Step at a Time*, *Internet Bible*, and *Small Business Computing For Dummies*.

To the fond memory of my uncle "Bing" Crosbie, the gentlest man I ever knew, and to his grandchildren, Elisabeth Anne Harper, Stephen Virgil Crosbie, and Joseph Andrew Crosbie, all of whom inherited Bing's good humor, caring nature, and kind heart.

— Al Stevens

Welcome to
Teach Yourself

Welcome to Teach Yourself, a series read and trusted by millions for nearly a decade. Although you may have seen the Teach Yourself name on other books, ours is the original. In addition, no Teach Yourself series has ever delivered more on the promise of its name than this series. That's because IDG Books Worldwide recently transformed Teach Yourself into a new cutting-edge format that gives you all the information you need to learn quickly and easily.

Readers told us that they want to learn by *doing* and that they want to learn as much as they can in as short a time as possible. We listened to you and believe that our new task-by-task format and suite of learning tools deliver the book you need to successfully teach yourself any technology topic. Features such as our Personal Workbook, which lets you practice and reinforce the skills you've just learned, help ensure that you get full value out of the time you invest in your learning. Handy cross-references to related topics and online sites broaden your knowledge and give you control over the kind of information you want, when you want it.

More Answers ...

In designing the latest incarnation of this series, we started with the premise that people like you, who are beginning to intermediate computer users, want to take control of their own learning. To do this, you need the proper tools to find answers to questions so you can solve problems now.

In designing a series of books that provides such tools, we created a unique and concise visual format. The added bonus: Teach Yourself books actually pack more information into their pages than other books written on the same subjects. Skill for skill, you typically get much more information in a Teach Yourself book. In fact, Teach Yourself books, on average, cover twice as many skills as other computer books — as many as 125 skills per book — so they're more likely to address your specific needs.

...In Less Time

We know you don't want to spend twice the time to get all this great information, so we provide lots of time-saving features:

▶ A modular task-by-task organization of information: Any task you want to perform is easy to find and includes simple-to-follow steps.

▶ A larger size than standard makes the book easy to read and convenient to use at a computer workstation. The large format also enables us to include many more illustrations — 500 screen shots show you how to get everything done!

▶ A Personal Workbook at the end of each chapter reinforces learning with extra practice, real-world applications for your learning, and questions and answers to test your knowledge.

▶ Cross-references appearing at the bottom of each task page refer you to related information, providing a path through the book for learning particular aspects of the software thoroughly.

▶ A Find It Online feature offers valuable ideas on where to go on the Internet to get more information or to download useful files.

▶ Take Note sidebars provide added-value information from our expert authors for more in-depth learning.

▶ An attractive, consistent organization of information helps you quickly find and learn the skills you need.

These Teach Yourself features are designed to help you learn the essential skills about a technology in the least amount of time, with the most benefit. We've placed these features consistently throughout the book, so you quickly learn where to go to find just the information you need — whether you work through the book from cover to cover or use it later to solve a new problem.

You will find a Teach Yourself book on almost any technology subject — from the Internet to Windows to Microsoft Office. Take control of your learning today, with IDG Books Worldwide's Teach Yourself series.

Teach Yourself
More Answers in Less Time

Search through the task headings to find the topic you want right away. To learn a new skill, search the Contents, chapter opener, or the extensive index to find what you need. Then find — at a glance — the clear task heading that matches it.

Go to this area if you want special tips, cautions, and notes that provide added insight into the current task.

Learn the concepts behind the task at hand and why the task is important in the real world. Time-saving suggestions and advice show you how to make the most of each skill.

After you learn the task at hand, you may have more questions, or you may want to read about other tasks related to that topic. Use the cross-references to find different information to make your learning more efficient.

Use the Find It Online element to locate Internet resources that provide more background, take you on interesting side trips, and offer additional tools for mastering and using the skills you need. (Occasionally you'll find a handy shortcut here.)

Copying and Moving Files

You can copy or move files and folders in Windows Explorer using two different methods: cut, copy, and paste or drag-and-drop.

The Windows Explorer Cut, Copy, and Paste buttons implement the Windows 98 Clipboard, a mechanism for exchanging data between applications and Windows 98 itself. Explorer uses the Clipboard as one way to copy folders, documents, and other files to other locations in the hierarchical file and folder system. The Clipboard is a temporary data storage bin. To move data using the Clipboard, you *cut* or *copy* data from a document into the Clipboard and *paste* data from the Clipboard into the same or another document.

For many people, using drag-and-drop is more convenient than using the Clipboard. You select a file or folder and then drag and drop the selected data to another location. To copy rather than move the data, press and hold Ctrl while you drag and drop the file or folder. (See the "Take Note" section for an exception to this method.) Another way to copy a file is to hold down the right mouse button when you drag the item onto a folder, release the mouse button when the item is over the desired folder, and select Copy Here from the shortcut menu.

You cannot have more than one file or folder with the same name in the same folder. If you try to move files or folders to a location that would result in

duplicates, Windows 98 asks you whether you want to replace the existing item with the new one. If you try to copy files in a manner that would produce duplicates, Windows 98 adds "Copy of" to the beginning of the filename.

TAKE NOTE

CUT WORKS DIFFERENTLY IN WINDOWS EXPLORER

In Windows Explorer, the Cut tool button works almost like the Copy tool button. Within an application, Cut deletes the original data after copying it to the Clipboard. With Explorer, Cut dims the icon of the original file or folder but does not delete the item itself. If you forget to paste the file or folder elsewhere, Windows Explorer simply leaves the file or folder in the original location. To delete the item, use the Delete tool button.

DRAGGING AND DROPPING BETWEEN DRIVES

Drag-and-drop works differently depending on whether you're dragging and dropping to the same drive or to a different one. If you drag a file or folder to a new location on the same drive, the file or folder is moved if you use the mouse alone; it is copied if you hold down the Ctrl key. If you drag a file or folder to a different disk drive, however, the file or folder is copied if you use the mouse alone and moved if you hold down the Shift key while you drag and drop.

CROSS-REFERENCE

See Chapter 7 for more on how the Clipboard deals with other types of data.

FIND IT ONLINE

See http://www.liquidmirror.com for info on Anywhere 98, a file copying/moving shareware program.

32

WELCOME TO TEACH YOURSELF

The current chapter name and number always appear in the top right-hand corner of every task page spread, so you always know exactly where you are in the book.

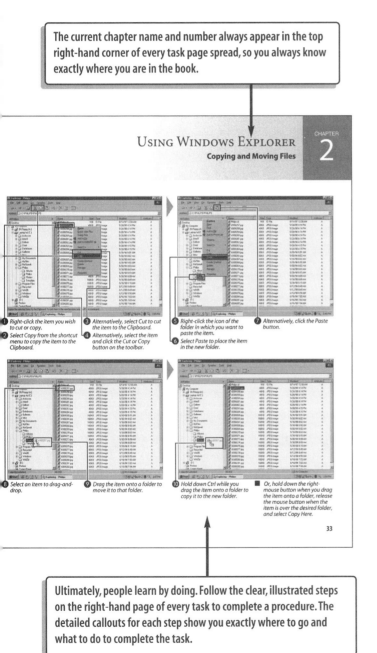

1 Right-click the item you wish to cut or copy.

2 Select Copy from the shortcut menu to copy the item to the Clipboard.

3 Alternatively, select Cut to cut the item to the Clipboard.

4 Alternatively, select the item and click the Cut or Copy button on the toolbar.

5 Right-click the icon of the folder in which you want to paste the item.

6 Select Paste to place the item in the new folder.

7 Alternatively, click the Paste button.

8 Select an item to drag-and-drop.

9 Drag the item onto a folder to move it to that folder.

10 Hold down Ctrl while you drag the item onto a folder to copy it to the new folder.

■ Or, hold down the right-mouse button when you drag the item onto a folder, release the mouse button when the item is over the desired folder, and select Copy Here.

33

Ultimately, people learn by doing. Follow the clear, illustrated steps on the right-hand page of every task to complete a procedure. The detailed callouts for each step show you exactly where to go and what to do to complete the task.

Who This Book Is For

This book is written for you, a beginning to intermediate PC user who isn't afraid to take charge of his or her own learning experience. You don't want a lot of technical jargon; you *do* want to learn as much about PC technology as you can in a limited amount of time. You need a book that is straightforward, easy to follow, and logically organized, so you can find answers to your questions easily. And you appreciate simple-to-use tools such as handy cross-references and visual step-by-step procedures that help you make the most of your learning. We have created the unique Teach Yourself format specifically to meet your needs.

Personal Workbook

It's a well-known fact that much of what we learn is lost soon after we learn it if we don't reinforce our newly acquired skills with practice and repetition. That's why each Teach Yourself chapter ends with your own Personal Workbook. Here's where you can get extra practice, test your knowledge, and discover ideas for using what you've learned in the real world. There's even a visual quiz to help you remember your way around the topic's software environment.

Feedback

Please let us know what you think about this book, and whether you have any suggestions for improvements. You can send questions and comments to the Teach Yourself editors on the IDG Books Worldwide Web site at **www.idgbooks.com.**

Personal Workbook

Q&A

① How do you display a specific folder when you open Windows Explorer?

_____

_____

_____

② How do you run a program that doesn't appear on your Start menu?

_____

_____

③ What will happen if you try to place a second copy of a file in a folder?

_____

_____

_____

④ What type of Windows Explorer view should you select if you want to sort the file listing according to the file attributes?

_____

_____

⑤ Windows Explorer file listings are always divided into what two groups?

_____

_____

⑥ How can you add a background image to a folder's Windows Explorer display?

_____

_____

_____

⑦ How can you keep the standard button toolbar and still gain the most space for the Windows Explorer file listing?

_____

_____

_____

ANSWERS: PAGE 353

42

After working through the tasks in each chapter, you can test your progress and reinforce your learning by answering the questions in the Q&A section. Then check your answers in the Q&A appendix at the back of the book.

Another practical way to reinforce your skills is to do additional exercises on the same skills you just learned without the benefit of the chapter's visual steps. If you struggle with any of these exercises, it's a good idea to refer to the chapter's tasks to be sure you've mastered them.

USING WINDOWS EXPLORER
Personal Workbook

CHAPTER 2

Read the list of Real-World Applications to get ideas on how you can use the skills you've just learned in your everyday life. Understanding a process can be simple; knowing how to use that process to make you more productive is the key to successful learning.

EXTRA PRACTICE

1. Open Windows Explorer and explore your \Windows\Desktop folder.

2. Experiment with expanding and collapsing the folder tree.

3. Copy Autoexec.bat from your hard disk to a disk in drive A.

4. Cycle through the different view detail levels.

5. Customize one of your folders by adding a background image or color.

6. Move your Windows Explorer toolbars around to see which arrangement takes the least space.

REAL-WORLD APPLICATIONS

✔ You install a program but then don't find it listed anywhere on your Start menu. You use Windows Explorer to locate and run the program.

✔ You're working on a project on your office PC and realize that you need to take the file with you on a business trip. Using Windows Explorer, you make a copy of your data file on a floppy disk.

✔ You have a new digital camera and you've downloaded a large number of images to your PC. You use Web page view to preview the images to decide which ones to keep and which ones to discard.

Visual Quiz

How does this view differ from the standard Windows Explorer view, and how can you make Windows Explorer display image previews like this?

43

Take the Visual Quiz to see how well you're learning your way around the technology. Learning about computers is often as much about how to find a button or menu as it is about memorizing definitions. Our Visual Quiz helps you find your way.

Acknowledgments

Thanks to Paul Clapman of Microsoft Corporation, whose patience and wisdom during the extensive Windows 98 beta program helped attain the success of their product and of our book.

Contents

CONTENTS

CONTENTS

CONTENTS

CONTENTS

Teach Yourself®
Microsoft®
Windows® 98

PART

I

Getting Started

If you're just getting started using Windows 98, you're in for a lot of fun. Windows 98 makes using a PC easy and enjoyable.

This first part of the book is all about getting a quick start with the basics of Windows 98. You learn how to open programs, how to identify and use the various things you see scattered around your screen, and how to find your files. Along the way you'll become comfortable with the way things work in Windows 98, and you'll gain the confidence to do even more interesting things with Windows 98.

Specifically, this part introduces you to the Windows 98 desktop and teaches you the meaning of its various objects — objects that you can use to perform useful tasks such as finding document files you've saved. Next, you learn about Windows Explorer, the built-in Windows 98 program that enables you to view all the files and folders that are available on your PC. Finally, you learn how to use the Recycle Bin, a real lifesaver that gives you a second chance when you make a mistake.

CHAPTER 1

MASTER THESE SKILLS

▶ Using the Start Menu

▶ Using Desktop Icons

▶ Examining My Computer

▶ Using the My Documents Folder

▶ Using the Quick Launch Toolbar

▶ Using the System Tray

▶ Exploring the Network Neighborhood

▶ Switching Between Windows

▶ Using Windows 98 Help

Windows 98 Basics

Windows 98 is an operating system, which is a computer program that manages two interfaces: the one between the user and the applications and the one between the applications and the computer's devices and files. Windows 98 provides you with access to all the parts of your computing environment — documents, files, applications, and so on. It also lets you set up and use printers and other hardware devices. If you're on a network, Windows 98 also provides access to network servers.

Windows 98 continues the Windows 95 desktop metaphor but with significant improvements. The Windows 98 environment is centered around windows. A *window* is a rectangular area onscreen that presents information. You open windows when you need them, and close, or minimize, them when you don't need to view their contents. Individual windows can be resized and moved about the screen. Windows 98 uses small graphical *icons*, or pictures, to represent objects. Most icons also have text labels.

You can *select* an object in several ways. If the object is not a menu selection, you *click* the object: Move the mouse cursor onto the icon and press the left mouse button once. A selected icon is highlighted; its label is darkened and has a dotted line. A selected object is ready to be chosen. You *choose* an object to activate its associated command by *double-clicking* its icon: Move the mouse cursor onto the icon and press the left mouse button rapidly twice. If the object is a menu selection or command button, however, you choose it with a single click.

To *drag and drop* an object onto another object, move the mouse cursor onto the icon of the object to be dragged. Press and hold the left mouse button while you move the mouse cursor to the destination object's icon. Then release the mouse button.

If you move the mouse over an object on the desktop or in a window and click the right mouse button, Windows 98 displays a menu called a *context menu*, or *right-click* menu, with the object's common commands.

You'll learn more about all these terms as you try the tasks for yourself.

Using the Start Menu

The Start menu is a list of options that pops up when you click the Start button at the lower-left corner of your Windows 98 desktop. The Start menu provides you with access to most of your programs, to your most recent documents, to the folders and Web sites you have designated as your favorites, and to the settings options that control how your system operates.

The Start menu contains three kinds of selections: commands, cascaded menus, and dialog box selections. Command selections run applications programs immediately. The Windows Update and Help commands in the figures on the facing page are command selections. When you click the command, the application starts.

Selections with a small arrow at the end of the label have pop-up cascaded menus. Programs, Favorites, Documents, Settings, and Find are cascaded menu selections. If you move the mouse cursor to one of them, a submenu pops up. Windows 98 uses this method to implement hierarchical menus.

Cascaded menus can contain the same three selection types as the Start menu. In the first figure on the facing page, the Programs menu is open, as is the Accessories menu in the Programs menu. WordPad, an application program, is selected. If you click it once, WordPad will run.

Menu selections that have three dots (. . .) next to the label will open dialog boxes. Run, Log Off, and Shut Down are dialog box selections. Dialog boxes are special boxes that appear on your screen to display messages or to accept input from you.

TAKE NOTE

▶ YOU CAN MOVE THE START BUTTON

Although it's usual for the Start button to appear at the lower-left corner of your Windows 98 desktop, you can move it to the upper-left or upper-right corner. The Start button moves with the taskbar — the long horizontal bar at the bottom of the desktop. If you drag your taskbar to a different screen location, the Start button also moves.

▶ STOP BY STARTING

It's important that Windows 98 be shut down properly before you turn off your PC. Although it may seem that you need only turn off the switch, you may damage your files and lose some of your work if you don't close Windows 98 correctly.

▶ LEFT-HANDED USE OF THE MOUSE

References to right- and left-clicking and right and left mouse buttons are somewhat inaccurate. If you configure your mouse for left-handed use, the left mouse button is for opening context menus and the right mouse button is for choosing, selecting, and dragging. The industry has resisted requests for nomenclature that does not specifically refer to the left-right position of the buttons.

CROSS-REFERENCE

See "Opening Programs and Folders" in Chapter 2 for more about opening programs not on the Start menu.

FIND IT ONLINE

For the latest on Windows 98, see **http://www.microsoft. com/windows98/default.asp.**

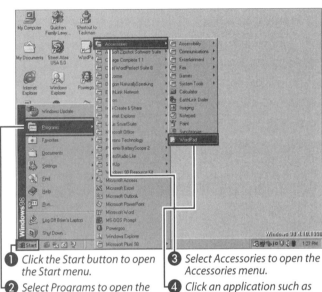

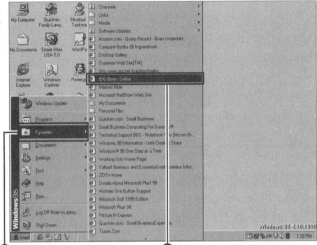

① Click the Start button to open the Start menu.

② Select Programs to open the Programs menu.

③ Select Accessories to open the Accessories menu.

④ Click an application such as WordPad to start the application.

⑤ Select Favorites to open your list of favorite folders and Web sites.

⑥ Click an item to open it.

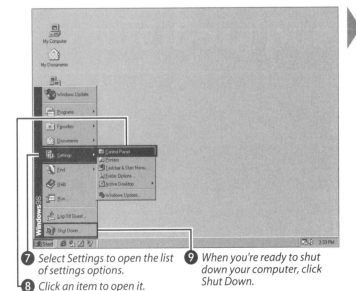

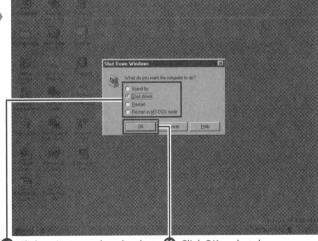

⑦ Select Settings to open the list of settings options.

⑧ Click an item to open it.

⑨ When you're ready to shut down your computer, click Shut Down.

⑩ Click an item to select the shut down option you want to use.

■ Desktop PCs generally don't offer the Stand by option.

⑪ Click OK to shut down your computer.

Using Desktop Icons

The Windows 98 desktop displays a group of icons along the left side. These icons enable you to access your applications, files, documents, and, if you are on a network, other computers.

The My Computer icon provides access to the files, folders, printers, and so on that are on your PC. The My Documents icon provides access to the document files you create and save. The Internet Explorer icon provides access to the World Wide Web. The Network Neighborhood icon provides access to the shared files and printers of other computers on your local network; it may not appear if you aren't connected to a network. The Recycle Bin icon is where you place discarded items from the desktop and file folders. The Outlook Express icon provides access to an e-mail and newsgroup application. If you use a different e-mail program or if you chose not to install the program, Outlook Express may not appear.

You can usually determine the purpose of the other icons on your desktop by looking at the labels that appear under each of them. Most of the remaining icons are program icons that will run the associated programs when you click the icon. The "Take Note" section contains more information about clicking icons to activate programs and documents.

Some of the icons on your desktop have a small arrow at the lower-left corner. The arrow is a symbol that the icon is a *shortcut* to an application or document. Shortcut icons may also include the words "Shortcut to" in their label, but not all of them do. Shortcuts also save disk space because they are actually only small files that point to the appropriate program or document file. You don't need to have a second copy of the program or document.

TAKE NOTE

▶ **SINGLE-CLICKS AND DOUBLE-CLICKS**

In Windows 98 you have the option of setting up your system to open programs and documents with a double-click or a single-click. In Chapter 5 you learn more about this option. For now, remember that if the text under an icon is underlined, a single-click will open the program or document. If the text is not underlined, use a double-click to open it.

▶ **ALIGNING ICONS ON THE DESKTOP**

Your Windows 98 desktop may not be as neat as you'd like, especially if you've added many icons to it. Use the desktop shortcut menu, as shown on the facing page, to align the icons into orderly rows and columns without any overlap.

CROSS-REFERENCE

See "Changing to a Single-Click Mouse" in Chapter 5 for more information on controlling your desktop.

FIND IT ONLINE

See **http://www.zdnet.com/wsources/content/ 0598/feat_tips_desktop.html** for more on the Desktop.

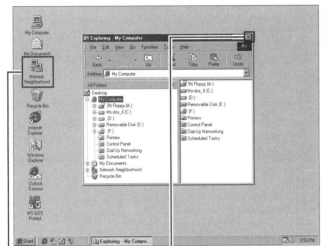

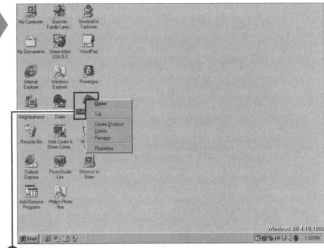

1 *Double-click an item to open it.*

■ *If the icon labels are underlined, single-click to open items.*

2 *Click the Close button to close an item you opened.*

3 *Right-click an item to view its shortcut menu.*

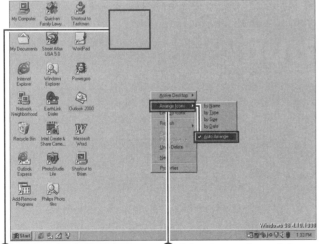

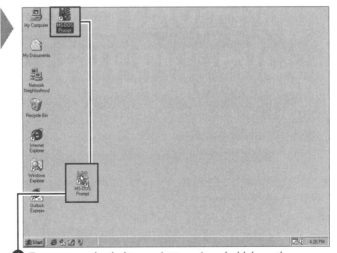

4 *To view the desktop shortcut menu, right-click a blank space on the desktop.*

5 *Select Arrange Icons ⇨ Auto Arrange to align the icons in neat rows and columns.*

6 *To rearrange the desktop, point to an icon, hold down the left mouse button, and drag the icon to a new location.*

Examining My Computer

The My Computer icon on the desktop opens a view into the resources of the local computer. The contents of My Computer depend on the resources on your PC. A typical configuration includes one floppy disk drive, one hard disk drive, and one CD-ROM drive. My Computer generally includes icons to open the Control Panel, access the Printers folder, open the Dial-Up Networking folder, and schedule tasks using the Scheduled Tasks folder. In the figures on the facing page, another object, Infrared Recipient, is shown. Your PC may include additional items, depending on its configuration.

My Computer contains an icon for each of the drives on your PC, including the A drive and CD-ROM drives. You can view the contents of a drive by double-clicking the drive's icon. Each item on the disk drive is represented by an icon. Folder icons are subdirectories in the file system. Other icons represent documents, data files, applications, shortcuts to devices and other PCs on the network, and so on.

If you double-click a document icon, the application with which it was created opens and loads the chosen document. If you double-click an application, it executes immediately. If you double-click an object that is not a folder, a recognized document, or an application, Windows 98 asks you which application should be used to process the object. To close a folder, click the Close button — the button with an X in the upper-right corner of the open folder's window.

The Printers folder in My Computer contains icons for your installed local and network printers and an application that lets you install additional printers. The Control Panel in My Computer contains many applets that let you manage the configuration of Windows 98 and your PC. The Dial-Up Networking folder in My Computer contains your modem and direct cable connections with which you connect to other computers and, perhaps, the Internet. The Scheduled Tasks folder in My Computer is where you post tasks that Windows 98 is to run at a scheduled time or at scheduled intervals. You learn more about these items later in this book.

TAKE NOTE

► LEARN MORE EASILY

Use the Web Page view to see more information about each of the items in the My Computer window. When you view the folder as a Web page, Windows 98 provides a description of an item when the item is selected.

► LEARN ABOUT YOUR SYSTEM

You can learn more about your system through the My Computers' Properties dialog box.

► YOU CAN'T REMOVE MY COMPUTER

You can't remove the My Computer icon from your desktop because it is an important system-level object.

CROSS-REFERENCE

See "Opening Programs and Folders" in Chapter 2 for more information on opening folders.

FIND IT ONLINE

See **http://www.winmag.com/win98/** for Windows 98 tips and information.

❶ *Double-click the My Computer icon to open the My Computer window.*

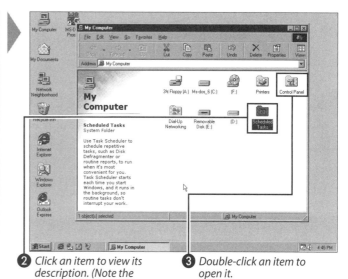

❷ *Click an item to view its description. (Note the description displays on the left side of the window.)*

❸ *Double-click an item to open it.*

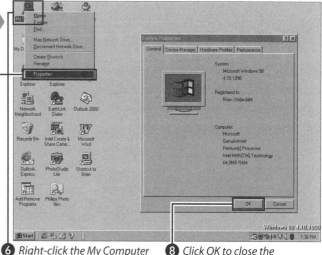

❹ *Right-click an item to view its shortcut menu.*

❺ *Click the Close button to close My Computer.*

❻ *Right-click the My Computer icon to view its shortcut menu.*

❼ *Select Properties to display the System Properties dialog box.*

❽ *Click OK to close the dialog box.*

Using the My Documents Folder

The folder labeled My Documents on the desktop is where Microsoft suggests that you store your document files. Many applications default to this location when you choose to open or save documents. Nothing requires you to use this convention; you can store documents any place you choose in the file system, including on drives other than the one where Windows 98 is installed and where the My Document folder resides.

Even though you can use other folders than the My Documents folder to store your work, you may want to use this folder for one reason: If all your document files are stored in one location, you're less likely to lose track of where you've stored things. Nevertheless, you need not keep all your document files in a single folder. You may wish to use the My Documents folder as the master folder and create additional folders within the My Documents folder to hold the files for individual projects. The figures at the lower left and lower right on the facing page show you how to add new folders to the My Documents folder.

In Chapter 2 you learn more about files and folders, and in Chapter 3 you learn more about using the Recycle Bin. Because the My Documents folder is no different from any other folder, the skills you learn in those two chapters will help you maintain this folder.

TAKE NOTE

▶ MOVING THE MY DOCUMENTS FOLDER

By default, Windows 98 creates a folder on your C drive named My Documents. If you'd rather save your documents in a different location — such as on your network — you can change the location of the My Documents folder. Right-click the My Documents icon, select Properties from the shortcut menu that pops up, and specify a new location in the Target text box. If you can't remember the exact name of the new location, click the Browse button to find the folder you wish to use.

▶ USE EXPLORER VIEW

By default, the My Documents folder opens in the My Computer view. You can also open the folder in Explorer view by selecting Explore from the My Documents right-click shortcut menu. If you have created subfolders within the My Documents folder, you may prefer to use the Explorer view so that you can better organize your files.

▶ USE MY DOCUMENTS FOR SAFETY

Saving all your document files in the My Documents folder offers the benefit of making it faster and easier to back up your files. You need not hunt around to find the files you wish to back up if they're all located in the My Documents folder.

CROSS-REFERENCE

See "Sending Objects to the Recycle Bin" in Chapter 3 for more on deleting unneeded files.

FIND IT ONLINE

For more on My Documents, see http://www.windows-help.net/windows98/troubl-02.shtml.

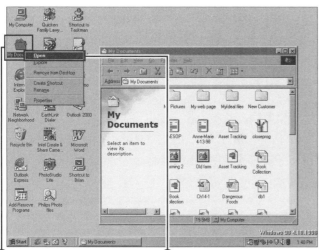

① Right-click the My Documents icon to open the shortcut menu for the My Documents folder.

② Select Open to open the folder.

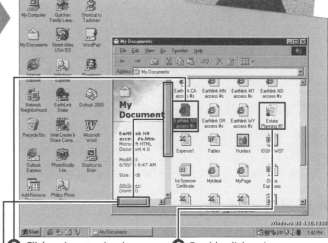

③ Click an item to view its description.

④ If necessary, drag the scroll bars to view the complete description.

⑤ Double-click an item to open it in the application in which it was created.

⑥ To create a new folder within the My Documents folder, select File ➪ New ➪ Folder.

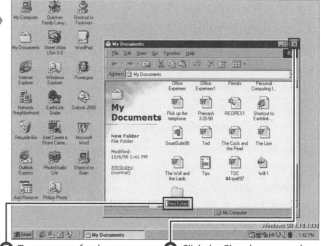

⑦ Type a name for the new folder and press Enter.

⑧ Click the Close button to close the My Documents folder.

Using the Quick Launch Toolbar

The Quick Launch toolbar is a small toolbar that normally sits just to the right of the Start button. The Quick Launch toolbar contains buttons that quickly open, or launch, certain applications. If you move the mouse cursor over a button and linger a few seconds, you see that button's *ToolTip* description appear. A ToolTip is a small message that tells you something about the icon.

The Quick Launch toolbar normally has four buttons. The Internet Explorer tool button launches Internet Explorer exactly as the Internet Explorer icon on the desktop does. The Outlook Express tool button launches Outlook Express—a program that provides e-mail and newsgroup services. The Show Desktop tool button minimizes all open windows to buttons on the taskbar so that you can view the desktop. The View Channels tool button launches the Channel View application, which shows you the Windows 98 channels on the Internet.

You can easily start your programs from their desktop icons or by using the Start menu, so you might wonder why you would need yet another way to run programs, especially these four programs. You probably *don't* need another way to run programs, and it's true that these four aren't likely to be at the top of your list. But the Quick Launch toolbar offers a bit more than meets the eye at first glance.

For example, you can add your own programs to the Quick Launch toolbar and gain the ability to launch them quickly. You can also remove some of the existing icons from the Quick Launch toolbar. In these ways you can customize the Quick Launch toolbar and make it more useful. The figures on the facing page show you how to make these changes.

Before you modify the Quick Launch toolbar, read the "Take Note" section on this page. This is especially important if you decide to drag one of the four default buttons from the toolbar. They exhibit slightly unusual behavior that may leave you a little confused if you don't know what's happening.

TAKE NOTE

▶ MAKE MORE ROOM

If you add too many of your own icons to the Quick Launch toolbar, you'll soon run out of space. To adjust the size of the toolbar, drag the edge of the toolbar right or left. If you still don't have enough room, drag the top of the toolbar up to create a second row.

▶ CORRECTING MISSING ICONS

If you drag items from the Quick Launch toolbar and later decide you'd like them back, you may discover that the icons are missing. You may need to manually copy the program items into the Quick Launch toolbar folder: C:\Windows\Application Data\Microsoft\Internet Explorer\Quick Launch. You should find any items you dragged from the toolbar in the C:\Windows\Desktop folder. They will have the file extension SCF.

CROSS-REFERENCE

See "Moving and Hiding the Taskbar" in Chapter 4.

FIND IT ONLINE

For another good site featuring Windows 98 tips, go to http://www.winfiles.com.

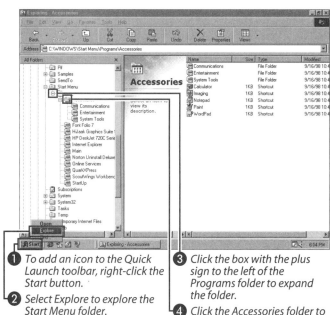

❶ To add an icon to the Quick Launch toolbar, right-click the Start button.

❷ Select Explore to explore the Start Menu folder.

❸ Click the box with the plus sign to the left of the Programs folder to expand the folder.

❹ Click the Accessories folder to open it.

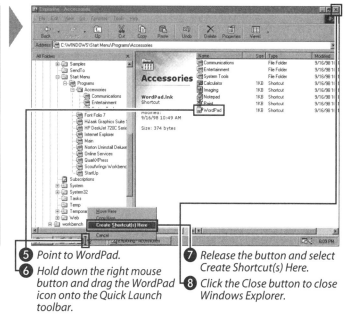

❺ Point to WordPad.

❻ Hold down the right mouse button and drag the WordPad icon onto the Quick Launch toolbar.

❼ Release the button and select Create Shortcut(s) Here.

❽ Click the Close button to close Windows Explorer.

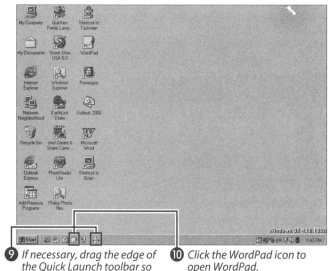

❾ If necessary, drag the edge of the Quick Launch toolbar so that you can see all the icons.

❿ Click the WordPad icon to open WordPad.

⓫ To remove the WordPad icon from the Quick Launch toolbar, point to the icon and hold down the left mouse button.

⓬ Drag the WordPad icon to your desktop and release the mouse button to move the icon there.

■ To completely remove the WordPad icon, drop it here.

Using the System Tray

The small pane at the right end of the taskbar is called the *system tray*. The system tray usually contains several icons. Which icons it contains depends on what software and hardware you have installed on your PC. You'll probably have at least three icons in your system tray: the Task Scheduler icon, the Volume Control icon, and the Time icon. The Task Scheduler icon launches the Windows 98 Task Scheduler. The Volume Control icon launches the Windows 98 Volume Control applet. The Time icon lets you constantly view the time of day. You can view the date by moving the mouse cursor to the icon and waiting a few seconds. Its ToolTip (discussed in a moment) displays the current date.

System tray icons represent programs or services that are currently running on your computer. For example, if you use a laptop computer, your system tray may include an icon for PC Card status whenever a PC Card is inserted into one of the slots. Clicking this icon will give you the option of stopping the card so that you can safely remove it from your system without shutting down your computer.

If you're not sure of the purpose of a system tray icon, hold your mouse pointer over the icon for a few seconds. Windows 98 will pop up a ToolTip that tells you about the icon. If you still aren't clear about the icon's purpose, right-click the icon. This action pops up a shortcut menu, which gives you additional clues about the icon's purpose.

TAKE NOTE

MAKE CHANGING SCREEN SETTINGS EASY

You can add an icon to your system tray that makes changing your screen settings much easier. To do so, right-click a blank space on your desktop, select Properties, click the Settings tab, and then click the Advanced button. Make sure the check box labeled "Show settings icon on task bar" is checked. Click the OK buttons until you've closed all the dialog boxes. The new screen settings icon will look like a small monitor on your system tray. You can click this icon to change the settings.

WATCH THE MODEM STATUS ICON

If you use a modem, you'll probably see a modem status icon on the system tray whenever the computer is connected. This icon has two green spots that become bright green when data is flowing to or from your PC. If both spots stay dark for a long time, your connection may be stalled, and you may wish to try reloading the current page or going to a different site. If neither works, you may need to restart your Internet connection.

CROSS-REFERENCE

See "Changing Desktop Resolution" in Chapter 4.

FIND IT ONLINE

See **http://www.mjmsoft.com/** for information on a couple of system tray utilities.

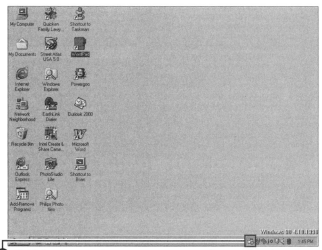

1 *Hold the mouse pointer over a system tray icon to view the ToolTip for the icon.*

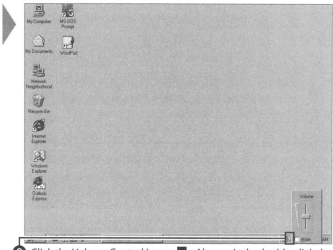

2 *Click the Volume Control icon to display the master volume control.*

■ *Alternatively, double-click the Volume Control icon to display the more detailed volume control window.*

3 *Right-click a system tray icon to display the icon's shortcut menu.*

■ *In this case the shortcut menu for the Time icon is displayed.*

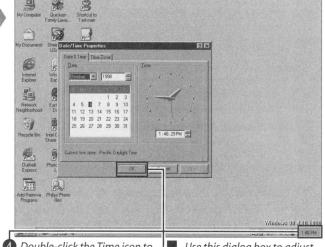

4 *Double-click the Time icon to display the Date/Time Properties dialog box.*

■ *Use this dialog box to adjust the system date, time, and time zone settings.*

5 *Click OK to close the dialog box.*

Exploring the Network Neighborhood

The Network Neighborhood icon is on the desktop if your computer is part of a local network or is equipped so that it can be connected to one. When you choose this object, it opens a window that displays the computers and shared printers in your network. The Network Neighborhood displays an icon that represents the entire network and icons for each computer on the network. The Network Neighborhood initially shows you only the computers in your own *workgroup*. The Entire Network folder contains icons for all the workgroups in the network.

If you're used to a quick response when you browse the folders and files on your local system, you may be surprised by the delays you encounter when you're browsing the Network Neighborhood. You may also find it necessary to refresh the screen to see changes someone made on his or her system while you were browsing the network. When you select a new folder or make changes, the view will reflect the current status of the folder, but the view may not automatically update when someone else makes changes such as adding or deleting files.

When you're browsing the Network Neighborhood, you may not be able to treat network resources in quite the same way you would be able to

if they were on your PC. For example, someone may share a folder but may not allow you to do anything except read the files in the folder. You may need to choose a different location for saving files to avoid seeing error messages.

TAKE NOTE

UNDERSTANDING THE ENTIRE NETWORK ICON

Your Network Neighborhood window will always include an icon named Entire Network. Usually, opening the entire network is the same as opening the Network Neighborhood, especially if you have a small network. The Entire Network icon is useful only if your computer is part of more than one workgroup and you need to view a workgroup other than the one you logged onto when you started Windows 98.

SHARING NETWORK RESOURCES

If you have a network but you can't see any of the disk drives or printers on any of the computers on your network, it may be that none of the folders or printers has been set up for sharing on the network. Network Neighborhood can show only shared resources. If no one on the network is willing to share anything, nothing will be available in the Network Neighborhood window.

CROSS-REFERENCE
See "Sharing Your Files" in Chapter 16.

SHORTCUT
Press F5 to refresh the Network Neighborhood view.

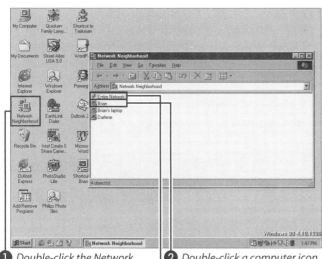

1 *Double-click the Network Neighborhood icon to open the Network Neighborhood window.*

2 *Double-click a computer icon to view the shared resources on that computer.*

3 *Alternatively, double-click the Entire Network icon to view available workgroups.*

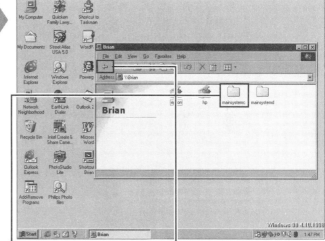

4 *Double-click a shared resource such as a folder icon to view its contents.*

5 *Alternatively, click the Back button to return to the previous window.*

6 *Double-click a folder to open the folder.*

7 *Click a shared resource to view its description.*

8 *Click the Close button to close the Network Neighborhood window*

Switching Between Windows

In Windows 98 you may have several windows displayed on the desktop. Each window represents an independently running program or an open disk drive folder. Only one window at a time interacts with you, the user. That window is said to be *active* or to have the *focus*. Usually the most recent window you open is active. You can change the focus to another window whenever you choose. An active window displays on top of the others, and receives the keystrokes that you type.

To make a different window active, simply click anywhere in it. A second method of switching to another window involves using the keyboard to open up the task list (a small window) that shows you icons and text descriptors of all open windows on your desktop. You use the keyboard to select the window you want to make active. You experiment with this method in the exercise on the facing page. Another way to switch to another window is by clicking a window button in the taskbar (the long horizontal bar at the bottom of the desktop).

The taskbar contains several elements: the Start menu button, buttons for open windows, and several icons at either end of the taskbar. The middle section of the taskbar contains buttons that represent open

windows on the desktop. When you opened the My Computer window, the Printers window, and so on, you may have noticed that buttons were added to the taskbar. The button that seems to be pushed in represents the active window. The buttons that seem to be popped out are open, but inactive.

TAKE NOTE

► JUMP BETWEEN TWO PROGRAMS

If you quickly press and release Alt+Tab, you'll return to the last open window. If you have several programs open, you can quickly switch back and forth between two of them by using this technique without waiting for the task list to display.

► FORCE STALLED WINDOWS TO CLOSE

If you find that your system stops responding, press Ctrl+Alt+Del and look for an item that says "Not Responding." Select the item and click the End Task button to close the item that has stopped working. You may need to restart your system to restore proper operation.

CROSS-REFERENCE

See "Closing Programs" in Chapter 6.

SHORTCUT

Press Alt+F4 to close an active window.

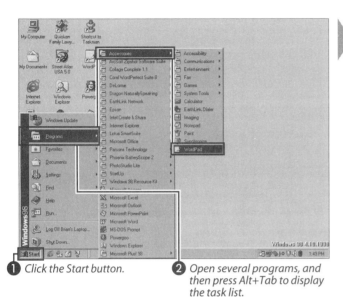

1 Click the Start button.

2 Open several programs, and then press Alt+Tab to display the task list.

3 Press Tab until you have highlighted the window you wish to make active, and then release the Alt key.

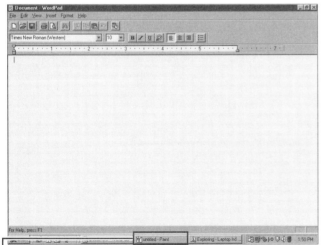

4 Alternatively, click a button on the taskbar to switch to the associated window.

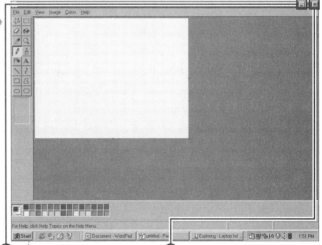

5 Click the Minimize button to hide the current window.

6 Click the Close button to close the current window.

Using Windows 98 Help

Even experienced Windows users sometimes need help using Windows. No one can know everything about using an operating system, and that is why Microsoft includes a good source of online help.

Windows 98 provides a new help system that displays help screens as Web pages. Anyone who has browsed the Internet should feel at home in the Windows 98 help system. Windows 98 also incorporates the World Wide Web into the new help system. If you can't find what you need in the Windows 98 help system, you can click the Web Help button shown in the figures on the facing page. You'll see a brief explanation of the Microsoft online technical support system along with a link you can click to go to the Support Online Web site.

The Windows 98 help system is also the place you should go if you're having trouble with your computer or Windows 98. As the upper-right figure on the facing page shows, the final topic on the Contents tab of the Windows Help window is Troubleshooting. When you open this item you can select the Windows 98 troubleshooter that best describes your situation. Each troubleshooter has a series of screens that ask you for information about the type of problem you're encountering. As you answer the questions, the troubleshooter makes suggestions and attempts to narrow the possibilities until the problem is solved.

Although most people find online help useful, sometimes you may prefer having a printed set of instructions. This is especially true if you're trying to perform a complex task such as installing new hardware or adjusting the way Windows 98 works. You can print a copy of the currently displayed help window from the Options menu. Often the dialog box will display an additional option: printing only the current page or printing the entire topic. Be careful when selecting the option to print the entire topic. You may discover that a topic runs to dozens of pages, and it's hard to stop the printing once it has started.

TAKE NOTE

OLD HELP FILES STILL WORK

Even though Windows 98 has a new help system style, you can still use the help system for your old programs. Many applications continue to use the help formats of Windows 3.1 and Windows 95, and Windows 98 continues to support these formats.

USE THE HELP BUTTON

Some windows have a Help button in the button group in the window's upper-right corner. A Help button has a question mark icon and provides *context-sensitive* help — information about using a specific object in the window. When you click the Help button, the mouse cursor changes to a pointer with a question mark. If you click an item in the window, the system displays helpful information about that item.

CROSS-REFERENCE

See "Using the Start Menu" earlier in this chapter.

FIND IT ONLINE

Go to **http://www.microsoft.com/support/ siteinfo/default.htm** for online support info.

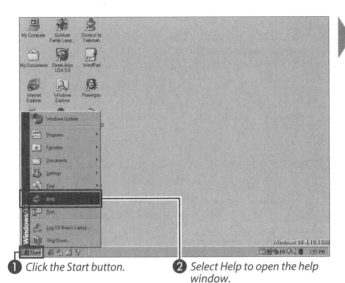

1 *Click the Start button.*

2 *Select Help to open the help window.*

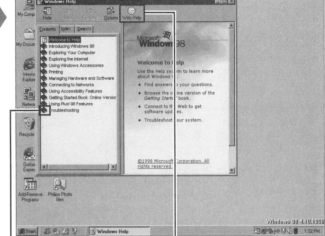

3 *Click the icon for the subject you wish to view.*

■ *Many subjects include additional subtopics. Continue clicking topics to reach the one you want.*

4 *Alternatively, click Web Help to access help resources on the Internet.*

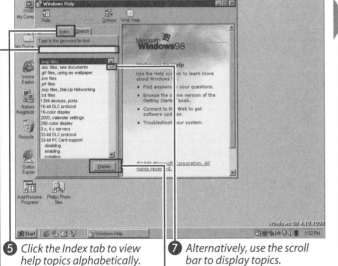

5 *Click the Index tab to view help topics alphabetically.*

6 *To go directly to a topic, enter the topic in this text box.*

7 *Alternatively, use the scroll bar to display topics.*

8 *If necessary, click the Display button to display the topic.*

9 *Click the Search tab to search for help topics.*

10 *Type in a keyword.*

11 *Click the List Topics button.*

12 *Double-click a topic to view the topic.*

Personal Workbook

Q&A

1 In addition to clicking the Start button, what else can you do to display the Start menu?

_____

_____

2 What does a small arrow next to an item on the Start menu mean?

_____

_____

3 What do three periods following a menu item mean?

_____

_____

4 What does a small diagonal arrow on a desktop icon mean?

_____

_____

5 What does it mean if the icons on your desktop are underlined?

_____

_____

6 What can you do if you add icons to the Quick Launch toolbar but can't see them?

_____

_____

7 How can you find out what a system tray icon does?

_____

_____

8 How can you quickly switch between two programs without using your mouse?

_____

_____

9 What is the purpose of the Entire Network icon?

_____

_____

10 How can you print a help topic?

_____

_____

ANSWERS: 353

EXTRA PRACTICE

1. Open Windows Explorer using the Start menu.

2. Open a program using one of the desktop icons.

3. Use My Computer to determine the free space on drive C.

4. If you have a network, use the Network Neighborhood to locate any shared printers.

5. Find the modem troubleshooter in Windows help.

6. Use the Time icon on the system tray to check the current system date and time.

REAL-WORLD APPLICATIONS

✔ You have been assigned the task of writing a memo to announce a staff meeting later today. To prepare the memo, you use the Start menu or the desktop icon to open your word processor.

✔ Your two middle-school children often use your computer for their homework assignments. To make it easy for them to locate their documents, you have them save their work in the My Documents folder.

✔ You like to check your e-mail often, so you keep your e-mail program open all the time. When you're working on a spreadsheet, it's easy to switch quickly between the two programs using Alt+Tab.

Visual Quiz

How can you display this folder? What must you do to make the folder display the message shown here?

_____

_____

_____

_____

_____

_____

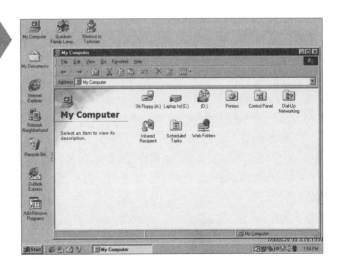

CHAPTER 2

Using Windows Explorer

Windows Explorer is the vehicle through which you view the contents of folders on your desktop and hard drive. As its name suggests, Windows Explorer enables you to explore the hierarchical system of disk drives and folders on your PC. (*Folders* represent the directories and subdirectories of individual drives.) Although Windows Explorer also enables you to view other resources on a local network, this chapter teaches you about Windows Explorer as it relates to your local computer.

Whenever you are looking at anything other than the desktop, a menu, an application window, a wizard, or a dialog box, chances are that what you are looking at is being presented in Explorer.

Explorer, like most other Windows 98 components, is a *window:* a rectangular area on the screen that presents information. You open windows when you need them, and close or minimize them when you don't need to view what they have to offer. For example, if you

need to see the contents of your C drive, you open the Explorer window, and then close it when you were through. Individual windows can be resized and moved about the screen. You can choose any of several different "looks" for Windows Explorer. These views vary in the way information is shown. You may see a simple group of icons or a folder tree with details about each file and folder. Windows Explorer can show folders as if they were Web pages, giving you a preview of the contents of many files.

Folders are arranged in a tree-like structure. Each folder can contain additional subfolders that branch off of it. These branches can extend several levels deep, but too many levels can make exploring your disk drives harder than necessary.

In this chapter, you learn how to navigate in Windows Explorer, how to set Windows Explorer to display different types of information, and how to use it to copy and move files. The chapter also explains how to sort file lists and how to set Explorer's toolbars to your preference.

Opening and Closing Windows Explorer

There are several ways to open Windows Explorer. In this section you learn about a few of the more common ones. One problem with having many different ways to start Windows Explorer is that it's easy to become confused by the way this application works. For example, when you right-click the Start button and choose Explore, Windows Explorer opens and displays the contents of the C:\Windows\Start Menu folder. In effect, Windows Explorer is exploring the Start Menu folder and not the root directory of drive C. (The *root* is the topmost directory of a drive. Windows Explorer displays the root directory of a drive as an actual drive, instead of a folder.) Likewise, if you right-click the Recycle Bin icon on your desktop, then choose Explore, a window opens that allows you to view the contents of the Recycle Bin.

The sidebar on the facing page lists additional command line options you may find useful when you start Windows Explorer using the command line. If you often explore a particular folder on your PC, you may want to use a Windows Explorer trick to make this task easier. While Windows Explorer is open, use the right mouse button to drag the folder onto your desktop. Choose Create Shortcut Here. Windows Explorer will place an icon for the folder on your desktop. Double-clicking the new icon will open the folder.

TAKE NOTE

▶ WINDOWS EXPLORER IS ALWAYS RUNNING

Windows Explorer is always running whenever you're using the Windows 98 graphical user interface (or GUI). The only time Windows Explorer isn't running is when you start Windows 98 in MS-DOS mode. As soon as you restart the Windows 98 desktop, however, Windows Explorer also restarts. In this chapter, *opening* Windows Explorer means displaying the Windows Explorer window.

▶ LEAVE WINDOWS EXPLORER OPEN

You may find that it's handy to have Windows Explorer always available. Rather than close Windows Explorer, leave it out of your way but open by clicking the Minimize button (the third button from the right) on the Windows Explorer title bar.

▶ RESTORE WINDOWS EXPLORER TO THE START MENU

Because you can rearrange your Windows 98 Start menu using drag-and-drop techniques, it's easy to accidentally delete an important item, such as Windows Explorer, from your Start menu. If this happens, right-click the Start menu, choose Explore, and then drag Explorer.exe onto the Start button. When the Start menu opens, drag Windows Explorer to the desired location on the menu.

CROSS-REFERENCE

See Chapter 1 for more information about using the Start menu.

FIND IT ONLINE

See **http://www.mijenix.com/powerdesk98.htm** for a utility designed to enhance Windows Explorer.

Command Options

Windows Explorer has command-line options you can use to create a shortcut that opens Windows Explorer in the way you specify. These options are /n to open Windows Explorer in a new window, /e to use the Windows Explorer view with the folder tree, /root to specify the folder you want to be the root folder, and /select to select a specific object. Click the Start button and select Run to display the Run dialog box. Then just type the command and press Enter. For example, if you type **explorer /n /e,/root,c:\windows** in the Run dialog box command line, Windows Explorer will open a new window that shows c:\windows as the root folder.

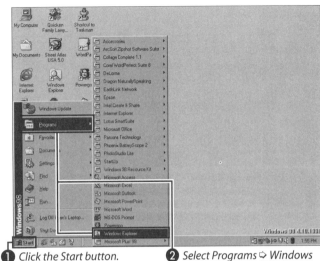

① *Click the Start button.*

② *Select Programs* ⟿ *Windows Explorer to open Windows Explorer.*

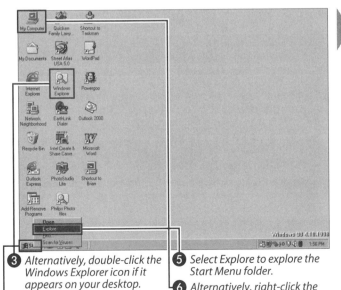

③ *Alternatively, double-click the Windows Explorer icon if it appears on your desktop.*

④ *Alternatively, right-click the Start button.*

⑤ *Select Explore to explore the Start Menu folder.*

⑥ *Alternatively, right-click the My Computer icon on your desktop, and select Explore.*

⑦ *With Windows Explorer open, select File* ⟿ *Close to close the window.*

⑧ *Alternatively, click the Close button to close the window.*

Opening Folders and Programs

When you open Windows Explorer, you'll see a hierarchical tree structure labeled All Folders in the left pane. The tree represents your computer and its resources, and displays your desktop at the top. (All Folders is one of several Explorer views you can display in the left pane. The other Explorer views relate to Internet access of the World Wide Web.)

Compare the tree's icons with those on your desktop. You will see that the desktop icons My Computer, My Documents, Internet Explorer, Network Neighborhood, Recycle Bin, and any folders you have added are represented in the tree. All these icons represent things that contain other things. The only icons on the desktop that are not also on the tree represent such things as shortcuts and documents that do not themselves contain other things.

Notice in the figures on the facing page that the C: entry in the tree is expanded to show what the C drive contains. Those same items appear in the right pane of the window, where the folder contents are shown. Observe also that some folders in the tree have plus (+) icons, others have minus (-) icons, and still others have neither. The folders with a plus icon have subfolders but are not expanded to show their subfolders. Folders with a minus icon also contain folders, but are expanded so the subfolders are displayed. Folders with no icons contain no subfolders, although they may contain documents and application files.

Use Explorer's All Folders view to navigate through and explore your PC's file system. If you are adventurous you may also want to explore Network Neighborhood and Internet Explorer. To open a folder, click its icon in the left-hand pane. The currently active folder is shown with an open folder icon. Inactive folder icons look like a closed folder. Only one folder can be open at a time (although the My Documents folder always appears to be open even if it is not the active folder).

TAKE NOTE

► QUICKLY EXPAND AN ENTIRE BRANCH

To quickly expand an entire branch and all folders it contains, press Num Lock+* (asterisk). To collapse the entire branch, press the left arrow key.

► START PROGRAMS THAT AREN'T ON THE START MENU

Even though you'll probably find most of your important programs somewhere on the Start menu, some programs may appear to be missing. You can still run such a program by double-clicking its icon in the Windows Explorer window.

CROSS-REFERENCE

See Chapter 6 for more information about running programs.

FIND IT ONLINE

For another tip on using Explorer, see **http://www.annoyances.org/cgi-bin/ce-showtopic/004_019**.

Resize Windows Explorer Panes

You may need to resize the panes after opening Windows Explorer if the folder title and description are truncated. To resize the panes, drag the separator between the two panes right or left as needed. You can instead use the horizontal scroll bar (at the bottom of the pane) to view the covered part of a folder name if you don't want to resize the panes.

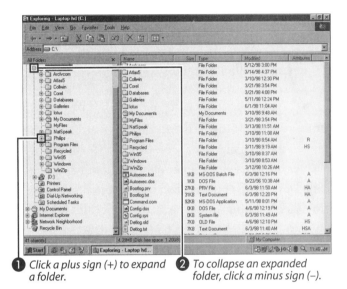

1 Click a plus sign (+) to expand a folder.

2 To collapse an expanded folder, click a minus sign (–).

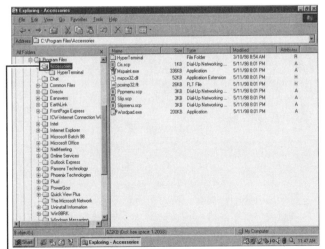

3 Click a folder icon to open the folder and make it active.

■ Notice that the contents of the folder you just opened, including the subfolder HyperTerminal, appear in the right-hand pane.

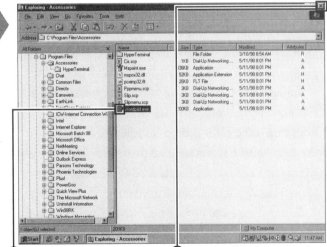

4 Double-click an application's icon to run the program.

5 Click the Close button to close Windows Explorer.

Copying and Moving Files

Y(ou can copy or move files and folders in Windows Explorer using two different methods: cut, copy, and paste or drag-and-drop.

The Windows Explorer Cut, Copy, and Paste buttons implement the Windows 98 Clipboard, a mechanism for exchanging data between applications and Windows 98 itself. Explorer uses the Clipboard as one way to copy folders, documents, and other files to other locations in the hierarchical file and folder system. The Clipboard is a temporary data storage bin. To move data using the Clipboard, you *cut* or *copy* data from a document into the Clipboard and *paste* data from the Clipboard into the same or another document.

For many people, using drag-and-drop is more convenient than using the Clipboard. You select a file or folder and then drag and drop the selected data to another location. To copy rather than move the data, press and hold Ctrl while you drag and drop the file or folder. (See the "Take Note" section for an exception to this method.) Another way to copy a file is to hold down the right mouse button when you drag the item onto a folder, release the mouse button when the item is over the desired folder, and select Copy Here from the shortcut menu.

You cannot have more than one file or folder with the same name in the same folder. If you try to move files or folders to a location that would result in duplicates, Windows 98 asks you whether you want to replace the existing item with the new one. If you try to copy files in a manner that would produce duplicates, Windows 98 adds "Copy of" to the beginning of the filename.

TAKE NOTE

CUT WORKS DIFFERENTLY IN WINDOWS EXPLORER

In Windows Explorer, the Cut tool button works almost like the Copy tool button. Within an application, Cut deletes the original data after copying it to the Clipboard. With Explorer, Cut dims the icon of the original file or folder but does not delete the item itself. If you forget to paste the file or folder elsewhere, Windows Explorer simply leaves the file or folder in the original location. To delete the item, use the Delete tool button.

DRAGGING AND DROPPING BETWEEN DRIVES

Drag-and-drop works differently depending on whether you're dragging and dropping to the same drive or to a different one. If you drag a file or folder to a new location on the same drive, the file or folder is moved if you use the mouse alone; it is copied if you hold down the Ctrl key. If you drag a file or folder to a different disk drive, however, the file or folder is copied if you use the mouse alone and moved if you hold down the Shift key while you drag and drop.

CROSS-REFERENCE

See Chapter 7 for more on how the Clipboard deals with other types of data.

FIND IT ONLINE

See **http://www.liquidmirror.com** for info on Anywhere 98, a file copying/moving shareware program.

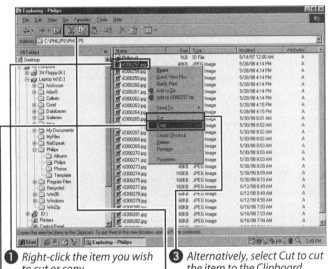

❶ *Right-click the item you wish to cut or copy.*

❷ *Select Copy from the shortcut menu to copy the item to the Clipboard.*

❸ *Alternatively, select Cut to cut the item to the Clipboard.*

❹ *Alternatively, select the item and click the Cut or Copy button on the toolbar.*

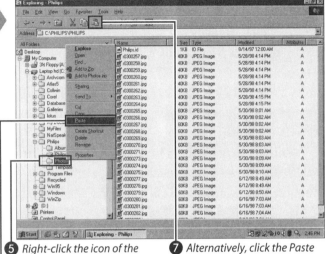

❺ *Right-click the icon of the folder in which you want to paste the item.*

❻ *Select Paste to place the item in the new folder.*

❼ *Alternatively, click the Paste button.*

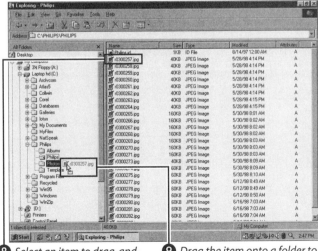

❽ *Select an item to drag-and-drop.*

❾ *Drag the item onto a folder to move it to that folder.*

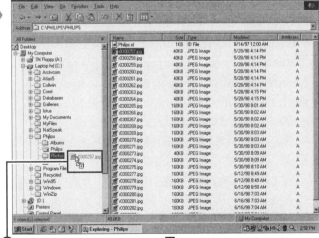

❿ *Hold down Ctrl while you drag the item onto a folder to copy it to the new folder.*

■ *Or, hold down the right-mouse button when you drag the item onto a folder, release the mouse button when the item is over the desired folder, and select Copy Here.*

Controlling the View Detail Level

Some operating systems, particularly older ones, provide one way to execute commands, view file lists, and so on. Windows Explorer takes a different approach. Rather than make you view file lists in only one predetermined way, Windows Explorer enables you to pick the view that best suits you and the task at hand.

Windows Explorer has four types of views you can select. The Large Icons view displays folder contents using the same large icons you normally see on your desktop. In this view the icons are displayed in rows beginning in the upper-left corner of the screen. All the folders are shown first, followed by any files. The Small Icons view is similar to the Large Icons view except for the size of the icons. You can see many more files onscreen in the Small Icons view than in the Large Icons view. The List view uses the same small icons as the Small Icons view but sorts the icons in columns rather than in rows. The final view option is the Details view. In Details view you can see the icon, the file or folder name, the file size, the object type, the date the file was last modified, and, optionally, the file's attributes.

As shown in the final figure on the facing page, Windows Explorer has a number of optional settings. One of these settings controls how Windows Explorer displays hidden and system files. Generally, these types of files are marked as hidden or system files for your protection because accidentally deleting them could cause your system to stop working. If you select the radio button labeled "Do not show hidden or system files," you'll protect those files from accidental deletions and may save yourself many problems.

TAKE NOTE

▶ USE DETAILS VIEW TO CONTROL SORTING

If you want to sort the file listing as discussed in the next section ("Sorting the File Listing"), you'll probably want to use the Details view rather than one of the other views. The Details view shows information in addition to the icon and filename; sorting any of the other types of views will probably result in a confusing display.

▶ MAKE ALL FOLDERS LOOK THE SAME

When displaying a folder, Windows Explorer usually uses the same settings you selected the last time you visited the folder. If you like, you can make all the folders look the same, as shown in the final figure on the facing page.

CROSS-REFERENCE

See Chapter 9 for more information about how to find files.

FIND IT ONLINE

For suggestions on configuring Explorer, see **http:// cpcug.org/user/clemenzi/technical/WinExplorer/ WinExplorerCookBook.htm**.

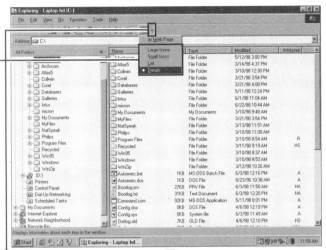

❶ Click the down-arrow at the right of the Views button.

❷ Select the type of view from the drop-down list.

■ Note that the right-hand pane shows the Details view, with small icons.

❸ Alternatively, click the Views button to cycle through the view types.

❹ Select View ➪ Folder Options to display the Folder Options dialog box.

■ Note in the right-hand pane the view is set to Large Icons.

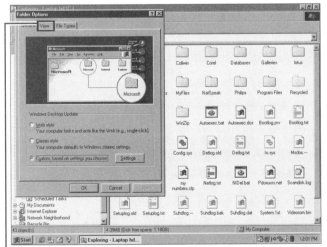

❺ Click the View tab.

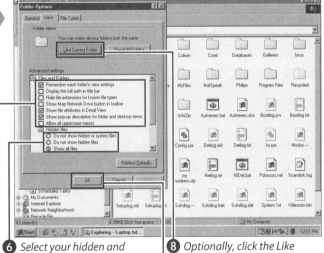

❻ Select your hidden and system file settings.

❼ Select the file and folder view options.

❽ Optionally, click the Like Current Folder button to apply the selected settings to all folders.

❾ Click OK to complete the task.

Sorting the File Listing

Searching through a list is much easier when it is sorted. That's why phone books are sorted alphabetically. It would be impossible to find a phone number if the names were shown at random. Similarly, it would be difficult to search unsorted file listings to locate a specific file from the hundreds or thousands of files on a typical hard disk.

If you're used to the standard way Windows Explorer displays file listings, you may not realize the value of some of the alternative sorting options. Suppose you saved a file yesterday and now can't remember the filename. How might you go about finding it? You could start at the top of the list and work your way down, hoping that one of the file-names would jog your memory. But a better way would be to sort the files according to when they were created or modified. That would let you concentrate on a few files — the ones you worked with yesterday — and you'd be more likely to find the correct file quickly.

When Windows Explorer is set to the Details view, column headers are displayed above each column in the file listing. These headers do more than identify the columns. If you click one of them, Windows Explorer will sort the file listing in ascending order based first on the column you clicked and then on the

filename. If you click the column header a second time, Windows Explorer changes to a descending sort.

No matter which sort order you choose, Windows Explorer always separates the files and folders into two groups. The folders may appear first or last — depending on the sort order you selected — but they are never mixed in with the files.

TAKE NOTE

▶ **SORT BY FILE ATTRIBUTES**

If you only use the Arrange Icon options to sort the file view you'll miss out on a useful sorting option. If you set the Details view options to show file attributes, you can click the Attributes column header and sort the listing by file attributes. You may find this quite handy, especially if you want to locate all the files with the "A" attribute, which indicates those files have not been backed up.

▶ **THE FOLDER TREE SORT ORDER**

No matter what sort order you choose for the file and folder listing, Windows Explorer always sorts the folder tree in alphabetical order.

▶ **CHECK FILE SIZES AND DATES**

If you run short of disk space, you can sort the files by size to see which files are using the most space. You can also sort by the modified date to see which files you haven't used for a long time.

CROSS-REFERENCE

See Chapter 9 for more information about how to find files.

SHORTCUT

Press Ctrl+End to move to the end of the listing. Use Ctrl+Home to move to the beginning.

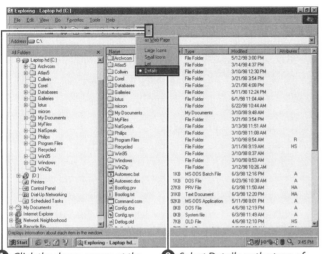

① *Click the down-arrow at the right of the Views button.*

② *Select Details as the type of view from the drop-down list.*

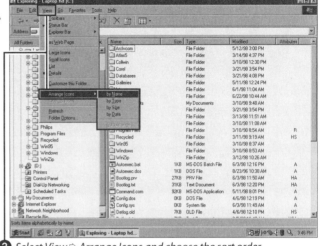

③ *Select View ▷ Arrange Icons and choose the sort order.*

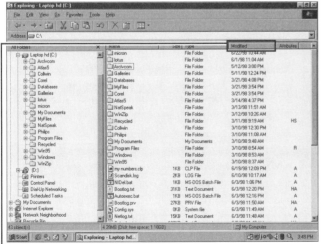

④ *Alternatively, click a column heading to sort the file listing in order of the values in the column.*

■ *This will sort the listing by the dates in the Modified column.*

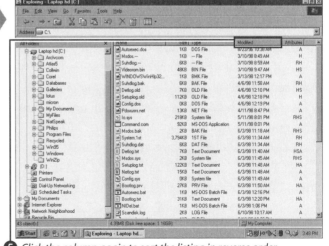

⑤ *Click the column again to sort the listing in reverse order.*

Viewing Folders as Web Pages

Windows 98 gives you a new way to view the folders on your hard disk: as Web pages. This way of viewing your computer reduces the distinction between your local files and those on the Internet. This change may also make it less confusing to move between your local computer and the Internet, because Explorer will work the same in both places.

The Web pages you see on the Internet are documents written in *Hypertext Markup Language* (HTML). HTML documents may contain background images, colored text, hypertext links you can click to travel to other Web pages, and features that you wouldn't normally associate with the way you view your folders. When you choose to view your folders as Web pages you may need to adopt a new way of thinking about your PC.

When you first switch to the Web page view, you probably won't notice much difference in the appearance of your folders. To make a folder look different you must customize it as discussed in the "Take Note" section on this page. But you will notice significant differences when you look in certain folders, especially those that contain graphics files. If you select a graphics file, Windows Explorer will display a thumbnail preview of the file so that you don't have to open the file to see what it contains. You can go from file to file viewing each one in turn. This is a fast way to find a specific file.

TAKE NOTE

SOME FOLDERS CHANGE IN WEB PAGE VIEW

In Web page view some folders look different when you visit them. Your Windows folder, for example, displays a warning message rather than the file list. The message reads "Modifying the contents of this folder may cause your programs to stop working correctly. To view the contents of this folder, click Show Files." To see the files in your Windows folder in Web page view, you must click a link labeled Show Files.

USE WEB PAGE VIEW TO SEARCH CLIP ART

You can use Web page view to search through your collection of clip art files. As long as Windows Explorer recognizes the clip art files as graphics files, it will generate an image preview of each file in turn as you move through the file listing.

CUSTOMIZING THE VIEW

The View ➪ Customize this Folder command gives you a number of options that make a significant change in the appearance of your folders. You can choose to fully customize the folder with HTML, add a background image, or remove all customization. If you choose to fully customize the folder, Windows 98 will open the Notepad accessory application and display the page's HTML code. You might prefer to write down the filename and then open the HTML file in FrontPage Express, where you can customize the file visually.

CROSS-REFERENCE

See Chapter 14 for more information about including Web content in folders.

FIND IT ONLINE

For more on new features in Windows 98, see **http://www.pcworld.com.hk/public/CoverFeatures/ cover0798.htm**.

① Select View ➪ as Web Page to change to Web page view.

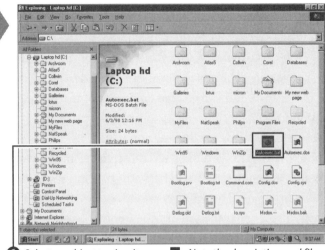

② Select an object to view its description and file details.

■ Note the description and file details of the object appear on the left side of the right-hand pane.

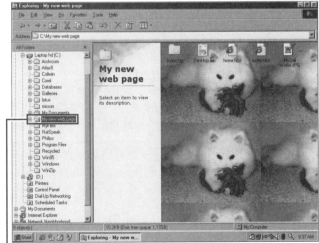

③ To view file customizations such as a background image, colors, or links, select a folder that has been customized.

■ In this case the folder has been customized to show a background bitmap image.

④ Select a folder that contains graphics files.

⑤ To display a thumbnail view of an image, select a graphics file.

■ Notice the thumbnail view for the selected image appears on the left side of the right-hand pane.

Controlling the Toolbars

You have learned that you can make changes in the way Windows Explorer displays file listings, but that's not the extent of the changes you can make in its appearance. You can change the layout of the Windows Explorer toolbars to make the program more convenient for the way you work.

Windows Explorer has several screen elements you can control: the toolbars, the status bar, and several Explorer bars. The toolbars are three elements you can display near the top of the Windows Explorer window. The main button toolbar, usually displayed at the top, presents the standard buttons that provide one-click access to common commands. The address bar shows the current location information — the full tree structure for the file or folder you have selected. Alternatively, it can show links you can click to quickly access Internet sites. It also enables you to specify a new address to display. The status bar, which appears at the bottom of the Windows Explorer window, shows information about the current folder. The Explorer bar you have chosen to view appears at the left of the window; you can view the folder tree or any one of several Internet-related bars.

You may not find the address bar and the links bar very useful for browsing your computer. These elements are generally more useful for browsing the Internet. To display the information that appears in the address bar in the Windows Explorer title bar, select the check box labeled "Display the full path in title bar" on the View tab of the Folder Options dialog box. Eliminating this toolbar will save space for the folder window. Read the "Take Note" section for other space-saving tricks.

TAKE NOTE

▶ STACK YOUR TOOLBARS

The Windows Explorer toolbars can eat up a lot of space in the Windows Explorer window. You can regain some of that space by stacking the toolbars. As the second figure on the facing page shows, you can drag any of the toolbars onto another toolbar or even onto the Windows Explorer menu bar. If you choose a blank space for the destination, you may even be able to see everything you need in both toolbars you place in the same row.

▶ HIDE TEXT LABELS

The standard button toolbar has optional text labels you can choose to display if you need extra help figuring out the purpose of the toolbar buttons. But if you choose to hide the text labels, the standard button toolbar uses a lot less space. You can still learn what each button does by pausing the mouse pointer over a button and waiting for the ToolTip to appear.

CROSS-REFERENCE

See "Controlling the View Detail Level" earlier for more information about customizing the view.

SHORTCUT

Click the X in the upper-right corner of an Explorer bar to hide the bar.

① *Select View ⇨ Toolbars to display the toolbar selections.*

② *Click any of the toolbar options to change the display.*

③ *Optionally, drag a toolbar to a new location and size in the toolbar area.*

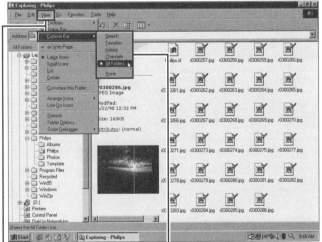

④ *Select View ⇨ Explorer Bar to display the Explorer bar options.*

⑤ *Select one of the Explorer bars to display at the left side of the Windows Explorer window.*

⑥ *Right-click one of the toolbars.*

⑦ *Click Text Labels to toggle the display of text labels.*

Personal Workbook

Q&A

1 How do you display a specific folder when you open Windows Explorer?

_____

_____

_____

2 How do you run a program that doesn't appear on your Start menu?

_____

_____

3 What will happen if you try to place a second copy of a file in a folder?

_____

_____

_____

4 What type of Windows Explorer view should you select if you want to sort the file listing according to the file attributes?

_____

_____

5 Windows Explorer file listings are always divided into what two groups?

_____

_____

_____

6 How can you add a background image to a folder's Windows Explorer display?

_____

_____

_____

_____

7 How can you keep the standard button toolbar and still gain the most space for the Windows Explorer file listing?

_____

_____

_____

_____

ANSWERS: PAGE 354

EXTRA PRACTICE

1 Open Windows Explorer and explore your \Windows\Desktop folder.

2 Experiment with expanding and collapsing the folder tree.

3 Copy Autoexec.bat from your hard disk to a disk in drive A.

4 Cycle through the different view detail levels.

5 Customize one of your folders by adding a background image or color.

6 Move your Windows Explorer toolbars around to see which arrangement takes the least space.

REAL-WORLD APPLICATIONS

✔ You install a program but then don't find it listed anywhere on your Start menu. You use Windows Explorer to locate and run the program.

✔ You're working on a project on your office PC and realize that you need to take the file with you on a business trip. Using Windows Explorer, you make a copy of your data file on a floppy disk.

✔ You have a new digital camera and you've downloaded a large number of images to your PC. You use Web page view to preview the images to decide which ones to keep and which ones to discard.

Visual Quiz

How does this view differ from the standard Windows Explorer view, and how can you make Windows Explorer display image previews like this?

_____

_____

_____

_____

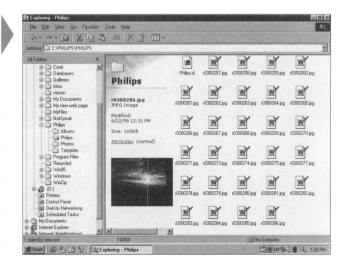

CHAPTER 3

Using the Recycle Bin

The Recycle Bin stores deleted objects. You can delete folders, files, documents, applications, and so on. Instead of deleting those objects from the file system, Windows 98 puts them in the Recycle Bin, unless you specifically tell Windows 98 to do otherwise.

You might want to think of the Recycle Bin as a safety net. If you accidentally delete files or folders or if you delete things on purpose and later discover you need them, the Recycle Bin gives you a second chance. When objects go into the Recycle Bin, Windows 98 actually saves them for a specific period of time rather than removing them immediately. You won't see these objects at their normal locations in Windows Explorer or on your desktop, but Windows 98 remembers where they belong in case you need to restore them. (Actually, Windows 98 won't allow you to restore files anywhere except to their original locations.)

Of course, if Windows 98 really saved everything you tried to throw out, you'd eventually run out of disk space. Even the largest of hard disks wouldn't be big enough to keep every file indefinitely. Sooner or later, depending on the Recycle Bin settings, Windows 98 must throw out some old stuff to make room for newer items you've discarded. This way, the items you're most likely to want to restore — the most recently deleted ones — will be in the Recycle Bin when you need them. The longer a file sits in the Recycle Bin, the less likely it is you'll discover you need the file back. For that matter, the longer a file sits in the Recycle Bin, the less likely it is you'll remember what the file was in the first place. At any rate, this is the logic behind the Recycle Bin's default settings.

From a practical standpoint, you'll probably want to do some hands-on Recycle Bin management. That is, you'll likely want to make certain that the Recycle Bin isn't so full of items you'll never need again that you have a difficult time finding the item you need. Depending on the Recycle Bin settings, you could find the Recycle Bin overflowing with hundreds or thousands of temporary junk files you'll never need again, and the one critical file you accidentally deleted last week may have been bumped to make room for them.

Sending Objects to the Recycle Bin

The Recycle Bin gives you something that's rare in life — a second chance in case you make a mistake. Unless you never make mistakes, the Recycle Bin can really save the day. It is easy to click the Delete icon or to press the Delete key on your keyboard. Without the Recycle Bin to serve as a temporary safe haven for files, these simple actions could cause major problems. The Recycle Bin stores deleted files, enabling you to restore them if needed. Once you know how to use the Recycle Bin, accidentally deleting a file will no longer cause a moment of panic. Restoring an important file will become a routine task.

Don't worry — using the Recycle Bin to protect yourself from yourself doesn't take a lot of extra work. Most of the time you won't do anything special to use the Recycle Bin instead of directly deleting files or folders.

As you see in the "Take Note" section, using the Recycle Bin is actually somewhat easier than not using it. Windows 98 operates that way on purpose. If you have to work harder to use the Recycle Bin, you probably use it only rarely, and chances are you won't use it when you really need it. If you know you are going to need to restore a file, you probably won't delete it in the first place.

CROSS-REFERENCE

See "Setting Recycle Bin Properties" in this chapter for more on controlling how the Recycle Bin works.

FIND IT ONLINE

For a tip on renaming the Recycle Bin, see **http://hardware.pairnet.com/howto/renamerecyclebin.html**.

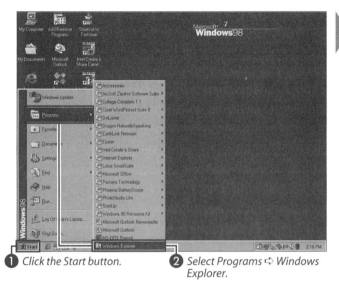

① Click the Start button.

② Select Programs ⇨ Windows Explorer.

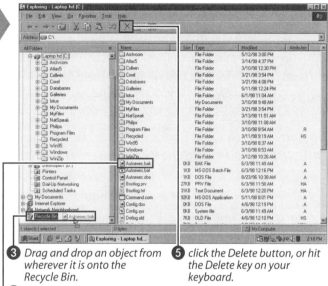

③ Drag and drop an object from wherever it is onto the Recycle Bin.

④ Alternatively, select the object and…

⑤ click the Delete button, or hit the Delete key on your keyboard.

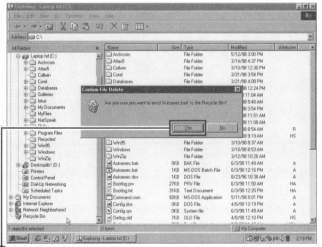

⑥ Click Yes to delete the file.

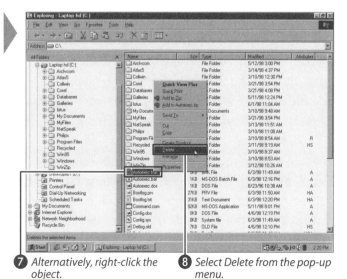

⑦ Alternatively, right-click the object.

⑧ Select Delete from the pop-up menu.

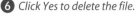

47

Viewing and Restoring Recycle Bin Contents

The Recycle Bin would not be very useful if you couldn't tell what it contained. You may be able to restore or delete everything at once, but that would be inefficient if you wished to restore only one file of hundreds the Recycle Bin may contain.

Once you've moved files or folders to the Recycle Bin, you can open it to view its contents. You can choose specific files or folders to restore or delete permanently. You can also choose to restore or remove all the files at once. Unless you're diligent about managing the contents of the Recycle Bin, however, it's more likely you'll want to work with individual files and folders.

The Recycle Bin is different from the other folders on your hard disk. You can't delete the Recycle Bin because that would cause problems for Windows 98. Another difference is that the Recycle Bin is the only place where two files can appear to have the same name without conflict, the reason being you may decide to delete identically named files from different folders. The files don't really have the same name — the folder name is actually part of every file's name — but in the Recycle Bin you'll see only the filename without the folder name. Fortunately, because the Recycle Bin remembers each file's origin, you can easily determine which copy of the file you wish to restore.

By default, files contained in the Recycle Bin are shown as icons without any detailed information. To learn more about a file, such as its original location, you can select the file. But as shown in the figures on the facing page, you can select the Details view and thereby make the Recycle Bin show complete information about every Recycle Bin object.

TAKE NOTE

▶ RECOGNIZING WHEN THE BIN HOLDS DELETED FILES

When the Recycle Bin contains deleted objects, its desktop icon changes. The empty Recycle Bin icon looks like an empty wastebasket. Once the Recycle Bin contains files or folders, its icon looks more like a wastebasket full of papers. The change is subtle, so it's easy to miss.

▶ THERE'S NO RECYCLE BIN FOR FLOPPY DISKS

Once you get used to using the Recycle Bin to protect you from accidental file deletions, you may be surprised to discover that Windows 98 doesn't have a Recycle Bin for files you delete from floppy disks. That's because the Recycle Bin stores the deleted files on the disk, and there isn't enough room to allow deleted files to remain on the floppy disk.

CROSS-REFERENCE

See "Emptying the Recycle Bin" later for information on making the Recycle Bin more manageable.

SHORTCUT

You can delete an object by dragging it onto the Recycle Bin icon on the desktop.

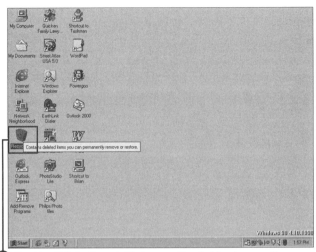

1 *Double-click the Recycle Bin icon on the desktop to open the Recycle Bin.*

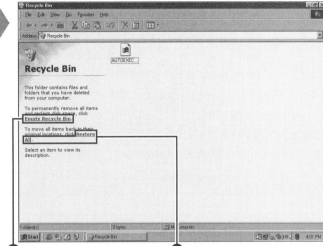

2 *Click Empty Recycle Bin to permanently delete everything from the Recycle Bin.*

3 *Alternatively, click Restore All to return all objects to their original locations.*

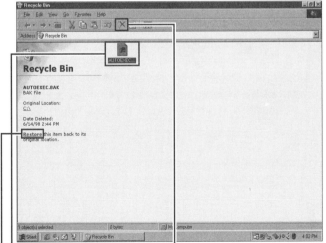

4 *Click an object to view its description.*

5 *Click Restore to return the selected object to its original location.*

6 *Alternatively, click the Delete button to permanently delete the file.*

7 *Click the down-arrow next to the Views button.*

8 *Select Details to view details on all Recycle Bin objects.*

Emptying the Recycle Bin

Emptying the Recycle Bin is like taking out the trash from your house or apartment. Everyone knows the job must be done, but few people want to be bothered with it until there's no other choice.

Windows 98 will automatically remove the oldest items when the Recycle Bin becomes too full to accept newer ones. This arrangement prevents the Recycle Bin from completely filling up your hard disk, so you need not empty the Recycle Bin yourself unless you want to do so. But letting Windows 98 handle the Recycle Bin contents automatically may not be the best idea.

By default, Windows 98 sets the size of your Recycle Bin to 10 percent of the size of your hard disk. On a typical 2GB hard disk, this means that 200MB of disk space may be set aside to hold the Recycle Bin contents. Depending on the size of the typical files on your system, this amount of space could represent hundreds or even thousands of files. Although that presents no problem for your computer, it makes it more difficult for you to find the file you need to restore.

You can choose to remove all of the Recycle Bin contents in one step, or you can select individual objects to delete (or restore). Remember, though, once you delete items from the Recycle Bin, they're gone forever and can't be restored.

TAKE NOTE

▶ INVERT YOUR SELECTION

When you first open the Recycle Bin you have the option of completely emptying it by deleting all the objects. If you'd rather save some of the items in case you may need them in the future, the best course is to select the files and folders you want to keep, choose Edit ⇨ Invert Selection, and then click the Delete button. Inverting the selection removes the objects you selected and adds all the others to the selection. This technique makes it easy to remove objects you won't ever need from the Recycle Bin.

▶ CONTROL THE RECYCLE BIN VIEW

In addition to changing to the details view, you may want to sort the Recycle Bin file listing to help determine which files to delete and which ones to restore. The easiest way to sort the file listing is to click one of the column heads that appear in the details view. When you click a column head, the view is sorted using the selected column. Click the column again to sort the items in reverse order.

CROSS-REFERENCE
See "Setting Recycle Bin Properties" (next) for information on controlling the Recycle Bin.

FIND IT ONLINE
For advanced file maintenance, check out Norton Utilities at **http://www.symantec.com/nu/**.

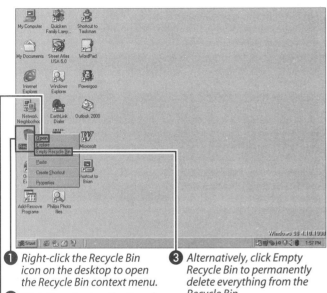

① Right-click the Recycle Bin icon on the desktop to open the Recycle Bin context menu.

② Click Open to view the Recycle Bin contents.

③ Alternatively, click Empty Recycle Bin to permanently delete everything from the Recycle Bin.

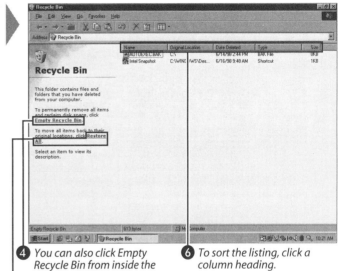

④ You can also click Empty Recycle Bin from inside the Recycle Bin dialog box.

⑤ Alternatively, click Restore All to return all objects to their original locations.

⑥ To sort the listing, click a column heading.

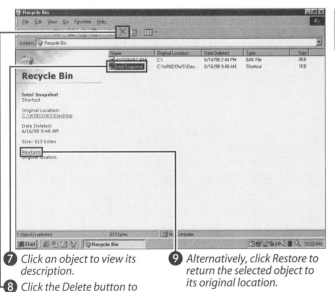

⑦ Click an object to view its description.

⑧ Click the Delete button to permanently delete the selected file.

⑨ Alternatively, click Restore to return the selected object to its original location.

⑩ Another way to permanently delete the file is to select File ➪ Delete.

Setting Recycle Bin Properties

You may find it convenient to have the Recycle Bin automatically protect you when you mistakenly delete files or folders, but you may not be happy with the default Recycle Bin settings. You may want to set aside more or less than the default 10 percent of your hard disk space for the Recycle Bin. You may be annoyed by the message box telling you that files will be moved to the Recycle Bin. You may want to use different settings for different drives, or perhaps you'd rather work without the Recycle Bin safety net altogether.

One of the most useful Recycle Bin property changes you can make is to eliminate the dialog box that appears when you delete an object. Normally, Windows 98 asks you to confirm that you want to move the object to the Recycle Bin. The first few hundred times you see the message you may find it helpful, but eventually you may tire of it. In that case, you can change a setting and thereafter skip the dialog box. Then when you delete an object, Windows 98 will send it straight to the Recycle Bin without reconfirming your action.

You can also choose to skip the Recycle Bin and delete files directly. It's hard to make a good case for using this option, because it eliminates any chance to recover from an accidental file deletion. If you like,

you can combine this with reducing the Recycle Bin size to the minimum effective size, which is 1 percent of your hard disk space.

TAKE NOTE

▶ **WHY USE DIFFERENT DRIVE SETTINGS?**

Most people don't need to set the Recycle Bin properties differently for different hard drives, but you may have reason to if you've set aside one hard disk for a special purpose such as creating master layouts for CD-ROM discs. If you need to dedicate an entire hard disk to the CD-ROM layout, you may be concerned about running out of space if the Recycle Bin uses up its allotted 10 percent of the disk space.

▶ **ELIMINATING THE DESKTOP RECYCLE BIN ICON**

The Recycle Bin is one of the icons that automatically appears on your Windows 98 desktop and seems to be impossible to remove. If you right-click the Recycle Bin icon you won't find an option for removing it. But if you prefer to have the cleanest desktop possible, you can take advantage of the options on the Desktop tab of the TweakUI dialog box. TweakUI should be an option in your Control Panel, but if it's not, look in the \tools\reskit\power-toy folder on your Windows 98 CD-ROM to install it.

CROSS-REFERENCE

See "Sending Objects to the Recycle Bin" earlier for information on skipping the Recycle Bin.

FIND IT ONLINE

See **http://www.microsoft.com/windows98/ basics/ features/tuningup/maintain.asp** for info on Disk Cleanup, a Windows 98 program for deleting files.

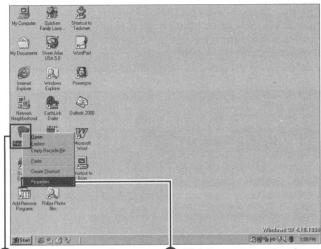

① Right-click the Recycle Bin icon on the desktop to open the Recycle Bin context menu.

② Click Properties to view the Recycle Bin Properties dialog box.

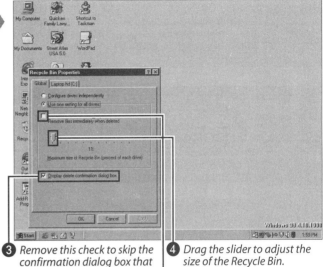

③ Remove this check to skip the confirmation dialog box that appears each time you delete a file from the Recycle Bin.

④ Drag the slider to adjust the size of the Recycle Bin.

⑤ Check here to delete files without using the Recycle Bin.

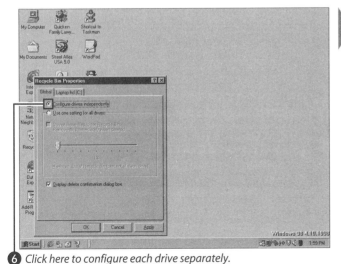

⑥ Click here to configure each drive separately.

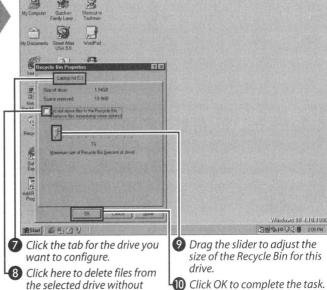

⑦ Click the tab for the drive you want to configure.

⑧ Click here to delete files from the selected drive without using the Recycle Bin.

⑨ Drag the slider to adjust the size of the Recycle Bin for this drive.

⑩ Click OK to complete the task.

Personal Workbook

Q&A

1 How can you bypass the Recycle Bin, and delete a file permanently?

_____

_____

_____

2 Why is it more dangerous to delete files from floppy disks than from hard disks?

_____

_____

_____

3 What two methods can you use to determine the original location of files in the Recycle Bin?

_____

_____

4 How much space will the default size Recycle Bin take on a 2GB hard disk?

_____

_____

_____

5 How do the Delete and Cut toolbar buttons differ?

_____

_____

_____

_____

6 How can two objects in the Recycle Bin appear to have the same name?

_____

_____

_____

_____

7 How can you change the Recycle Bin sort order?

_____

_____

_____

_____

ANSWERS: PAGE 354

EXTRA PRACTICE

1 Drag several files onto the Recycle Bin icon.

2 Move several files to the Recycle Bin using the Delete button on the Windows Explorer toolbar.

3 View the contents of the Recycle Bin.

4 Select and restore one of the files in the Recycle Bin.

5 Select and delete one of the files in the Recycle Bin.

6 Restore the remaining files in the Recycle Bin.

7 Prevent the delete confirmation dialog box from appearing when you delete files.

REAL-WORLD APPLICATIONS

✔ You start running short on disk space, and you need to remove a bunch of your old files. You'll likely discover that you deleted at least one file in error and will need to use the Recycle Bin to restore the file.

✔ You allow someone else to use your computer, and you discover that your friend accidentally deleted some of your important files. You use the Recycle Bin to rescue your work.

✔ You've been assigned to prepare a confidential report that must be deleted from the hard disk. After you make a backup on a floppy disk, you hold down the Shift key when you delete the file. This technique prevents the copy from being moved to the Recycle Bin, where it could otherwise be retrieved by an unauthorized person.

Visual Quiz

How do you display this dialog box? Which part of the dialog box do you use to control how much disk space the Recycle Bin uses? Where would you place a check mark if you didn't want deleted items to go to the Recycle Bin?

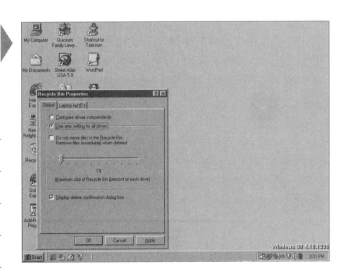

_____

_____

_____

_____

_____

PART

II

Customizing Windows 98

Do you like to have things you can call your own? Do you like to do things your own way? If you do, this part of the book is for you. Here, you learn how to change the way Windows 98 looks and how it works.

There are many things you can do to customize Windows 98. If you don't like the colors on your screen, you learn how to change them. If the words on your screen are too small and hard to read, you learn how to fix that, too. Do you want to liven things up with moving images when your computer is idle? Or how about changing the sounds Windows 98 makes when it displays a message? You can easily customize these and many other Windows 98 features, and this part explains how to do it.

This part also shows you how to apply the accessibility options. These options can make a PC much easier to use, especially for people who have trouble using the standard PC conventions.

CHAPTER 4

MASTER THESE SKILLS

▶ **Configuring the Desktop Background**

▶ **Changing Desktop Colors**

▶ **Using a Screen Saver**

▶ **Adding Active Desktop Content**

▶ **Changing Desktop Resolution**

▶ **Moving and Hiding the Taskbar**

▶ **Putting New Objects on the Desktop**

Changing the Look of Windows 98

For many reasons, you may prefer that your Windows 98 desktop look different than everyone else's desktop. Windows 98 has many looks, all of them based on options that you select. This chapter explains how you can change the look of things on the screen for your personal preferences.

You can do quite a bit to change the appearance of Windows 98. Some of the changes you can make include displaying a picture, called *wallpaper*, as a background on the desktop. You can also use different colors, add a screen saver so that your computer looks as if it's doing something when you aren't using it, and change the screen resolution. In this chapter you learn how to make all these modifications as well as a number of other changes. If you share your PC with other people, you may find that not everyone enjoys your tastes in the appearance of Windows 98. If so, each person who uses the PC can configure his or her preferences and enter

his or her name and password when starting Windows 98. In this way the system will look just as it did the last time your colleague used the computer, and any appearance changes you make will affect the PC only when you're using it.

Most of the changes you make as you follow along in this chapter affect only the Windows 98 appearance. Be aware, however, that a few of the options can also affect how Windows 98 operates. For example, if you activate a screen saver and you specify a password, you must remember the password if you want to get back to Windows 98 once the screen saver is running. If you move or hide the taskbar, other users may not realize what they must do to open the Start menu. This may result in someone shutting down Windows 98 incorrectly, perhaps causing you to lose any work you haven't saved. When in doubt, use caution with changes that make it difficult for someone to access the standard Windows 98 screen elements.

Configuring the Desktop Background

Do you like the background that appears on your Windows 98 desktop, or would you rather have something more distinctive? Would you prefer to have bright wallpaper or a favorite picture in the background? There's no reason you can't have the look you prefer on your Windows 98 screen.

Windows 98 uses the term *wallpaper* to describe desktop background images. All the desktop icons appear in front of the wallpaper. Anything else on your desktop, such as the Channel Bar or any active content, also sits in front of the wallpaper. Even though your desktop wallpaper sits on the desktop behind everything else, some wallpaper images can make it difficult to see desktop icons, especially if the wallpaper is loaded with a number of dark colors. If you encounter this type of problem with your favorite wallpaper, you may want to try centering the image rather than tiling or stretching it.

Windows 95 allowed you to add an image to your desktop, but only if the image was in Windows Bitmap (BMP) format. Windows 98 allows you to design your desktop by enabling you to use JPEG images. JPEG images are easy to find and use far less disk space than Windows Bitmap images. Most of the images you find on the Internet are JPEG images.

Most digital cameras produce JPEG images. You must enable the Active Desktop in order to use JPEG images as your Windows 98 desktop wallpaper, as explained later in this chapter. If the Active Desktop isn't activated, Windows 98 will offer to activate it when you choose a JPEG image to show on your desktop.

TAKE NOTE

STRETCH WITH CARE

Your Windows 98 desktop is measured in units called *pixels*. Digital images are also usually measured in pixels. It is likely that most images aren't the same size as your desktop, so you may end up with blank space around a desktop image, or the image may extend beyond the edges of the screen. Windows 98 offers you the option to stretch the image to fit, but unless the image is in the same 4-wide-by-3-high ratio as your screen, this will probably distort the image when it appears on the desktop.

WALLPAPERED FOLDERS

Wallpaper the background of folders by opening a folder and selecting View ➪ Customize this Folder. Select the wallpaper background option, choose a background, and follow the remaining instructions.

CROSS-REFERENCE

See "Changing Desktop Resolution" later in this chapter.

FIND IT ONLINE

See **http://www.nasa.gov/gallery/photo/index.htm** for a great source of graphics.

CHANGING THE LOOK OF WINDOWS 98
Configuring the Desktop Background

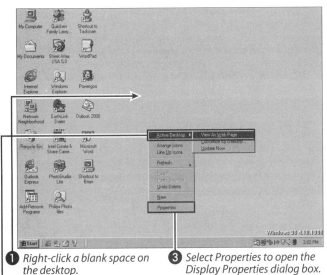

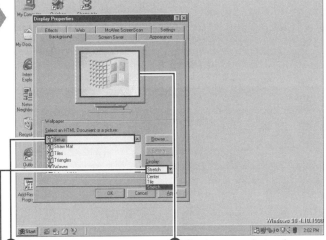

❶ Right-click a blank space on the desktop.

❷ Select Active Desktop ➪ View As Web Page to enable JPEG images and HTML documents to be used as wallpaper.

❸ Select Properties to open the Display Properties dialog box.

❹ Choose an image to use as wallpaper.

❺ Select the method of displaying the image from the drop-down Display list box.

❻ Preview your choices here.

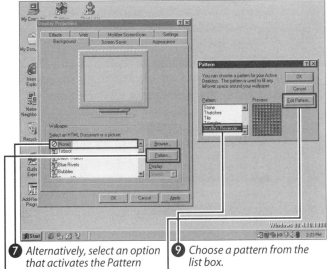

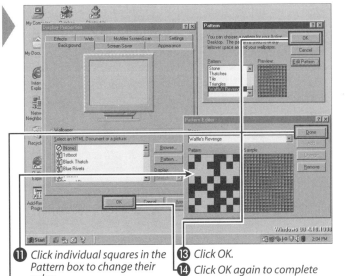

❼ Alternatively, select an option that activates the Pattern button.

❽ Click Pattern to open the Pattern dialog box.

❾ Choose a pattern from the list box.

❿ Click Edit Pattern to open the Pattern Editor dialog box if you wish to edit your selection.

⓫ Click individual squares in the Pattern box to change their color.

⓬ Click Done.

⓭ Click OK.

⓮ Click OK again to complete the task.

Changing Desktop Colors

Just as you have many options for background wallpaper images on your Windows 98 desktop, you also have a broad range of options when it comes to configuring colors for many of the elements of your Windows 98 screen. If you prefer a given screen element to be pale blue or fluorescent green, you can configure it accordingly. If you need a high-contrast color scheme to make the screen more readable, you can have that, too. The Take Note section on this page contains more information on the available high-contrast color schemes.

Once you've created a color scheme that you like, click the Save As button in the Appearance tab of the Display Properties dialog box. In this way you'll be able to return quickly to your scheme if someone else uses your PC and changes the color selections. If you save your color scheme when you first open the dialog box, you can experiment at will and conveniently undo any changes you've made.

Keep in mind that the changes you make on the Appearance tab of the Display Properties dialog box apply to items that Windows 98 can control. Generally, these changes will not affect such things as the text fonts, sizes, and colors that appear in programs such as word processors. In most cases you must make those adjustments within the programs themselves.

TAKE NOTE

USE HIGH CONTRAST FOR VISIBILITY

If you have difficulty viewing the Windows 98 screen, you may want to try using one of the Windows 98 high-contrast color schemes. These color schemes are designed to help make the Windows 98 screen much easier to view, especially in poor lighting conditions or for visually impaired Windows 98 users. Each of these color schemes includes two optional settings that display text in either large or extra large characters. You may need to experiment with the high-contrast color schemes to see which one works best for you. And, on the flip-side, you may want to hand-select desktop colors that are muted, ot toned down. Less glaring colors can help prevent eyestrain.

BE CAREFUL WHEN CHOOSING TEXT COLORS

Windows 98 enables you to select text colors that match the background colors of a screen element. If you pick text colors that are the same as the background colors, you won't be able to see the text. Choosing that option could make it virtually impossible to use Windows 98. If you accidentally set your text colors this way, choose another one of the Windows 98 color schemes to reset the colors so that you can see message text.

SHORTCUT

Click screen elements in the preview window to place them in the Item list box.

FIND IT ONLINE

See **http://windowsupdate.microsoft.com/default.htm** for additional desktop themes.

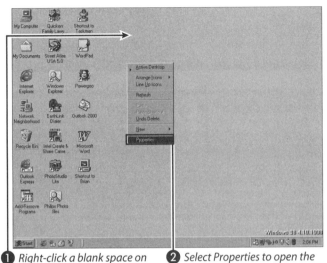

❶ *Right-click a blank space on the desktop.*

❷ *Select Properties to open the Display Properties dialog box.*

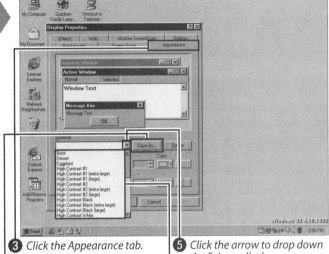

❸ *Click the Appearance tab.*

❹ *Click Save As to save your current color scheme before you make any changes.*

❺ *Click the arrow to drop down the Scheme list box.*

❻ *Choose a color scheme from the list.*

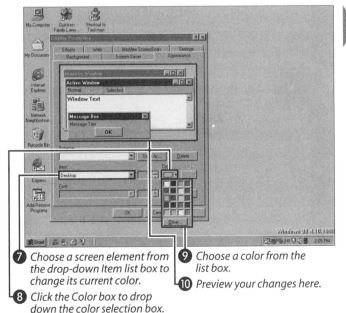

❼ *Choose a screen element from the drop-down Item list box to change its current color.*

❽ *Click the Color box to drop down the color selection box.*

❾ *Choose a color from the list box.*

❿ *Preview your changes here.*

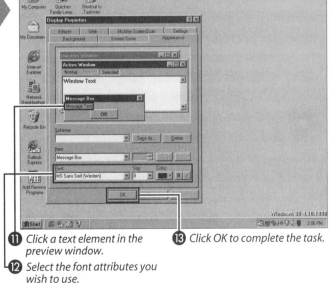

⓫ *Click a text element in the preview window.*

⓬ *Select the font attributes you wish to use.*

⓭ *Click OK to complete the task.*

Using a Screen Saver

With a name like *screen saver* you may think that this Windows 98 accessory would serve an important purpose in saving your monitor from some type of damage. Screen savers were first developed to prevent images from being permanently burned in on the screen. Thanks to advancements in monitor technologies, you don't need a screen saver because no damage occurs from normal computer use. Screen savers today exist for two primary purposes: they look nice and they can provide a small measure of security. Be sure to read the "Take Note" section, however, before you count on a screen saver too heavily for security.

A Windows 98 screen saver can save you money if your monitor is equipped with energy-saving features. Virtually all PCs come with monitors that go into a very low power standby mode when they receive the appropriate signal from the computer. The monitor generally uses the most power of all your computer's components. Automatically shutting down the monitor may save more than half the power otherwise consumed by your system. This arrangement enables you to leave the system turned on to receive incoming faxes or so that Windows 98 can perform routine system maintenance while the computer is idle . Leaving the system turned on may also be a little easier on your computer's components.

The screen savers that come with Windows 98 are optional. If you don't see any choices in the Screen Saver list box, open the Add/Remove Programs item in the Control Panel and use the Windows Setup tab to add the screen savers.

TAKE NOTE

▶ DON'T DEPEND ON SCREEN SAVER SECURITY

If you use a screen saver and a password to prevent other people from accessing your PC, don't depend too heavily on the security provided by the screen saver password. If someone is determined to access your files, he or she can bypass the screen saver simply by turning off the PC and then restarting it. If you need to secure your files against access, you'll need much stronger security measures.

▶ POWER MANAGEMENT OPTIONS VARY

Your power management options may not be the same as those shown in the Power Management Properties dialog box in the lower-right figure on the facing page. Laptop computers generally have more extensive power management options than do desktop systems. Even so, using the power management options that are available on your system is a good way to conserve energy.

CROSS-REFERENCE

See "Installing Accessory Applications" in Chapter 12.

FIND IT ONLINE

Search for screen savers at **http://www.yahoo.com/ Business_and_Economy/Companies/Computers/ Software /.**

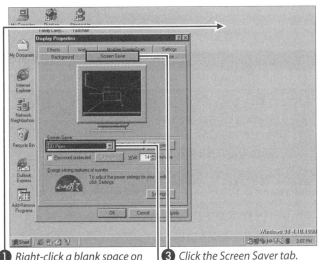

1 Right-click a blank space on the desktop.

2 Select Properties to open the Display Properties dialog box.

3 Click the Screen Saver tab.

4 Choose a screen saver from the Screen Saver list box.

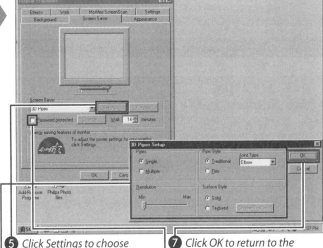

5 Click Settings to choose options for the screen saver you just selected.

6 Choose the options you prefer.

7 Click OK to return to the Display Properties dialog box.

8 Click the Password protected check box to set a password.

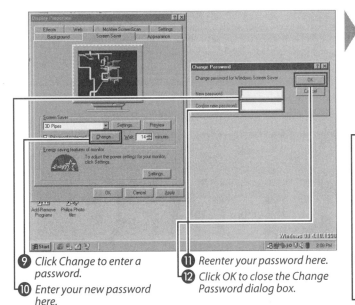

9 Click Change to enter a password.

10 Enter your new password here.

11 Reenter your password here.

12 Click OK to close the Change Password dialog box.

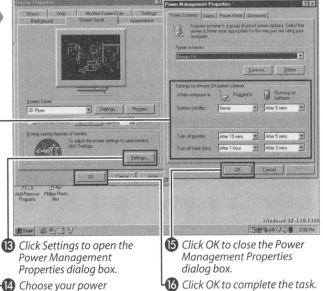

13 Click Settings to open the Power Management Properties dialog box.

14 Choose your power management settings. (These setting options vary.)

15 Click OK to close the Power Management Properties dialog box.

16 Click OK to complete the task.

Adding Active Desktop Content

Information has always been crucial, and today is highly accessible, in part because of Windows 98. You can have information delivered to your desktop so you'll always be aware of current weather conditions, sports scores, breaking news stories, or the latest stock market conditions. What makes all this possible is the Windows 98 *Active Desktop* — an active link between your desktop and information on the Internet.

Active Desktop content is usually updated automatically at intervals you specify. If you have a dedicated, full-time Internet connection, you can have content delivered as quickly as it's updated on the Web site.

The figures accompanying this task show one example of the available Active Desktop content. At the Microsoft Active Desktop Gallery Web site you'll find a frequently updated set of options that you can choose for your desktop. When you visit the Web site you'll find a large variety of interesting items in addition to the MSNBC weather map selected for this example.

The first time you access Microsoft's Active Desktop Gallery Web site, you'll see one or more security warnings as shown in the lower-left figure on the facing page. These security warnings tell you that in order for you to continue, certain program files must be downloaded and then run on your PC. Downloading programs and running them on your system can pose a risk. If you don't allow the programs to be installed and run, you won't be able to download active content for your desktop.

The lower-right figure on the facing page shows that you can choose content from several different categories. As you click on each of the category buttons, you'll see the options currently available in that category.

Continued

TAKE NOTE

ACTIVE CONTENT REQUIRES WEB PAGE VIEW

If you want to add any active content to your Windows 98 desktop, you must select the "View my Active Desktop as a web page" check box that appears on the Web tab of the Display Properties dialog box.

TRUSTING DIGITAL CERTIFICATES

When Internet Explorer displays a security warning, it also provides information about the authenticity of the content based on *digital certificates* — electronic identifications that verify the publisher of the content. You can click the More Info button to learn more about the digital certificate and the content publisher. To eliminate future security warnings for a content publisher such as Microsoft, you can check the "Always trust content from Microsoft Corporation" check box. In this way, any content that has a valid digital certificate verifying the publisher as Microsoft can be downloaded without further approval.

CROSS-REFERENCE

See "Viewing Channels" in Chapter 14.

FIND IT ONLINE

The Active Desktop Gallery is at
http://www.microsoft.com/ie/ie40/gallery/.

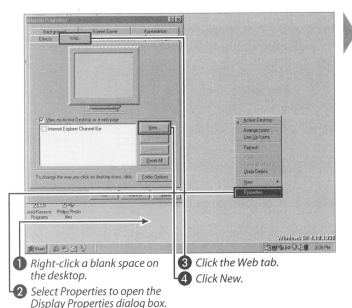

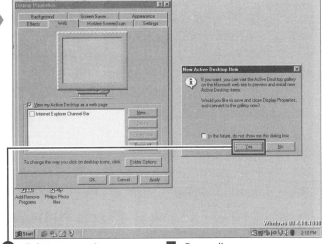

1 *Right-click a blank space on the desktop.*

2 *Select Properties to open the Display Properties dialog box.*

3 *Click the Web tab.*

4 *Click New.*

5 *Click Yes to continue.*

■ *Depending on your connection you may need to confirm that you want to connect to the Internet.*

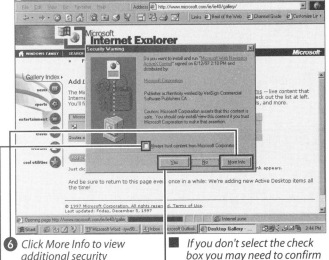

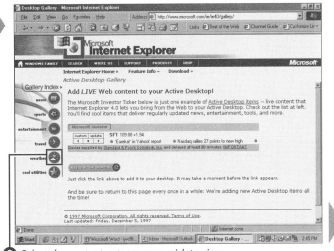

6 *Click More Info to view additional security information.*

7 *Check this box if you wish to prevent this message from appearing in the future.*

■ *If you don't select the check box you may need to confirm several security warnings.*

8 *Click Yes to continue.*

9 *Select the content category you wish to view.*

Adding Active Desktop Content

Continued

Some of the Active Desktop Gallery categories have several options that you can choose, whereas others may be more like the weather category shown on the facing page. To learn more about each of the items in a category, click the item to view a sample and a description.

Active content is useful only if it's updated regularly. A weather map may look nice when you first add it to your desktop, but it will soon become outdated. You probably don't want last week's weather map taking up space on your desktop. That's where *subscriptions* enter the picture. Subscriptions are schedules for updating your active content. You might, for example, schedule the weather map for an update every morning just before you begin work. Or you might decide to have the updates occur more often, especially for content such as a news wire or a stock ticker.

Most subscriptions are free, but there's no guarantee that they'll remain that way in the future. As companies try to figure out how to make the Internet profitable, you can expect that interesting content will be available on a pay-as-you-go basis.

After you've added active content to your desktop, you'll notice that the objects you've added don't appear to have menus or other means of controlling them. This is deceptive. Active desktop objects have menus — the trick is in how to make those menus appear. Move the mouse pointer over an active desktop object; you'll notice a thin gray border around the object. Move the mouse pointer to the top edge of the object, and the top border will expand enough so that you can see a small down-arrow in the upper-left corner. Click the arrow to expose the menu hidden at the top of the object. Select Properties to pop up a standard Windows 98 dialog box that will enable you to control how the object is updated. If you want to remove the object from your desktop, click the small Close button in the upper-right corner of the object's header bar.

CROSS-REFERENCE
See "Starting Internet Explorer" in Chapter 14.

SHORTCUT
Activate or deactivate Active Desktop content on the Web tab of the Display Properties dialog box.

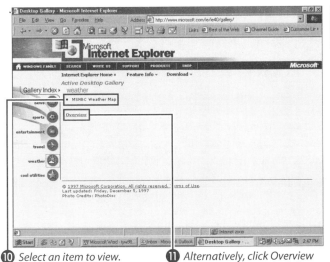

⑩ Select an item to view.

⑪ Alternatively, click Overview to return to the main Gallery.

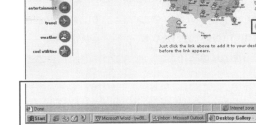

⑫ Click Add to Active Desktop.

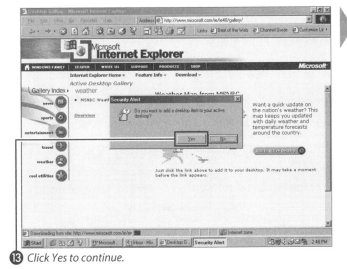

⑬ Click Yes to continue.

⑭ Click OK to begin downloading the content to your desktop.

■ Wait for the download to complete before you continue.

⑮ Click the Close button to close Internet Explorer.

■ The weather map or other active content you selected should now appear on your desktop.

Changing Desktop Resolution

The image you see on your Windows 98 desktop is measured in units known as *pixels*, which is shorthand for "picture elements." The number of pixels that are displayed is called the *screen resolution*. As PCs have become more powerful and monitor sizes have grown, screen resolution has increased considerably. Several years ago the VGA resolution of 640×480 pixels was standard, but today's systems typically use higher-resolution settings such as 800×600; $1,024 \times 768$; $1,280 \times 1,024$; or even $1,600 \times 1,200$ on very large monitors.

Depending on your monitor, you may discover that your screen takes on a strange appearance when you change the resolution settings. The Windows 98 desktop may not fill the screen, or the desktop may be too wide or too tall. If this happens, you need to adjust your monitor's controls to make the screen look normal. In most cases, though, modern monitors can store several different settings; if you change back to your original resolution you probably won't have to readjust the screen.

When you change to a higher resolution, you may find that your PC cannot display as many colors as it can at lower resolutions. This is a function of the amount of memory in your display adapter and generally cannot be changed without replacing the adapter. Even so, a 2MB graphics card can display more than 65,000 colors at $1,024 \times 768$ resolution.

CROSS-REFERENCE
See "Changing Desktop Colors" earlier in this chapter.

FIND IT ONLINE
See **http://www.windows98.org/resources.html** for more configuration tips.

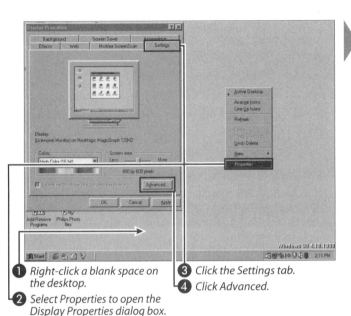

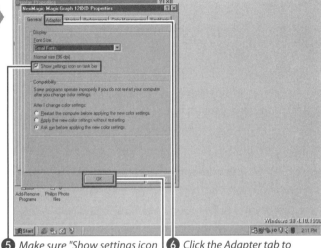

① *Right-click a blank space on the desktop.*

③ *Click the Settings tab.*

④ *Click Advanced.*

② *Select Properties to open the Display Properties dialog box.*

⑤ *Make sure "Show settings icon on task bar" is selected.*

■ *This lets you change screen resolution by clicking an icon on the system tray.*

⑥ *Click the Adapter tab to locate an option to set monitor refresh rate. Use caution when changing this setting.*

⑦ *Click OK to continue.*

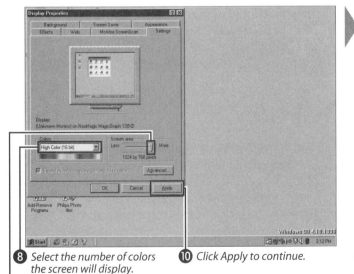

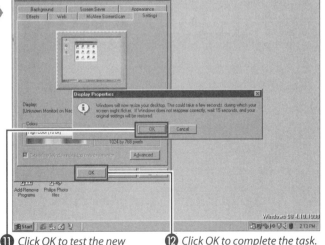

⑧ *Select the number of colors the screen will display.*

⑩ *Click Apply to continue.*

⑨ *Drag the slider to the desired resolution setting.*

⑪ *Click OK to test the new setting.*

■ *If acceptable, click Yes within 15 seconds when Windows 98 asks whether you want to keep the new setting.*

⑫ *Click OK to complete the task.*

Moving and Hiding the Taskbar

The long horizontal bar that usually appears at the bottom of the desktop is the taskbar. The taskbar often contains several elements: the Start menu button, the Quick Launch toolbar, buttons for open windows, and the system tray.

When you have many windows open, the taskbar may not be long enough to hold all the window buttons, or it may not be long enough for you to read the title on each button. There are several ways around this problem. You can make the taskbar larger so that there is room for two or more rows of buttons, or you can also move the taskbar to either side or the top of the screen. When the taskbar is at either side of the screen, it is usually large enough to hold many more buttons. Or you can remove the Quick Launch toolbar and the clock to create a bit of extra screen space.

You can do other things to the taskbar. You can add toolbars to it, cause it to hide itself, and allow applications to overlap it. Hiding the taskbar or allowing applications to overlap it provides you with more screen real estate and may be especially useful when you need all possible room for workspace. (On a related note, some applications, such as Internet Explorer, enable you to hide their title bars, toolbars, and menus so that nothing interferes with what you see.)

If the taskbar is hidden you can usually redisplay it by moving the mouse pointer off the edge of the screen where the taskbar is hiding. This doesn't work if the Auto hide check box (shown in the upper-left figure on the facing page) is checked. That's how software installation programs often try to prevent you from getting to the taskbar. The "Take Note" section tells you how to work around this problem.

TAKE NOTE

▶ FINDING THE TASKBAR

Programs sometimes hide the taskbar to prevent you from doing anything else while they're running. This is most common with software installation programs. There are times, however, when you need to do something else, such as explore your hard disk to find a place to install a program. When the taskbar is hidden, press the Windows key if your keyboard has one to pop up the Start menu and display the taskbar. This works no matter where the taskbar is hiding.

▶ USING THE ADDRESS BAR

If you know the URL of a Web page you'd like to visit, the quickest way to go directly to the site is to add the Address toolbar to the taskbar and then enter the URL into the Address bar. After you type the address and press Enter, Internet Explorer opens and takes you directly to the Web site, bypassing any start pages that Internet Explorer normally opens first.

CROSS-REFERENCE
See "Changing Desktop Colors" earlier in this chapter.

SHORTCUT
To pop up the hidden taskbar any time, press Ctrl+Esc or press the Windows key on your keyboard.

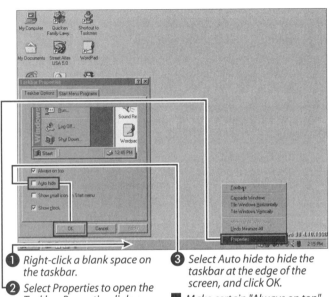

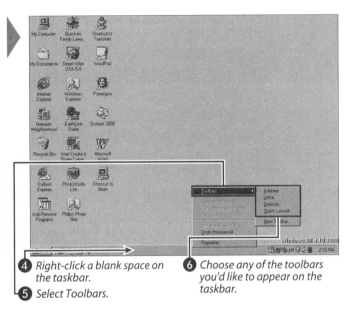

① Right-click a blank space on the taskbar.

② Select Properties to open the Taskbar Properties dialog box.

③ Select Auto hide to hide the taskbar at the edge of the screen, and click OK.

■ Make certain "Always on top" is checked.

④ Right-click a blank space on the taskbar.

⑤ Select Toolbars.

⑥ Choose any of the toolbars you'd like to appear on the taskbar.

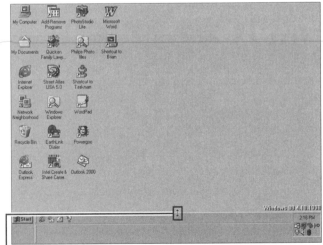

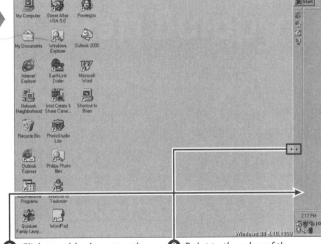

⑦ Drag the top of the taskbar up or down to change its size.

■ When the taskbar is at the top or bottom of the screen, it will resize only in increments equal to the height of the taskbar buttons.

⑧ Click on a blank spot on the taskbar and drag the taskbar to one edge of the screen.

⑨ Point to the edge of the taskbar. When the mouse pointer changes to a double-headed arrow, drag the edge to resize the taskbar.

Putting New Objects on the Desktop

Your Windows 98 desktop is a handy place. Anything on your desktop is easy to find and easy to open. This makes your desktop the perfect place to keep things that you need to use often. That's one of the reasons many of your programs place an icon on your desktop. That's also why you'll want to create your own desktop objects.

If you look at your desktop, you'll probably discover that most of the icons represent application programs rather than documents. If you think about the way you work with your computer, you'll see that this arrangement may not be ideal. When you work on a task, you're most likely thinking about what you want to accomplish.

Windows 98 is designed to help you think in terms of documents rather than only in terms of the tools you'll use to create documents. When you install programs on your system, Windows 98 keeps a record of the types of documents each program understands. So if you want to open a document you don't need to worry about first opening the program that created the document. Instead, Windows 98 will open the appropriate program along with your document. Double-click the document icon, and your document will open.

TAKE NOTE

USING SHORTCUTS

Putting a shortcut — rather than the actual document — on the desktop provides an added measure of safety. If you delete a shortcut, only the shortcut is deleted, and your document remains in its original location. If you've placed the document itself on your desktop, you might accidentally delete the document. The figures on the facing page show you how easy it is to create a shortcut to your documents. Don't forget, though, that your desktop already contains an icon for the My Documents folder. Even if you don't create shortcuts to all your documents, you can store them in the My Documents folder, where they're only a few clicks away.

KEEP YOUR DESKTOP NEAT

If you start adding a lot of extra things to your desktop you'll probably end up with a mess. To maintain some order you can right-click the desktop and select Arrange Icons ➪ Auto Arrange. This action will make all the icons line up in neat rows and columns without overlapping. Any new icons you add later will automatically arrange themselves, too. And don't forget another important bit of housekeeping — deleting things you no longer need.

CROSS-REFERENCE

See "Viewing and Restoring Recycle Bin Contents" in Chapter 3.

FIND IT ONLINE

Download icons for your desktop at
http://www.screensandthemes.com/Icons/index.html.

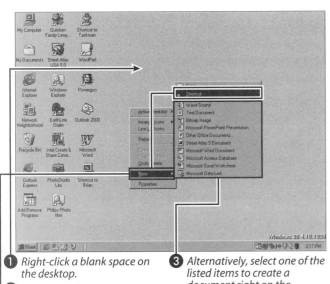

① Right-click a blank space on the desktop.

② Select New ➪ Shortcut to open the Create Shortcut dialog box.

③ Alternatively, select one of the listed items to create a document right on the desktop.

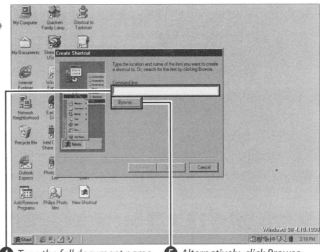

④ Type the full document name (including the path) in the Command line text box.

⑤ Alternatively, click Browse.

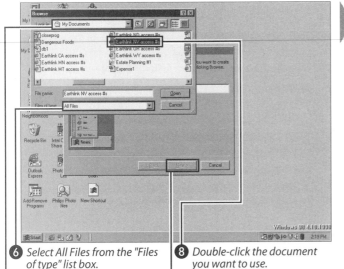

⑥ Select All Files from the "Files of type" list box.

⑦ Choose the folder containing the document from the "Look in" list box.

⑧ Double-click the document you want to use.

⑨ Click Next to continue.

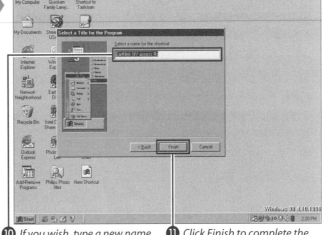

⑩ If you wish, type a new name for the document shortcut.

⑪ Click Finish to complete the task.

Personal Workbook

Q&A

1 What do you need to activate before you can use a JPEG image as your desktop wallpaper?

_____

_____

2 What is the fastest way to choose a desktop element on the Appearance tab of the Display Properties dialog box to change the element's color?

_____

_____

_____

3 How can someone bypass your screen saver password?

_____

_____

_____

4 What is the name of the process that automatically updates Active Desktop content?

_____

_____

5 What will happen if you change the screen resolution setting but don't click the Yes button?

_____

_____

6 How can you make a hidden taskbar pop up without moving the mouse?

_____

_____

7 How can you find a hidden taskbar using the mouse?

_____

_____

8 What setting will make the taskbar hide even from the mouse?

_____

_____

9 What will Windows 98 do when you double-click on a document on the desktop?

_____

_____

ANSWERS: PAGE 355

EXTRA PRACTICE

1 Add the Setup image as your desktop wallpaper.

2 Change the desktop to bright red.

3 Try out a different screen resolution setting.

4 Add a news ticker to your desktop.

5 Move the taskbar to the left side of your screen.

6 Place a shortcut to one of your documents onto your desktop.

REAL-WORLD APPLICATIONS

✔ You are planning an open house for your customers. To promote your company image, you use a picture of your company logo as the wallpaper on everyone's desktop.

✔ Your sister sends you a digital photograph of your new nephew, but it's too large to view on your screen. You increase your screen resolution to view the entire image.

✔ You assist at the computer center for an elementary school. To help the youngest students learn how to use a computer, you select a high-contrast color scheme that uses larger text.

Visual Quiz

This image shows the 3D FlowerBox Setup dialog box. How can you display this dialog box? What purpose does it serve?

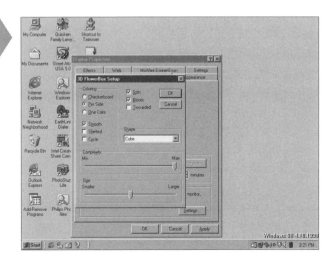

_____

_____

_____

_____

_____

CHAPTER 5

MASTER THESE SKILLS

- Changing to a Single-Click Mouse
- Configuring the Mouse
- Configuring Your Keyboard
- Adding Sounds to System Events
- Setting the Accessibility Options
- Adding New Hardware

Changing the Way Windows 98 Works

hanging the appearance of Windows 98 is fun, but changing how Windows 98 works can help make you more productive. Computers are, after all, tools to help you do things more efficiently. They should work with you and not make you work harder.

Many of the changes you can make to Windows 98 are small and subtle. By themselves, they probably won't make much difference, but, taken as a whole, small changes can add up to real improvements.

If everyone were identical, there would be no need to customize the way Windows 98 works. The same settings would be optimal for all PC users and nothing would need adjustment. In the real world, however, people are different. You may be the world's fastest typist and want to configure your keyboard for lightning-fast response. But if you're a hunt-and-peck typist, that setting would make your keyboard repeat characters too quickly. Perhaps you're helping someone with special needs who requires extra help using a computer. In this chapter you learn how to deal with all these issues to make your Windows 98-based PC easier to use.

You can access each of the settings discussed in this chapter through the Windows 98 Control Panel. The Control Panel is the one central location where you'll find the tools you need to configure and control nearly all aspects of how your PC runs under Windows 98. The Control Panel contents can vary depending on your system's configuration. You may not have all the icons shown in this chapter's figures, and your Control Panel may include others that aren't shown here. You need not be concerned about this difference; you'll have the ones you need for this chapter. (There may be one exception: If the Accessibility Options icon isn't in your Control Panel, you may need to use the Windows Setup tab of the Add/Remove Programs dialog box to add the Accessibility options.)

None of the changes you make in this chapter will pose any danger to your system, and all of them are easy to reverse if you decide you don't like the results. That's not the case, however, for all the changes you can make through the Control Panel. Some Control Panel options can cause major problems if you make changes just to see what will happen. When in doubt, don't change anything you don't understand.

Changing to a Single-Click Mouse

Have you ever wondered why your mouse works differently when you're browsing the Internet than it does when you're browsing the folders on your PC? Why, for example, does a single mouse click take you from place to place on the Internet, but you must double-click to do most tasks when you're accessing things on your computer? The answer is that it doesn't have to be different — you can set up your mouse to work the same way in both places.

Windows 98 uses the terms *classic style* and *Web style* to indicate the two types of mouse behavior. In the classic style, a single click of the left mouse button selects an object, and a double-click opens it. This style is consistent with the way most people are used to a mouse working. In the Web style, moving the mouse over an object selects the object, and a single click opens it. When you're browsing the Web, moving your mouse over a link selects the link and a single click opens the link.

When the mouse is set up for Web style, selecting multiple objects can be a bit of an adventure, at least until you're used to the process. First, you move the mouse pointer over an object, and then you hold down either the Shift key or the Ctrl key depending on whether you wish to select a contiguous range or several individual items. Next, you move the mouse

pointer to the next (or last) item you wish to select. The tricky part comes when you don't want to select everything between the first and last items. To accomplish this you must move the mouse pointer carefully so that it touches only the items you want to select. If you select an item in error, move the mouse pointer onto the object and then away from it.

TAKE NOTE

▶ SINGLE CLICKS MAY TAKE PRACTICE

If you decide to configure your mouse to use single-clicking rather than double-clicking, you may find that it takes a little bit of practice to get used to the change. You may, for example, discover that you're opening files when you meant only to add them to a selection. This can be especially true if you use a laptop system that has a touchpad that you use both for moving the mouse pointer and, by tapping the touchpad, for clicking the left mouse button.

▶ USE DETAILS OR LIST VIEW WITH WEB STYLE

If you select the Web style, you'll soon discover that it's much easier to use the Windows Explorer details and list views than to use the small or large icons views.

CROSS-REFERENCE
See "Configuring Mouse Speed" later in this chapter.

FIND IT ONLINE
If you have a three-button mouse be sure to visit http://www.digconsys.com/.

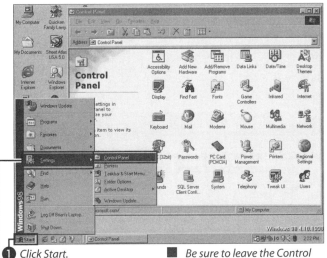

1 Click Start.

2 Select Settings ➪ Control Panel.

■ Be sure to leave the Control Panel open when you complete this task. You'll need it for the other tasks in this chapter.

3 Select View ➪ Folder Options to open the Folder Options dialog box.

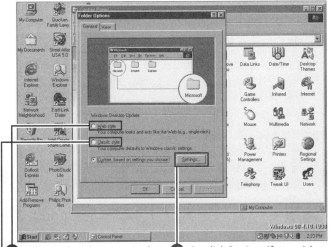

4 Select Web style to use single mouse clicks to open objects.

5 Alternatively, select Classic style to use double mouse clicks to open objects.

6 Or, click Settings if you wish to customize the mouse settings.

■ If you chose to customize your options in Step 6, proceed to Step 7.

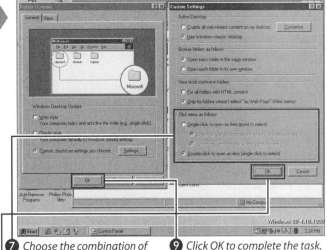

7 Choose the combination of settings that suits your needs.

8 Click OK to close the Custom Settings dialog box.

9 Click OK to complete the task.

Configuring the Mouse

If it ever seems that your mouse is sluggish or that it doesn't recognize double-clicks properly, this task shows you how to adjust it. You'll also learn how to liven up your mouse pointers and find some alternatives to the hourglass.

One difference between Windows-based PCs and the Macintosh has always been the mouse. The Mac mouse has a single button compared with most PC mice, which have two buttons. The extra button on the PC mouse makes it easy to access context-sensitive menus by right-clicking an object. But left-handed PC users may not always find the normal mouse button orientation to be as comfortable as they'd like. Fortunately, it's easy to swap the functions of the two mouse buttons, as shown on the facing page.

Instead of the plain little mouse pointer you're used to seeing, you can configure your mouse pointer to take on a different appearance. Windows 98 can also use *animated cursors:* mouse pointers that use an animated picture to provide an indication of what is happening. For example, you can replace the static hourglass icon with an animated substitute that flips over to show the passage of time. You'll find a number of animated cursors in the C:\Windows\Cursors folder, and you'll find many additional animated cursors on the Web. Enter the term *animated cursors* in your search engine —

include the quotation marks — and press the Search button. We've given you a start with the link listed on this page. Animated cursors designed for Windows 95 will work fine in Windows 98.

CROSS-REFERENCE
See "Configuring Your Keyboard" later in this chapter.

FIND IT ONLINE
You'll find lots of animated cursors at
http://www.animalbytes.com/Cursors/.

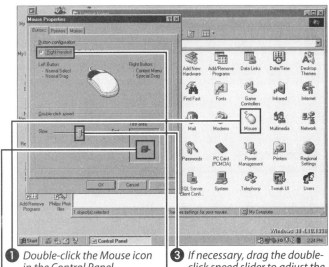

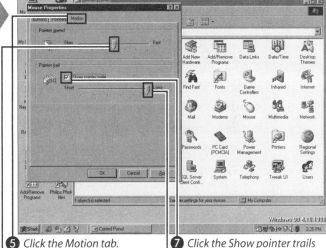

1 *Double-click the Mouse icon in the Control Panel.*

2 *Double-click in the test area to test double-click speed. If the clown doesn't pop up, adjust the double-click speed.*

3 *If necessary, drag the double-click speed slider to adjust the double-click speed.*

4 *Choose Right-handed or Left-handed to swap mouse button functions.*

5 *Click the Motion tab.*

6 *Drag the slider right or left to adjust the mouse speed.*

7 *Click the Show pointer trails check box if you wish to add trails behind your mouse pointer.*

8 *Drag the slider to adjust the length of the mouse trails.*

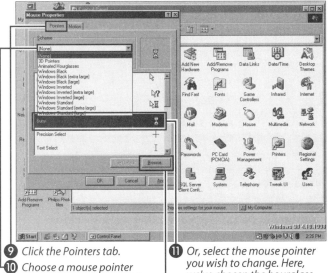

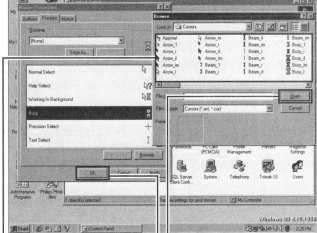

9 *Click the Pointers tab.*

10 *Choose a mouse pointer scheme to preview it. Click Apply when you've decided on one.*

11 *Or, select the mouse pointer you wish to change. Here, we've chosen the hourglass.*

12 *To see additional mouse pointers from which you can choose, click Browse.*

13 *Choose one of the available mouse pointers.*

■ *When you choose a pointer, the Preview window will show a sample.*

14 *Click Open to apply your choice of mouse pointers.*

15 *Click OK to complete the task.*

Configuring Your Keyboard

The keyboard is your direct link to your PC, so your keyboard should work with you rather than against you. In this section you look at several adjustments you can make to the way your keyboard works with Windows 98.

The *repeat delay* is the measure of how long you must hold a key down before that character is repeated. Fast typists usually appreciate a short delay time, but too short a time can be frustrating for someone who types more slowly because characters may repeat too soon. You'll want to adjust this setting to the shortest delay that is compatible with your typing style.

The *repeat rate* is a measure of how many times per second characters are repeated once you've held the key down long enough to begin repeating characters. In other words, do you want the repeating characters to zip quickly across your screen, or do you prefer a slower rate that is easier to control? Adjusting this setting requires striking a balance between a rate that's too fast — forcing you to delete the extra characters — and one that's so slow that it's faster to strike the same key repeatedly yourself.

The *cursor blink rate* doesn't affect your typing speed. Rather, this setting controls how quickly the cursor blinks on and off. The rate you select is a matter of personal preference, although too slow a cursor blink rate may give the false impression that your computer is operating more slowly than it really is.

The language settings are most useful if you're bilingual and produce documents in more than one language. The language settings also enable you to adjust the keyboard layout.

TAKE NOTE

CHANGING YOUR KEYBOARD LAYOUT

You can use the language settings to choose an alternative keyboard layout, such as one of the Dvorak keyboard layouts. Some people claim that typing on a Dvorak keyboard is faster than typing on a standard QWERTY keyboard layout, but this may depend on how you learned to type. Popular legend has it that the standard keyboard layout was designed in the days of the early manual typewriter with the purpose of keeping people from typing faster than the typewriter's mechanics could accommodate. Whether this story is true is open to debate.

THE KEYS WON'T MATCH

Of course, changing keyboard layouts won't actually move the keys on your keyboard. If you choose to use an alternative keyboard layout, remember that what is shown on the keys won't be the same characters that will appear when you type. If you share your PC with another user, switch the keyboard to the standard layout when you're finished using the system.

CROSS-REFERENCE
See "Setting the Accessibility Options" later in this chapter.

FIND IT ONLINE
You'll find Dvorak keyboard information at **http://www.dvorakint.org/**.

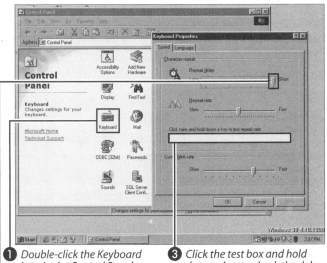

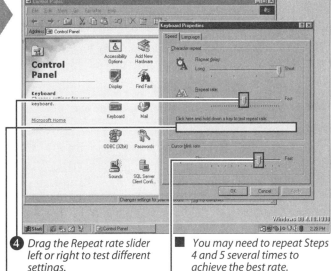

① *Double-click the Keyboard icon in the Control Panel.*

② *Drag the Repeat delay slider left or right to test different settings.*

③ *Click the test box and hold down a key to check the delay setting.*

■ *You may need to repeat Steps 2 and 3 several times to achieve the best rate.*

④ *Drag the Repeat rate slider left or right to test different settings.*

⑤ *Click the test box and hold down a key to check the rate setting.*

■ *You may need to repeat Steps 4 and 5 several times to achieve the best rate.*

⑥ *Drag the slider right or left if you wish to adjust the cursor blink rate.*

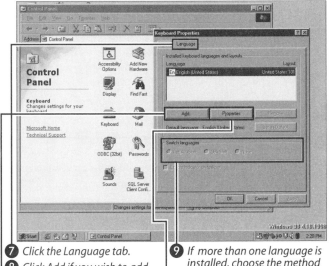

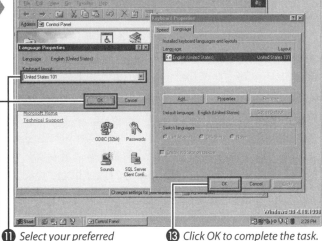

⑦ *Click the Language tab.*

⑧ *Click Add if you wish to add additional languages.*

⑨ *If more than one language is installed, choose the method for switching between languages.*

⑩ *Click Properties to choose a new keyboard layout option.*

⑪ *Select your preferred keyboard layout.*

⑫ *Click OK to close the Language Properties dialog box.*

⑬ *Click OK to complete the task.*

85

Adding Sounds to System Events

Windows 98 has a set of system events, such as opening and closing Windows 98, signaling an error, and so on. You can associate sound files with these events so that when a system event occurs, the sound clip calls your attention to the event. You're probably already familiar with many of these sounds; by default, Windows 98 uses a sound file named "The Microsoft Sound" to announce that Windows 98 has opened.

Sound files contain digital representations of actual audio recorded from various sound sources. The sound sources can be microphones and line inputs. Sound files have the filename extension .WAV, and the quality of the sound they store depends on parameters used when the sound files are recorded. The higher the quality, the more disk storage a sound file requires. Sound files can be monaural (one channel) or stereophonic (two channels). You can build sets of sound-to-event associations and record them as schemes by using the Save As button in the Sounds Properties dialog box. Later, you can select a scheme from the Schemes drop-down list box.

It's a good idea to use short sound clips to signal events. Windows 98 comes with a number of sounds that you'll find in the \Windows\Media folder, or you can use Sound Recorder to create your own sound files. For example, to assist someone with limited vision or a small child who might otherwise have a difficult time reading on-screen messages, you might record short sound files that identify system events and then attach those files to the events.

If you work in an office where constant noises from your PC might be disruptive, use common sense in assigning sounds to system events. You probably don't want a message that says "You Bozo!" whenever you make a mistake. In fact, you may choose less obtrusive sounds to assign to a minimum number of events.

TAKE NOTE

▶ SPEAKER QUALITY MATTERS

You can't expect the tiny speakers that often come free with new systems to be worth much more than what they cost you. If you care about sound quality you'll need to upgrade your speakers. Even a set of speakers from an old stereo system will usually sound better than the ones that come with most systems. For the best sound, you may need to connect your sound card to an external amplifier.

▶ WHO OWNS THE COPYRIGHT?

Many of the sound files you'll find on the Internet are illegal copies of sounds from popular movies and TV shows. You can probably use these files on your own PC, but unless you have permission from the copyright owner, it's not a good idea to distribute sound clips you didn't create yourself.

CROSS-REFERENCE

See "Recording Sounds with Sound Recorder" in Chapter 11.

FIND IT ONLINE

See **http://www.yahoo.com/Computers_and_ Internet/Multimedia/Sound/Archives/WAV/** for links to sound file collections.

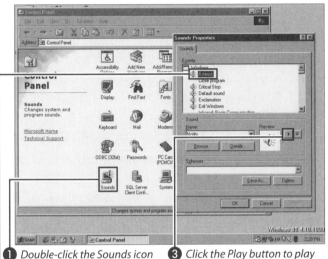

1 Double-click the Sounds icon in the Control Panel.

2 Select an event that has a speaker icon indicating that a sound has been assigned to the event.

3 Click the Play button to play the sound.

4 To open the Name drop-down list box, click the down-arrow at the right of the list box.

5 Select a new sound for the event.

6 Click the Play button to test the new sound.

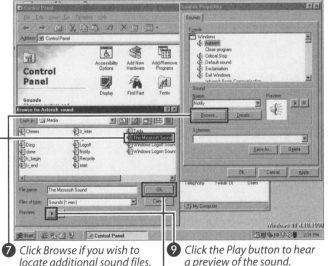

7 Click Browse if you wish to locate additional sound files.

8 Select a sound file.

9 Click the Play button to hear a preview of the sound.

10 Click OK to assign the new sound and close the dialog box.

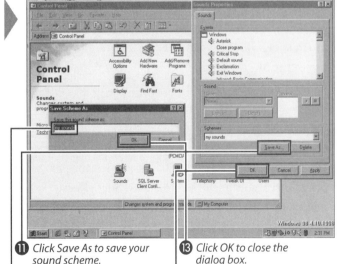

11 Click Save As to save your sound scheme.

12 Type a name for the sound scheme.

13 Click OK to close the dialog box.

14 Click OK to complete the task.

Setting the Accessibility Options

Using a computer can be more complicated for a person who has vision, hearing, or mobility restrictions. The accessibility options available in Windows 98 are designed to make the services of the computer more accessible and turn a Windows 98-based PC into a valuable tool.

If the Accessibility Options icon isn't in your Control Panel, you may need to use the Windows Setup tab of the Add/Remove Programs dialog box to add the Accessibility options.

The accessibility options include a number of useful tools. The figures on the facing page show the keyboard-related accessibility options. These figures also show you how to customize these options to the needs of an individual user.

StickyKeys and FilterKeys can be a help to someone who has limited mobility or who types using a touch stick. *StickyKeys* enables a user to simulate the use of the Shift, Ctrl, and Alt keys in combination with another key. When StickyKeys is active, you can first press Shift, Ctrl, or Alt, release it, and then press the next key you would normally press at the same time. For example, rather than hold down Ctrl while you press A, you can press Ctrl, release it, and then press A to accomplish the same task. StickyKeys makes it possible to type and to use the menu shortcuts found in many programs even if you are able to press only one key at a time.

FilterKeys causes Windows 98 to ignore keys you press in error or keys you hold down so long that they are repeated in error. You can tell Windows 98 to ignore key repeat. In this way, no matter how long a key is held down it won't repeat. You can also choose to have Windows 98 ignore repeated pressing of the same key unless there is a delay between pressing the keys.

ToggleKeys plays sounds when the Caps Lock, Num Lock, or Scroll Lock key is pressed. These keys can have an adverse effect on the way your PC operates, but if you have limited vision you might not realize that you pressed them in error.

Continued

TAKE NOTE

▶ FINE-TUNE THE OPTIONS

If you assist someone who needs accessibility options, be sure to take the time to fine-tune the settings to meet his or her needs. It may not occur to the accessibility options user to ask for assistance in adjusting these options for optimal performance, but a few extra minutes of setup time will pay many dividends.

▶ TURNING ON THE OPTIONS

The keyboard accessibility options use shortcuts to turn on the options. The upper-right, lower-left, and lower-right figures on the facing page show the shortcuts.

CROSS-REFERENCE
See "Configuring Your Keyboard" earlier in this chapter.

FIND IT ONLINE
See **http://www.microsoft.com/enable/default-u.htm** for more on accessibility.

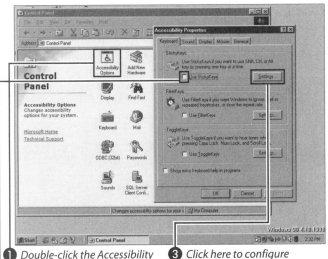

1 *Double-click the Accessibility Options icon in the Control Panel.*

2 *Click the Use StickyKeys check box to enable this option.*

3 *Click here to configure StickyKeys.*

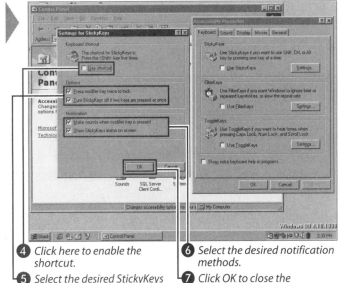

4 *Click here to enable the shortcut.*

5 *Select the desired StickyKeys options.*

6 *Select the desired notification methods.*

7 *Click OK to close the dialog box.*

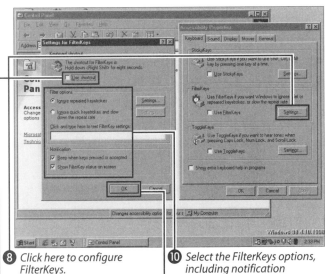

8 *Click here to configure FilterKeys.*

9 *Click here to enable the shortcut.*

10 *Select the FilterKeys options, including notification method.*

11 *Click OK to close the dialog box.*

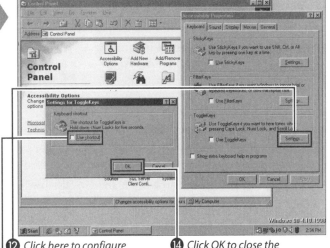

12 *Click here to configure ToggleKeys.*

13 *Click here to enable the shortcut.*

14 *Click OK to close the dialog box.*

Setting the Accessibility Options

Continued

In addition to the keyboard options, the accessibility options include a number of other tools for making your PC easier to use. The figures on the facing page provide a quick look at the extent of these additional options.

The sound options are designed to assist Windows 98 users who have a hearing impairment. These options supplement the sounds that Windows 98 normally uses to advise you of system events. Rather than simply playing a sound, when you activate *SoundSentry,* Windows 98 will flash the title bar or window border to alert you of the event. *ShowSounds* displays text captions in addition to audible messages from your programs.

The display options use a high-contrast color scheme to make the screen easier to read. You can choose the color scheme that is the easiest to read; the default high-contrast color scheme displays white lettering on a black background.

Users who have difficulty using a mouse may find that the *MouseKeys* option makes life simpler. When you enable this option you can use the arrow keys on your numeric keypad to move the mouse pointer. To make the MouseKeys pointer work more like a real mouse pointer, you can press and hold Ctrl to speed up the movement or Shift to slow down the movement.

On the General options tab shown in the lower-right figure on the facing page, you'll find the option to allow the accessibility features to expire if they aren't used for a period of time. Because the accessibility options can be confusing to users who aren't familiar with them or who don't expect them, this option makes it easier to share a PC in which the accessibility options have been activated. You can set the accessibility features to turn off after 5 to 30 minutes.

TAKE NOTE

▶ **ALTERNATIVE INPUT OPTIONS**

Users who cannot use a standard keyboard or mouse can still use a Windows 98-based PC. *SerialKey* devices connect to the PC's serial port and enable the user to communicate with the system using specially adapted devices. For example, one type of device enables a user to interact with the computer completely through eye movements. Many other devices are available. You'll find good information on the Internet. The two Web sites listed at the bottom of the page provide a good starting point for your search.

▶ **CONSIDER VOICE RECOGNITION**

Voice recognition is another option that may assist users who have difficulty using the keyboard. Although Windows 98 does not offer any built-in voice recognition capabilities, modern PCs are powerful enough to enable voice recognition software to do a creditable job. Dragon Naturally Speaking (http://www.dragonsys.com/) is one example of this type of software that seems to work well, especially when used with the included high-quality headset.

CROSS-REFERENCE

See "Adding Sounds to System Events" earlier in this chapter.

FIND IT ONLINE

See **http://www.lctinc.com/doc/egwin95.htm** for information on the Eyegaze system.

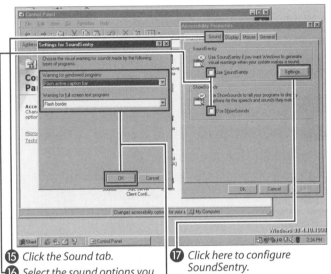

⑮ Click the Sound tab.

⑯ Select the sound options you wish to enable.

⑰ Click here to configure SoundSentry.

⑱ Configure the SoundSentry, and then click OK to close the dialog box.

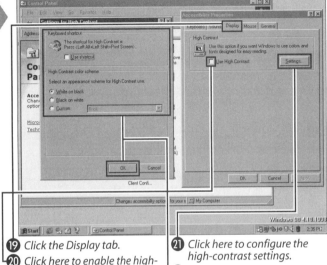

⑲ Click the Display tab.

⑳ Click here to enable the high-contrast display.

㉑ Click here to configure the high-contrast settings.

㉒ Enable the shortcut, select the color scheme, then click OK.

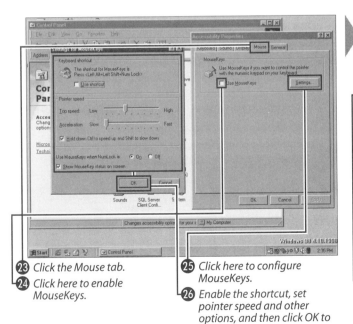

㉓ Click the Mouse tab.

㉔ Click here to enable MouseKeys.

㉕ Click here to configure MouseKeys.

㉖ Enable the shortcut, set pointer speed and other options, and then click OK to close the dialog box.

㉗ Click the General tab.

㉘ Select the check box to enable SerialKey devices, and click Settings to configure your device.

㉙ Select the serial port and baud rate for your SerialKey device, and click OK to close the dialog box.

㉚ Click OK to complete the task.

Adding New Hardware

Adding new hardware to your computer can be an adventure. To work with almost any peripheral device, your system needs the services of special software called a *driver*. Usually, you don't have to worry about drivers; they're typically installed automatically when Windows 98 is installed on your system. But if you add new hardware, you may need to tell Windows 98 that you've added something new so that it can load the correct driver software.

The figures on the facing page are a little different from those that accompany most of the tasks in this book. Rather than attempt to detail each step that you may encounter, these figures present an overview of the hardware installation task. The reason for this is simple: There are thousands of different pieces of hardware you could add to your PC, and the process varies somewhat depending on what you're installing. Therefore, we've chosen the screens that best illustrate the important things you need to know about adding new hardware.

Most hardware components you buy today conform to a standard called Plug and Play — when you install them, Windows 98 will know how to configure them. For peripherals you add inside your PC, Windows 98 will likely recognize the new components on your system as soon as you turn your computer back on. If it doesn't, or if you add an external component, you'll need to use the procedures shown on the facing page to install the correct drivers.

TAKE NOTE

▶ GO USB IF POSSIBLE

When you add new hardware peripherals to your PC, you probably would like the entire process to be as painless as possible. There's a good way to accomplish this, at least if your PC is relatively new. If your PC has Universal Serial Bus (USB) ports, all you need to do to install a new USB-based peripheral is to plug in the USB cable. When you do, Windows 98 will display a message telling you it has detected a new USB peripheral and has loaded the software for it. You can then use the new piece without any further action.

▶ USE WINDOWS UPDATE

The driver software accompanying that new piece of hardware you just bought may not be the latest version. Once you've installed new hardware, it's a good idea to visit the Windows 98 Update Web site to see whether newer versions of the driver are available. Click the Start button and select Windows Update to check for newer drivers. You must have Internet access to use Windows Update.

CROSS-REFERENCE

See "Using Windows Update" in Chapter 14.

FIND IT ONLINE

See **http://www.intel.com/design/usb/** for more information on USB peripherals.

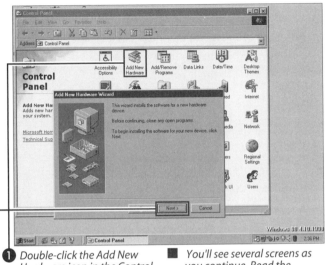

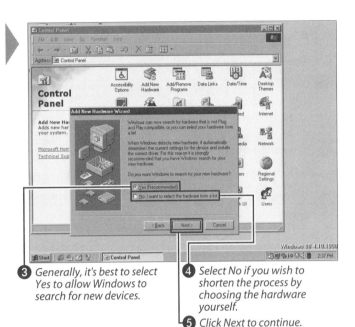

① *Double-click the Add New Hardware icon in the Control Panel.*

② *Click Next to continue.*

■ *You'll see several screens as you continue. Read the messages on each, take appropriate action, and click Next to continue.*

③ *Generally, it's best to select Yes to allow Windows to search for new devices.*

④ *Select No if you wish to shorten the process by choosing the hardware yourself.*

⑤ *Click Next to continue.*

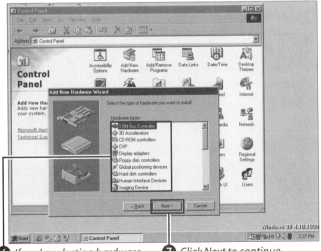

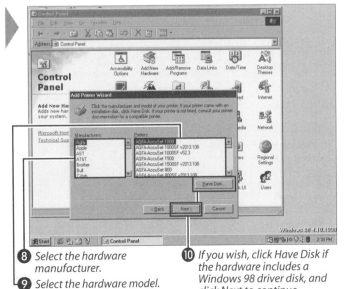

⑥ *If you're selecting hardware manually, select the type of hardware.*

⑦ *Click Next to continue.*

⑧ *Select the hardware manufacturer.*

⑨ *Select the hardware model.*

⑩ *If you wish, click Have Disk if the hardware includes a Windows 98 driver disk, and click Next to continue.*

■ *At this point Windows 98 will load the new driver software.*

93

Personal Workbook

Q&A

1 How can you tell, by looking at your desktop, whether your mouse is configured for single-clicking?

_____

_____

2 What can you do to make your mouse pointer easier to follow?

_____

_____

3 How can you change your keyboard layout without actually moving any keys?

_____

_____

_____

4 Where do you go to assign sounds to Windows 98 events?

_____

_____

5 What option do you activate to allow the Shift, Ctrl, or Alt key to be pressed once and act as if it were being held down while the next key is pressed?

_____

_____

6 How can you cause Windows 98 to make a sound when the Caps Lock key is pressed?

_____

_____

7 What type of peripheral installs automatically when you plug in its cable?

_____

_____

8 What are animated mouse pointers called?

_____

_____

9 Where do you find the options that enable you to configure Windows 98?

_____

_____

ANSWERS: PAGE 356

EXTRA PRACTICE

1 Change your mouse to operate as a single-click mouse.

2 Change your settings so that icons are underlined only when you point to them.

3 Set your keyboard repeat rate to the fastest position and see how quickly keys repeat.

4 Change the sound that plays when Windows 98 starts.

5 Activate the StickyKeys option and type a short note using a combination of uppercase and lowercase characters.

6 Add long pointer trails to your mouse and practice moving the mouse around the screen.

REAL-WORLD APPLICATIONS

✔ You are an editor assisting a novelist who has limited mobility and can't press two keys at the same time. To help your client use his word processor efficiently, you activate the StickyKeys option.

✔ You work in a courtroom, where it is important to be as quiet as possible. You silence Windows 98 and use the SoundSentry and ShowSounds options.

✔ You purchase a new printer so that you can produce color brochures for your garden club. To make sure that you have the correct drivers loaded, you use the Windows 98 Add New Hardware wizard.

Visual Quiz

How can you display this dialog box? What purpose does it serve?

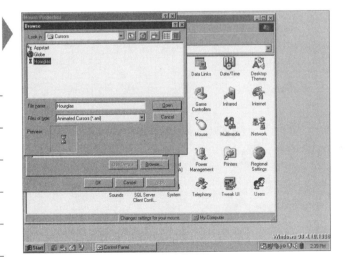

_____

_____

_____

_____

_____

PART

III

Using Programs and Documents

A personal computer can be a powerful tool, but only if you know how to use programs and work efficiently with your documents. In this part you learn important tasks such as installing new programs, using the various program elements that enable you to work with programs, and communicating with them. You learn how to open your document files and, even more important, how to save your files.

After you've learned how to create documents, you learn how to put your work on paper by using Windows 98 printers. You find out how you can control the way your printer works, too.

Documents often have a nasty habit of hiding when you need them the most. The final chapter in this part teaches you how to use Windows 98 to find all the important files that you know are hiding somewhere on your system. After you complete this part, you'll never again have to worry about losing your work, because you'll know how to find your documents no matter where they are.

CHAPTER **6**

Using Programs

Windows 98 gives you access to *computer applications* (or *programs*) — the software you run to process the documents and other data that store your information. Examples of applications are word processors, spreadsheets, and system utilities.

Windows 98 includes many small applications to support word processing, graphical composition, and so on. These applications are called *applets* or sometimes *accessory* applications. You won't mistake these accessory applications for full-featured programs, but you'll likely find them useful.

Windows 98 is a multitasking operating system, and that means you can have many applications running at the same time. Windows 98 applications are typically interactive and need user interaction to do anything. Consequently, only one application is *active* at a time. The active application runs in a window and is said to *have the focus*, which means your keystrokes and mouse clicks act on that application. To change the focus between interactive applications, you select an application's window.

Some applications can be running in the background without your attention. Windows 98 keeps a number of tasks going that you never see. At other times, you will launch an application that takes time to complete, let it run in the background, and switch the focus to something else.

This chapter covers some program basics. It starts by showing you how to install new programs and then explains how to make your programs easier to use. You also learn how to use common elements that you'll find in most programs. Of course, this chapter doesn't show you how to use specific programs, but it explains what you need to open and navigate within programs.

If you've used Windows 95, you may be surprised by some of the Windows 98 changes you learn about in this chapter. Windows 98 incorporates changes that may not be obvious but make Windows 98 easier to use. "Adding an Entry to the Start Menu" shows one good example of this type of change: the new drag-and-drop menus.

Installing Programs

Most applications install themselves with little interaction from you; you put the CD-ROM in your computer's CD-ROM drive, and Windows 98 automatically starts the application's Setup program by using the Windows 98 AutoPlay feature. After that, you may have to answer some questions about the installation and occasionally click OK. When the installation is completed, the application is installed on your hard disk, and the necessary commands are added to your Start menu's Programs submenu.

Although most programs are now distributed on CD-ROM, not all come that way. Applications distributed on a floppy disk cannot use the Windows 98 AutoPlay feature, and you must launch the application's setup program manually. Applications that you download from the Internet typically arrive as a single executable file that expands into a setup configuration and then runs its own setup program. You can download and execute the installation file in one step, or you can download it, save it to disk, and manually execute it later.

The figures on the facing page show how to install programs using the Add/Remove Programs icon in the Control Panel. This procedure doesn't depend on the Windows 98 AutoPlay feature, although enabling AutoPlay may make installing new programs a bit easier.

If you decide to uninstall a program, you can do so from the Install/Uninstall tab of the Add/Remove Programs dialog box, which you open from the Control Panel.

TAKE NOTE

▶ WHAT IF CD-ROMS DON'T PLAY AUTOMATICALLY?

Some PCs have the AutoPlay feature disabled. Even though the application CD-ROM includes the AutoPlay commands to automatically install the application, the PC does not use the commands when you load the CD-ROM into the drive. You can use the Paranoia tab of Tweak UI to control whether AutoPlay is enabled. If Tweak UI does not appear in your Control Panel, look in the \tools\reskit\powertoy folder on your Windows 98 CD-ROM for the readme file that tells you how to install this option.

▶ AVOID WINDOWS 3.x PROGRAMS

If possible, you should avoid installing programs designed for Windows 3.0, 3.1, and the like on your Windows 98 system. Programs designed for Windows 3.x generally do not register themselves properly with Windows 98, and this can make it difficult (if not almost impossible) to later uninstall them. In addition, older programs may incorrectly overwrite critical system files, something that can cause your PC to become unstable and crash-prone.

CROSS-REFERENCE

See "Starting Programs Automatically" later in this chapter.

FIND IT ONLINE

WinSite, at **http://www.winsite.com/**, has a large inventory of software specifically for Windows.

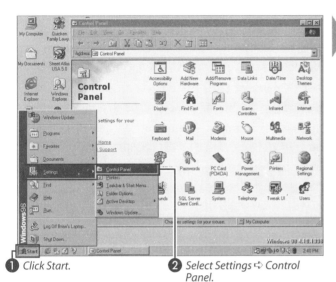

1 Click Start.

2 Select Settings ⇨ Control Panel.

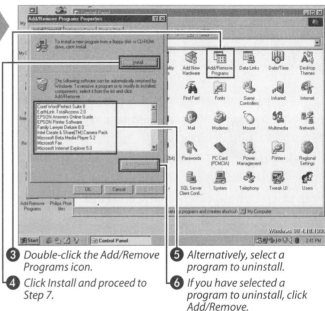

3 Double-click the Add/Remove Programs icon.

4 Click Install and proceed to Step 7.

5 Alternatively, select a program to uninstall.

6 If you have selected a program to uninstall, click Add/Remove.

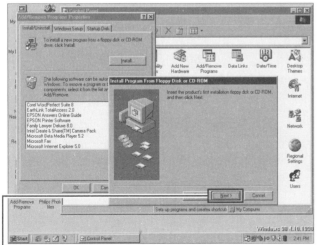

7 Make certain the installation CD-ROM or disk is in the drive and click Next to continue.

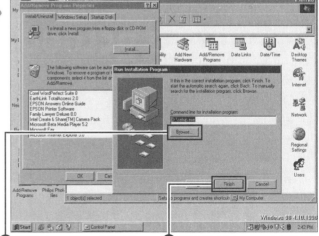

8 If Windows 98 can't find the correct installation program, click Browse to locate it.

■ You may need to locate the program manually.

9 Click Finish to complete the task.

■ Depending on the program, you may need to answer some questions to finish the installation.

Adding a Program Shortcut to the Desktop

Windows 98 gives you several ways to start an application. How you do it depends on how the application was installed, how you configure your work environment, or simply how you choose to do it. You can start an application from an entry on the Start/Programs menu or from a shortcut located on the desktop or in a folder. You can automatically run a program when you turn on your computer or have it run at a scheduled time. You can also run programs by choosing the application's executable file in the folder where the application resides or by choosing a document file of the type that the application processes.

Adding a shortcut to your desktop is a good way to make your favorite programs easily accessible. Just click the shortcut to run your program.

Adding a desktop shortcut is easy, but you need some information that may not be readily apparent. You may have to do some detective work to find out the information you need to know to create some shortcuts.

To create a desktop shortcut, you need to know how to locate your programs. The first place to look is in your Start menu. If the program you want to use is on the Start menu, you can right-click the program item, select Properties, and look at the Target text box. If the program isn't on the Start menu, try to find it in the \Program Files folder. If you still don't have any luck, you can use the Find search tool in Windows Explorer. Once you've located the program, move the mouse cursor to a background location on the desktop. Right-click to open the desktop's context menu and select New ⇨ Shortcut. With the path and name of the executable in the Create Shortcut dialog box, click Next to open the Select Program Folder dialog box and create the shortcut.

TAKE NOTE

THE TWO-STEP METHOD

If you want to add a desktop shortcut and you know which executable file to use, simply right-click the executable's icon in a folder window. Then, choose Send To ⇨ Desktop as Shortcut.

TAKE THE EASY WAY

When you install new programs on your system, the installation procedure often gives you the option of having an icon placed on your desktop. It's easier to allow this desktop icon to be created than to create your own later. If you don't want all your program icons to remain on your desktop, consider creating a new desktop folder and dragging the unwanted icons onto the folder. In that way, you'll be able to restore any of the icons if you later decide you need them.

CROSS-REFERENCE
See "Putting New Objects on the Desktop" in Chapter 4.

SHORTCUT
You can use the Find tool to locate programs.

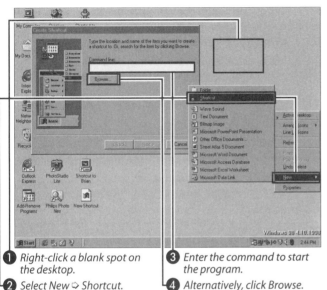

1 Right-click a blank spot on the desktop.

2 Select New ➪ Shortcut.

3 Enter the command to start the program.

4 Alternatively, click Browse.

5 Click the down-arrow at the right side of the "Look in" list box.

6 Find the folder containing the program file and click the folder to open it.

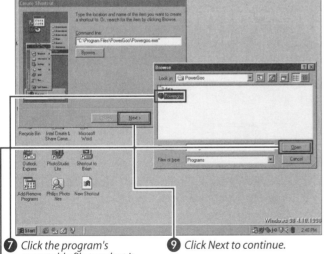

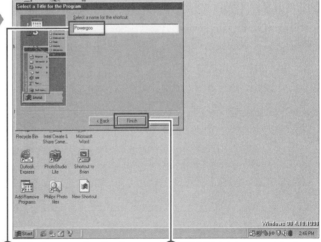

7 Click the program's executable file to select it.

8 Click Open to close the Browse dialog box and place the proper command in the "Command line" text box.

9 Click Next to continue.

10 Edit the name for the shortcut if you wish. This name will appear in the label of the program's icon.

11 Click Finish to complete the task.

Starting Programs Automatically

You can configure your system to start an application whenever you start the computer. Perhaps you want to run your mail reader to collect all unread e-mail or download the latest quotes for the stocks in your portfolio, or maybe you want a warning when your laptop computer's battery is running low. There are many reasons you would want to run programs at system startup.

Often, programs you install set themselves up to run automatically whenever you start your system. In that way, it will be convenient to use the program whenever your PC is running. It's easy for you to add other programs that also will start automatically.

The Windows 98 Start menu includes an item called StartUp that is located on the Programs submenu. Anything that appears in the StartUp menu will automatically load whenever you start Windows 98. The StartUp menu is actually a shortcut to the C:\Windows\Start Menu\Programs\StartUp folder. You can add items to the StartUp menu by copying them to the folder, or you can add them directly to the menu.

If you've used Windows 95, you may be surprised by the ease with which you can add things to your Windows 98 Start menu. In the past it was necessary to access the C:\Windows\Start Menu folder using Windows Explorer and make your changes in Windows Explorer. In Windows 98 you can use drag-and-drop to drag an item onto the Start button; you wait for the Start menu to pop up and then drag the object where you want it. When you release the mouse button, the new object will appear on the menus just where you dropped it. If you dropped the object into the StartUp menu, the program will run, the document will open in the appropriate application, or the folder will open in Windows Explorer the next time you start Windows 98.

TAKE NOTE

▶ **THE STARTUP FOLDER ISN'T THE ONLY WAY**

Placing a shortcut in the C:\Windows\Start Menu\Programs\StartUp folder is not the only method of automatically starting programs. Certain programs must run without the possibility that you will disable them. Such programs are usually started by the *Registry*, a system database that controls the way Windows 98 operates. That's why some programs will run even though there is no mention of them in the StartUp menu.

▶ **USE SHORTCUTS**

Make certain you place shortcuts — and not program files — in the C:\Windows\Start Menu\Programs\StartUp folder. In that way you won't accidentally lose a program if you remove one from the folder to prevent it from running automatically at startup.

CROSS-REFERENCE

See "Copying and Moving Files" in Chapter 2.

FIND IT ONLINE

See **http://www.annoyances.org/win98/features/registry.html** for more on the Registry.

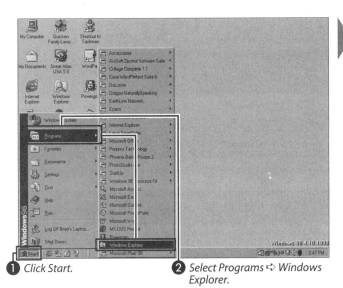

1 Click Start.

2 Select Programs ⇨ Windows Explorer.

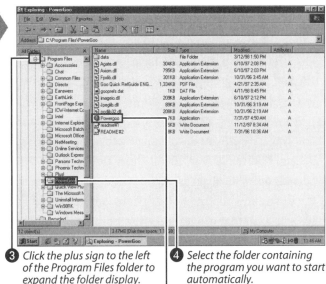

3 Click the plus sign to the left of the Program Files folder to expand the folder display.

4 Select the folder containing the program you want to start automatically.

5 Select the program icon.

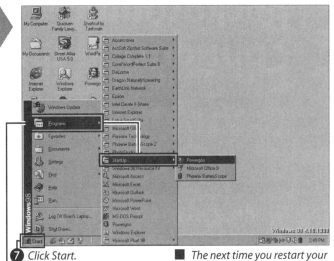

6 Drag the program icon onto the Start button, wait for the Start menu to open, and drop the icon in the Programs ⇨ StartUp menu.

■ Make sure you drag the icon into the open StartUp menu (don't drop it into the Programs menu).

7 Click Start.

8 Select Programs ⇨ StartUp to verify that you dropped the icon in the correct location.

■ The next time you restart your system, the program you selected should start automatically.

Adding an Entry to the Start Menu

Sometimes you want easy access to programs but you don't want to add them to the StartUp menu. One way to gain quick access to programs is to add a program's shortcut to the Start menu.

You can add shortcuts to your Start menu in several ways. When you install a new program, you'll usually find that a Start menu shortcut has been added automatically. You can also add shortcuts using the drag-and-drop method — shown in the preceding section — so that programs start automatically whenever you start Windows 98. In addition, you have the option of opening Windows Explorer and creating shortcuts in any of the folders that lie under the C:\Windows\Start Menu folder. Yet another method is shown in the figures on the facing page.

Using the Taskbar Properties dialog box to add programs to your Start menu isn't necessarily a better way to change your Start menu. It's just another way that Windows 98 provides to do so. Choosing the "best way" to accomplish most Windows 98 tasks is often subjective. By showing you several methods, this book helps you make your own choice.

As you browse your PC looking for programs to add to your Start menu, keep in mind that not all items that are listed as applications are intended to be run manually. In some cases, items that are listed as applications are actually a part of another program.

Although you usually won't do any harm by attempting to run these applications, there's no guarantee that it's safe to try to run an application you don't recognize. You should be able to recognize most of your programs by their file names, but, when in doubt, try right-clicking the application and selecting Properties. This action should provide some additional clues about the program's purpose.

TAKE NOTE

▶ DRAG IT!

Drag a file and drop it on the Start button to add a shortcut to the top of the Start menu, or drag it but don't drop it if you want to position it yourself.

▶ KEEP THE PROGRAMS MENU CLEAN

You may be tempted to move any new program shortcuts or folders onto the Programs menu. If you do this, though, you'll soon discover that the menu will become too large to be manageable. It's better to use some of the existing folders, such as the Programs ⇨ Accessory folder, to help organize your Start menu. You'll find additional folders, such as Communications, Entertainment, System Tools, and so on in the Programs ⇨ Accessory folder. Often, these folders would be the best location for your new program shortcuts. If none of the existing folders seems to be a good fit, you can always add new folders to the Start menu tree as necessary.

CROSS-REFERENCE

See "Starting Programs Automatically" earlier in this chapter.

FIND IT ONLINE

See **http://www.worldowindows.com/w98t-tech.html** for a Start menu troubleshooting tip.

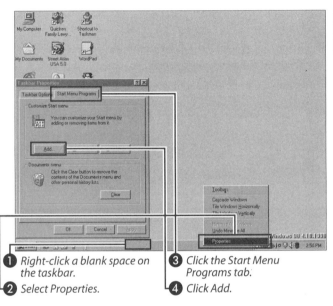

1 Right-click a blank space on the taskbar.

2 Select Properties.

3 Click the Start Menu Programs tab.

4 Click Add.

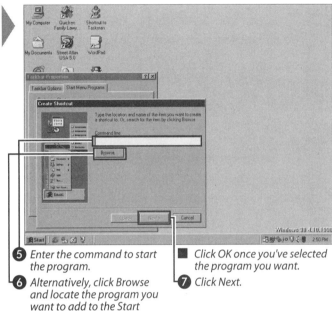

5 Enter the command to start the program.

6 Alternatively, click Browse and locate the program you want to add to the Start menu.

■ Click OK once you've selected the program you want.

7 Click Next.

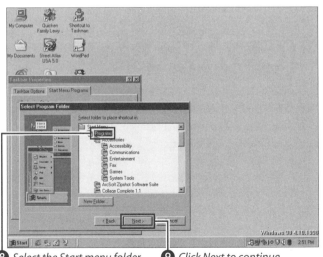

8 Select the Start menu folder where you want to place the new program item.

9 Click Next to continue.

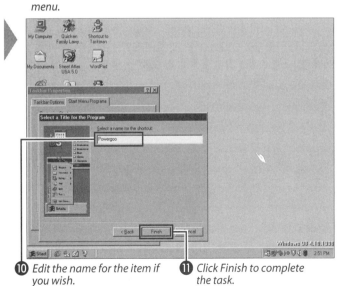

10 Edit the name for the item if you wish.

11 Click Finish to complete the task.

Using Menus

Programs in the Windows 98 environment use menus extensively. The Windows 98 menu architecture is consistent across applications and within the Windows 98 accessory and utility programs. Most applications have a menu bar at the top of the application window just under the title bar; this menu bar contains the titles of pull-down menus. These titles vary from application to application, but standards exist. For example, most applications have File and Help menus.

The File menu typically contains commands to open and close documents, print documents, open recently used documents, and exit the application. Applications in which you create or use text and graphical documents usually have an Edit menu to support cut, copy, and paste operations with the Clipboard. Edit menus may also include commands for searching documents and for search and replace operations. Applications use the View menu to control the appearance of visible items in the application. It can be useful to control how the parts of the application appear on the screen. Sometimes you don't need to see everything in an application, and the View menu provides commands to select and deselect viewing options. Most applications have a Help menu to provide access to the Windows 98 Help system.

Regardless of the nature and content of menus, they all work the same way: You use mouse and keyboard commands to navigate the menus and choose from them. There are three menu operations to learn: selecting a menu, moving from menu to menu, and choosing a command from a menu.

Many menu items have an underline under one of the characters. For example, the F in the File menu item is usually underlined. If you press the Alt key to activate the menu bar, you then press the underlined character to activate the associated menu or menu selection. Some menu items also work with a shortcut, or *hotkey* combination. Many of these hotkeys are common to a wide range of Windows 98 programs. Ctrl+C is a common hotkey that copies a current selection to the Clipboard. Ctrl+Z usually selects Edit ⇨ Undo.

CROSS-REFERENCE
See "Adding an Entry to the Start Menu" earlier in this chapter.

SHORTCUT
Press Esc to back out of a menu.

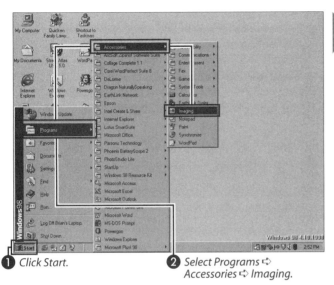

1 Click Start.

2 Select Programs ⇨ Accessories ⇨ Imaging.

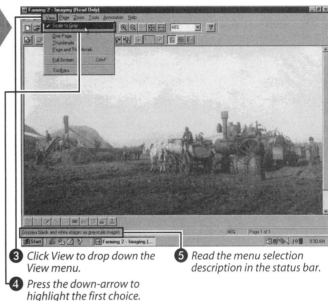

3 Click View to drop down the View menu.

4 Press the down-arrow to highlight the first choice.

5 Read the menu selection description in the status bar.

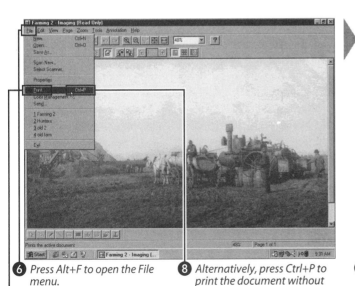

6 Press Alt+F to open the File menu.

7 Click Print.

8 Alternatively, press Ctrl+P to print the document without opening the menu.

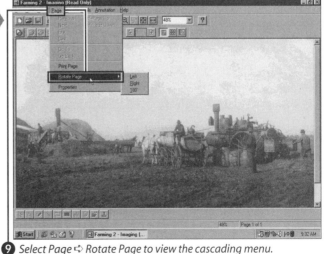

9 Select Page ⇨ Rotate Page to view the cascading menu.

Using Scroll Bars

When you display data in a window's workspace, the display often extends beyond the area covered by the window. A word processing document, for example, is usually much longer than the allotted space. Graphics as well as many text files can be wider than the window. To view the hidden data, you must *scroll* the window horizontally and vertically. Horizontal and vertical scroll bars enable you to do this with the mouse.

Sometimes an application has scroll bars, but they are disabled when you start the program. The scroll bars are inactive as long as the longest line of text does not go past the right margin of the window's workspace and the number of lines in the document does not exceed the height of the work space. If you add text so that the document is longer or wider than the workspace, the scroll bars become active. The scroll bars contain scroll boxes whose size may depict the percentage of the total document that is visible.

To scroll the workspace up or down, move the mouse cursor to a scroll arrow in the vertical scroll bar. Press and hold the left mouse button. The workspace scrolls up or down, and the scroll box moves in the opposite direction. To scroll the workspace left or right, use the horizontal scroll bar. You can use the cursor to drag a scroll box along the scroll bar. In many programs the scroll box moves in increments proportional to the length or width of the workspace. To page up or down, point the mouse cursor just ahead or below the scroll box in the scroll bar. Click to scroll forward or back one page of text.

To scroll one line at a time with the keyboard, press the arrow keys to move in any of the four directions. When the cursor reaches the edge of the workspace, the window will move. To move one page at a time using the keyboard, press the PgUp and PgDn keys to page through the workspace vertically. Press Ctrl+PgUp and Ctrl+PgDn to page horizontally.

TAKE NOTE

DRAG TO DISPLAY DOCUMENT POSITION

Many Windows 98 applications report the document position when you drag the scroll box.

SCROLLING WITH THE MOUSE WHEEL

Some mice have a wheel between the two buttons. You can turn the wheel to scroll, and often you can hold down the wheel to power scroll in the direction you move the mouse. These types of mice require special drivers in order for the wheel to work, and applications must support that particular driver as well.

CROSS-REFERENCE

See "Configuring Mouse Speed" in Chapter 5.

FIND IT ONLINE

See http://www.sundog.demon.co.uk/index.html for a software alternative to scrollbars.

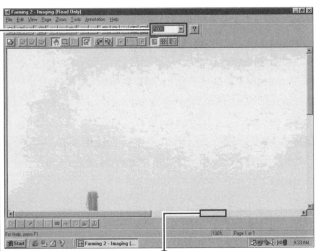

1 If necessary, select a zoom percentage that activates the scroll bars.

2 Click a blank space in the scroll bar to scroll one screen in that direction.

3 Drag the scroll box in the direction you want to scroll.

4 To scroll one line at a time, click the arrow at either end of a scroll bar.

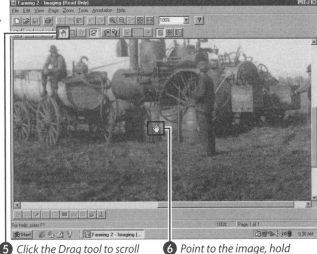

5 Click the Drag tool to scroll the image by dragging.

6 Point to the image, hold down the left mouse button, and drag the image to scroll.

Using Common Dialog Box Controls

Windows 98 programs use dialog boxes for data entry. You enter text and select options by using controls on the dialog box. Controls are data entry components such as command buttons, radio buttons, list boxes, text boxes, and so on.

Many dialog boxes are *modal:* The dialog box keeps the focus as long as the dialog box is open. You cannot select another component of the program, such as a menu or toolbar button, while the dialog box is open. You can tell whether a modal dialog box is open: Clicking outside it in the application that opened it has no effect. You can switch to a different application, but when you return to the original application, the modal dialog box is still in control.

A *modeless* dialog box lets you change the focus to other parts of the application without closing the dialog box. The Spell Check dialog box in some word processors is one example of a modeless dialog box.

Dialog boxes have several kinds of controls. They may have tabs that select different dialog functions, command buttons that execute commands immediately, check boxes where you select options, and radio buttons that allow one choice to be selected. At any given time you can enter data into only one control. The one that is currently accepting input has the focus. To enter data into another control, you must change the focus to the new control. To change the focus to another control, click the desired control,

press the Tab key to move forward, or press Shift+Tab to move backward. Some control labels include underlined letters to identify the control's shortcut key. Press the letter to move to the control or to select its value. The dialog box indicates the active control by surrounding its label with a dotted line, by using different shading, or, in the case of a text control, by moving the keyboard cursor to the control.

TAKE NOTE

▶ ESCAPE FROM DIALOG BOXES

If you open a dialog box, make several selections, and then decide you don't want to make any changes, look for a Cancel button. If you don't see one, you'll probably see a Close button (the X in the upper-right corner). If these two options aren't available, you can usually press Esc to back out of dialog boxes without entering any changes.

▶ USE THE HELP BUTTON

Most Windows 98 dialog boxes have a help button — a button with a question mark — near the right side of the title bar. If you're not certain what a dialog box control does, click the help button to change the mouse pointer into a question mark, and then click the question mark on the control. You'll see a quick help tip about the control.

CROSS-REFERENCE

See "Opening Windows 98 Help" in Chapter 1.

SHORTCUT

Press the up or down arrow to adjust a spin control value.

① *Select a command, such as File ⇨ Print, that displays a dialog box.*

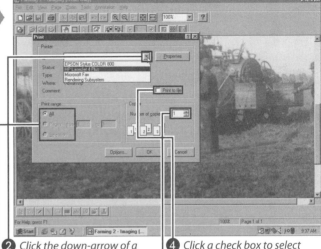

② *Click the down-arrow of a drop-down list box to display the contents.*

③ *Click one of a set of radio buttons to select one option and deselect the others.*

④ *Click a check box to select or deselect the option.*

⑤ *Click an up or down arrow to change the value of a spin box.*

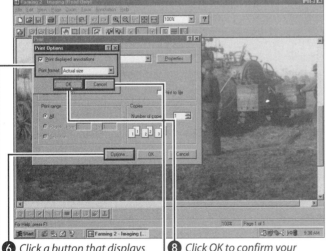

⑥ *Click a button that displays an additional dialog box.*

⑦ *Make your selections in the dialog box.*

⑧ *Click OK to confirm your choices and close the dialog box.*

⑨ *Alternatively, click Cancel to abandon your choices and close the dialog box.*

⑩ *Click Properties to display the Properties dialog box.*

⑪ *Click a tab to view the options on that dialog box tab.*

⑫ *Click OK to close the dialog box.*

⑬ *Click OK to complete the task.*

Closing Programs

Now that you know all the ways to start an application, you must learn how to stop, or terminate, one. Terminating an application is usually an orderly procedure. The application is notified that it is to be terminated, and it takes steps to accommodate an orderly exit. If the application has open documents that need to be saved, for example, it does so, perhaps asking you first whether it should.

Applications typically store information in the Windows 98 Registry to record such data as a list of most recently used documents, the size and position of applications windows, user option settings, and so on. When you terminate an application in an orderly manner, this information is stored. If the program isn't shut down properly, the information is not stored and you may lose data.

Most applications have a File menu, and most File menus have an Exit command from which you can terminate the application. In addition, most applications have a title bar at the top of their main window, and most application title bars have a Close button at the right end, a button with an X icon, which terminates the application.

Of course, there's a keyboard shortcut to shut down an application. Give it a try when you want to rest your mousing hand. Hit Alt+F4 to close a program.

TAKE NOTE

▶ POWERING DOWN

The most drastic way to end an application, and Windows 98 itself, is to power down the computer (turn it off) or press the computer's reset button. This action is the last resort when things stop working. Sometimes it is necessary when Windows 98 itself has become unstable, usually because of an errant application. None of your applications will initiate their termination procedures, and all your unsaved work will be lost. Disk file records that are being held in a memory cache are not written to the disk. The potential exists for corruption of the file system. Consequently, when you restart the computer, Windows 98 senses that its previous termination was an abrupt power interruption and runs the ScanDisk utility to ensure that the file system integrity was not corrupted by the untimely shutdown.

▶ USING THE TASK LIST

Windows 98 maintains a Task List of running tasks. You can view the running tasks and terminate one by using the Task List. To terminate a program, press Ctrl+Alt+Del to open the Close Program dialog box. Select the task you want to terminate and click End Task. This technique is the way you terminate an errant application that refuses to be terminated by using the more conventional procedures. When you stop a program this way, Windows 98 does not signal the task to initiate termination procedures. Any changes you made to the application's data are probably lost.

CROSS-REFERENCE
See "Switching Between Programs" in Chapter 1.

FIND IT ONLINE
If you are looking for a good source of shareware programs, go to **http://www.galttech.com**.

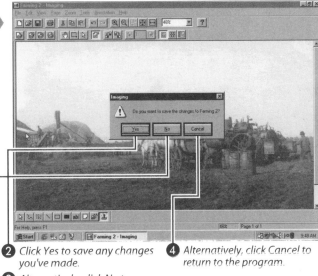

1 Select File ➷ Exit to begin an orderly shutdown.

2 Click Yes to save any changes you've made.

3 Alternatively, click No to abandon any changes and close the program.

4 Alternatively, click Cancel to return to the program.

5 Click the system menu icon.

6 Select Close to close the application.

7 Alternatively, click the Close button.

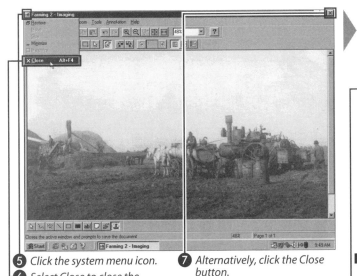

■ If an application has stopped responding, press Ctrl+Alt+Del to display the Close Program dialog box.

8 Select the application that has frozen.

9 Click End Task to close the program.

10 Alternatively, click Shut Down to close Windows 98.

Personal Workbook

Q&A

1 Why should you avoid installing Windows 3.*x* programs on your Windows 98 system?

_____

_____

_____

2 If you have items you want to start automatically whenever you start Windows 98, where should you place them?

_____

_____

_____

3 Why is it best to place shortcuts rather than actual programs on your desktop?

_____

_____

4 How does setting your mouse for single- or double-clicking affect menu selections?

_____

_____

5 What is a hotkey?

_____

_____

6 What does the size of the scroll box indicate?

_____

_____

7 How many options can you select at the same time from a group of radio buttons?

_____

_____

8 How many options can you select at the same time from a group of check boxes?

_____

_____

9 Why is it important to close programs correctly?

_____

_____

ANSWERS: PAGE 357

EXTRA PRACTICE

1 Install a new program using the Add/Remove Programs dialog box.

2 Add a shortcut to WordPad to your desktop.

3 Set up WordPad to start automatically when you start Windows 98.

4 Experiment with the hotkeys on the WordPad menus.

5 Open the Print dialog box and try out the various controls.

6 Try the different methods of closing WordPad.

REAL-WORLD APPLICATIONS

✔ You get a CD-ROM that contains several programs, each in its own folder. To install each individual program, you use the Add/Remove Programs dialog box.

✔ You depend on e-mail orders to support your home-based business. To make certain you get your e-mail frequently, you add your e-mail program to the StartUp folder so that it starts whenever you run Windows 98.

✔ You've just downloaded a new crossword puzzle game from the Internet. You like to work on this game in your spare moments while you're on hold. You add the program shortcut to the Start menu so that you can start it easily.

Visual Quiz

How can you display this dialog box? What purpose does it serve? What are the items in the list box?

_____

_____

_____

_____

_____

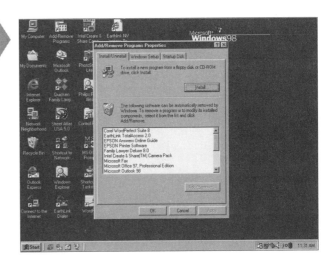

CHAPTER 7

MASTER THESE SKILLS

- ▶ Opening Documents
- ▶ Opening Recently Used Documents
- ▶ Saving Documents
- ▶ Selecting Text
- ▶ Cutting, Copying, and Pasting to the Clipboard
- ▶ Dragging and Dropping Data

Working with Documents

Virtually everything you do in Windows 98 involves some type of *document*, at least in the way Windows 98 defines documents. Windows 98 calls all your data files documents. Anything you create with a word processor — image files, address databases, and so on — are considered to be documents.

Windows 98 supports a *document-centric* work environment by letting you put documents on the desktop and in folders, use drag-and-drop operations to move documents, and automatically launch applications from documents. This means you can stop thinking about which tools — programs — you need to use and concentrate on what you want to produce — your documents. It also means that when you work with your documents, you'll use the same general techniques no matter what applications created the documents. That's one of the important advantages of Windows 98 and one way that it makes your PC easier to use.

Some of the material in this chapter may seem familiar, especially if you've been using a PC for some time. However, even highly experienced computer users are often surprised to discover better or easier ways of doing things. Windows 98 has many subtle improvements that make it easier to use your system.

If you think in terms of the documents rather than the tools, you'll find that many tasks are easier to manage. When documents are your focus, you'll probably think more about how projects are organized. If you're preparing a report on a certain project, for example, you'll naturally want to keep all the report materials together, just as you would if you were manually filing paper documents. How is this different from the old ways of working with a computer? Consider where you might store a spreadsheet file, a word processor document file, a graphics file, and so on. If you think in terms of the individual tools, you probably would have a separate folder for each type of program, and you'd store the separate pieces of your report in all those different folders. What a mess! Contrast that with the document-centric approach, in which all the pieces of a report are together in one place. It's easy to see why this approach makes sense.

Opening Documents

Documents are central to Windows 98. As a result, you usually don't need to think about which particular application was used to create a document. In most cases, Windows 98 already knows how a document was created. So when you open the document, Windows 98 opens the correct application program for the document.

Windows 98 doesn't force you to work its way, but it makes it easy for you to do so. As mentioned in Chapter 1, Windows 98 creates a special folder — My Documents — that appears on your Windows 98 desktop. By default, most programs offer the My Documents folder as the location for saving your files. Unless you have a good reason to do otherwise, it is an excellent idea to use this folder as the location where you store your files.

You can create new folders within My Documents and use these new folders to organize your projects. To take advantage of this feature, keep all the files for a project in one folder, no matter what application program produced the files. Then you'll know just where to begin when you need to work on the project. The "Take Note" section offers another reason why it's a good idea to use the My Documents folder as the base for your projects.

TAKE NOTE

▶ DON'T CHANGE FILE EXTENSIONS

How does Windows 98 know which application to open when you open a document? The answer is the *file extension*: the three characters that follow the period at the end of the filename, such as .doc for a Word document.

Most of the time Windows 98 doesn't display the file extensions, so you may not realize they exist. When you save a document file, most application programs add the appropriate file extension automatically. Each program uses a set of file extensions that is registered with Windows 98. If you change the extension on an existing file, Windows 98 may not recognize the new extension, or it may confuse it with the extension that is registered for another type of file. This could result in Windows 98 making an attempt to open the document in the wrong application or requiring you to manually select the correct program to open the file.

▶ BACKING UP IS EASY TO DO WITH MY DOCUMENTS

If you use the My Documents folder for saving your document files, you'll find there is a significant advantage in having all your documents in one place. Rather than hunt all over your hard disk, you can back up the My Documents folder contents and be assured that you've protected all your important work files. Be sure to include all the folders that are contained in the My Documents folder. In that way you'll also back up the documents you've organized by project.

CROSS-REFERENCE
See "Opening the My Documents Folder" in Chapter 1.

FIND IT ONLINE
For instructions on accessing My Documents from the Start Menu, see http://www.zdtips.com/w98/hpc-f.htm.

1 *Double-click the My Documents icon on your desktop to open the folder.*

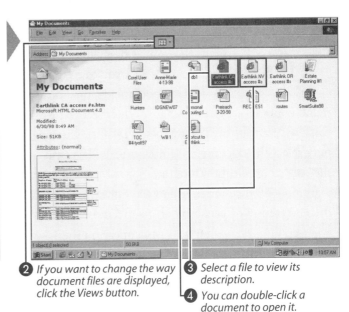

2 *If you want to change the way document files are displayed, click the Views button.*

3 *Select a file to view its description.*

4 *You can double-click a document to open it.*

5 *Select File ➪ New ➪ Folder to create a new folder within the My Documents folder.*

■ *Use folders within the My Documents folder to organize your projects.*

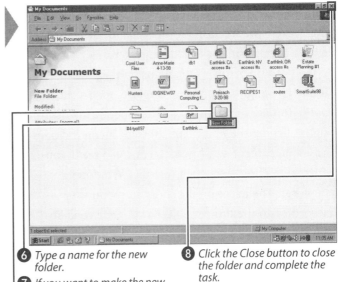

6 *Type a name for the new folder.*

7 *If you want to make the new folder the active folder, double-click it.*

8 *Click the Close button to close the folder and complete the task.*

Opening Recently Used Documents

Windows 98 maintains a list of documents that you've opened recently. To make it easy for you to reopen any of these documents, the Start menu contains a Documents list. When you want to work with any of the documents in this list, you need only select the document. Windows 98 will open it in the correct application program.

Windows 98 stores shortcuts to your documents in the C:\Windows\Recent folder. The 15 most recently accessed document shortcuts can appear on the Documents list. If you work with a large number of documents in the course of a day, it's easy for important documents to get bumped off the list. To keep this from happening you may want to manually delete unimportant documents from the list, as shown in the figures on the facing page. Also, read the "Take Note" section on this page to learn another reason for pruning your Documents list.

You can open any of the items on the Documents list by clicking the item. You can also open a shortcut menu for any of the items on the Documents list by right-clicking the item. This shortcut menu includes the same context-sensitive choices you'd see if you opened the item's shortcut menu in Windows Explorer. The items on the shortcut menu vary according to the type of object you've selected. You'll always see an Open choice, a Delete choice, and a Properties choice along with several other choices.

Open is always the first choice at the top of the shortcut menu, and selecting Open is the same as clicking the item. Use Delete to remove the shortcut without affecting the actual document file.

TAKE NOTE

▶ DON'T ALWAYS BELIEVE THE DOCUMENTS LIST

Just because an item is on the Start menu's Documents list doesn't mean that you'll be able to open the document file. What this list actually shows is a list of shortcuts to the documents you've used recently. If you delete the document file, the shortcut may remain in the list for some time until it is bumped off by newer documents. Similarly, if you move the document file without opening the file, the shortcut probably won't point to the correct file location.

▶ CONTROLLING YOUR DOCUMENTS LIST

The Documents list is a history of the documents you have recently used. Anyone who examines your Documents list can easily see which document files you've been using. In some cases you may prefer that certain documents not appear on this list. For example, you may not want your boss to know that you've been working on your resume. As the figures on the facing page show, you may wish to delete certain documents from the Documents list to protect your privacy.

CROSS-REFERENCE
See "Sending Objects to the Recycle Bin" in Chapter 3.

FIND IT ONLINE
Search the IDG site, at **http://www.idg.net** , for Windows 98 tips and more.

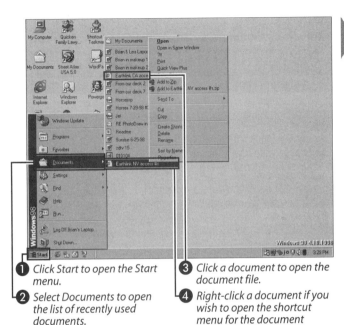

❶ Click Start to open the Start menu.

❷ Select Documents to open the list of recently used documents.

❸ Click a document to open the document file.

❹ Right-click a document if you wish to open the shortcut menu for the document shortcut.

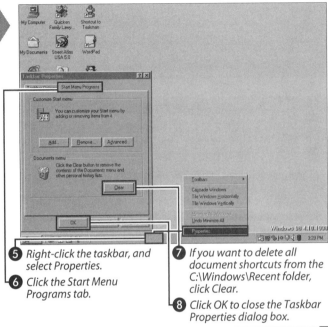

❺ Right-click the taskbar, and select Properties.

❻ Click the Start Menu Programs tab.

❼ If you want to delete all document shortcuts from the C:\Windows\Recent folder, click Clear.

❽ Click OK to close the Taskbar Properties dialog box.

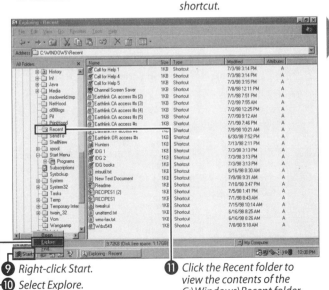

❾ Right-click Start.

❿ Select Explore.

⓫ Click the Recent folder to view the contents of the C:\Windows\Recent folder.

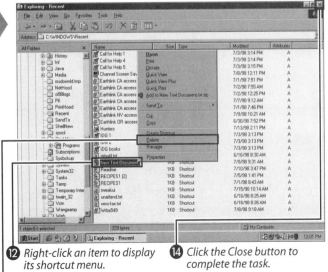

⓬ Right-click an item to display its shortcut menu.

⓭ If you want to remove the shortcut, select Delete.

⓮ Click the Close button to complete the task.

Saving Documents

Virtually any program you use in Windows 98 gives you the option to save the documents you create. In almost every case, programs follow certain guidelines that specify where common commands should be located so it will be easier to use different programs. When programs adhere to these standard conventions, you don't have to hunt through the menus to find the command you need.

One of the standard conventions followed by Windows 98 programs is to include a File ⇨ Save command so you can easily save your work. Generally, you'll also find a File ⇨ Save As command so that you can save your work under a new name, in a different location, or even as a different type of file. For example, you might save a word processing document in the word processor's native file format and then save a second copy in another format so you can more easily share the file with someone who uses a different word processor.

The figures on the facing page show some examples of how you can use the File ⇨ Save As command to save your document files. The options that are available in your application programs vary according to which program you're using and which file translation options you've installed. In some cases it may be necessary to use a custom installation option to add the file filters you need.

TAKE NOTE

BEWARE OF PORTED PROGRAMS

Not every computer uses Windows. A small percentage of systems use something called the Mac OS. Because the market for Windows 98 programs is much larger, many of the companies that write software for the Mac OS translate, or *port*, their software from the Mac version to create a version that runs on Windows 98. Unfortunately, a number of these companies don't spend the time to create a program that follows the Windows program guidelines, and you may have to work a bit harder to use the resulting ported program. Moreover, it's difficult for most people to determine which programs are simple ports from Mac OS programs. Graphics programs are often the worst offenders.

BE CAREFUL WHERE YOU SAVE FILES

Most Windows 98 programs remember the last location where you opened or saved files, and they offer the same location when you save a new file. Although this practice is usually convenient, it can cause problems. If you open a file that you've received as part of an e-mail message, Windows 98 generally stores the file in the C:\Windows\Temp folder. If you don't notice this, it's easy to misplace files that you know you've saved. Always check the location before you save a new file for the first time.

CROSS-REFERENCE

See "Copying and Moving Files" in Chapter 2.

SHORTCUT

Saving an unnamed file is the same as selecting File ⇨ Save As.

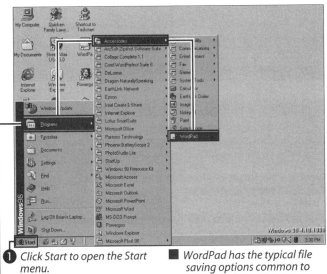

❶ Click Start to open the Start menu.

❷ Select Programs ➪ Accessories ➪ WordPad.

■ WordPad has the typical file saving options common to most Windows 98 programs.

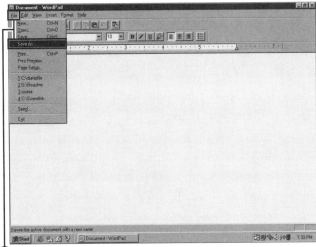

❸ Select File ➪ Save As to open the Save As dialog box.

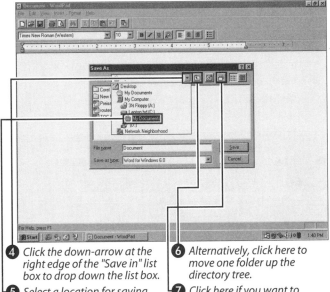

❹ Click the down-arrow at the right edge of the "Save in" list box to drop down the list box.

❺ Select a location for saving the file.

❻ Alternatively, click here to move one folder up the directory tree.

❼ Click here if you want to create a new folder to hold the file.

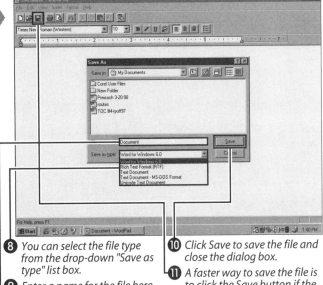

❽ You can select the file type from the drop-down "Save as type" list box.

❾ Enter a name for the file here.

❿ Click Save to save the file and close the dialog box.

⓫ A faster way to save the file is to click the Save button if the file has already been saved.

125

Selecting Text

Windows 98 uses the *Clipboard* to temporarily store data that you wish to copy or move from one place to another. Often you may be copying or moving data only within a document, but the Clipboard also enables you to copy and move data between different applications. You may, for example, want to copy a Web page address from Internet Explorer into a letter that you plan to e-mail to someone. Copying the address rather than retyping it reduces the possibility of typing errors.

To send text to the Clipboard, you must first select the text. To select a block of text with the mouse, move the cursor to the first character of the block. Next, press and hold the left mouse button and drag the cursor to the last character of the block. As you move the mouse, the text is highlighted to indicate the range of the selected block. When you have selected the text block that you want to send to the Clipboard, release the mouse button.

To select text using the keyboard, move the keyboard cursor to the first character of the block. Next, press and hold the Shift key and move the cursor with the arrow keys. As you move the cursor, the text is highlighted to indicate the range of the marked block. To clear the marking of a block, release the Shift key and move the cursor.

Most Windows 98 programs make it somewhat easier to select text by using *automatic word selection*.

When automatic word selection is enabled, you don't have to start at the beginning of a word. Instead, you can start dragging the pointer anywhere within the first word of your selection; the selection automatically expands to select complete words as soon as you drag the pointer onto a new word. The figures on the facing page demonstrate how this feature works in WordPad. Other Windows 98 applications are similar. Automatic word selection usually does not work when you are selecting text using the keyboard.

You can usually select all the text in a document by clicking Edit ➪ Select All. Most programs use Ctrl+A as a shortcut for this command. In Windows Explorer you use this shortcut to select the entire contents of a folder.

TAKE NOTE

▶ DOUBLE-CLICK TO SELECT

To select only a single word, double-click the word. In most applications this action selects the entire word along with the space following the word. If the word is followed by punctuation, only the word itself is selected.

▶ SELECT TEXT TO CHANGE ATTRIBUTES

If you wish to change the character formatting — such as bold, italics, or font size — in a document, select the text before selecting the attribute.

CROSS-REFERENCE

See "Cutting, Copying, and Pasting to the Clipboard" later in this chapter.

FIND IT ONLINE

See **http://www.sharewarejunkies.com/win_clipboard.htm** for a list of Clipboard utilities.

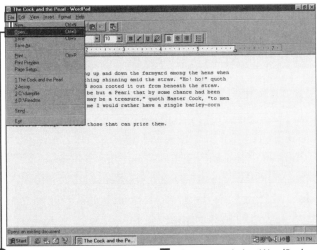

1 Select File ➪ Open.

■ Open an existing WordPad document that you can use to practice selecting text.

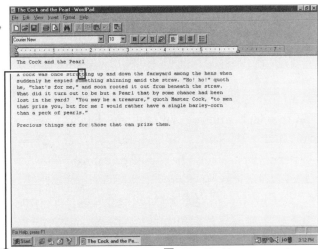

2 Move the mouse pointer over the middle of a word.

■ WordPad has automatic word selection enabled by default, so you don't need to begin at the start of a word if you wish to select multiple words.

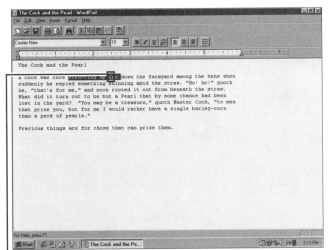

3 Hold down the left mouse button as you drag the mouse pointer across several words.

■ As you move to the second word, it is also automatically selected. The selection expands one word at a time as you continue dragging.

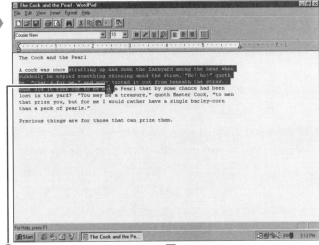

4 Continue holding down the left mouse button and drag the pointer down several rows.

■ As you extend the selection downward, it encompasses all words from the first selected word to the final selected word.

Cutting, Copying, and Pasting to the Clipboard

After you select data, you can cut or copy it to the Clipboard. Cutting deletes the data block from the sending application's document. Copying leaves the data in the sending application's document. Once you have data on the Clipboard, you can paste the data to a new location in the same or in another document. Many types of data can also be copied or cut from one application and pasted into a different application.

To copy the selected data to the Clipboard, open the application's Edit menu and choose the Copy command. To cut the selected data to the Clipboard, open the application's Edit menu and choose the Cut command. To insert Clipboard data into an application, first position the application's insertion point — the keyboard cursor in a text application — where you want the data to be pasted. Next open the application's Edit menu and choose the Paste command. To replace a block of data with data from the Clipboard, first select the data to be replaced. Then open the application's Edit menu and choose the Paste command.

Data you copy to the Clipboard can exist in several formats. When you paste the data into a document, it is pasted using whichever format contains the most information about the data that is compatible with the document. For example, if you copy text from your word processor, the font and attribute information for the selected text is also copied to the

Clipboard. If you paste the data back into a word processing document, all the original selection's attributes are retained in the copy. But if you paste the data into a text document in Notepad, only the text is pasted because plain text documents don't retain any character formatting information. If you'd like more control over how the data is pasted into the document, choose the Edit ➪ Paste Special command. The Paste Special dialog box enables you to select which of the data formats will be used when the data is pasted into your document.

TAKE NOTE

▶ DON'T LOSE YOUR DATA ON THE CLIPBOARD

Any new data you copy to the Clipboard replaces any existing data that may already be on the Clipboard. If you cut earlier data from a document and haven't already pasted it into a new location, you'll lose the older data when the new data is sent to the Clipboard.

▶ ENHANCE YOUR CLIPBOARD WITH CLIPBOARD VIEWER

Windows 98 includes a useful tool for enhancing the Clipboard. The Clipboard Viewer enables you to save Clipboard contents for future use, effectively enabling you to store several items in sequence on the Clipboard. See "Using Clipboard Viewer" in Chapter 12 for more information on this handy Windows 98 accessory.

CROSS-REFERENCE
See "Dragging and Dropping Data" later in this chapter.

FIND IT ONLINE
For a tip on using the Clipboard efficiently, see
http://malektips.envprogramming.com/98w0026.html.

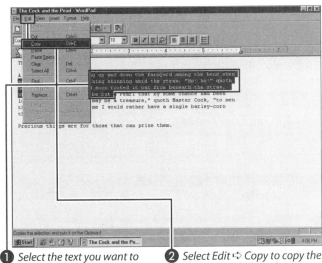

① Select the text you want to copy or cut.

② Select Edit ➪ Copy to copy the text to the Clipboard.

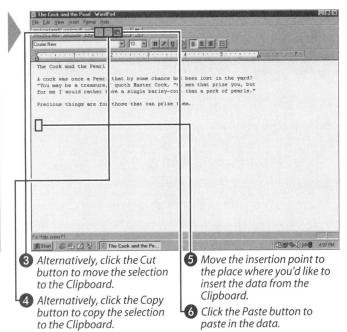

③ Alternatively, click the Cut button to move the selection to the Clipboard.

④ Alternatively, click the Copy button to copy the selection to the Clipboard.

⑤ Move the insertion point to the place where you'd like to insert the data from the Clipboard.

⑥ Click the Paste button to paste in the data.

⑦ Alternatively, select Edit ➪ Paste Special to open the Paste Special dialog box.

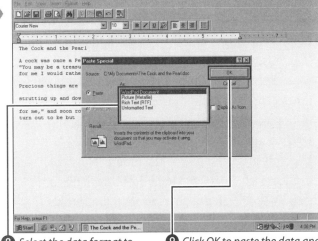

⑧ Select the data format to paste into the document.

⑨ Click OK to paste the data and complete the task.

Dragging and Dropping Data

With some Windows 98 applications, you can exchange data using drag and drop, which is more convenient than the Clipboard. You select data in a document in one application and then drag and drop it into another document – even one in another application. Not all applications support drag-and-drop data exchange. WordPad does, but Notepad does not.

The accompanying figures show how you can drag and drop data between two WordPad documents. To try this example, first open two copies of WordPad. Not all Windows 98 programs enable you to open two copies of the program at the same time. Some programs can detect that a copy is already open, and they open a second document within the first copy of the program rather than open a new copy of the program. You can still drag and drop between two documents within the same copy of the application, but you must open both document windows at the same time. The method for opening two document windows in an application varies, but you'll likely find an option on the Window menu to allow this.

Drag and drop can be confusing initially. You select the data and release the mouse. Next you point to the selected data and hold down the left mouse button while you drag the mouse pointer to the destination location. If you don't wait for the mouse pointer to return to the standard arrow pointer after

selecting the data, you won't be able to move the selected block. You'll end up changing the selection instead of dragging the data to the new location. Usually it's best to select the data, move the mouse slightly, and then point to the selection before you press and hold the left mouse button to initiate the drag.

CROSS-REFERENCE
See "Adding an Entry to the Start Menu" in Chapter 6.

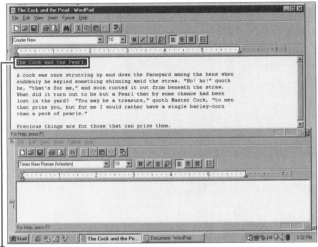

1 Select the text you want to drag and drop.

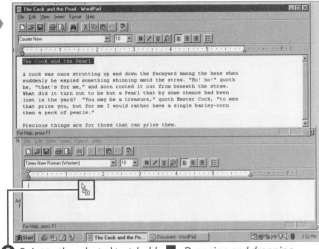

2 Point to the selected text, hold down the left mouse button, and drag the pointer to the desired location.

■ Dragging and dropping between two applications copies the text unless you hold down Alt.

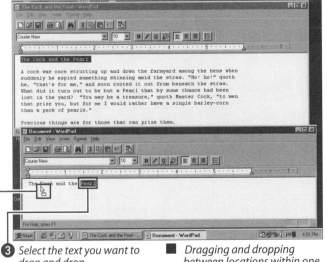

3 Select the text you want to drag and drop.

4 Point to the selected text, hold down the left mouse button, and drag the pointer to the destination.

■ Dragging and dropping between locations within one document moves the text unless you hold down Ctrl.

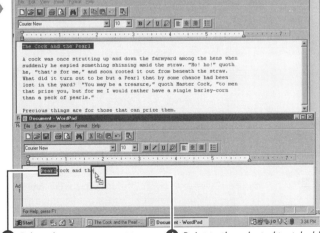

5 Select the text you want to drag and drop.

■ Text you just moved or copied will already be selected.

6 Point to the selected text, hold down the left mouse button, hold down Ctrl, and drag the pointer to the destination.

131

Personal Workbook

Q&A

1 Why must you be careful about changing file extensions on your document files?

_____

_____

2 Where can you quickly find a list of the documents that were most recently opened on your PC?

_____

3 What happens to data that you've copied to the Clipboard when you copy additional data to the Clipboard?

_____

4 How can you copy data using drag and drop within a single document?

_____

_____

5 What happens when you drag and drop data between two different documents without holding down any keys?

_____

_____

6 What is the fastest method of selecting an entire paragraph?

_____

_____

7 What shortcut can you use to copy selected text to the Clipboard?

_____

8 What shortcut can you use to paste text from the Clipboard?

_____

9 How can you control the format of data you paste from the Clipboard?

_____

_____

10 If you are unable to open a document that appears on the Documents list, what might be the cause?

_____

_____

ANSWERS: PAGE 358

EXTRA PRACTICE

1 Open several documents by selecting them from the My Documents folder.

2 Examine the Documents list to see the list of your most recently used documents.

3 Remove one of the documents from the Documents list.

4 Go to the My Documents folder and confirm that the document file you removed from the Documents list is still in the folder.

5 Copy some text to the Clipboard and then paste it into a new location in your document.

6 Copy some new text to the Clipboard and paste it to confirm that the original text is no longer available.

REAL-WORLD APPLICATIONS

✔ You are working on a project that has numerous document and graphics files. To organize the files, you create a new folder called Project in the My Documents folder.

✔ You decide to touch up your resume at work. When you go to lunch, you remove the file from the Documents list so that no one will know you were looking for another job.

✔ You're creating a complex report that includes several text files you created in Word, a photo you've retouched in Imaging, and some graphs you drew in a drawing program. After you complete work on the different pieces, you drag and drop them into one document to consolidate them.

Visual Quiz

How can you display the active folder? What purpose does it serve? How can you learn more about the items in the folder?

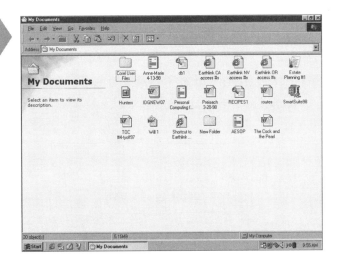

CHAPTER 8

Printing Documents

In spite of many predictions of the paper-less office, most documents are printed. The printer you find attached to almost every PC seems to be an indispensable peripheral.

This chapter describes how to print documents. Windows 98 has built-in support for converting your work to hard copy. When you have everything set up, printing is as simple as making a few menu selections or dragging and dropping documents onto devices.

Most applications print reports and documents. The File menus of these applications have Print and Page Setup commands. If you've used earlier versions of Windows, you're accustomed to these conventions. What the hard copy output looks like is between you and your application. No operating system can turn you into a great document designer or report writer. But assuming that you can piece together the parts that make a great-looking report on the screen, Windows 98 can turn your report into hard copy no matter what kind of printer you have.

This chapter assumes that your printer is installed and properly connected to your computer. If you haven't installed your printer, please refer to the "Adding New Hardware" section in Chapter 5 before continuing. The Add New Printer icon in the Printers folder makes adding a printer easy. Be sure your printer is working correctly before you try the exercises in this chapter.

Some of the dialog boxes in this chapter may not exactly match what you see when you access your printer. Printer manufacturers often include their own printer management software, which may replace some of the standard Windows 98 dialog boxes. This arrangement provides you with easier access to the features unique to your printer. If you encounter such differences, try to locate the options mentioned in the text and ignore those things that don't match. You can always make adjustments after you have a better understanding of the basics. The default settings for your printer's advanced settings will probably be acceptable while you practice.

Even though you'll probably use extra paper practicing the tasks in this chapter, remember that most programs let you preview the appearance of your document onscreen before you print. Using this option is an excellent way to save paper. Look for the Print Preview command on the File menu or on the Print dialog box.

Setting Printer Properties

In the early days of computing, people were happy to have any sort of printed output. If you had a printer, you considered yourself lucky, and you didn't spend much time worrying about the appearance of the printed output. The world has changed since then, and today's PC printers can do things no one dreamed about a few years ago.

Today's printers often have several *properties*—such as resolution, paper, and color settings—that you can adjust to get the desired type of output. The combination of properties you select may represent a compromise between the highest quality of printing and speed, or between the cost per page of output and the purpose of the document you're printing. You might, for example, choose to use a lower-resolution setting to quickly produce proof copies of a report and then switch to a high-quality setting to print the final report. The higher-quality setting might take several times as long to print and could also cost several times as much per page for toner or color ink. For day-to-day printing you might decide on a combination of settings that falls in the middle of these two extremes.

There are a number of ways to access the properties of your printer. The figures on the facing page demonstrate how to access the printer properties through the Printers folder. You can also access the printer properties by clicking the Properties button in the Print dialog box. You usually have access to more properties when you use the Printers folder as your starting point.

The lower-left and lower-right figures on the facing page show two versions of the printer Properties dialog box. Notice that the two dialog boxes share some common features, but they also differ to reflect differences between two types of printers. You may need to explore a little to find the printer property settings you want to adjust. For example, the types of settings shown on the Graphics tab for the HP LaserJet are found instead on the Main tab for the Epson printer.

TAKE NOTE

SHARING YOUR NETWORK PRINTER

If your PC is connected to a network and you have file and printer sharing enabled, your printer Properties dialog box will include an additional tab labeled Sharing. Before anyone else on your network can share your printer, you must enable sharing by selecting the "Shared as" radio button on this tab.

PRINT A TEST PAGE

Be sure to print a test page whenever you install a new printer driver. Printing a test page not only ensures that your printer is working properly, but also provides you with a list of the printer drivers currently in use.

CROSS-REFERENCE

See "Sharing a Printer" in Chapter 16.

FIND IT ONLINE

Check out **http://windowsupdate.microsoft.com** for printer driver updates.

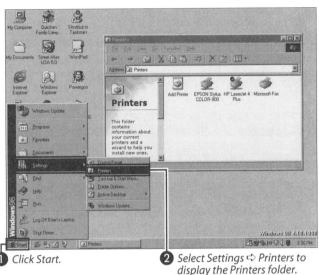

1 Click Start.

2 Select Settings ⇨ Printers to display the Printers folder.

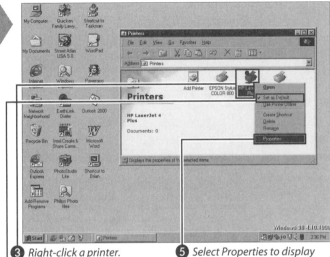

3 Right-click a printer.

4 You can select Set as Default to make this the printer used for most printing.

5 Select Properties to display the Properties dialog box for the selected printer.

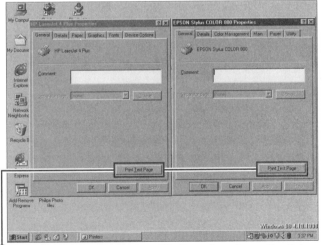

6 Click Print Test Page to make certain the printer is working correctly.

■ Two printer Properties dialog boxes are shown to illustrate similarities and differences between different printer models.

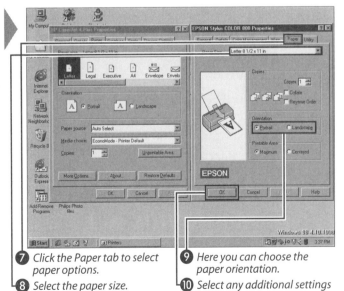

7 Click the Paper tab to select paper options.

8 Select the paper size.

9 Here you can choose the paper orientation.

10 Select any additional settings you want and click OK to close the dialog box and complete the task.

137

Putting a Printer on the Desktop

In earlier chapters you learned you can easily place a shortcut to a program, a document, or a folder on your desktop. A desktop shortcut makes it easy to access these objects. You can also put a shortcut to a printer on the desktop. If you do a lot of printing from documents or if you frequently check the status of queued print documents, having the printer available on the desktop is convenient.

If the document is of a type that Windows 98 recognizes, Windows 98 opens the program that created the document, prints the document, and then closes the program. Be sure to read the "Take Note" section to learn how you can make this process even more convenient.

In addition to providing an easy method of printing documents, a desktop printer icon enables you to quickly check the printer's status. Windows 98 generally *spools* print jobs — that is, it stores the data being sent to the printer on disk. In this way, you don't have to wait for the printer to finish so that you can continue working. In addition, Windows 98 *queues* print jobs so that you can send more than one document to your printer; each one prints in turn as the previous job is completed. By double-clicking the printer icon, you can display the printer status dialog box as shown in the lower-right figure on the facing page. If there are print jobs in line for the printer, you can pause, delete, or postpone them using this dialog box. You can also see who is printing to your printer, if you are sharing it.

TAKE NOTE

▶ USING THE QUICK LAUNCH TOOLBAR

If you find a printer shortcut on your desktop handy, you'll see there's an even more convenient place for a printer shortcut: the Quick Launch toolbar. Placing a printer shortcut on the Quick Launch toolbar offers all the advantages of placing the shortcut on your desktop and adds another important benefit. Because the Quick Launch toolbar is almost always visible, you can use a printer shortcut on this toolbar even when it may not be convenient to use a shortcut on your desktop.

▶ PRINTING REQUIRES THE RIGHT APPLICATION

A desktop shortcut makes it easy to print documents because you can print simply by dragging the document icon and dropping it on the printer icon. But this technique works only if you have the correct application program installed on your PC. You must have the application that created the document, and that application must be one designed for Windows 98 (or Windows 95).

CROSS-REFERENCE

See "Opening Documents" in Chapter 7.

SHORTCUT

Add a desktop shortcut to your printer so you can print documents by dragging the document icon and dropping it onto the printer icon.

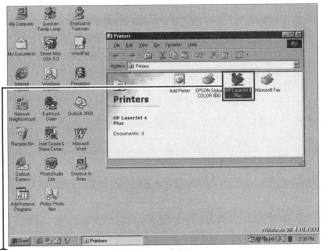

1 Point to the printer in the Printers folder.

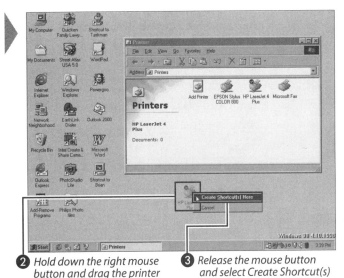

2 Hold down the right mouse button and drag the printer icon onto your desktop.

3 Release the mouse button and select Create Shortcut(s) to add the printer shortcut to your desktop.

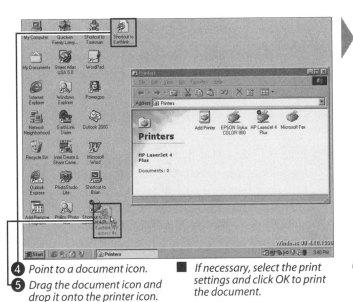

4 Point to a document icon.

5 Drag the document icon and drop it onto the printer icon.

■ If necessary, select the print settings and click OK to print the document.

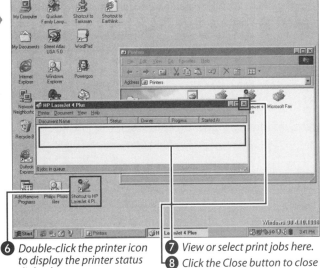

6 Double-click the printer icon to display the printer status dialog box.

7 View or select print jobs here.

8 Click the Close button to close the dialog box and complete the task.

Printing a Document

Although you can print a document by dragging its icon onto the printer icon, you'll probably print most documents from within the application that you used to create them. This is true especially if you want to change any of the default print settings. Dragging a document onto a printer icon usually doesn't allow you much latitude in adjusting the document print options.

You print from applications by using the Print, Print Preview, and Page Setup commands on the application's File menu. Not all applications have all three of these commands, but this command set is typical. Most programs' toolbars also provide a Print icon so you don't have to wade through the menus to print a document. Using the Print icon, however, may not always give you the opportunity to adjust the print settings.

Although the default settings of individual programs vary, most programs enable you to specify certain page setup options. Typically, these options include the orientation of the printing — portrait or landscape — along with the paper size and the margin settings. The upper-right figure on the facing page shows the Page Setup dialog box that WordPad displays when you select File ➪ Page setup. When you adjust the page setup options, the on-screen view of the document will likely change to reflect the new settings. If you're trying to control the final document appearance, it's best to make the page setup changes before you begin formatting your document.

The File ➪ Print command usually displays a Print dialog box similar to the one shown in the lower right figure on the facing page. You can use this dialog box to select a different printer, change the printer properties, select the page range you wish to print, and choose the number of copies to print. To print multiple copies of the same document, it's usually more efficient to select the number of copies in the Print dialog box than to issue several print commands.

TAKE NOTE

► SELECT YOUR PRINTER FIRST

Correct page setup depends on the printer. Different printers have different features that affect the page layout, so if you have more than one printer installed, select the printer before trying to change the page settings. Otherwise, you may find that the page settings change when you select the correct printer.

► BE CAREFUL WITH MARGIN SETTINGS

Most printers have limitations regarding how close they can print to the edge of a page. If you set the print margins too small, you may get a warning from the application program, or there may be no warning and your document may be printed minus the characters closest to the edges of the page.

CROSS -REFERENCE

See "Printing to a File" later in this chapter.

FIND IT ONLINE

For a tip on printing labels, see **http://www.toweroffice. co.za/label_printing_tips.html**.

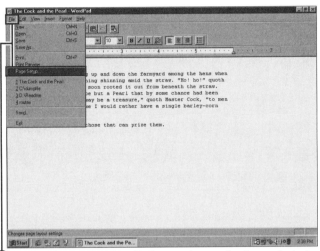

1 Open a document in WordPad or another application and select File ➪ Page Setup.

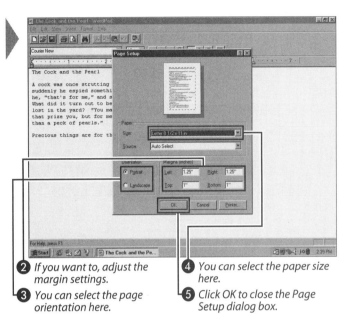

2 If you want to, adjust the margin settings.

3 You can select the page orientation here.

4 You can select the paper size here.

5 Click OK to close the Page Setup dialog box.

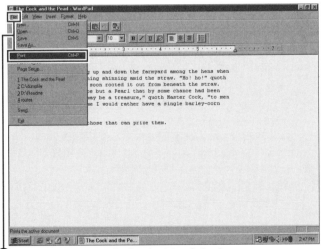

6 Select File ➪ Print to display the Print dialog box.

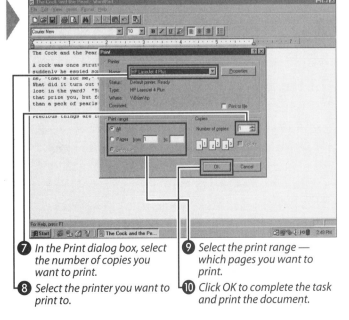

7 In the Print dialog box, select the number of copies you want to print.

8 Select the printer you want to print to.

9 Select the print range — which pages you want to print.

10 Click OK to complete the task and print the document.

Printing to a File

At times you will want to print to a file instead of to a printer. This concept often confuses new users. The document itself is a file, so what is the difference between the document file and the file to which you print?

The document file contains data in a format that the application understands. A file to which you print contains data in a format that the printer understands. In other words, the character stream in a printer file is exactly what the computer sends to the printer to print the document.

Why would anyone want to print to a file rather than to a printer? There are several possible reasons. You may be preparing a file to send to a printing organization (also called a *printshop*). The printshop may typeset your document to film on a typesetting device and then print it on an offset printer. Your computer has the typesetting device installed in software but not physically attached.

You may want to print to a printer attached to someone else's PC (perhaps it has better graphical features or color), but that person's PC is not on a network and does not have your document-generating application installed. In that case, you would carry your file on a floppy disk to the other person's PC and copy it directly to the printer.

You may want to prepare a PostScript file to be read by a program such as GhostScript, which emulates the printer on the screen by reading the file and displaying the document pages.

TAKE NOTE

▶ INSTALL YOUR PRINTER FIRST

Before you can print to a printer file, you must install the printer. Otherwise, Windows 98 won't be able to create a print file for the correct printer. Print files work only with the printer they were created for.

▶ PRINTING THE PRINT FILE

Once you create the print file, you must use MS-DOS commands to print the file properly. The easiest way to do this is to create a batch file named PF.bat on your desktop. To do this, open the MS-DOS prompt, enter the following lines, and then press F6:

```
COPY CON \WINDOWS\DESKTOP\PF.BAT
<Enter>
COPY %1 /B LPT1
<Enter>
```

To print the file, drag the file icon onto the PF icon. Be sure you drag only print files onto the PF icon. If you drag other document files onto this icon, your printer is likely to start spewing out page after page of garbage. If you don't want to add the PF icon to your desktop, you can also print a file from the MS-DOS command prompt by replacing %1 in the preceding command with the name of the print file.

CROSS-REFERENCE
See "Printing to a Network Printer" in Chapter 16.

FIND IT ONLINE
For a comparison of printers, see **http://www.computers. com/cdoor/o,1,0-15-2,00.html?st.co.fd.nav.Printers**.

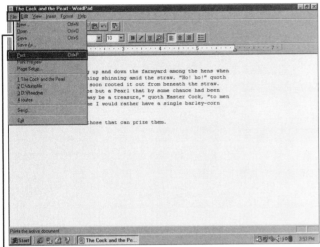

1 Select File ➪ Print to display the Print dialog box.

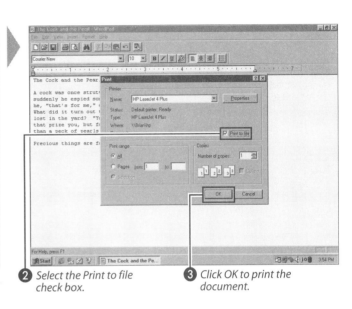

2 Select the Print to file check box.

3 Click OK to print the document.

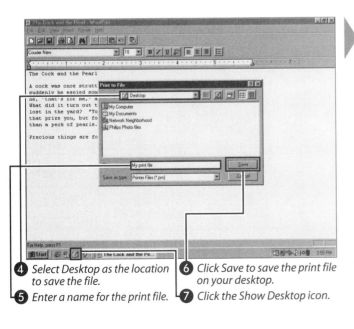

4 Select Desktop as the location to save the file.

5 Enter a name for the print file.

6 Click Save to save the print file on your desktop.

7 Click the Show Desktop icon.

8 Drag the print file onto the icon for your PF.bat MS-DOS batch file.

■ If necessary, copy the print file to a disk and print the file on the PC connected to the printer.

Personal Workbook

Q&A

1 How can you save paper while still seeing how your printed output will appear?

_____

_____

2 What must you do before someone on your network can use your printer?

_____

_____

_____

3 How can you print using a printer that isn't connected to your PC or your network?

_____

_____

4 What is the best way to print multiple copies of the same document?

_____

_____

5 What do the terms portrait and landscape refer to?

_____

_____

6 How can you make certain your documents will print on your preferred printer?

_____

_____

_____

7 Why do you have to specify the correct printer before printing to a file?

_____

_____

_____

8 What type of command do you use to print a print file?

_____

9 Why would you want to place a printer icon on your desktop?

_____

_____

_____

ANSWERS: PAGE 359

EXTRA PRACTICE

1. Open the printer Properties dialog box for your printer.

2. Print a test page.

3. Print a document by dragging and dropping it onto the printer icon on your desktop.

4. Print three copies of the same document using a single print command.

5. Change the paper orientation for your printer to landscape and print another copy of the same document.

REAL-WORLD APPLICATIONS

✔ You are creating a fancy advertising piece to promote your company's new product line. To show your boss how the piece will look, you create a print file that works with the PostScript printers at your local printshop.

✔ Your printer needs service, and you need to print documents while it's in the shop. You create print files of your documents so that you can use a friend's printer.

✔ You have a standard form that you print frequently, so you create a copy of the document on your desktop. Now you can easily print a copy simply by dragging and dropping the document onto your desktop printer icon.

Visual Quiz

How can you display this dialog box? What purpose does it serve? How can you change the type of paper?

_____

_____

_____

_____

_____

_____

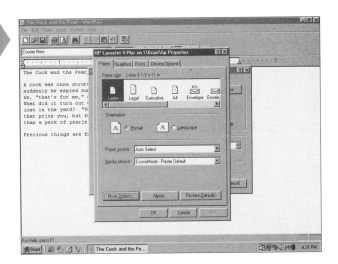

CHAPTER **9**

MASTER
THESE
SKILLS

▶ Searching for a File

▶ Specifying a Date Search

▶ Finding Specific File Types

▶ Saving a Search

Finding a File

It's easy to misplace things on your computer. Your hard disk may have hundreds of folders and thousands of files, and important files can disappear when you need them. This chapter shows you how to avoid (or lessen) the painful moment when you think you've lost hours of work.

Searching for things on your PC is easy. Windows 98 provides the Find feature, a powerful and flexible search tool. With this tool you can quickly do a simple search or, with a little more work, a complex search that can find, for example, every file that contains a specific phrase or that was created within a specified time period. You can combine several criteria to narrow your search as needed.

If libraries worked the way the Windows 98 Find tool works, you'd be able to ask for a list of every book that mentions your first name in any context. You could then narrow your search to only those books whose subject is beauty or honesty and that were published in the year before you were born. You could then check out the resulting titles to see whether any of them may have had an influence on the name your parents chose.

Libraries don't work that way, at least not yet. But your Windows 98–based PC provides that kind of search power, and this chapter shows you how to harness it. You start with a basic file search and then learn to use more qualifications to narrow your search. You'll be able to locate files based on words or phrases contained in the name, by the date the file was created, or by looking for specific types of files. Finally, you learn a few tricks about saving a search for future use. One of these tricks helps you bypass a trap that many experts fall into.

Of course, not even the most powerful search tool can find files that aren't there. Search tools are no substitute for making backup copies of important files. Accidents happen, hard disks can crash, and the one file that will almost certainly be damaged or destroyed will be the file you can't do without but haven't yet gotten around to copying. If you've turned to this chapter because you're in panic mode over a lost file, be sure to also read Chapter 18.

Searching for a File

It's easy to lose a file or two simply by not paying attention. You click the Save button or select File ⇨ Save, but you fail to notice where the file was being stored. Everyone who uses computers has probably lost more than one file simply because he or she didn't pay close enough attention. Fortunately, Windows 98 can find a file that you know you saved but can't find.

If you've been working with computers for a while you may remember when you could use only 11 characters to name your files: 8 characters for the filename and 3 characters for the file extension. Windows 98 gives you the capability to use much longer and more descriptive names for your files. These longer filenames should make it harder to misplace files. After all, the purpose of a file named "Letter to Dad asking for more money.doc" should be easy to determine, wouldn't you say? But if this file were lost somewhere on your hard disk, its long filename could also complicate your efforts to locate it.

You can use two different approaches to search for words or phrases in filenames. If you know the exact title of the file, you can search for only that specific phrase. But if you're not certain of the exact filename you can search for part of the name. Unfortunately, you may quickly discover that your carefully crafted long filename can cause all sorts of problems in searching. The figures on the facing page demonstrate why this is so. Clearly, Windows 98 has found a lot of files that aren't what you want, and the list is too long to be helpful in finding the file.

Searching for a filename becomes complicated if you've saved the file using a long filename that includes spaces. That's because Windows 98 assumes that you want to search for any of the words you specified. As the lower-left figure on the facing page shows, this probably won't accomplish what you had hoped. In fact, after a couple of hours of waiting for a complicated search to complete, you may decide that it would be faster to just look for the file yourself!

Continued

TAKE NOTE

MAKE YOUR SEARCH CASE-SENSITIVE

If you're certain about the capitalization of the words in your search string, you can force Windows 98 to find only the files that use the same capitalization. To do this, select Options ⇨ Case Sensitive.

CHECK THE "LOOK IN" LOCATION

Be sure to verify that the correct location is shown in the "Look in" list box. Windows 98 may modify this without warning you.

CROSS-REFERENCE
See "Sorting the File Listing" in Chapter 2.

FIND IT ONLINE
See **http://www.chami.com/tips/windows/ 122596W.html** for a tip on using Windows file searching capabilities.

Use Wildcards

You can also use *wildcards* to aid in your search. Use an asterisk (*) to take the place of any number of characters, or a question mark (?) to take the place of a single character. For example, TY*.DOC would find any files that start with the letters TY and use the DOC extension. TY??.DOC would also find any files that start with TY and use the DOC extension, but would limit the search to filenames that were exactly four characters in length. Each question mark in a wildcard specifies that there must be a character in that position.

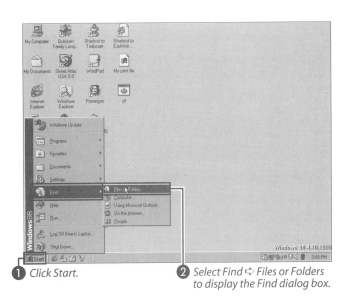

① Click Start.

② Select Find ➪ *Files or Folders to display the Find dialog box.*

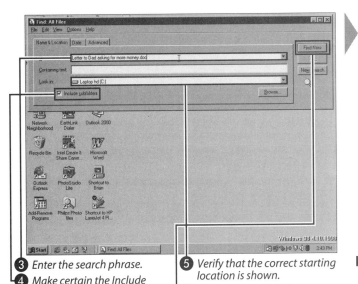

③ *Enter the search phrase.*

④ *Make certain the Include subfolders check box is selected.*

⑤ *Verify that the correct starting location is shown.*

⑥ *Click the Find Now button to begin the search.*

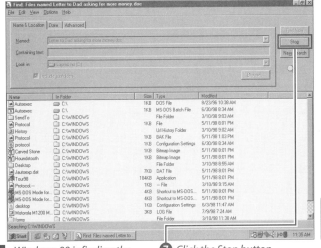

■ *Windows 98 is finding the wrong files. Each word in the search phrase is searched for individually, so many files match. Examine the listing to see why.*

⑦ *Click the Stop button.*

It's apparent that Windows 98 understood your search phrase differently than you intended. Rather than look for a file named "Letter to Dad asking for more money.doc" Windows 98 looked for any file that had any of the words anywhere in its name. "Autoexec" was found, for example, because it contains one of the search words — to — within the filename.

The upper-left figure on the facing page shows one way to correct this problem. Because you know the exact name of the file you wish to locate, return to the Named text box and enclose the name within quotation marks. Now Windows 98 will understand that you're specifying a complete filename and will search only for files having exactly that name. When you click the Find Now button, your search will conclude much faster because the search is no longer ambiguous.

Of course, even solutions to problems can introduce problems. By enclosing the search phrase within quotation marks, you've told Windows 98 that you know the exact name of the file you want to find. Suppose, though, that you are certain of only some of the words in the filename. You may know that the filename contains *more* followed by *money,* but you aren't certain about the rest of the name. In this case, enter your search phrase as *more?money.* The question mark substitutes for any single character, so Windows 98 will find all files that have the word

more followed by a single character — which could be a space — and then followed by *money.*

When you've found a file that was hiding in an unexpected location, you can use the File ⇨ Open Containing Folder command to see what else you may have saved there. Before using this command, you must first select the file in the list of found files.

TAKE NOTE

▶ DON'T USE SPACES IF YOU WANT TO FIND FILES

Because Windows 98 assumes that words separated by spaces in search phrases are separate search phrases, you can eliminate a lot of search problems by not including spaces in your filenames. You could, for example, use an underscore (_) between words rather than a space when you name files. Then when you search for files, use an underscore or a question mark between the words in the search phrase.

▶ QUICKLY CHECK YOUR RESULTS

The two bottom figures on the facing page show you how to use a handy Windows 98 accessory — Quick View — to verify that you've found the correct file. This accessory lets you view the contents of a selected file without opening the application that created the file. You may need to install Quick View if it does not appear on the context menu.

CROSS-REFERENCE
See "Specifying a Date Search" later in this chapter.

FIND IT ONLINE
See **http://home.cdarchive.com/ftp/shareware/ 05A.htm** for Windows file utilities.

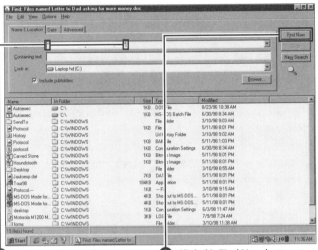

8 *When you know the exact filename, put it in quotation marks.*

9 *Click the Find Now button to restart the search.*

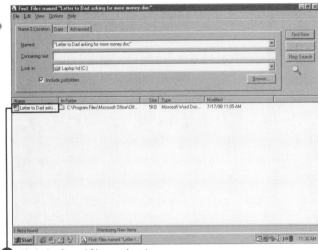

10 *Click the found file to select it.*

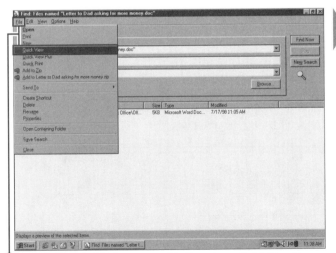

11 *Select File ⇨ Quick View to view the contents of the selected file.*

■ *If you have Quick View Plus installed, you can use that in place of Quick View.*

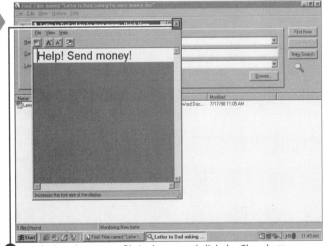

12 *Verify that the correct file is shown and click the Close button to complete this task.*

Specifying a Date Search

Searching for files by name is fine if you know most or all of the filename, but you may not always know the names of the files you'd like to locate. Windows 98 gives you many different ways to search for files. In this section you learn how to conduct a search based on the date the file was created or last modified.

Why would you want to search for files based on their file dates? Maybe you worked on a project last January, but you weren't very well organized at the time and now you can't remember the names of all the files you created. Or perhaps you installed a new program and you'd like to see a list of all the files that were added or changed during the installation. Maybe your collaborator used your PC last week but forgot to tell you where she saved an important report file. Each of these scenarios presents an opportunity to search for files based on a date range.

When you specify a date search, you can also specify whether you're searching for the time the file was created, modified, or last accessed. For document files you'll likely want to look for files that were modified within a time period. In that way, you can locate which files were changed, not only those that were originally created during the specified date range.

CROSS-REFERENCE

See "Copying and Moving Files" in Chapter 2.

SHORTCUT

Press Alt+I to start the search.

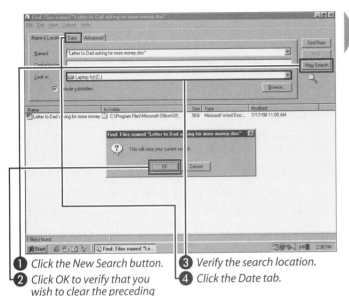

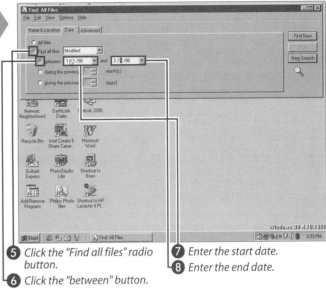

1. Click the New Search button.

2. Click OK to verify that you wish to clear the preceding search.

3. Verify the search location.

4. Click the Date tab.

5. Click the "Find all files" radio button.

6. Click the "between" button.

7. Enter the start date.

8. Enter the end date.

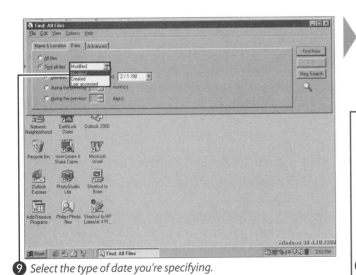

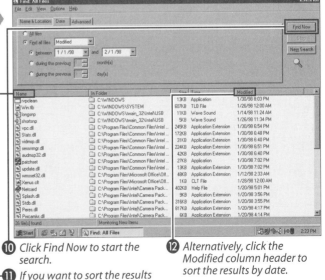

9. Select the type of date you're specifying.

10. Click Find Now to start the search.

11. If you want to sort the results by name, click the Name column header.

12. Alternatively, click the Modified column header to sort the results by date.

Finding Specific File Types

Until this point you've searched for files without regard to the type of file. This kind of search may not suit your needs because it often shows you long lists of files that are unrelated to the files you want to find.

When you're searching for a file on your PC, you're probably more concerned with the various document files that you create or modify than you are with all the other types of files found on your hard disk. For example, you're probably not looking for the hundreds of system files that are used by Windows 98 and your programs. Having those files displayed in the search results makes it harder to locate the document files you're trying to find.

To search for files by file type you use the options on the Advanced tab of the Find dialog box, as shown in the figures on the facing page. The "Of type" list box includes entries for every file type that is registered on your system. It does not, unfortunately, contain an entry for generic documents. If you wish to find document files, you must specify which type of document files you want to find. You can specify Microsoft Word document files, Lotus 1-2-3 spreadsheet files, or Paradox database files — but you cannot specify a search that finds all three at one time using the "Of type" list box entries.

The figures show a search for one type of file you may find useful — Wave sounds. To play the sound, double-click any of the files you find.

TAKE NOTE

▶ DON'T COUNT ON THE "CONTAINING TEXT" BOX

You may have noticed the "Containing text" box on the Name & Location tab of the Find dialog box. In theory, you should be able to use this text box to specify text that you'd like to find in a file — but don't count on it. Files are often encrypted when they are stored on your hard disk, and this makes it impossible to locate the actual text within the files. It's unlikely that you'll find what you want by using this text box. You can try, but don't count on the results being complete.

▶ BEWARE OF APPLICATIONS

You may be tempted to search for all applications when you open the "Of type" list box and see that option listed. If you try this, be forewarned that many of the items that will appear on the list of applications aren't intended for you to run manually. In fact, attempting to run some of the items in this list may lock up your computer or cause you to lose data. To find out more about a particular application file, right-click the file and choose Properties.

CROSS-REFERENCE

See "Saving a Search" later in this chapter.

SHORTCUT

Look for entries with "Image" in their file type to see all the image files you can open.

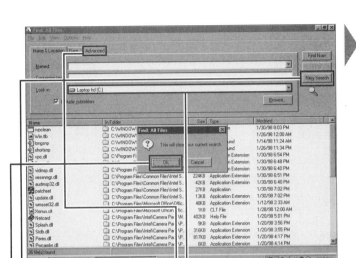

① Click the New Search button.

② Click OK to verify that you wish to clear the preceding search.

③ Verify the search location.

④ Click the Advanced tab.

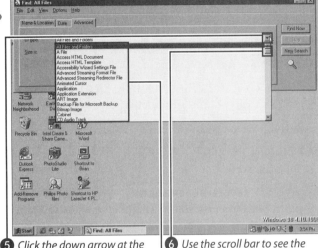

⑤ Click the down arrow at the right edge of the "Of type" list box.

⑥ Use the scroll bar to see the available file types.

⑦ Choose the type of file you wish to find.

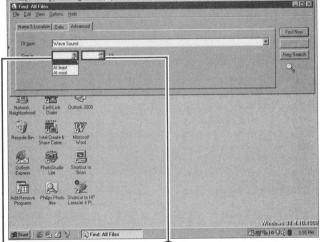

⑧ You can choose a file size option.

⑨ If you selected a file size option, choose the size you want.

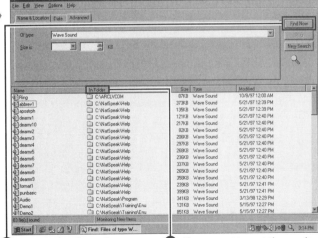

⑩ Click the Find Now button to start the search.

⑪ If you want to sort the results by folder, click the In Folder column header.

Saving a Search

After you've created a carefully crafted search, you may decide to save the search criteria for future reuse. For example, if you're working on a long-term project you may want to create a search that finds all the document files that you've used in the past week. After you've found these files it's easy to make a backup copy of them to protect against system failure or human error.

Unfortunately, the Windows 98 Find program has a subtle idiosyncrasy that may jump up and bite you. This section shows you how to avoid this "interesting feature" of the Find program. What is this little problem? If you want Windows 98 to save your entire set of search criteria you must actually perform a search before you save the search criteria. If you specify the search criteria but don't perform a search, Windows 98 will save the search for you, but it won't save any date criteria you specified. The next time you open the saved search to run it again, Windows 98 will revert to finding all files regardless of their dates. But if you perform a search and then save the search, Windows 98 will remember the date range you specified to use.

When you save a search, Windows 98 creates an icon on your desktop so you can later perform the same search by double-clicking the icon. The desktop icon will have the same name that is displayed in the Find dialog box title bar. For example, saving the

search shown in the figures on the facing page results in a desktop icon named "All Files." If you have Windows Explorer configured to show file extensions, the name will have the extension FND. You can save as many different searches as you like on your desktop. Each one will have a different name, although if you save multiple copies of the same search the names will differ only by having a number appended to the icon name.

TAKE NOTE

▶ SPECIFY YOUR COMPLETE SEARCH

If you're going to save a search for future use, be sure that you specify your complete search using all necessary options from each tab before you click the Find Now button. Windows 98 will save the complete set of search conditions only if you specify all of them before you perform the search. Remember that you must actually do the search before saving the search. Otherwise, you may find that your saved search is incomplete.

▶ CREATE A SEARCH FOLDER ON YOUR DESKTOP

If you save a large number of searches, you may want to create a new folder named "Search" on your desktop. You can then drag all the saved searches into the Search folder and reduce desktop clutter.

CROSS-REFERENCE

See "Specifying a Date Search" earlier in this chapter.

FIND IT ONLINE

See a list of filename extensions and what they mean at **http://stekt.oulu.fi/~jon/jouninfo/extension.html**.

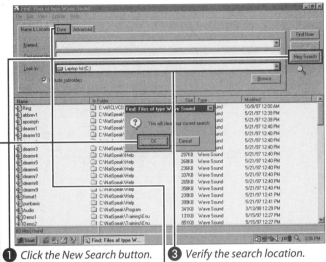

① *Click the New Search button.*

② *Click OK to verify that you wish to clear the preceding search.*

③ *Verify the search location.*

④ *Click the Date tab.*

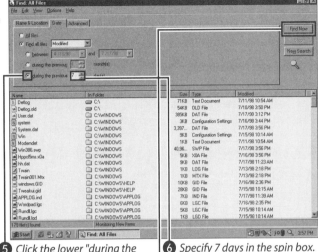

⑤ *Click the lower "during the previous" radio button.*

⑥ *Specify 7 days in the spin box.*

⑦ *Click the Find Now button to start the search.*

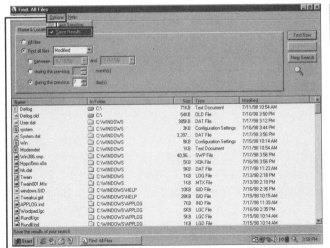

⑧ *Select Options ⇨ Save Results.*

■ *Make sure this option is checked. Options ⇨ Save Results is a toggle and will change its state each time you select it.*

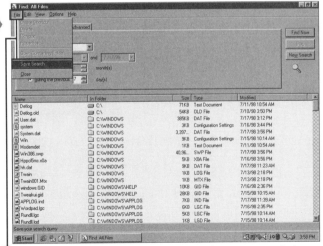

⑨ *Select File ⇨ Save Search to save the search icon on your desktop.*

Personal Workbook

Q&A

1 How can long filenames complicate the search for files?

_____

_____

2 How can you avoid problems with searching for filenames that include spaces?

_____

_____

3 What Windows 98 accessory enables you to quickly look at the contents of most of the files you find?

_____

4 What will happen if you don't click the New Search button between searches?

_____

_____

5 What usually happens to the search location when you click the New Search button?

_____

_____

6 How can you specify that you want to limit your search to files larger than a certain size?

_____

_____

7 What step must you take before saving a search for future use?

_____

_____

_____

8 How can you reuse a search you've saved?

_____

_____

_____

9 How can you find a file if all you know is two particular words occur together somewhere in the filename?

_____

_____

ANSWERS: PAGE 359

EXTRA PRACTICE

1 Search for all the files and folders on your system that contain "wind" in their name.

2 Find all the files *created* in the past month.

3 Find all the files *modified* in the past month.

4 Search for all the Bitmap image files on your hard disk.

5 Search for all the Cabinet files on your Windows 98 CD-ROM.

6 Find all the files that are more than 750K in size.

7 Create and save a search that finds all your word processor document files for the past two weeks.

REAL-WORLD APPLICATIONS

✔ You do a lot of work on your PC. To make it easy to back up your files, before you stop work for the day you locate all the files you've created that day.

✔ While you were on vacation for a week, someone else in the office borrowed your system. You search for the files that were created during your absence so that you can offer to let him have a copy of them.

✔ You suspect that someone has been modifying your files while you were away from the office for a few days. You do a search for files created or modified during that time.

✔ In working on the Ebenezer project, you included "Ebenezer" as part of the names of all the files. Now you search for all files using the project name to make certain you have backup copies of all of them.

Visual Quiz

How can you display this dialog box? What purpose does it serve? How can you change the search location to your CD-ROM drive?

_____

_____

_____

_____

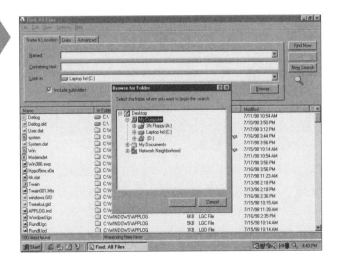

PART

IV

Using Windows 98 Accessories

If you think Windows 98 is all work and no play, wait until you try the examples in this part of the book. In addition to providing useful functionality, the Windows 98 accessories can be a lot of fun and can even make your PC lively.

In this part you learn how to make Windows 98 do some of the everyday computer chores for you so that you have more time to play. The Task Scheduler can take over some of the drudgery and let you concentrate on enjoying your computer. After that's out of the way, you learn how to use the multimedia accessories to add sound and motion to your system. If you want to, you can add special sounds to system events, play videos and view images on the screen, and even record your own sound files.

After you've had your fun with multimedia, you try out some of the other Windows 98 accessories and even learn how you can run MS-DOS programs, such as games, on your PC. If you don't have fun in this part, you're not trying!

CHAPTER 10

MASTER THESE SKILLS

▶ Adding a Scheduled Task

▶ Modifying a Scheduled Task

▶ Suspending and Resuming Tasks

Using Task Scheduler

Windows 98 makes your life simpler by providing a tool called the Task Scheduler. Task Scheduler is a background task that starts when you start Windows 98. Task Scheduler lets you schedule applications to run at regular intervals. Windows 98 itself uses Task Scheduler to schedule routine maintenance tasks when you use Maintenance Wizard (Chapter 19). These tasks include defragmenting your hard disk to improve performance and removing extraneous files.

You can also use Task Scheduler to run other applications on a regular schedule:

▶ Suppose you're a real estate agent who routinely connects to the local Board of Realty's database to gather new listings of properties for sale. You could run a communications program that uses programming scripts to control the interaction with the remote system.

▶ As an investor, you periodically monitor the activity of critical stocks in your portfolio. Here, too, you could use a program that goes online to download data and a stock analysis program to provide the results.

▶ You could use the computer to remind you when to take your medicine. You would use an event reminder program that displays or vocalizes a message.

▶ You want to back up your data files regularly. If you scheduled a backup program to automatically copy all your data files at regular intervals, you wouldn't have to worry about a system failure or user error causing you to lose your work.

To support such uses of Task Scheduler, you must have an appropriate application. Windows 98 does not include a script-driven communications program, a stock analysis program, or an event reminder, but such applications are available from other sources. Windows 98 does include a backup utility, which you will learn to use in Chapter 18. In this chapter you learn how to employ and configure the Task Scheduler using the standard types of tasks common to the Task Scheduler. Adding other types of tasks to the schedule is not very difficult, but you'll need to know how to program the application you wish to use.

Adding a Scheduled Task

The Task Scheduler runs programs at time intervals that you specify. Although this may sound like an ideal way to automate most tasks, the program you run must have the capability to do something without your input if it is to accomplish anything useful as a scheduled task. Merely opening a program that sits there waiting for you to do something probably won't be very useful.

When you install Windows 98, you have the option to schedule several system maintenance tasks such as defragmenting your hard drive at specified intervals. If you choose to use this option, Task Scheduler will have one or more tasks scheduled the first time you open the Scheduled Tasks folder. These scheduled tasks are good examples of the types of tasks you should consider when you decide to add new items to the schedule; when they are run, they accomplish a useful purpose whether you're around or not. For the sake of clarity, this exercise shows you how to add disk defragmenting as a scheduled task. You can safely add this task even if you have already allowed Windows 98 to schedule tasks.

The background component of Task Scheduler is always running, but to work with it, you must open the folder that contains scheduled tasks. There are several ways to access Task Scheduler. You can click the Start button and select Programs ⇨ Accessories ⇨ System Tools ⇨ Scheduled Tasks. Or you can open My Computer and double-click Scheduled Tasks. Or you can double-click the Task Scheduler icon in the group of icons at the right end of the Taskbar. Finally, you can right-click the Task Scheduler icon and select Open.

The figures on the facing page show you how to start adding a scheduled task using the Scheduled Task Wizard. The following pages show you how to complete this exercise.

Continued

TAKE NOTE

▶ SELECT TASKS CAREFULLY

When you select tasks you wish to schedule, make sure that the programs you select can perform a task without human intervention. Task Scheduler enables you to schedule almost any program that is installed on your PC, but few programs are appropriate for this purpose. Disk Cleanup, Disk Defragmenter, and ScanDisk are three good choices.

▶ BE PATIENT

When you click the Next button shown in the lower-left figure on the facing page, Windows 98 must determine which programs are available on your system before it can display the list as shown in the lower-right figure. If you have a large number of programs installed on your system, you may experience a long delay of perhaps several minutes while Windows 98 searches for the programs. Be patient and wait until the list of programs appears.

CROSS-REFERENCE

See "Modifying a Scheduled Task" later in this chapter.

SHORTCUT

Double-click the Task Scheduler icon on the System Tray to quickly open the Scheduled Tasks folder.

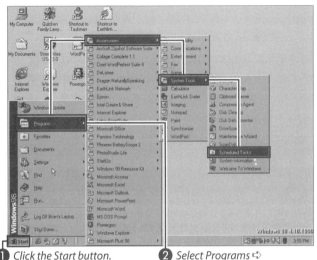

1 *Click the Start button.*

2 *Select Programs ⇨ Accessories ⇨ System Tools ⇨ Scheduled Tasks.*

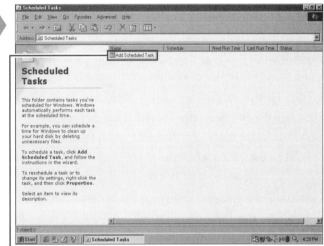

3 *Click Add Scheduled Task to open the Scheduled Task Wizard.*

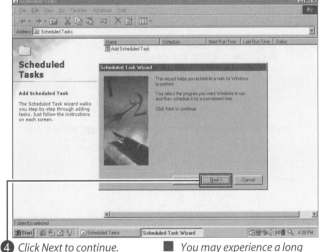

4 *Click Next to continue.*

■ *You may experience a long delay while Windows 98 searches for installed applications.*

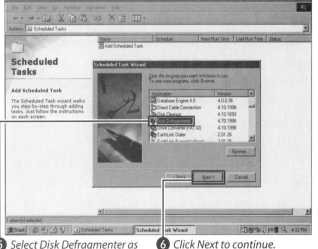

5 *Select Disk Defragmenter as the program you wish to schedule.*

6 *Click Next to continue.*

After you've selected a task you want to schedule, the next step is to select the schedule you want to use. As the upper-left figure on the facing page shows, you have a number of options from which to choose. The first three options — daily, weekly, or monthly — are usually the best choices, and their purpose is obvious. The remaining three are a bit less obvious, so let's take a look at them.

The "One time only" option seems to be a strange choice — why would you go to the bother of scheduling a task to run one time when you could just run it manually? Imagine that you know when an important online event is going to occur, but you aren't sure you will be available to participate and record it. This may be the perfect use for the "One time only" option.

The "When my computer starts" and "When I log on" options seem appropriate for a routine maintenance chore until you realize that when you turn your system on and log on, you probably don't want to wait for a long task to complete. You may, however, have something that can be done quickly, such as opening the latest office newsletter from your network server, and that would be a good choice.

The next step in choosing a schedule is to determine the time and day to run the task. You should select a time when running the task won't disrupt your use of your system, especially for tasks that may slow everything else down. Running the disk defragmenter is one task that may slow down other operations. You may want to choose to run these types of tasks at night or when you're at lunch.

As you learn in the next section, you can easily modify a schedule later.

TAKE NOTE

► YOUR SYSTEM MUST BE ON TO RUN SCHEDULED TASKS

Your PC can run scheduled tasks only if the system is running at the scheduled time. This shouldn't be a problem because modern PCs use very little power when the monitor is off, but if you're in the habit of always turning off your computer when you aren't using it, you'll have to change your thinking if you want to run scheduled tasks.

► SOME TASKS RUN FASTER IF THEY'RE RUN OFTEN

Certain tasks, such as defragmenting your hard disk, run faster when you run them often. That's because the more often the task is run, the less work the application must do to complete its task. If you seldom run Disk Defragmenter, it may take a long time to run the first time it is scheduled, but it will work quickly after that.

CROSS-REFERENCE

See "Modifying a Scheduled Task" later in this chapter.

FIND IT ONLINE

See **http://www.bugnet.com/** for the latest in PC bug fixes.

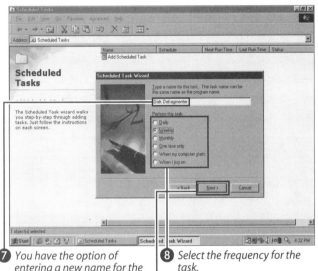

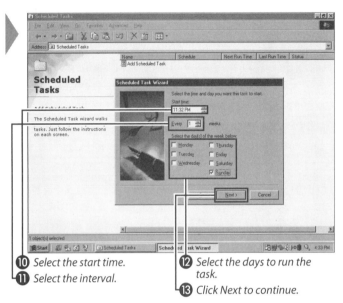

7 *You have the option of entering a new name for the task.*

■ *You may want to enter a descriptive name.*

8 *Select the frequency for the task.*

9 *Click Next to continue.*

10 *Select the start time.*

11 *Select the interval.*

12 *Select the days to run the task.*

13 *Click Next to continue.*

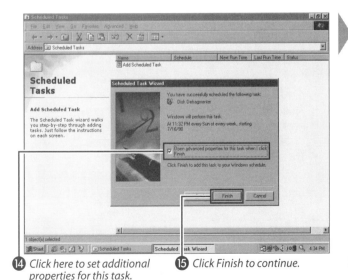

14 *Click here to set additional properties for this task.*

15 *Click Finish to continue.*

16 *Click the Settings button to set additional properties for this task.*

17 *Click OK to complete the task.*

Modifying a Scheduled Task

When you've added scheduled tasks you may discover that you'd like to tinker a little. Perhaps you've decided that the schedule needs revision, or perhaps the program's options need tweaking to improve the operations. Whatever the reason, you can easily make these adjustments at any time.

The figures on the facing page show how you can adjust the schedule for a task. The available adjustments to the runtime options vary according to the program you're running, so showing those options would be of limited value here. If you were trying to adjust the options for a different program, the options wouldn't be the same.

Most of the settings you can adjust will seem familiar because they're the same choices you selected when you first set up the task schedule. As the lower-right figure on the facing page shows, however, other interesting settings are also available. Here's more information about these options.

The Scheduled Task Completed section includes the option to delete the scheduled task after it completes. You might use this option for a task you want to run only one time, such as converting your hard drive to the FAT32 file system over a weekend when you aren't planning to be in the office. This section also lets you limit the amount of time a task can run. The default is 72 hours, but you can set whatever limits you prefer. This option may be useful if you want to run a task fairly often but also want it to end before you use your system for something else.

The Idle Time section delays or stops a task if you're using your system at the scheduled time. These options can help make scheduled tasks less obtrusive because they won't interfere with your use of your PC.

The Power Management settings are useful primarily on laptop systems where they can help save power by not allowing scheduled tasks to run when your computer is running on batteries. Not all systems will display all the Power Management options.

TAKE NOTE

WEEKLY DOESN'T HAVE TO MEAN EVERY WEEK

If you schedule tasks to run weekly, you don't have to run them every week. As the lower-left figure on the facing page shows, you can specify the number of weeks between each run. This option would be useful if you wanted to run a thorough disk check every two weeks and the standard test during alternate weeks. You also can apply this option if the schedule is monthly.

USE ADVANCED OPTIONS

If you need even more control over the event schedule, click the Advanced button on the Schedule tab. This button opens a dialog box that provides options such as setting a date range for scheduled tasks.

CROSS-REFERENCE
See "Checking for Errors with ScanDisk" in Chapter 18.

FIND IT ONLINE
Computer or technical terms got you confused? See http://www.pcwebopedia.com.

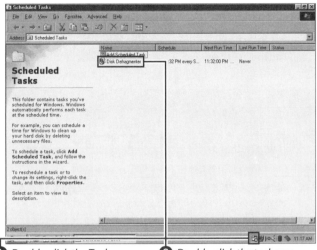

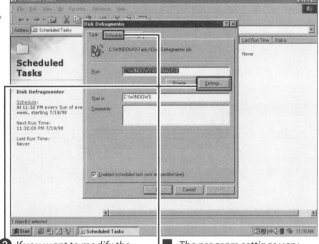

1 *Double-click the Task Scheduler icon to open the Scheduled Tasks folder.*

2 *Double-click the task you wish to modify.*

3 *If you want to modify the program settings, click Settings.*

■ *The program settings vary according to the program selected.*

4 *Click the Schedule tab.*

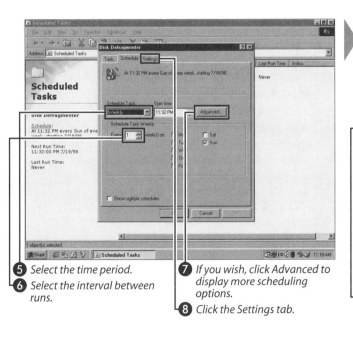

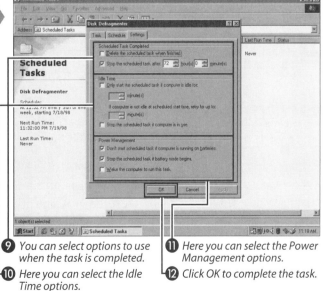

5 *Select the time period.*

6 *Select the interval between runs.*

7 *If you wish, click Advanced to display more scheduling options.*

8 *Click the Settings tab.*

9 *You can select options to use when the task is completed.*

10 *Here you can select the Idle Time options.*

11 *Here you can select the Power Management options.*

12 *Click OK to complete the task.*

Suspending and Resuming Tasks

If necessary, you can temporarily suspend a scheduled task. You can also remove tasks from the schedule, but in most cases it's best to suspend a task so that you can later resume the task without going through the setup process again. You may want to suspend a task for a variety of reasons. For example, perhaps you're going on vacation and won't be around to respond to notices about your stock portfolio.

In addition to suspending individual tasks, you can stop or pause the Task Scheduler. This option may be useful if you want to run a program that may not be able to run properly if a scheduled task initiates while it is running. Some game programs may fit into this category. You may also need to pause the Task Scheduler while you're installing some new programs or while creating a CD-ROM. Pausing the Task Scheduler is less extreme than stopping it. If you stop Task Scheduler, you can restart it by going to the Scheduled Tasks folder.

The Task Scheduler keeps a log that records the running of all scheduled events. The lower-right figure on the facing page shows a copy of this log. By viewing this log, you can determine whether the events you scheduled were completed successfully. If there were problems, you may need to suspend a task while you figure out how to correct the problem. See the "Take Note" section for more information about

using the reports in the log to correct problems. The events log is a file named Schedlog.txt in your C:\Windows folder.

TAKE NOTE

USE THE EVENTS LOG TO LOOK FOR CONFLICTS

If the scheduled events log shows that certain tasks are consistently unable to complete successfully, you can look for additional clues within the log. You may find, for example, that a conflict exists between two task schedules. If a scheduled task runs successfully but takes too long to complete, it may prevent a later task from completing in the time you've allotted. The solution may be to rearrange the schedule so that the two tasks don't overlap. You might, for example, run them on alternate days.

USE THE NOTIFY OPTION

If you'd like an onscreen notification that advises you when a scheduled task did not run, select Advanced ⇨ Notify Me of Missed Tasks. This option is a toggle. Each time you select it, the option changes from off to on or from on to off. If you are notified of tasks that did not complete, be sure to examine the events log to learn more about the problem that prevented the tasks from completing.

CROSS-REFERENCE
See "Checking for Errors with ScanDisk" in Chapter 18.

FIND IT ONLINE
See **http://www.raisin.com/typc** for advice on troubleshooting your computer.

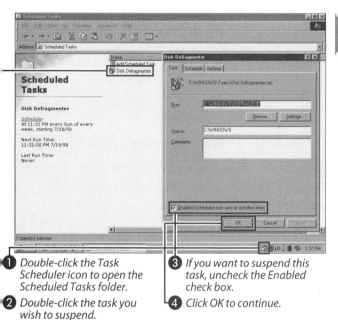

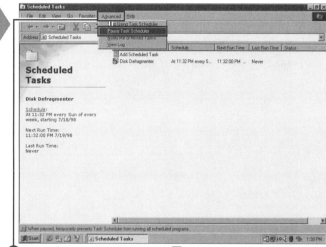

1 *Double-click the Task Scheduler icon to open the Scheduled Tasks folder.*

2 *Double-click the task you wish to suspend.*

3 *If you want to suspend this task, uncheck the Enabled check box.*

4 *Click OK to continue.*

5 *Select Advanced ➪ Pause Task Scheduler.*

■ *When paused, Task Scheduler still loads when you start Windows 98 but does not run any scheduled tasks.*

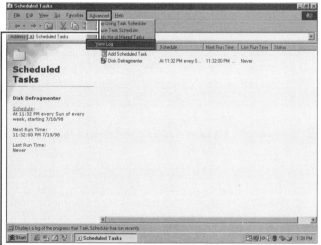

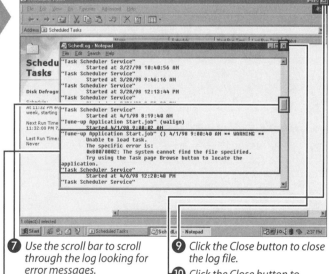

6 *Select Advanced ➪ View Log to view the events log.*

■ *You may also wish to select Advanced ➪ Notify Me of Missed Tasks so that you will know when you need to view the log.*

7 *Use the scroll bar to scroll through the log looking for error messages.*

8 *View error messages and make note of suggested corrections.*

9 *Click the Close button to close the log file.*

10 *Click the Close button to complete the task.*

Personal Workbook

Q&A

1 To be a good candidate for a scheduled task, what capability does a program need?

_____

_____

2 What is the quickest method of opening the Scheduled Tasks folder?

_____

_____

3 Why might you want to enter a descriptive name for a task?

_____

_____

4 What is the shortest interval you can specify for repeating a scheduled task?

_____

5 What do the Idle Time options do?

_____

_____

_____

6 How can you get an on-screen notification that advises you when a scheduled task did not run?

_____

_____

_____

7 How can you suspend a task?

_____

_____

8 If you receive a notice that a task did not run, how can you find the problem?

_____

_____

_____

9 How can you set a date range for scheduled tasks?

_____

_____

_____

ANSWERS: PAGE 360

EXTRA PRACTICE

① Add ScanDisk as a scheduled task.

② Modify the ScanDisk schedule to run the task every third day.

③ Suspend the ScanDisk task.

④ View the event log to see which events have been completed.

⑤ Resume the ScanDisk task but change the schedule to weekly.

⑥ Stop and then close Task Scheduler.

⑦ Restart Task Scheduler.

REAL-WORLD APPLICATIONS

✔ You use your system often, and you find that it slows down after you've saved your work many times. To restore the system performance, you schedule Disk Defragmenter to run regularly.

✔ The PC you're responsible for runs all day in an elementary school library, where it is subject to being bumped and jostled. You schedule ScanDisk to run nightly to look for disk errors.

✔ You are installing a large new graphics program, which will take a long time to install. To avoid conflicts with scheduled tasks, you stop Task Scheduler until you've completed the installation.

Visual Quiz

How can you display the dialog box at the right side of the figure? What purpose does this dialog box serve? How can you limit the task to run only during a specified month?

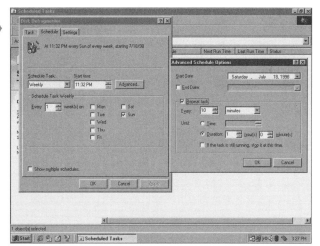

_____

_____

_____

_____

_____

CHAPTER **11**

Using Multimedia

Windows 98 includes extensive support for multimedia presentations: sound, music, video, graphics, and sound recording. Many Web pages, applications, and computer games are enhanced with multimedia. You can add multimedia components to your documents and Web pages, too. This requires the ability to record and play multimedia *clips*—the files containing multimedia information. You need sound, video, and music devices installed and properly configured to support multimedia.

Every Windows 98 system has multimedia capability. Your video monitor supports the playback of video clips. Many systems have a sound card to play the audio portion of video clips, play back audio clips, and—with a sound source attached to the sound card—to record audio clips. Many sound cards support the recording and playback of MIDI music clips.

Sound files contain digital representations of actual audio recorded from sound sources such as microphones. Sound files typically have the extension .WAV, and the quality of their sound depends on parameters determined when they are recorded. The higher the quality, the more disk storage a sound file requires.

Video files, which typically have the filename extension .AVI, contain video and, if desired, audio information. As with sound files, the resolution and format of the video data determine the amount of disk space required. Windows 98 supports other video file formats under the category ActiveMovie.

MIDI files, which have the filename extension .MID, contain data packets that a MIDI playback device can interpret into musical instrument sounds. Each packet in a MIDI file is one, two, or three bytes long, and the packets constitute messages to a MIDI playback system to turn notes on and off with a velocity or volume assigned to each note. Each packet is assigned to one of 16 channels. Each channel is assigned to one of 128 instrument sounds. Depending on the quality of the musical instrument simulations in the MIDI playback system, a well-constructed MIDI file can produce a realistic-sounding musical production.

MIDIs are smaller than audio and video files. The audio quality of the music is a function of the music samples or synthesis of the MIDI hardware system itself.

Playing Sounds

The ability to play sounds is a part of almost anyone's definition of multimedia. Windows 98 excels at playing sounds. When you first start your PC it plays a sound file, and it plays another one when you shut down your system.

Certain commercial multimedia applications play video, audio, and MIDI clips as integrated parts of their presentations. Windows 98 also includes playback capabilities. Windows 98 treats multimedia clips as documents. As with other documents, you choose the document's icon to launch an application that plays the clip in the document.

Your PC probably has a number of sound files that you can play. Most of them are probably stored in the C:\Windows\Media folder, although if you have installed an application that uses multimedia — such as a game or a program that you use to create multimedia presentations — you may find sound files elsewhere, too. The two most common types of sound files are wave sounds (WAV) and MIDI sequences (MID or RMI). You'll find these and other types of sound files on the Internet, but the tools built into Windows 98 won't be able to play all of them. You can find various shareware and freeware tools at many sites on the Internet to play other types of sound files that Windows 98 itself cannot play — such as RealAudio files.

The files that contain MIDI sequences are generally quite small compared with .WAV sound files. But because MIDI sequences are simply instructions to the musical instrument synthesizer on your sound card, the quality of MIDI sequences may vary widely on different PCs. Also, MIDI sequences are limited to music, whereas wave sounds can be a recording of any type of sound, even human speech. In fact, as you'll learn later in this chapter, you can record your own wave sound files easily using the tools that come with Windows 98. You need to buy specialized software to create MIDI sequence files.

TAKE NOTE

▶ FINDING SOUNDS ON YOUR WINDOWS 98 CD-ROM

Your Windows 98 CD-ROM is a good source of sound files. You can use the Windows 98 Find tool to search for sound files using *.wav for wave sound files and *.mid for MIDI sequence files. You'll find more than 250 sound files on the Windows 98 CD-ROM.

▶ STORING YOUR SOUND FILES IN ONE PLACE

If you download sound files from the Internet or copy sound files from a CD-ROM, store those files in the C:\Windows\Media folder. In that way, you'll easily be able to locate the sounds you've collected when you wish to use them in documents or attach them to events.

CROSS-REFERENCE

See "Finding a File" in Chapter 9.

FIND IT ONLINE

See **http://soundamerica.com/** for an extensive collection of sound files.

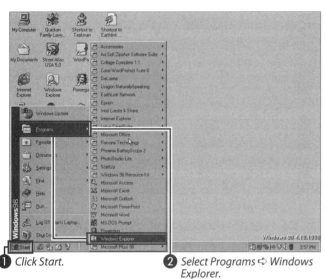

1 Click Start.

2 Select Programs ➪ Windows Explorer.

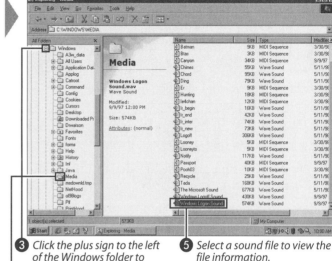

3 Click the plus sign to the left of the Windows folder to expand the folder (the folder is shown expanded here).

4 Click the Media folder to open the folder.

5 Select a sound file to view the file information.

■ You can double-click a sound file to play the sound.

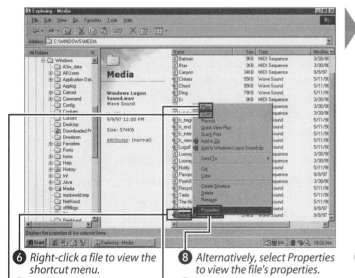

6 Right-click a file to view the shortcut menu.

7 Select Open to open the sound for playing.

8 Alternatively, select Properties to view the file's properties.

9 Alternatively, select Play to play and then close the file.

10 Click the play/pause button to play or pause the sound.

■ Hold the mouse pointer over any of the player controls to learn what it does.

11 Click the Close button to close the player and complete the task.

Viewing Videos

If a picture is worth a thousand words, how many words is a 90-second color video complete with stereo sound worth? It would be hard to answer such a question, but consider how far PCs have come in the past few years. The first PCs displayed monochrome text and not much else. Today's PCs can show movies in full motion, full color, and with high-quality sound.

Windows 98 supports several video formats. Video files, which have the filename extension .AVI, contain video and, optionally, audio information. As with sound files, the resolution and format of the video data determine the amount of disk space that a video file requires. Windows 98 supports several other video file formats under the category ActiveMovie. ActiveMovie, a new video standard introduced as an add-on to Windows 95, enhances the quality and playback of video clips. It also supports high-quality video formats such as QuickTime and MPEG-1.

Video files take a lot of disk space. The 90-second color video file with stereo sound takes between 11MB and 12MB, and that's for a video intended to be viewed in a small window and not full-screen. For full-screen video that is also capable of showing enough images per second to look like a television transmission, you would need even more disk space. A typical full-length motion picture would require several gigabytes of disk capacity.

Several methods are used to reduce the size of video files. Each has an impact on the quality of the image you see on your monitor, although you may not notice it unless the impact is quite pronounced. Reducing the size of the video window is the most common step used by video producers. A video that is sized at 320 x 240 pixels takes one-fourth the space of one that is 640 x 480 pixels. Video producers sometimes reduce the *frame rate*—the number of images displayed per second—to further reduce the file size. Your TV displays 30 frames per second. PC videos may reduce this to 10 frames or fewer per second. As the number of frames per second drops, videos tend to become choppy-looking.

TAKE NOTE

▶ FINDING VIDEOS ON YOUR WINDOWS 98 CD-ROM

Your Windows 98 CD-ROM is a good source of video files. In fact, when you insert the Windows 98 CD-ROM into the CD-ROM drive, one of the options you'll have is to view the videos that are supplied on the CD-ROM.

▶ DISTINGUISHING MPEG FROM AVI

If you look closely at the icons Windows 98 assigns to MPEG and AVI files, you'll notice a very small difference. The video camera in the MPEG icon is blue, whereas the one in the AVI icon is gray.

CROSS-REFERENCE
See "Configuring Multimedia Devices" in this chapter.

FIND IT ONLINE
See http://www.people.cornell.edu/pages/rc42/ mmedia.html for a collection of videos.

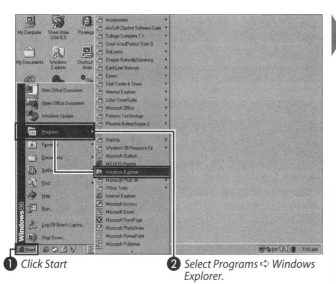

① Click Start

② Select Programs ➪ Windows Explorer.

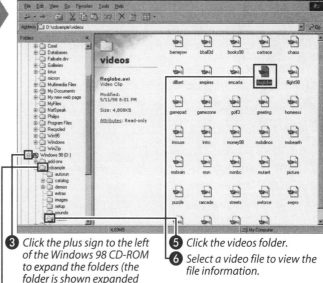

③ Click the plus sign to the left of the Windows 98 CD-ROM to expand the folders (the folder is shown expanded here).

④ Click the cdsample folder.

⑤ Click the videos folder.

⑥ Select a video file to view the file information.

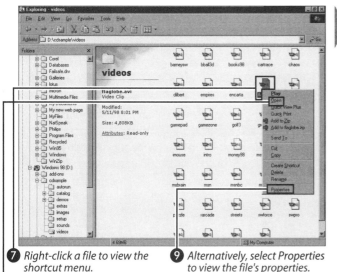

⑦ Right-click a file to view the shortcut menu.

⑧ Select Open to open the video for playing.

⑨ Alternatively, select Properties to view the file's properties.

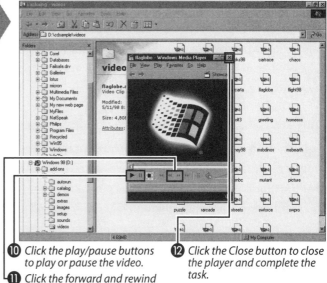

⑩ Click the play/pause buttons to play or pause the video.

⑪ Click the forward and rewind buttons to control the playback.

⑫ Click the Close button to close the player and complete the task.

Using CD Player

Many people enjoy listening to music while they're working. If you're one of them, you can make your CD-ROM drive do double duty. Music (or *audio*) CDs are completely compatible with your CD-ROM drive, and Windows 98 includes a handy accessory called CD Player that lets you play audio CDs on your PC.

Usually, CD Player automatically plays audio CDs that you insert into your CD-ROM drive. You can configure your system to prevent CD Player from playing automatically, but there's little reason to do so.

Each audio CD has a unique identification number that is contained on the CD. CD Player takes advantage of this by allowing you to enter the title, artist, and song titles, which are then stored so that the same information can be displayed the next time you insert the same audio CD. If you like, you can also enter a play list so that the songs are played in the order you prefer, even skipping pieces you don't want to hear.

As the figures on the facing page show, the CD Player interface was designed to look like the buttons and controls on the front of a CD player that you might find in a typical home stereo system. There are buttons for playing, pausing, and ejecting a CD, as well as buttons that enable you to skip forward and back. You can choose what information you'd like to

see on the front panel readout and even choose to play the tracks in random order. If you've entered the play list, CD Player also shows the name of the current track.

CROSS-REFERENCE

See "Configuring Multimedia Devices" in this chapter.

FIND IT ONLINE

See **http://www.cddb.com/downloads** for a list of CD player software.

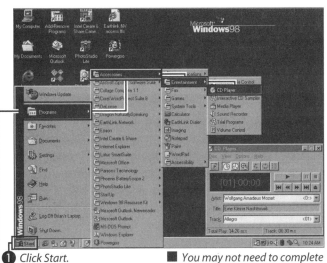

1 Click Start.

2 Select Programs ⇨ Accessories ⇨ Entertainment ⇨ CD Player.

■ You may not need to complete these steps because CD Player is normally set to start automatically when you insert an audio CD.

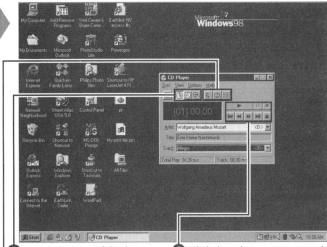

3 Select the type of display you wish to see.

4 If you wish to select a playback option, do so.

5 Click these buttons to control the playback functions.

■ Hold the mouse pointer over a control for a few seconds to learn what the control does.

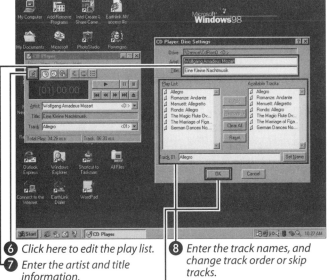

6 Click here to edit the play list.

7 Enter the artist and title information.

8 Enter the track names, and change track order or skip tracks.

9 Click OK to continue.

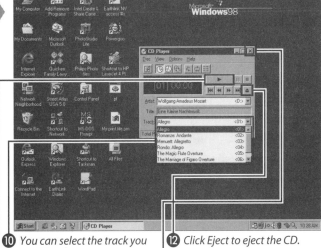

10 You can select the track you want to play.

11 Click the Play button to play the audio CD.

12 Click Eject to eject the CD.

13 Click the Close button to close the CD Player and complete the task.

Using Media Player

Media Player plays video clips, sound files, MIDI songs, and musical CDs from your CD-ROM drive. The figures on the facing page show how you can use Media Player to play back multimedia files.

To use Media Player, first select a playback device from the Device menu. The selections are typically ActiveMovie, Video for Windows, Sound, MIDI Sequencer, and CD Audio. There may be others depending on any other multimedia applications installed on your PC. You can also choose the Open command on the File menu. The kind of device will be determined by the kind of file that you select.

When you're viewing a video file, the Scale menu lets you change the scale displayed on the front of the Media Player between time and frames. You can drag the sliding pointer control back and forth to view individual frames. The Properties command on the Device menu lets you change the size of the playback window up to the complete screen size.

When you're playing an audio file, the Properties command on the Device menu lets you control the amount of memory used by Media Player to buffer sound files. If a sound file is breaking up, allocating more memory for it may make it play back more clearly.

If you choose a MIDI sequence, the Properties command lets you select whether to play the song through the internal MIDI system or through an external connection to a MIDI device. You can also choose the specific instrument settings.

The Media Player's Device menu also includes a selection named CD Audio for playing music CDs through the CD-ROM drive. You may never use the CD Audio function, however, because CD Player does a better job and enables you to use play lists.

To play something back, locate and select a file with the type that matches your selected device. Click the single right-pointing arrow button on the Media Player's toolbar. The Play button changes into a Pause/Resume button during playback.

TAKE NOTE

THE DEVICE LIST MAY VARY

If your system has no sound card or CD-ROM drive or if the MIDI drivers are not installed, some devices may not be available. The Device menu adjusts itself according to what is available. In addition, if a resource such as your CD-ROM drive was already in use when you started Media Player, that device may not show up in the device list until you restart Media Player.

ACTIVEMOVIE ENHANCES YOUR VIDEO CLIPS

ActiveMovie is a new video standard that enhances the quality and playback of video clips. It also supports high-quality video formats such as Quick-Time and MPEG-1.

CROSS-REFERENCE

Refer to "Using CD Player" in this chapter.

SHORTCUT

Press Ctrl+O to display the Options dialog box.

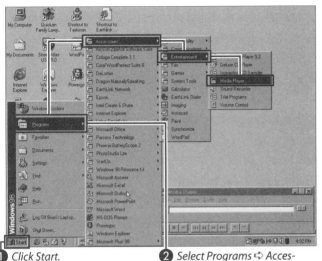

❶ Click Start.

❷ Select Programs ➪ Accessories ➪ Entertainment ➪ Media Player.

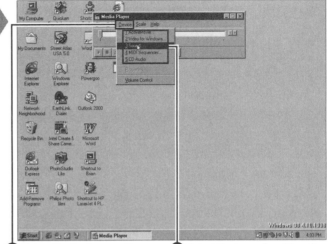

❸ Select Device to open the Device menu.

❹ Select the type of multimedia file you want to play.

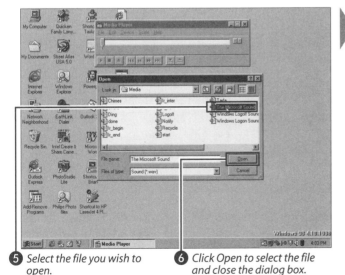

❺ Select the file you wish to open.

■ If necessary, you can use the "Look in" list box to select the correct location.

❻ Click Open to select the file and close the dialog box.

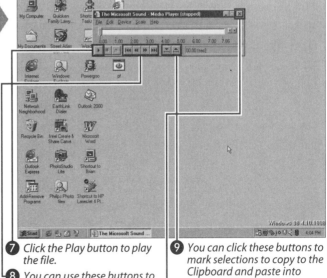

❼ Click the Play button to play the file.

❽ You can use these buttons to change tracks or to skip forward or back.

❾ You can click these buttons to mark selections to copy to the Clipboard and paste into other applications.

❿ Click the Close button to close the Media Player.

183

Recording Sounds with Sound Recorder

indows 98 also includes Sound Recorder, an application that lets you record sound files (.WAV) from a microphone, from line input, and from your PC's internal sound sources. You can, for example, record your own sound files that you can attach to system events, or you can record a greeting to send along with an e-mail message to wish someone a happy birthday.

Once you've recorded a sound file you can experiment with Sound Recorder. You can add effects such as echoing or reversing the sound. You can distort the sound by increasing or decreasing the playback speed. You can adjust the volume level up or down. Finally, you can clip out parts of a sound file and add them to another document or even add sounds to an existing sound file.

Recorded sound files can take a lot of disk space, especially if you select a high sound quality setting. Sound quality and file size are determined by several factors.

The *sample rate* is the number of sound samples per second that are recorded. The generally accepted guideline is to use a sample rate twice as high as the highest frequency you wish to record. CD quality uses a sample rate of 44,100 Hz. You can use a much lower rate, such as 11,025 Hz or even 8,000 Hz, if you're recording the human voice. The file size is directly proportional to the sample rate.

The *bit rate* determines the number of volume levels that can be recorded. 16-bit recordings can store 65,536 levels, whereas 8-bit recordings store only 256 levels. 16-bit recordings take twice the disk space as 8-bit recordings. 8-bit is fine for voice.

Stereo recordings take twice the space of mono recordings. Unless you are recording from a stereo source, the extra space is wasted.

The *format* is the method of compressing the sound file. Some formats provide better compression rates than others, but the most important factor in choosing a format is that the format be available on the system where you'll use the sound files.

Continued

TAKE NOTE

USING THE STANDARD QUALITY SETTINGS

You can select from the CD, Radio, and Telephone quality settings or select a format and attributes. The lower the quality, the less storage is required for a signal of a specific length. The standard quality settings are more likely to work on all PCs than format and attribute settings that you select.

CHOOSING YOUR SETTINGS BEFORE YOU RECORD

Choose the quality settings before you begin recording. After a sample has been recorded, you must start over if you want higher quality.

CROSS-REFERENCE

See "Adding Sounds to Events" in Chapter 5.

FIND IT ONLINE

See **http://www.microsoft.com/netshow** for online audio and video.

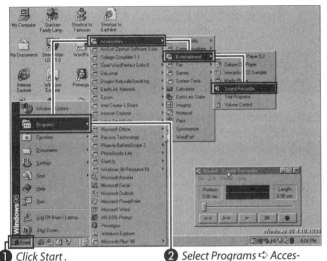

1 Click Start.

2 Select Programs ➪ Accessories ➪ Entertainment ➪ Sound Recorder.

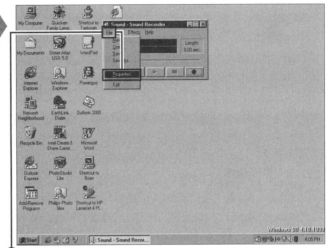

3 Select File ➪ Properties to set the recording properties before you begin recording.

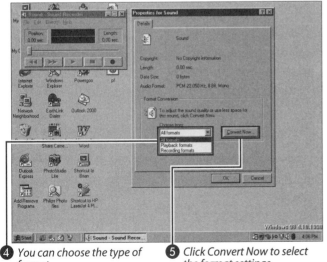

4 You can choose the type of format.

5 Click Convert Now to select the format settings.

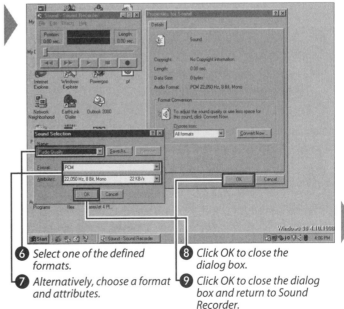

6 Select one of the defined formats.

7 Alternatively, choose a format and attributes.

8 Click OK to close the dialog box.

9 Click OK to close the dialog box and return to Sound Recorder.

185

After you've set the recording properties you're ready to record your sounds and apply any special effects you want to use. As the upper-left figure on the facing page shows, Sound Recorder depicts the recorded sounds by varying the thickness of the line in the viewing window in the middle of the Sound Recorder window. Thicker lines indicate higher volume levels.

The upper-right figure on the facing page shows the Effects menu. You can use the selections on this menu to modify sound files in a number of ways. You might, for example, record a message for someone and then use Effects ⇨ Reverse to reverse the recording so that it would seem like an unintelligible mess. Your intended recipient would then use his or her own copy of Sound Recorder to once again reverse the file and hear the message. To further enhance the confusion, you might also choose Effects ⇨ Increase Speed one or two times. Again, your intended recipient would need to apply the opposite effect to convert your message to near normal format.

You may find that you have "dead air" at the beginning or end of a recording. The lower-left figure on the facing page shows you how to truncate the recording to eliminate unwanted portions. Play the recording several times and note the exact position where the recording should begin or end. Make certain that you've placed the slider in the right place; you may want to check this several times to be sure.

Then select Edit ⇨ Delete Before Current Position or Edit ⇨ Delete After Current Position to eliminate the unwanted material and reduce the file size.

You can also combine several short clips by using the Edit ⇨ Insert File command.

TAKE NOTE

▶ TROUBLESHOOTING RECORDING PROBLEMS

If you click the Record button but Sound Recorder doesn't record any sound, first make certain that your microphone is plugged in correctly. The microphone jack looks just like the headphone jack, so you need to make certain you've plugged the microphone into the correct jack. If you aren't sure, check your user's manual.

If the microphone is plugged in correctly, check to make certain that the microphone input is enabled in the volume control, as shown in the next section of this chapter. There should not be a check mark in the Mute check box.

▶ MOST EFFECTS DEGRADE THE RECORDING

If you decide to use any of the available effects to modify your recording, you should know that virtually any changes you make will degrade the quality of the recording. If the quality of the recording is important, save a copy of the sound file under a new name and do your experiments on the copy.

CROSS REFERENCE

See "Using the Volume Controls" later in this chapter.

FIND IT ONLINE

Want to edit your sound files? See **http://www.idg.net/idg_frames/english/content.cgi?vc=docid_9-53600.html**.

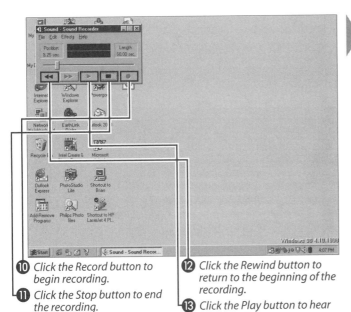

⑩ Click the Record button to begin recording.

⑪ Click the Stop button to end the recording.

⑫ Click the Rewind button to return to the beginning of the recording.

⑬ Click the Play button to hear the recording.

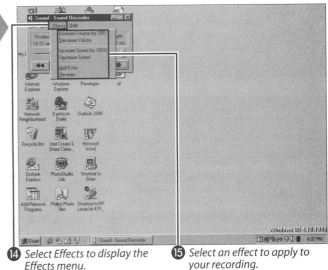

⑭ Select Effects to display the Effects menu.

⑮ Select an effect to apply to your recording.

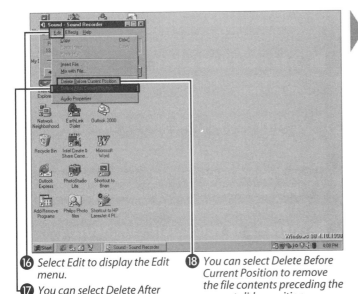

⑯ Select Edit to display the Edit menu.

⑰ You can select Delete After Current Position to remove the file contents following the current slider position.

⑱ You can select Delete Before Current Position to remove the file contents preceding the current slider position.

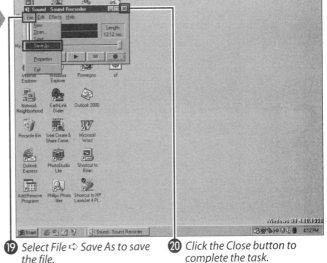

⑲ Select File ➪ Save As to save the file.

■ You will need to enter a name for the file.

⑳ Click the Close button to complete the task.

Using the Volume Controls

You probably already know that if you click the speaker icon in the system tray at the right side of the taskbar, a small volume control slider pops up so that you can adjust the sound level of your PC's speakers. In addition, Windows 98 has a more sophisticated volume control you can use to adjust each individual sound source independently. If you've ever been blasted by sound when you switch from one sound source to another, you'll appreciate this capability to balance the different sound sources.

In addition to adjusting the individual sound levels, you can adjust the left/right balance. Depending on your sound card, you may also be able to adjust the bass, treble, and loudness settings. As the lower-right figure on the facing page shows, you can also choose which of the individual volume controls will appear on the master volume control.

You can display the simple volume control by clicking the speaker icon or display the complete volume control by double-clicking the icon. After either volume control is displayed, you can adjust the volume by dragging the slider up or down. To turn the sounds off, click the Mute check box. Drag the horizontal sliders to adjust the left/right balance. If you have a set of powered speakers, you may need to experiment with the volume control settings to discover which settings produce the highest-quality sound. The amplifiers in some powered speakers may produce excess distortion if the volume level from your PC is too high. Too low a volume level from your PC may result in problems such as excess hum from the speakers.

TAKE NOTE

▶ ADJUSTING VOLUME LEVELS FOR RECORDING

If you are using Sound Recorder or another application to record a sound file, you may discover that the sound file includes unexpected background noise. In many cases this unwanted noise comes from the other input sources that connect to your sound card. As the figures on the facing page show, each of the individual sound sources has a Mute check box intended to silence that sound source. Unfortunately, many sound cards don't completely mute the sounds from a source even if this check box is selected. For the best results, reduce all unused sound sources to the lowest volume level in addition to selecting their Mute check boxes. Then adjust the remaining source to the proper level for recording.

▶ USE THE CORRECT VOLUME CONTROL SET

Make certain that you select the correct set of volume controls. Generally, you can select the set of controls either for playback or for recording. Depending on your sound card, choosing the incorrect set may make it more difficult to adjust the individual volume levels correctly.

CROSS-REFERENCE
See "Configuring Multimedia Devices" later in this chapter.

SHORTCUT
Use the Windows key along with the PageUp and PageDown keys to adjust speaker balance.

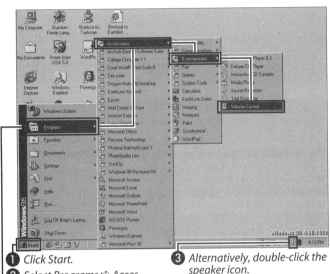

❶ Click Start.

❷ Select Programs ➪ Accessories ➪ Entertainment ➪ Volume Control.

❸ Alternatively, double-click the speaker icon.

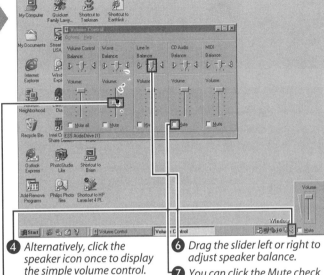

❹ Alternatively, click the speaker icon once to display the simple volume control.

❺ Drag the slider up or down to adjust the volume level.

❻ Drag the slider left or right to adjust speaker balance.

❼ You can click the Mute check box to silence the sound source.

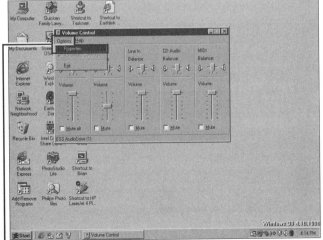

❽ Select Options ➪ Properties to display the Properties dialog box.

■ To adjust bass, treble, loudness, or other advanced settings, select Options ➪ Advanced Controls if this command is available.

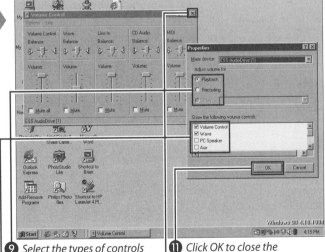

❾ Select the types of controls you wish to see.

❿ Select individual controls you wish to see.

⓫ Click OK to close the dialog box.

⓬ Click the Close button to complete the task.

Putting Multimedia Clips into Documents

When you think of documents you probably think of letters or forms that are printed on paper. This traditional form of document is still common and useful, of course, but now it is often supplemented by computerized documents. For example, you can include a voice message as part of a document. Windows 98 makes it easy to include multimedia clips in electronic documents.

You can add multimedia content to your electronic documents using several different methods. In this section you'll learn one of the easiest and quickest methods of adding a short voice message to a document. You'll use Sound Recorder to record a new sound to place in your document. If you prefer to add an existing multimedia file, you may want to use copy and paste or drag and drop to copy the multimedia content to your document.

Adding multimedia content greatly increases the size of the document. If you're adding a simple voice message, consider adjusting the sound object properties to use a lower sound quality that will result in a much smaller file size. For information about adjusting the properties for recording, refer to the section "Recording Sounds with Sound Recorder."

You can save some disk space by creating the multimedia object directly in your document, rather than adding an existing multimedia file to your document. That's because you'll have only one copy of the multimedia object — the one you created within the document — rather than two copies.

Don't forget to save your document after you've added the sound object. If you're using WordPad to create your document, WordPad reminds you if you attempt to close it without saving any changes.

TAKE NOTE

▶ PLAYING MULTIMEDIA CONTENT IN A DOCUMENT

After you've added a multimedia object to an electronic document, it's easy to play the sound or video; you simply double-click the sound or video icon in the document. If you're sending the document file to someone else, it's a good idea to include text to tell the recipient to double-click the icon to hear the sounds or to view the video.

▶ EDITING MULTIMEDIA CONTENT IN A DOCUMENT

If you add multimedia content such as a sound object to a document, you may discover that your first effort isn't quite what you'd like it to be. You can edit the sound object by right-clicking the object's icon and then selecting Wave Sound Object ⇨ Edit. This action reopens the sound object in Sound Recorder, where you can adjust the object or even record a completely new message. When you're finished editing the sound object, select File ⇨ Exit & Return to Document. This action closes Sound Recorder and updates the sound object.

CROSS-REFERENCE

See "Cutting, Copying, and Pasting to the Clipboard" in Chapter 7.

FIND IT ONLINE

See **http://viswiz.gmd.de/MultimediaInfo/#Guides** for more on multimedia and its uses.

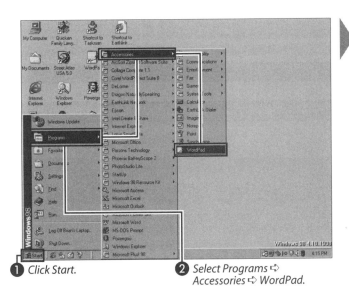

1 Click Start.

2 Select Programs ⇨
Accessories ⇨ WordPad.

3 Select Insert ⇨ Object.

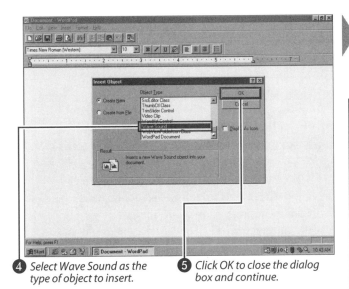

4 Select Wave Sound as the
type of object to insert.

5 Click OK to close the dialog
box and continue.

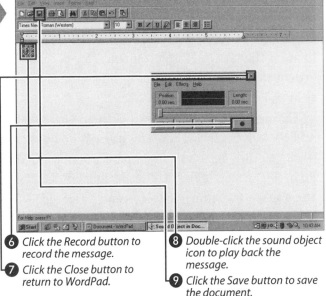

6 Click the Record button to
record the message.

7 Click the Close button to
return to WordPad.

8 Double-click the sound object
icon to play back the
message.

9 Click the Save button to save
the document.

Configuring Multimedia Devices

Getting the most from the devices installed in your PC requires that they be properly configured. You configure most multimedia devices using the Control Panel's Multimedia applet. The figures on the facing page show you how to open the Multimedia Properties dialog box and configure the audio options. The following pages continue the task by showing you how to configure the remaining multimedia options.

The upper-right figure on the facing page shows the Speakers tab of the Advanced Audio Properties dialog box. Select the configuration that most closely represents your speaker setup. This is especially important if you've spent a lot of money on speakers. Otherwise, Windows 98 may not take advantage of all the advanced features built into your speaker system.

The lower-left figure shows the Performance tab of the dialog box. Experiment here to find the best settings for your system. Faster computers are generally better able to handle the higher-quality settings at the right end of the two scales.

The lower-right figure shows a different Advanced Audio Properties dialog box. This dialog box appears when you click the Advanced Properties button in the Recording section of the Multimedia Properties dialog box. You use the settings in this second Advanced Audio Properties dialog box to adjust the settings used while you're recording audio files. Here, too, you may need to experiment with the settings to see which

ones work best on your system. You may want to try the highest-quality settings and see whether they work correctly on your PC. If you experience slowdowns or if the quality of your recordings suffer, you can back the settings off a notch and try again.

Continued

TAKE NOTE

▶ SELECTING PREFERRED DEVICES

Some PCs have more than one sound card installed. The "Preferred device" selections in the Audio tab of the Multimedia Properties dialog box identify the default sound card that applications use when the applications do not provide a way for you to select from the installed sound cards. Media Player, described earlier in this chapter, uses the default playback device. Sound Recorder, also described earlier in this chapter, uses the default recording device. If you want your applications to use the preferred devices only without the user option to change to an alternative device, check the "Use only preferred devices" selection.

▶ GETTING YOUR SPEAKER ICON BACK

If you don't see the speaker icon in the system tray, ensure that "Show volume control on the taskbar" is checked. This permits you to launch the Volume Control applet, described earlier in this chapter, from the taskbar. If the check box is selected and the speaker icon is still not visible, you may want to restart your system to refresh all the system tray icons.

CROSS-REFERENCE
See "Moving and Hiding the Taskbar" in Chapter 4.

SHORTCUT
Click Restore Defaults to return to the original settings.

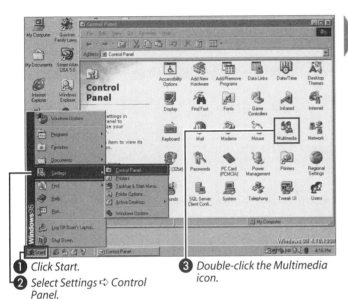

1 Click Start.

2 Select Settings ➪ Control Panel.

3 Double-click the Multimedia icon.

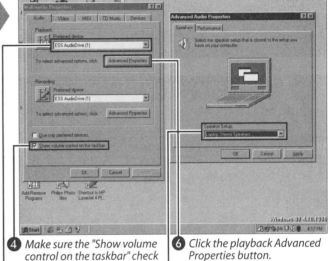

4 Make sure the "Show volume control on the taskbar" check box is selected.

5 If you want, choose the playback device.

6 Click the playback Advanced Properties button.

7 Select your speaker setup.

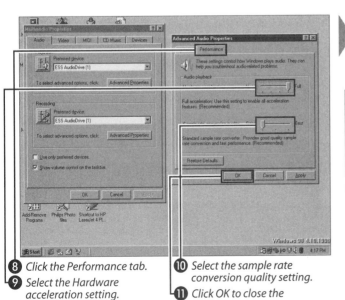

8 Click the Performance tab.

9 Select the Hardware acceleration setting.

10 Select the sample rate conversion quality setting.

11 Click OK to close the dialog box.

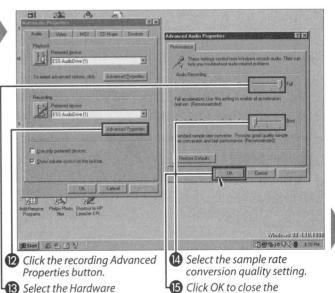

12 Click the recording Advanced Properties button.

13 Select the Hardware acceleration setting.

14 Select the sample rate conversion quality setting.

15 Click OK to close the dialog box.

The figures on the facing page continue the task from the preceding two pages. Here you'll set the remaining multimedia configuration options. You can also view the properties for all multimedia devices using the Devices tab of the Multimedia Properties dialog box.

The Video tab lets you choose whether to view videos in a window or full screen. If you choose any setting other than the original size setting, the quality of the display of most videos will be degraded. Videos that are expanded beyond their original size usually don't contain enough data to display correctly.

The MIDI tab is of most interest to musicians who create their own music using a PC and a synthesizer. MIDI sequence files assign certain sounds to specific instruments—just as each of the musicians in an orchestra has a specific part to play in a concert. The options on the MIDI tab let you change instruments so that, for example, you might have a drum playing all the piano parts, a piano playing all the oboe parts, and a saxophone playing all the guitar parts. Before you make adjustments to the MIDI settings, it is recommended that you have a thorough understanding of MIDI configurations.

The CD Music tab enables you to control how audio CDs are played on your system. If you have more than one CD-ROM drive, you may need to select the drive that is actually connected to your sound card. Most sound cards have a single CD audio input, so if you add a second CD-ROM drive and the drive letter changes for your original drive you'll need to make this adjustment to hear audio CDs. If the "Enable digital CD audio for this CD-ROM device" option is available, you may wish to try it. This will often result in better sound from audio CDs because the CD-ROM drive won't attempt to do a digital-to-analog conversion.

TAKE NOTE

VIEWING VIDEOS IN A WINDOW

I recommend viewing videos in a window. You can usually change the presentation for a video as it is being viewed, and the intentions of some multimedia applications that expect to have video presentations displayed in their windows are thwarted when Windows 98 expects to display videos full screen. For the same reason, I recommend viewing videos in their original size.

THE DEVICES TAB IS FOR INFORMATION ONLY

The Devices tab of the Multimedia Properties dialog box is for information only. If you select a device and click the Properties button, one of the options that will appear on the resulting dialog box is a Remove button. Clicking this button will display a message box informing you that you must use the System icon in Control Panel to actually delete the selected item.

CROSS-REFERENCE

See "Adding New Hardware" in Chapter 5.

SHORTCUT

The standard Windows 98 volume control is more accessible than the one on the CD Music tab.

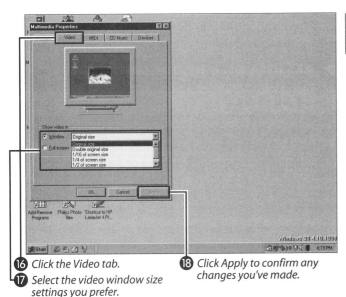

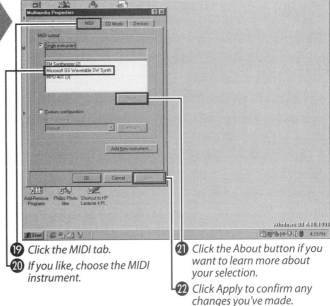

16 Click the Video tab.

17 Select the video window size settings you prefer.

18 Click Apply to confirm any changes you've made.

19 Click the MIDI tab.

20 If you like, choose the MIDI instrument.

21 Click the About button if you want to learn more about your selection.

22 Click Apply to confirm any changes you've made.

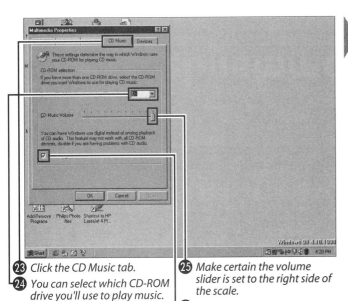

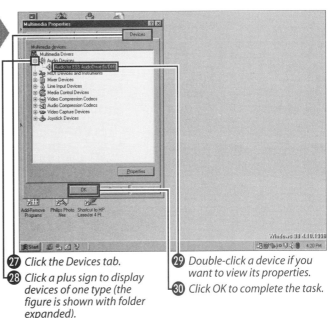

23 Click the CD Music tab.

24 You can select which CD-ROM drive you'll use to play music.

25 Make certain the volume slider is set to the right side of the scale.

26 Select "Enable digital CD audio for this CD-ROM device" if available.

27 Click the Devices tab.

28 Click a plus sign to display devices of one type (the figure is shown with folder expanded).

29 Double-click a device if you want to view its properties.

30 Click OK to complete the task.

Personal Workbook

Q&A

1 What are the two standard sound files the Windows 98 multimedia accessories can play?

_____

_____

2 Why are most video files shown in a small window?

_____

_____

_____

3 Which Windows 98 tool would you use to record a voice message?

_____

_____

_____

4 How can you make CD Player skip the same song on an audio CD every time you play the CD?

_____

_____

_____

5 What is the quickest method of displaying the full volume control?

_____

_____

_____

6 How does doubling the selected sample rate affect sound files you record?

_____

_____

7 What should you do if you don't see the speaker icon in the system tray?

_____

_____

_____

8 What type of files does the Sound Recorder produce?

_____

_____

_____

ANSWERS: PAGE 361

EXTRA PRACTICE

1 Find and play the Microsoft Sound.

2 Open several of the videos on your Windows 98 CD-ROM and experiment with the playback controls.

3 Open the full volume control and adjust each of the individual controls to suit your preferences.

4 Open a new document and add a voice note to the document.

5 Enter a play list for your favorite audio CD.

6 Play a MIDI sequence while you adjust the left/right speaker balance using the full volume control.

REAL-WORLD APPLICATIONS

✔ If you want to use sounds to enhance a presentation you're creating on your PC, you may want to preview the available sound files first.

✔ If you like to listen to music while you work, you may want to create play lists to play certain audio CDs in your favorite order.

✔ You have several sound sources connected to your sound card. You adjust the sound levels so that each one plays at the same relative sound level.

Visual Quiz

This is a slightly different control than the one you're probably used to seeing. How can you display this window? What purpose does it serve?

_____

_____

_____

_____

_____

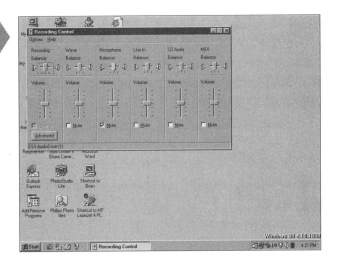

CHAPTER **12**

Using the Accessory Applications

This chapter tells you how to use the accessory applications, also called *applets*, that are included with Windows 98. Applets are small applications — productivity tools, utilities, a low end word processor, and a basic painting program. These applications add value to Windows 98 by providing you with functions for which you might otherwise have to buy another program, functions such as cutting and pasting information between documents, performing calculations, writing letters and memos, working with fax documents, and creating computer graphics. You shouldn't expect that any of these accessory applets will be the equal of an expensive, full-featured program, but you will probably find them useful in performing everyday tasks.

Not all these programs install automatically when you install Windows 98. Be sure to start with the section "Installing Accessory Applications" for more information on adding Windows 98 options.

Many people don't give much thought to what their computer can do until they discover that it can't easily handle a task that seems simple. That's one of the main reasons Windows 98 includes these accessories: to enable you to handle simple tasks without much difficulty. Many of the Windows 98 accessories are based, at least in their concept, on programs that computer users had to either purchase or create for themselves in earlier operating system versions. Some of the accessory programs that come with the package are actually slightly disguised "lite" versions of popular utility programs that Microsoft has licensed for Windows 98.

The Calculator accessory will not replace your favorite spreadsheet program, nor will the drawing tools in Paint rival those found in sophisticated graphics programs. But if all you need is to make some quick calculations or create a simple sign, you will find the Windows 98 accessory programs handy. In some cases they may be more suitable for the task at hand than the full-featured programs. For example, it is much easier to use the Calculator than to try to create a formula in an Excel spreadsheet, and it's faster to knock out a basic sign in Paint than to go through all the steps needed to make the same sign in PowerPoint. If you approach the Windows 98 accessory programs for what they are — bonus applications that can often get a simple job done quickly — they will prove to be useful.

Installing Accessory Applications

The default Windows 98 installation procedure does not install all the accessory applications and system services available to a user, and it installs ones that some users may not want. You may find that you want to install one that was omitted or remove one that you do not need.

Although you install Windows 98 accessory applications using the Add/Remove Programs dialog box, these components reside on a separate tab of the dialog box from the one you use to install most other programs. This tab, called the Windows Setup tab, includes a large number of options that enable you to customize your Windows 98 installation. If you're short on disk space, you can use this tab to remove everything that isn't essential to running Windows 98. But if you have ample room and want to try out everything that Windows 98 has to offer, you can go to the extreme of installing everything. Most people find a compromise somewhere between these two options.

You may be surprised to learn that the Windows Setup tab doesn't offer exactly the same set of options on all Windows 98 PCs. The available options can vary for several reasons. If your PC was upgraded from Windows 95, for example, you may have options for such items as Windows Messaging and Microsoft Fax, two Windows 95 components that didn't make it into Windows 98. Also, if you have any compressed drives on your system, the disk compression tools won't appear. This may sound strange until you think about it: If you have compressed drives, you don't want the option of uninstalling the very tools that enable you to access them.

TAKE NOTE

► SOME ACCESSORIES HAVE MULTIPLE PARTS

Some Windows 98 components, such as Screen Savers under Accessories, have multiple parts that you can add and remove. If an accessory has such components, the Details button is enabled and you can use it to open a Details dialog box. Use this dialog box to choose the parts you'd like to install.

► YOU MAY NEED YOUR WINDOWS 98 CD-ROM

Depending on what you have added or removed, the program may ask you to insert the Windows 98 CD-ROM so that it can copy some files. It might also ask you whether it can restart the computer so that the changes can take effect.

► WINDOWS MESSAGING AND MICROSOFT FAX

Even though Windows Messaging and Microsoft Fax didn't officially make it into Windows 98, both applications are available on your Windows 98 CD-ROM. Look in the \tools\oldwin95\message folder and choose either the intl (international) or us (United States) folder as appropriate. A file named Wmsfax.txt in the folder provides additional information about installing these two components.

CROSS-REFERENCE

See Chapter 6 for more information about installing programs.

FIND IT ONLINE

For Windows 98 updates, visit **http://windowsupdate.microsoft.com/default.htm**.

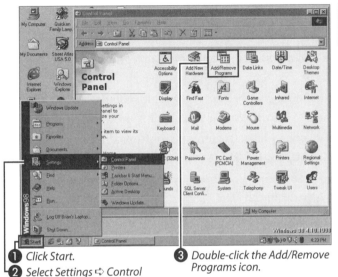

1 Click Start.

2 Select Settings ⇨ Control Panel.

3 Double-click the Add/Remove Programs icon.

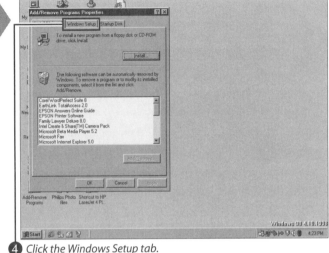

4 Click the Windows Setup tab.

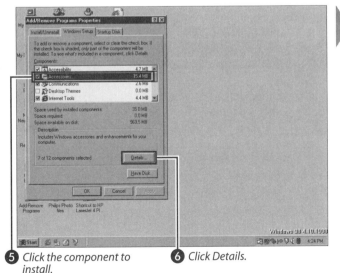

5 Click the component to install.

6 Click Details.

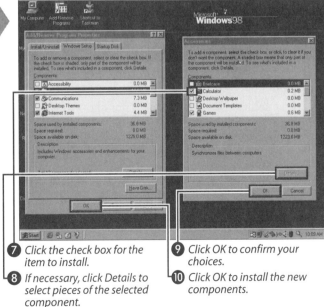

7 Click the check box for the item to install.

8 If necessary, click Details to select pieces of the selected component.

9 Click OK to confirm your choices.

10 Click OK to install the new components.

Using the Calculator

alculator is an on-screen calculator. Two calculators are built into the application: the standard calculator and the scientific calculator. The standard calculator resembles a typical pocket calculator, with add, subtract, multiply, and divide functions, a square root function, a percent function, a reciprocal function, and memory. The scientific calculator has many additional functions like those you'd find on a sophisticated calculator used by a scientist or engineer. Change to the scientific calculator by choosing Scientific on the View menu.

Each Calculator command has a button on the Calculator display and a corresponding key on the PC's keyboard. If you want to use the keyboard, you'll probably find it easier to use the numeric keypad; make certain the Num Lock indicator is lit.

To enter numbers into the calculator, use your mouse to click the digit buttons, or type the numbers on your keyboard. The other buttons on the Calculator serve various functions: The period button (.) enables you to begin entering digits to the right of the decimal place; Backspace removes the last digit you entered; CE clears the current entry from the display without modifying the current calculation; and the C button zeros out the Calculator. The arithmetic operators (+, -, *, and /) and the = operator work like those in a standard calculator. (The Enter key and the = key on the keyboard also do what the on-screen = command button does —

display the result of the operation.) The remaining buttons, sqrt, 1/x, and +/-, compute the square root, calculate the reciprocal, and change the sign, respectively, of whatever number is displayed.

The Calculator has a one-value memory. When the memory is other than zero, the box immediately above the / and sqrt function buttons displays an M. The MC button resets memory to zero, and MR displays the value in memory. MS stores the value currently displayed into memory, and M+ adds the value currently displayed to whatever value is in memory.

TAKE NOTE

▶ USING THE SCIENTIFIC CALCULATOR

The scientific calculator is considerably more complex than the standard calculator. It includes such engineering functions as the capability to convert between the decimal, hexadecimal, octal, and binary number systems. It also includes statistical functions, Boolean operators, modulus calculations, integer calculations, parentheses, and trigonometric functions.

▶ USE COPY AND PASTE

The easiest way to transfer data between the calculator and other applications is to use copy and paste. If you use the calculator to perform a complex calculation, you can avoid the risk of typing errors: Use Ctrl+C to copy the result to the Windows 98 Clipboard and then use Ctrl+V to paste the number into your document.

CROSS-REFERENCE

See Chapter 7 for more information about using the Clipboard.

FIND IT ONLINE

See **http://www.507pm.com/kw25.htm** for an advanced Windows calculator.

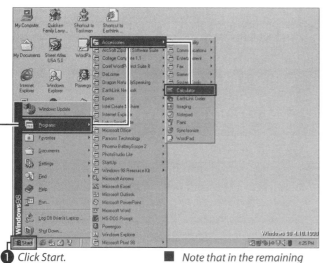

① *Click Start.*

② *Select Programs ⇨ Accessories ⇨ Calculator.*

■ *Note that in the remaining tasks you follow a similar procedure to start each of the accessories.*

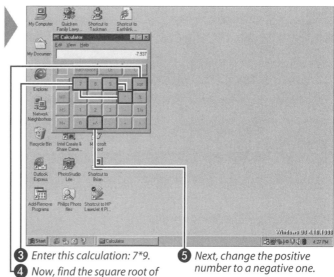

③ *Enter this calculation: 7*9.*

④ *Now, find the square root of the result.*

⑤ *Next, change the positive number to a negative one.*

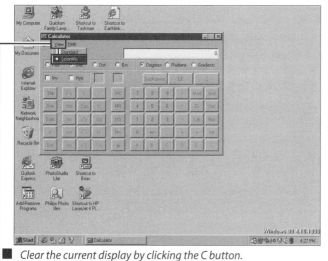

■ *Clear the current display by clicking the C button.*

⑥ *To switch the type of calculator, select View ⇨ Scientific.*

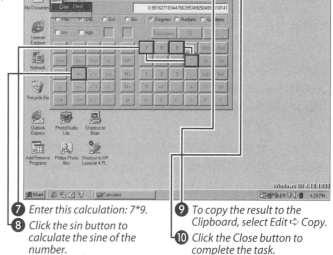

⑦ *Enter this calculation: 7*9.*

⑧ *Click the sin button to calculate the sine of the number.*

⑨ *To copy the result to the Clipboard, select Edit ⇨ Copy.*

⑩ *Click the Close button to complete the task.*

Using Clipboard Viewer

You've already learned that you cut and copy data from documents to the Clipboard and paste data from the Clipboard into documents. The Clipboard Viewer lets you view the data in the Clipboard and save the data to Clipboard data files. (Clipboard Viewer is not installed automatically when you install Windows 98. You must add it to the System Tools options using Add/Remove Programs in the Control Panel.) The figures on the facing page show the Clipboard Viewer application.

Most users generally ignore the Clipboard except to use it for cut, copy, and paste operations in applications. The Clipboard Viewer gives you more control over the Clipboard and makes it more useful. You can use the Clipboard Viewer to change the Clipboard from a one-piece-at-a-time accessory to one that saves Clipboard contents for future use.

The Clipboard is normally a one-trick pony. Whatever you copy to the Clipboard replaces whatever was already there, and if you forgot to paste the data into another application, it's gone forever. The Clipboard Viewer changes that by adding new commands that let you save the current Clipboard's contents into a file and load data into the Clipboard from a file saved earlier. You can copy data to the Clipboard, save it in a CLP file for future use, and then copy something else to the Clipboard. When you're ready to use the data you saved, you open the CLP file in Clipboard Viewer and paste the data just as if you had just copied it.

TAKE NOTE

▶ CLIPBOARD FORMATS

When you copy data to the Clipboard, the Clipboard contents can contain many different formats. This multitude of formats is one of the reasons the Clipboard is useful. To understand why this is so, consider what happens when you copy text from a Word document to the Clipboard. The most complete data format on the Clipboard is Word document format, which Word, of course, has no problem understanding. But if you tried to paste that text into a simple text editor such as Notepad, you wouldn't be able to use the Word document format because Notepad doesn't understand it. Notepad understands plain text format and imposes that format on the pasted data. The Clipboard, on the other hand, tries to use the best format an application can accept.

▶ CLEAR THE CLIPBOARD

If Windows 98 or an application is reporting insufficient memory problems and the Clipboard holds a large block of text or a large graphic, you can free some memory by using the Clipboard Viewer Edit menu's Delete command to free the memory that the Clipboard is using. You can accomplish almost the same thing by simply copying a single character to the Clipboard.

CROSS-REFERENCE

If Clipboard Viewer is not already installed, see "Installing Accessory Applications."

FIND IT ONLINE

See http://www.cyber-matrix.com/clipmag.htm for another Clipboard extender.

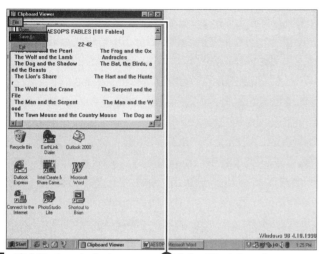

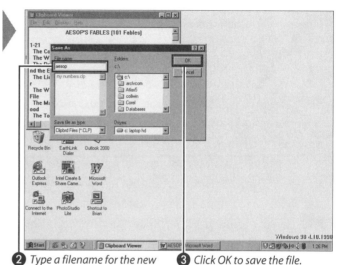

■ Click Start, and select
Programs ➪ Accessories ➪
System Tools ➪ Clipboard
Viewer.

■ Copy something to the
Clipboard.

➊ Select File ➪ Save As to save
the Clipboard contents.

➋ Type a filename for the new
file.

➌ Click OK to save the file.

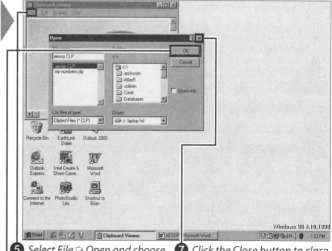

■ Copy some other type of data to the Clipboard.

➍ Click the Clipboard Viewer window to make it the active window.

➎ Select File ➪ Open and choose
the file you saved earlier.

➏ Click OK to open the file.

➐ Click the Close button to close
Clipboard Viewer.

Using Notepad

Notepad is a text editor suitable for memos, short letters, and various Windows 98 text file types. Notepad can support text files as large as about 50,000 characters. The File menu has the usual New, Open, Save, and Save As commands. You can launch Notepad by clicking a text file with the extension .TXT.

Notepad is easy to use. Because it supports only plain text files, there's no formatting to worry about and all you need to do is type whatever text you want. You use the mouse or the keyboard to move around within your document. Because Notepad has no formatting options, Notepad documents cannot contain bold, italic, or any other type of character formatting.

Windows 98 uses a number of files that must always be plain text files. These include MS-DOS batch files such as Autoexec.bat, system configuration files such as Config.sys, setup files that use the INF extension, and log files that use the LOG extension. These files cannot contain anything except plain text — otherwise they will be unusable. Notepad is the perfect editor for these types of files because it does not attempt to alter their format and always saves new files as plain text files. If you were to attempt to create one of these files in a word processor program such as WordPad or Microsoft Word, you would have to remember to specifically save the file as a plain text file.

When you try to print text files in Notepad, you may discover that short and long lines of text alternate in the printout. This problem is usually caused by the default margin settings Notepad uses. Often, text documents have too many characters per line to fit within the default margins, and this accounts for the odd appearance of the printouts. You can select File ⇨ Page Setup to adjust the margins to enable the printed text to better fit the page. When you're changing margins, consider the capabilities of your printer. Many printers cannot print closer than 0.25 inches from the edge of the paper.

TAKE NOTE

USE WORD WRAP

Use the Edit ⇨ Word Wrap option for letters, memos, and documents. The paragraphs reform themselves as you change the size of the window. When Word Wrap is on, the horizontal scroll bar disappears, and you can see text that would normally extend past the right side of the Notepad window. Word Wrap is off by default when you first run Notepad.

USE WORDPAD IF NOTEPAD IS TOO SMALL

If you attempt to open a text file that is too large for Notepad, Windows 98 will ask whether you want to open it in WordPad. There's no penalty for doing so, and WordPad will remember that the file is a plain text file.

CROSS-REFERENCE

See Chapter 7 for more information about using other types of documents.

SHORTCUT

Press F5 to insert the current time and date into a Notepad document.

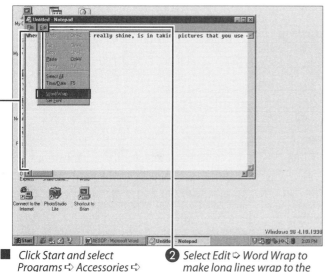

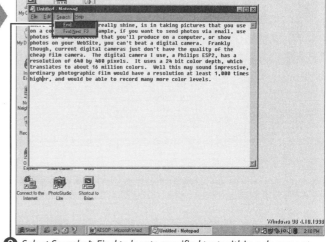

■ Click Start and select Programs ➪ Accessories ➪ Notepad.

❶ Type your text in the document window.

❷ Select Edit ➪ Word Wrap to make long lines wrap to the width of the Notepad window.

❸ Select Search ➪ Find to locate specified text within a document.

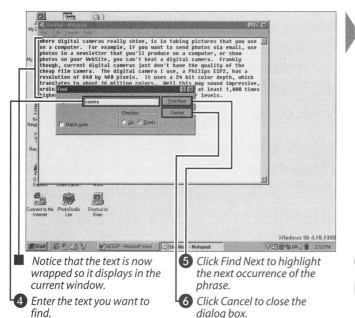

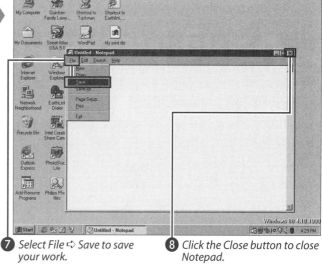

■ Notice that the text is now wrapped so it displays in the current window.

❹ Enter the text you want to find.

❺ Click Find Next to highlight the next occurrence of the phrase.

❻ Click Cancel to close the dialog box.

❼ Select File ➪ Save to save your work.

■ Enter a name for the file and then click Save to save the file.

❽ Click the Close button to close Notepad.

207

Creating Documents in WordPad

WordPad is a word processor with many of the features of Word. WordPad will read and edit WordPad documents in Word format, so even if you do not have the bigger program, you can work with documents that were prepared in Word. You can also create documents that Word users can read and modify. WordPad, of course, isn't as elaborate as Word, but it allows you to do many things you can't do in Notepad, such as format text.

WordPad may be a good choice if you need to open Word documents but you normally use a different word processor such as Word Pro or WordPerfect. WordPad will show the formatting in Word documents correctly — which may not always be the case with those other word processors.

When you start WordPad, you see the WordPad screen shown in the figures on the facing page. The vertical bar in the upper-left corner of the workspace is the insertion point, where you type text and insert graphics. After you enter some text, you move the insertion point around within the document by using the mouse or the keyboard. WordPad orients its display to the printed page, trying to show the document on the screen as it will appear on paper. The initial right and left page margins are set to 1.25 inches on 8.5 x 11 inch paper, and the default screen font for some printers needs more than a window's width to display 6 inches of text.

WordPad has a ruler that you can toggle on and off. Using the ruler you can control indenting of the first line of a selected paragraph, every line except the first line of a selected paragraph, or an entire paragraph. The ruler also enables you to set and clear tab stops.

WordPad also lets you set the font and font size from its Format bar. You can select whether the font should be displayed in boldface, italics, with underscores, and in a different color. The Format bar also has buttons for setting justification and for setting bullets into the left margins of selected text.

Continued

TAKE NOTE

▶ OPEN WORD DOCUMENTS

If Word is not installed on your computer, Word documents are associated with WordPad, and double-clicking one of them will launch WordPad. If Word is installed, double-clicking WordPad documents will open them in Word.

▶ USE TEXT DOCUMENT FORMAT WHEN NECESSARY

If you use WordPad to create or modify a text file such as an MS-DOS batch file, be sure to use File ⇨ Save As and select Text Document from the "Save as type" list box. Otherwise, WordPad will save the file as a Word document, and the batch file will not function.

CROSS-REFERENCE

See Chapter 8 for information about printing documents.

FIND IT ONLINE

Find more fonts at **http://www.fontsnthings.com/**.

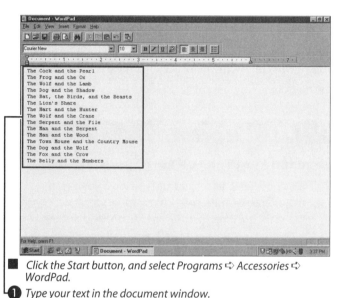

■ Click the Start button, and select Programs ⇨ Accessories ⇨ WordPad.

❶ Type your text in the document window.

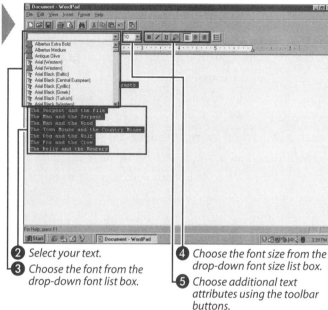

❷ Select your text.

❸ Choose the font from the drop-down font list box.

❹ Choose the font size from the drop-down font size list box.

❺ Choose additional text attributes using the toolbar buttons.

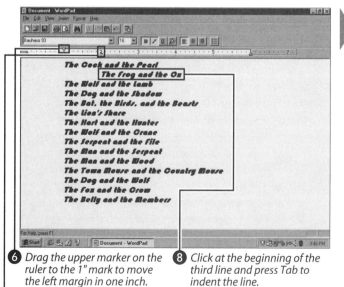

❻ Drag the upper marker on the ruler to the 1" mark to move the left margin in one inch.

❼ Click the 2" position on the ruler to set a tab stop.

❽ Click at the beginning of the third line and press Tab to indent the line.

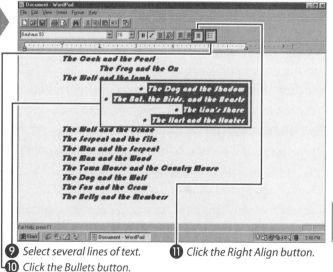

❾ Select several lines of text.

❿ Click the Bullets button.

⓫ Click the Right Align button.

Creating Documents in Wordpad

Continued

One of the advantages of using a word processor rather than a simple text editor is a word processor lets you create a document that has special graphical treatment of document elements such as typefaces and illustrations. Although no one would argue that WordPad is the equal of a full-blown word processor such as Microsoft Word, WordPad has many more capabilities than a simple text editor such as Notepad. In a WordPad document, you can use different fonts, font sizes, font styles, and even colors for the text. You can also embed objects such as bitmap images to enhance your WordPad document. None of these options is available in a plain text document.

WordPad can also save documents in different formats. By default, WordPad documents are saved in Word 6 format, but you can also select Rich Text Format (RTF), which preserves the text formatting you've applied. WordPad also offers several plain text formats that differ in the specific character set used in the document. Unless you use accented characters such as those you may find in many European languages, any of the plain text formats work well.

The figures on the facing page aren't intended to show you everything about creating complicated documents in WordPad. That would take a full book all by itself. Rather, the figures show you some of the WordPad capabilities you can use to spice up a document quickly. For example, you can use the font options to select a large and easy-to-read font and then add a graphic image of an arrow to create a quick garage sale sign.

When you insert an object into a WordPad document, the appearance of WordPad may change while you're working with the object. To return WordPad to the normal appearance, click outside the object.

TAKE NOTE

▶ USE TRUETYPE FONTS

It's a good idea to select TrueType fonts (marked by the double T's in the font list) to use in your WordPad documents. TrueType fonts look the same on the screen as they do in the printed document, and they can be scaled to many different sizes without degrading the appearance of the text.

▶ INSERTING OBJECTS

When you choose Insert ⇨ Object you'll probably see a few types of objects that you don't recognize. Although you may wish to experiment with some of them by seeing what appears when you insert them into a document, many the object types aren't intended for general use. Object types are quite often specific to one of the programs installed on your PC and won't work correctly in a WordPad document. Generally, though, they won't do any harm, and you may enjoy playing around to see what is available. Inserting an object places the object into your document. If you double-click the inserted object, you can edit the object. Whether you are able to edit the object directly in the document or in the application that created the object depends on the properties of the two applications.

CROSS-REFERENCE

See Chapter 7 for more information about working with documents.

FIND IT ONLINE

Find clip art at **http://www.bizart.com/**.

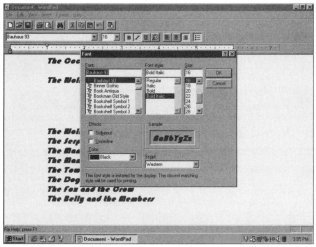

■ Select some text you wish to change the font of, and select Format ➪ Font to display the Font dialog box.

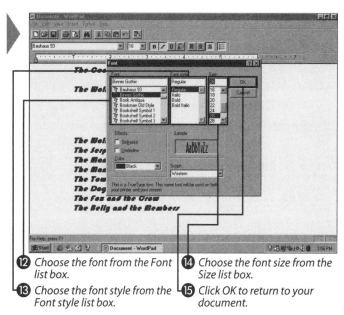

⑫ Choose the font from the Font list box.

⑬ Choose the font style from the Font style list box.

⑭ Choose the font size from the Size list box.

⑮ Click OK to return to your document.

⑯ Select Insert ➪ Object to display the Insert Object dialog box.

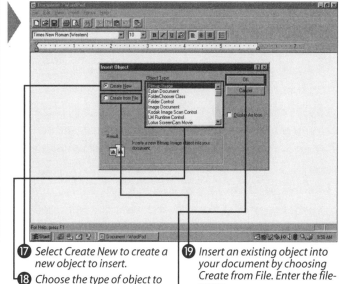

⑰ Select Create New to create a new object to insert.

⑱ Choose the type of object to insert. If you click OK now, an object of the type you selected is inserted.

⑲ Insert an existing object into your document by choosing Create from File. Enter the filename.

⑳ When you've selected a file to insert, click OK.

Configuring WordPad Document Options

Although WordPad doesn't have many options, you can configure it so that when you start a new document you don't have to make many changes to set up things the way you prefer. In that way you can begin working on your document without having to specify your preferences each time. You can decide which settings you want WordPad to use as its default settings, and new documents will automatically use those settings.

In WordPad you can select such options as the default measurement unit, the parts of WordPad that appear on your screen, word wrap settings, and the way WordPad selects blocks of text when you manipulate your mouse a certain way. For example, if you create a form that needs to fit a specific layout, choosing the correct unit of measure will be a big help. And turning off automatic word selection may make it easier to select parts of words because WordPad normally tries to help out by selecting entire words as soon as you have selected parts of two or more words.

You can select other options, such as fonts and styles for individual documents, but WordPad doesn't save these settings to use for new documents. If you want that level of convenience you'll need to step up to a more powerful word processor such as Microsoft Word. The "Take Note" section has a handy tip for setting font and style options for the entire document.

Even if WordPad makes you reselect these options for each new document, you can still save time and work by doing it once for the whole document.

TAKE NOTE

▶ WORDPAD ISN'T ALONE

WordPad isn't the only program that enables you to specify your preferences. Many of the programs you use on your PC have similar types of configuration settings. Usually you'll find a User Setup, Preferences, or Options choice on the File or View menu. You may need to experiment to find where the program default settings reside. In some complex programs they may be under more than one menu option.

▶ SET DOCUMENT OPTIONS WHEN YOU BEGIN

Because WordPad doesn't save many of the document options, such as fonts and styles, that you may wish to use as your default settings, you may want to set those options yourself when you begin a new document. One handy way to make certain your settings will apply to the entire document is to press Ctrl+A to select the entire document before you make any setting changes. WordPad will then use the new settings throughout the document, even applying them to new text you add later. You may also wish to apply your settings to a blank document and use it as the basis for new documents. In this way, you can create your own customized document template.

CROSS-REFERENCE

See the preceding section for more information about selecting document style options in WordPad.

SHORTCUT

Press Ctrl+S to quickly save your WordPad document.

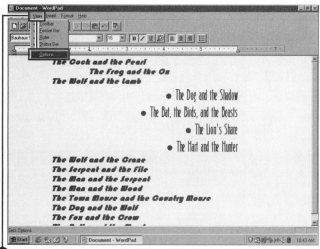

① *With WordPad open, select View ⇨ Options to display the Options dialog box.*

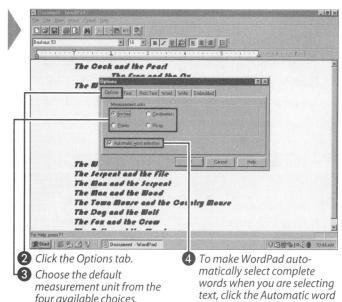

② *Click the Options tab.*

③ *Choose the default measurement unit from the four available choices.*

④ *To make WordPad automatically select complete words when you are selecting text, click the Automatic word selection" check box.*

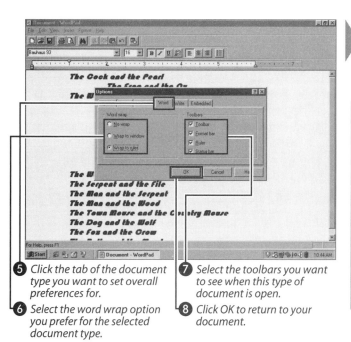

⑤ *Click the tab of the document type you want to set overall preferences for.*

⑥ *Select the word wrap option you prefer for the selected document type.*

⑦ *Select the toolbars you want to see when this type of document is open.*

⑧ *Click OK to return to your document.*

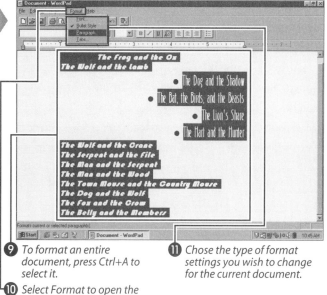

⑨ *To format an entire document, press Ctrl+A to select it.*

⑩ *Select Format to open the format options menu.*

⑪ *Chose the type of format settings you wish to change for the current document.*

Using Imaging for Windows

If you have a scanner, the Imaging accessory will come in handy as a tool you can use for scanning graphics images. If you don't have a scanner, you can use the Imaging application as a tool to view and annotate faxes you receive. After you've added notes and modifications to a fax, you can then respond or forward the fax as needed.

Scanners often come with a software package that includes a simple faxing program, so you may wonder why you would need to use Imaging. A simple faxing program may be good enough if all you want to do is to send someone an unaltered copy of a single page, but you may need to scan and fax multiple pages or may need to add annotations to a page. It's possible to send each page individually, and you can scribble some notes on the original document before you scan it, but using Imaging is probably easier and won't damage or compromise your original document.

Although Imaging can open many different types of image files, the program saves files in only three file formats: TIFF (files that have the extension .tif), Microsoft Fax (extension .awd), and Windows Bitmap (extension .bmp). Of the three, Microsoft Fax format will usually result in the smallest file size. This format is monochrome rather than color, and it is also limited to a relatively low resolution. Other programs that produce TIFF files are often able to produce smaller TIFF files than is possible with Imaging because

Imaging does not apply any compression when saving files. If you decide to save Imaging files in the TIFF or Windows Bitmap format, you must have plenty of disk space available. You may be surprised by the often very large sizes of these types of files.

Continued

TAKE NOTE

▶ IMAGING SUPPORTS TWAIN SOURCES

To scan an image directly into the Imaging application, you need to use a TWAIN image source. Usually this means using a scanner, but Imaging will use any available TWAIN image source. In addition to scanners, certain digital cameras and USB video cameras also function as TWAIN image sources. Select File ⇨ Select Scanner to see which TWAIN image sources are installed on your system.

▶ SEND A FAX

Once you've scanned in and annotated the images you want to send as a fax, you can use the File ⇨ Print command to send a fax. Select FAX as your printer before you click the OK button in the Print dialog box. Remember to set the printer selection back to your normal system printer when you're finished sending the fax. If you forget this step, you may be surprised the next time you try to print a document.

CROSS-REFERENCE
See the section "Using Paint" later in this chapter for more about creating and modifying image files.

FIND IT ONLINE
See **http://www.eastmansoftware.com/products/ImagingPro/pr_pro_index.htm**. for an advanced version of Imaging.

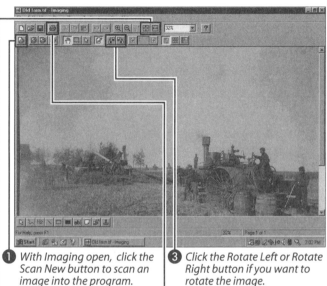

1 *With Imaging open, click the Scan New button to scan an image into the program.*

2 *To adjust the image zoom percentage, select Best Fit or Fit to Width.*

3 *Click the Rotate Left or Rotate Right button if you want to rotate the image.*

4 *Click the Print button to print a copy of the image.*

5 *Click the Append Scanned Page button to add a second page.*

6 *Click the Page and Thumbnails View button to show both pages in thumbnail view and the current page.*

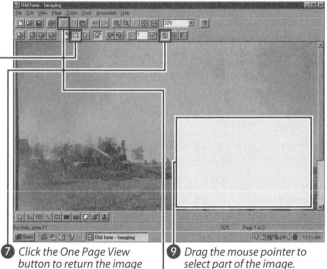

7 *Click the One Page View button to return the image to full size.*

8 *Click the Select Image button so you can select part of the image to cut.*

9 *Drag the mouse pointer to select part of the image.*

10 *Click the Cut button to cut the selected area to the Clipboard.*

11 *Click the Undo button to restore the cut area to the image.*

Using Imaging for Windows

Continued

There's more to Imaging than just scanning and faxing. When you send or receive faxes, you often want to add a notation to draw someone's attention to an important part of the image or to respond to something in the text. Imaging has tools designed to make annotating an image easy. You can add lines, text, highlighting, or even a yellow sticky note to the scanned image.

Annotations you add to an image may not appear if you save the image and then attempt to open the file in another application unless you first make your annotations a permanent part of the image. The "Take Note" section includes a tip on showing or hiding annotations. There you find more information about making annotations permanent.

The annotation toolbar has a number of interesting tools you can use to add your notes to an image. If you're not certain about the function of one of the buttons, move your mouse over the button. You'll see a description of the button in the status line. If you wait a few seconds, a small text box with the name of the tool will appear. If you're still not sure whether you've selected the correct tool, it doesn't harm anything to go ahead and try it out. If you don't like the results you can remove the annotation. Imaging also enables you to reverse the last thing you did by using the Undo button, and the Redo button will redo the last thing that was undone. The Cut, Copy, and Paste buttons also work in the usual way when you have selected an annotation.

CROSS-REFERENCE

See Chapter 8 for more information about printing your documents.

Solving Print Problems

Some images may not print properly unless you select the first print format. Select File ➪ Print to display the Print dialog box and then click the Options button in the Print dialog box before printing. If the image is too large, you may need to select the Fit to page option. The other options are Actual size and Pixel to pixel. The Pixel to pixel option may not print quite as you might expect, as the actual size of the image will vary according to the resolution of your printer. Higher resolution printers will likely print Pixel to pixel images in a very small size.

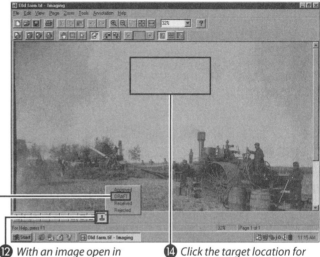

⑫ *With an image open in Imaging, click the Rubber Stamp tool button.*

⑬ *Select the text you want for the rubber stamp.*

⑭ *Click the target location for the Rubber Stamp.*

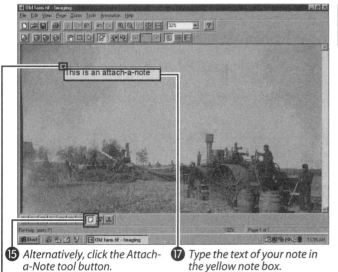

⑮ *Alternatively, click the Attach-a-Note tool button.*

⑯ *Click the location for the attach-a-note.*

⑰ *Type the text of your note in the yellow note box.*

⑱ *To add the annotation to the image layer, select Annotation ➪ Make Annotations Permanent.*

⑲ *Click the Save button to save your work. If you haven't already saved the image, you'll need to provide a filename.*

Using Paint

Paint is a graphical composition program that you use to create color pictures. You can incorporate these pictures into documents and presentations by importing the graphics files into a word processor or slide show program.

You create and modify pictures by using the tools in the toolbox to create colorful effects. The toolbox is initially on the left side of the application window, and the color box is at the bottom. Both are floatable and dockable, which means you can drag and drop them anywhere on the desktop. This feature releases more of the application window for the workspace, permitting you to view more of the picture you are working on.

The Paint toolbox contains buttons that select drawing tools. The tools in the top row enable you to select a region on the screen to move, cut, copy, or modify. The eraser tool erases parts of the picture with the background color. You erase by dragging the mouse cursor across the picture. The Fill tool fills the portion of the picture that you point to with the foreground color. The portion filled is defined by the color boundaries of whatever you point to. The Pick Color tool sets the foreground and background colors to the color in the picture that you click on. The Magnifier tool zooms in on the picture to enable you to work with smaller details. The Pencil tool draws as you drag the pencil cursor around the screen. The

Brush tool is similar to the Pencil tool except that you can select from several brush shapes in the options box. The Airbrush tool sprays a pattern as you drag the tool around the picture. The Text tool lets you define a rectangle into which you can type text. The Line tool enables you to draw straight lines by dragging the cursor. The remaining Paint tools draw curves, rectangles, many-sided shapes, ellipses, and rounded rectangles.

TAKE NOTE

▶ PAINT FILE FORMATS

In addition to the standard Windows 98 Bitmap (.bmp) format, the Paint application can save files in JPEG (.jpg) and GIF (.gif) formats, which are often used for images on Web pages. If you intend to use an image on a Web page, select either JPEG or GIF when you save the file. Most Web browsers cannot open BMP files.

▶ USE THE PICK COLOR TOOL

If you want to match a color exactly, select the Pick Color tool and then click the right or left mouse button on a patch of the desired color. The Paint drawing tools will use the selected color as their right- or left-click color, respectively.

▶ USE PAINT TO OPEN FILES

Paint is also a handy application in that it allows you to open, view, print and edit a variety of image file formats.

CROSS-REFERENCE

See "Using Imaging for Windows" earlier for information about another Windows 98 graphics tool.

FIND IT ONLINE

See http://baderb.jerseycape.net/bitmapc.htm for the Bitmap of the Month Club.

Sharing Images with Imaging

Paint and Imaging can only share images if you use the BMP file format. Use File ⇨ Save As and select Bitmap before you save the file you wish to share. Both programs can use additional file formats, but BMP is the only one that both programs can open and save. For example, if you open a JPG or GIF file in Imaging, you won't be able to make any changes or save the file. Paint cannot use Imaging's default TIF format.

■ *Open Paint by clicking the Start button and selecting Programs ⇨ Accessories ⇨ Paint.*

■ *Use File ⇨ Open to open an existing image file.*

❶ *Select the Magnifier tool from the toolbox.*

❷ *Move the mouse pointer to select an area to magnify.*

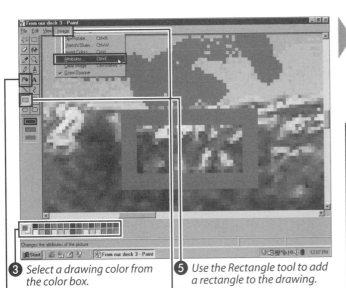

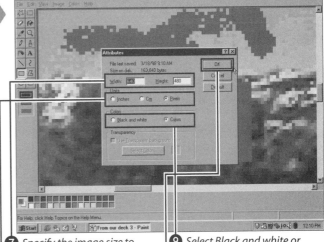

❸ *Select a drawing color from the color box.*

❹ *Select the Airbrush tool from the toolbox and drag the tool across your drawing.*

❺ *Use the Rectangle tool to add a rectangle to the drawing.*

❻ *Select Image ⇨ Attributes.*

❼ *Specify the image size to resize your drawing.*

❽ *Select the unit of measurement — choose Pixels for easier sizing of on-screen images.*

❾ *Select Black and white or Color (choose Black and white for images you'll print on a monochrome printer).*

❿ *Click OK to return to Paint.*

Personal Workbook

Q&A

1 Where should you go to install missing Windows 98 accessories?

_____

_____

2 How can you transfer data between the calculator and other applications?

_____

_____

_____

_____

3 How can you save Clipboard contents for future use?

_____

_____

_____

4 When is Notepad the best choice for editing files?

_____

_____

5 What can you do if the lines of text in a Notepad document extend past the right edge of the window?

_____

_____

_____

_____

6 How can you add a picture to a WordPad document?

_____

_____

_____

_____

7 What must you do if you want to edit an image from Imaging in Paint?

_____

_____

_____

_____

ANSWERS: PAGE 362

EXTRA PRACTICE

1. Look on the Windows Setup tab of the Add/Remove Programs dialog box to see what other accessories you can install.

2. Balance your checkbook using Calculator.

3. Copy several images to the Clipboard and save each of them individually using Clipboard Viewer.

4. Open a text file in Notepad.

5. Create a new Word format document in WordPad.

6. Open an image file in Imaging and add a DRAFT marking using the Rubber Stamp tool.

7. Open an image file in Paint and edit it with the Eraser tool.

REAL-WORLD APPLICATIONS

✔ You find yourself on a committee that is exchanging information via fax, and you need to mark the documents with an "Approved" stamp before sending it to someone else. You use the Rubber Stamp tool in the Imaging application to add the stamp quickly and easily.

✔ You are working on a report that includes several complex calculations. You use the Calculator to make certain you haven't made any mathematical errors.

✔ Someone sends you a Word document, but you don't have Microsoft Word installed on your PC. You use WordPad to open, edit, and print the document.

Visual Quiz

What is the purpose of this dialog box? How do you display it? Why isn't the Format Bar option checked?

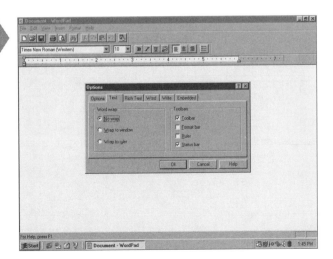

_____

_____

_____

_____

_____

_____

CHAPTER **13**

MASTER
THESE
SKILLS

▶ Opening and Closing the MS-DOS Window

▶ Using MS-DOS Commands

▶ Configuring Programs for MS-DOS Mode

▶ Restarting in MS-DOS Mode

Using MS-DOS

Windows 98 provides various powerful tools to help you perform almost any task on your computer. Most PC users don't need anything else.

As powerful as the Windows 98 *graphical user interface* (GUI) may be, though, it's not possible to do everything by clicking a mouse. Accomplishing some tasks is too difficult or even impossible without access to the *command line,* the old standby from the earliest days of personal computing.

Before the advent of GUIs like Windows, PCs used DOS (short *for disk operating system*) to control how the PC operated. (Today, Microsoft's MS-DOS has become the industry standard.) To use an MS-DOS-based PC you entered commands at the *MS-DOS prompt* (often called the *DOS prompt* or the *command prompt*). For example, to copy a file named MYFILE.DOC from the C drive to a floppy disk in the A drive, you might use the following command:

COPY C:\MYFILE.DOC A:

MS-DOS commands often seemed esoteric and confusing, especially to newcomers. It was hard to remember all the subtle variations to a command. Clearly, MS-DOS had to be replaced if most people were to have a chance to use PCs effectively. Windows was one solution. You can use Windows 98 without entering a command at the MS-DOS command prompt.

If the Windows 98 GUI can handle almost any computing task, why should you be interested in knowing about using MS-DOS? The answer is simple. There are a few things you can't do (or can't do easily) without using MS-DOS. For example, if you want to print a listing of the files in a folder, Windows 98 doesn't provide an easy way to do it without using the command prompt. And if you're a game player, some of the hottest PC games won't run unless you start the computer in MS-DOS mode.

Windows 98 gives you a complete set of MS-DOS commands. Almost anything that was possible to do from the command prompt on MS-DOS-based PCs is still possible on a Windows 98 PC. A few obsolete commands are no longer available, but they've been replaced by more efficient ways of doing things directly from the Windows 98 GUI.

Opening and Closing the MS-DOS Window

indows 98 provides two primary methods of accessing MS-DOS. The easiest and most straightforward method is to use the MS-DOS Prompt item that appears on the Start menu. When you select this command, Windows 98 displays the *MS-DOS window*, where you can enter commands. The MS-DOS window can appear as an actual window, or it can be expanded to full-screen view. Nearly all tasks that require the use of MS-DOS can be done using the MS-DOS window. Later in this chapter you learn how to use the more extreme method of accessing MS-DOS.

To Windows 98, the MS-DOS window is simply another program that you can run on your PC. When you select Programs ⇨ MS-DOS Prompt from the Start menu, you're actually running a program named Command.com that is normally found in the C:\Windows folder. Command.com is a special type of program, called a *command processor*, that executes the commands you enter at the command prompt.

The MS-DOS window is versatile. You can shrink the window down so much that it is virtually impossible to read any of the text in the window, or you can expand it to cover the entire screen. You can control the number of lines displayed in the window. Typically, you can choose 25, 43, or 50 lines depending on your needs. To change the number of lines displayed in the MS-DOS window, right-click the MS-DOS Prompt icon, select Properties, choose the size from the "Initial size" list box on the Screen tab, and click OK.

When you're finished working in the MS-DOS window, close the window by typing **EXIT** and pressing Enter, or by clicking the Close button in the upper-right corner of the window.

TAKE NOTE

▶ RUNNING MS-DOS PROGRAMS FROM ICONS

Some MS-DOS programs run in an MS-DOS window, but typically you can start the program by double-clicking the program icon. Sometimes when you run an MS-DOS program this way you'll encounter behavior that may seem a little confusing. Rather than the MS-DOS window closing when the program completes, you may see an MS-DOS window that shows the program name and the message "finished" in the title bar. When you see the "finished" message in the title bar, you can close the window by clicking the Close button at the upper-right corner of the window.

▶ MS-DOS PROGRAMS MUST BE SHUT DOWN PROPERLY

To avoid losing data, you must shut down MS-DOS programs properly. If the MS-DOS window shows the program name but does not show the "finished" message, choose the proper command from the program's menus to exit the program before you attempt to close the MS-DOS window. Otherwise, any files the program had open may be corrupted and you may lose data.

CROSS-REFERENCE

See "Using MS-DOS Commands" next in this chapter.

FIND IT ONLINE

For more on MS-DOS, see
http://www.cit.ac.nz/smac/os100/.

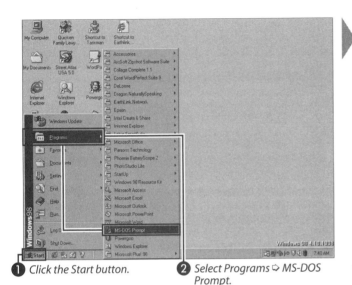

❶ Click the Start button.

❷ Select Programs ➪ MS-DOS Prompt.

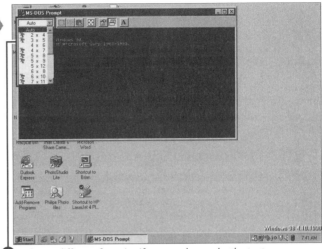

❸ Select a different font size if you need to make the text in the MS-DOS window easier to read.

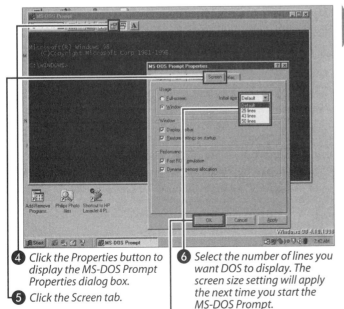

❹ Click the Properties button to display the MS-DOS Prompt Properties dialog box.

❺ Click the Screen tab.

❻ Select the number of lines you want DOS to display. The screen size setting will apply the next time you start the MS-DOS Prompt.

❼ Click OK.

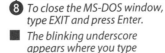

❽ To close the MS-DOS window, type EXIT and press Enter.

■ The blinking underscore appears where you type commands. Commands can be upper- or lowercase.

❾ Alternatively, click the Close button to close the MS-DOS window.

Using MS-DOS Commands

By itself, opening and closing the MS-DOS window doesn't accomplish very much. To do anything useful at the MS-DOS prompt, you need to enter MS-DOS commands. In the earlier example, you typed the EXIT command to close the command processor and the MS-DOS window. In this section you learn how to use other, more useful MS-DOS commands. Be sure to see the "Take Note" section to learn how you can find out more about the individual MS-DOS commands.

Using MS-DOS commands can sometimes be confusing. You may enter a command that you're certain is correct only to be greeted with the message "Bad command or file name." This rather cryptic message is simply telling you that MS-DOS cannot find an internal command or a program that matches what you typed on the command line. This doesn't necessarily mean that what you typed was incorrect — only that MS-DOS cannot find it. You may need to give MS-DOS a little help.

One way to give MS-DOS the help it needs to find a program is to include the complete *path* to the program. For example, if Myprog.exe is in the C:\Allmine folder, you could type the command as **C:\allmine\myprog** and press Enter. Sometimes this may not work because the program you want to run may not be able to find all its data files. In that case you'll need to use the CD — Change Directory — command to change to the program's folder before

you execute the program. In this example you would first type **CD \allmine** and press Enter, and then type **myprog** and press Enter.

The figures on the facing page show a few examples of using MS-DOS commands. Be sure to read the "Take Note" section that follows to learn how you can get more information about using MS-DOS commands.

TAKE NOTE

▶ GET HELP WITH MS-DOS COMMANDS

It's difficult to remember all the options for each of the MS-DOS commands. Fortunately, Windows 98 provides you with help in the form of a small MS-DOS program that describes each of the MS-DOS commands and shows you all the options for each one. To get help with the MS-DOS commands, run Help.com in the \Tools\Oldmsdos folder on your Windows 98 CD-ROM. You can also copy the files from this folder to your hard disk if you want to make it easier to access the MS-DOS help file. You may want to copy the files to the C:\Windows\Command folder. At a minimum you must copy three files: Help.com, Help.hlp, and Qbasic.exe.

▶ MS-DOS PROGRAM EXTENSIONS

MS-DOS recognizes three extensions as being programs that can be executed. A program must have an EXE, COM, or BAT extension to be run at the MS-DOS prompt.

FIND IT ONLINE
See **http://support.microsoft.com/support/c.asp** for online support of MS-DOS.

FIND IT ONLINE
For more on DOS commands, see **http://www.compucure.com/msdos.htm**.

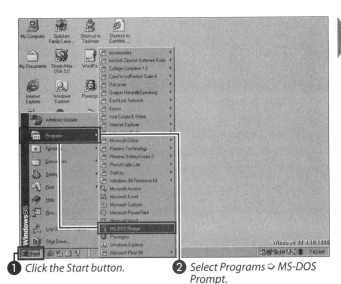

1 Click the Start button.

2 Select Programs ⇨ MS-DOS Prompt.

3 Type **DIR** and press Enter.

■ This command shows you a listing of the files in the current folder.

■ You can enter MS-DOS commands in any combination of upper- and lowercase characters.

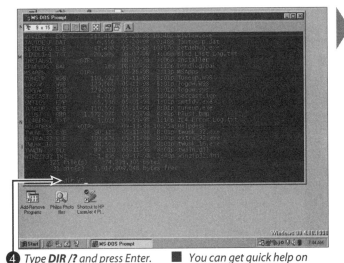

4 Type **DIR /?** and press Enter.

■ You can get quick help on MS-DOS commands by adding /? after the command name before you press Enter. Don't use /? with any other parameters.

5 View the parameters (or switches) you can add to the command to modify how the command functions.

6 Optionally, enter a new command using the optional parameters.

7 Click the Close button to close the MS-DOS window.

227

Configuring Programs for MS-DOS Mode

Y ou should be able to run most MS-DOS programs either by double-clicking the program icon in Windows Explorer or by entering the proper command at the MS-DOS prompt. Unfortunately, a few poorly written programs — mostly games — won't run properly unless they have complete control of your computer. For them there's *MS-DOS mode,* an operating mode that reduces your multitasking, GUI-based Windows 98 PC to a simple computer that can do only one thing at a time. Read on to learn how to configure your system to run programs that require MS-DOS mode.

Using MS-DOS mode is different from using the MS-DOS window. When you run a program in an MS-DOS window, you can run other programs at the same time and even share data using the Windows 98 Clipboard. The MS-DOS window appears as one of the buttons on the taskbar, and you can switch back and forth between programs. When you run programs in MS-DOS mode, on the other hand, the Windows 98 GUI shuts down, multitasking shuts down, all the Windows 98 services shut down, and only the MS-DOS mode program can be run.

Configuring a program to run in MS-DOS mode should be a last resort when you've already tried to run the program in an MS-DOS window but have encountered problems. Sometimes you can run an old MS-DOS program full-screen in the MS-DOS window without going to the extreme measure of

using MS-DOS mode. If so, you won't have to save all your work and shut down all your other applications so that the MS-DOS program can be run.

The figures on the facing page show how to configure Msd.exe — one of the programs in the \Tools\Oldmsdos folder on your Windows 98 CD-ROM — to run in MS-DOS mode. For this example I'm assuming that you have a copy of Msd.exe on your desktop. This is not a requirement, but it makes it a little easier to run the program.

TAKE NOTE

NO PROPERTIES FOR MS-DOS MODE PROGRAMS

Even though the Properties dialog box includes several tabs that you can use to set the properties for MS-DOS programs, most of these settings are ignored for programs that run in MS-DOS mode. After your PC is switched into MS-DOS mode, Windows 98 has no way to control how your programs function.

USE AS FEW CONFIGURATION OPTIONS AS POSSIBLE

When you configure a program to run in MS-DOS mode, use as few of the configuration options as possible. Each configuration option uses a certain amount of memory, and memory is always in short supply in MS-DOS mode. Be especially wary of the Direct Disk Access option that enables an MS-DOS mode program to directly modify your disk data structures.

CROSS-REFERENCE

See "Restarting in MS-DOS Mode" next in this chapter.

FIND IT ONLINE

See http://pw2.netcom.com/~stotzerm/sysdos.html for DOS tips.

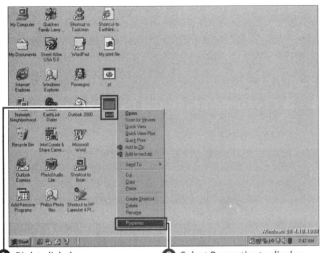

1 Right-click the program you wish to configure for MS-DOS mode.

2 Select Properties to display the Properties dialog box.

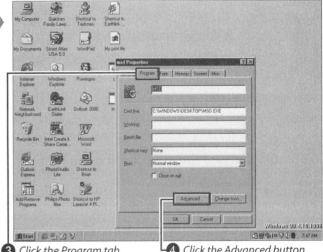

3 Click the Program tab.

■ The Font, Memory, Screen, and Misc tabs do not apply to MS-DOS mode programs.

4 Click the Advanced button.

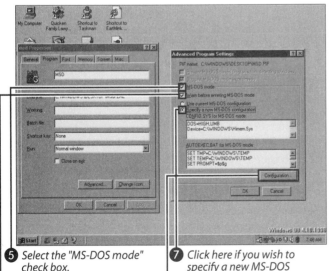

5 Select the "MS-DOS mode" check box.

6 Select the "Warn before entering MS-DOS mode" check box. If you don't, you may lose data.

7 Click here if you wish to specify a new MS-DOS configuration.

8 Click the Configuration button.

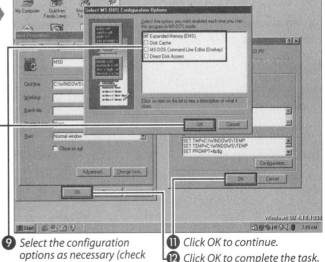

9 Select the configuration options as necessary (check the DOS program's documentation for details).

10 Click OK to continue.

11 Click OK to continue.

12 Click OK to complete the task.

Restarting in MS-DOS Mode

Once you've configured a program to run in MS-DOS mode, you're almost ready to restart your system in MS-DOS mode. Before you run an MS-DOS mode program, however, you should first save all your work and close any programs running on your PC. This is especially important if you chose not to select the "Warn before entering MS-DOS mode" check box in the Advanced Program Settings dialog box (see the preceding section). If this check box is not selected, you won't have any warning before your computer changes operating modes, and you run a high risk of losing data.

When you run a program configured to use MS-DOS mode, Windows 98 shuts down while the program is running. When you exit the program, Windows 98 automatically restarts. Any programs or services that you have set up to automatically load when you start Windows 98 will reload, but you'll have to restart any other programs.

While your computer is running in MS-DOS mode you won't have access to any of the Windows 98 services. If your printer or your modem uses Windows-based drivers, for example, you won't be able to use the printer or modem. In some cases you may need to edit the CONFIG.SYS and AUTOEXEC.BAT settings in the Advanced Program Settings dialog box in order to make your system function correctly. The documentation for the

MS-DOS mode program should provide information about any special settings that may be required. You also will not be able to run more than one program at a time — MS-DOS mode is not multitasking.

TAKE NOTE

YOUR MOUSE MAY NOT FUNCTION IN MS-DOS MODE

If you're used to using your mouse in Windows 98 you may be unpleasantly surprised to discover that your mouse does not work while you're running programs in MS-DOS mode. In most cases it is necessary to load *real mode* drivers if you wish to use your mouse in MS-DOS mode. You'll probably have to dig deep to find out how to configure real mode drivers for your mouse. Those types of drivers are not needed in Windows 98, and your mouse manufacturer may not provide easily accessible information about how to use the mouse in MS-DOS mode.

YOU CAN RESTART YOUR SYSTEM IN MS-DOS MODE

If you must run in MS-DOS mode for a task that cannot be completed while the Windows 98 GUI is running, you can use a different option for restarting your PC in MS-DOS mode. Click the Start button and choose Shut Down. Then click the "Restart in MS-DOS mode" radio button and choose OK. Your system will shut down and restart in MS-DOS mode. When you are finished using MS-DOS mode, type **EXIT** or press Ctrl+Alt+Del to restart Windows 98.

CROSS-REFERENCE

See "Configuring Programs for MS-DOS Mode" earlier in this chapter.

FIND IT ONLINE

See **news://msnews.microsoft.com/microsoft.public. win95.msdosapps** for more on MS-DOS.

You May Need MS-DOS Mode for Special Purposes

You may need to use MS-DOS mode for tasks that cannot be completed in Windows 98 such as updating your PC's BIOS or changing a Windows 98 system file. Some files cannot be updated while they are in use, and MS-DOS mode is the only way you can access the files.

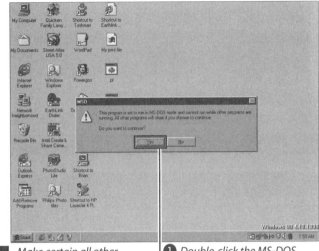

■ *Make certain all other programs are shut down.*

❶ *Double-click the MS-DOS mode program icon.*

❷ *Click Yes to continue.*

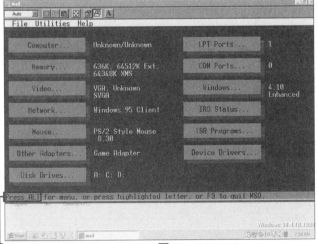

❸ *Press the Alt key to activate the menu.*

■ *Your MS-DOS mode program may require you to use other methods to activate the menus. There's little consistency in MS-DOS mode programs.*

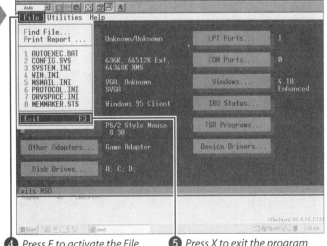

❹ *Press F to activate the File menu.*

❺ *Press X to exit the program and restart Windows 98.*

■ *Or you can press F3 in place of Steps 4 and 5.*

Personal Workbook

Q&A

1 How can you switch a program that is running in an MS-DOS window to full-screen view?

_____

_____

_____

2 What should you do if the MS-DOS window says "finished" in the title bar?

_____

_____

_____

3 What types of files does MS-DOS recognize as programs?

_____

_____

_____

4 What does the message "Bad command or file name" mean?

_____

_____

5 What happens to your Windows 98 programs when you enter MS-DOS mode?

_____

_____

_____

_____

6 How many programs can you run at one time in MS-DOS mode?

_____

_____

_____

7 What do you type to close the MS-DOS window?

_____

8 What type of drivers must you load to run things such as your mouse in MS-DOS mode?

_____

_____

_____

ANSWERS: PAGE 363

EXTRA PRACTICE

1. Open the MS-DOS window.

2. Run the Help.com program from your Windows 98 CD-ROM.

3. Look in the help window for information about using the DIR command.

4. Use the DIR command to view the file listing in your Windows folder with the listing sorted by name and paused after each page of files.

5. Set up Msd.exe to run in MS-DOS mode.

6. Restart your system in MS-DOS mode and then restart Windows 98.

REAL-WORLD APPLICATIONS

✔ Your supervisor wants you to print a list of all the 75 files in the Smith Project folder. To print the list, you use the MS-DOS window.

✔ Your computer manufacturer releases a BIOS update for your PC. To run the program successfully, you restart your system in MS-DOS mode.

✔ In the sale bin at your local computer store, you discover a great baseball game that runs only in MS-DOS mode. To run it, you create a special MS-DOS mode configuration for it.

Visual Quiz

Why does this dialog box show the message rather than enable you to set the properties? How can you change these properties?

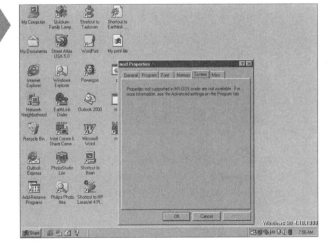

_____

_____

_____

_____

_____

PART

V

Windows 98 Connectivity

Some people say that the whole world is becoming connected, but you're probably more concerned about getting yourself connected. If so, you've come to the right place in this part of the book. If you can't wait to start browsing the Internet, look no further — you'll find it here.

This part will also have you sending and receiving e-mail in no time at all. E-mail is today's most exciting way to communicate because your messages travel almost instantly to almost anywhere in the world. You even learn how to include more than a simple text message so that you can send pictures or other file attachments along with your messages.

If you have more than one PC, you also learn the basics of Windows 98 networking in this part. You discover how you can use Windows 98 networking features to enable remote access to your system even if you don't have a network.

Finally, this part concludes by showing you how to make two computers talk to each other without using the Internet. If you want to communicate directly with another system, HyperTerminal may be your best option.

CHAPTER 14

Connecting to the Internet

This chapter is about using Windows 98 to "cruise the information superhighway" — in other words, to use the Internet. It is not a comprehensive guide to accessing the information content on the Internet. Entire books have been dedicated to that subject; one that we recommend is the *Internet Bible* published by IDG Books Worldwide, Inc. This chapter is specifically about using the features of Windows 98 Internet Explorer to explore the Internet.

The Internet is an international network of interconnected computers called *servers*. They cooperate by using intercomputer data exchange protocols that they all understand. You do not have to know anything at all about how they achieve this, only that they do.

Users of the Internet access its servers from workstations and personal computers. You typically connect to a particular *ISP*— Internet service provider — server that hosts your Internet access. Your computer is logged on to the ISP server and becomes a workstation on the Internet. Each new connection involves a login to the computer. Fortunately, most users need

not know the details of logging in to computers in order to access the Internet. Windows 98's Internet Explorer and the World Wide Web take the pain out of it.

The World Wide Web is the view of the Internet with which most users are familiar. The Web provides a graphical way to view the Internet. A *Web site* consists of *pages*. A Web site can have many pages; typically the main page is called the *home page.*

A Web page typically consists of text, pictures, and links to other Web pages. *Links* are instructions that tell your system the address of another Web page (or other resource) to load when you click the link.

As we mentioned before, users view Web pages and navigate the Web's links via Web browser programs running in their local computers. The Internet Explorer (IE) browser is an integrated component of Windows 98. IE gives you a similar user interface for browsing the Web that you use for navigating your computer's files and folders and for navigating a local network.

Adding an Internet Connection

To use the Internet and the World Wide Web, you need several things. You need a physical connection to an Internet server, either via a modem or your organization's local or wide area network. If you're using a modem, you need an account with an ISP. You'll also need your Internet account and connection properly configured for Windows 98. (If your organization provides Internet access through its network, your organization *is* your ISP. Consult your network administrator for assistance.)

This discussion assumes that you will access the Internet through a modem, and that your modem is already installed. This section also assumes that you do not already have an Internet account set up on your system.

The figures on the facing page show how to use the Internet Connection Wizard to connect to Microsoft via your modem and get a list of ISPs in your area who will provide service.

You'll likely have a number of choices if you decide to sign up with an ISP on Microsoft's list. Depending on your location, however, you may need to check with more than one of the services to find one with a local access number. Paying long distance charges on top of your monthly access fees could result in huge bills very quickly. It's also advisable to do some outside research on Internet providers in your area. Consider it similar to signing up for a long distance phone plan. It's best to be well-versed in all your options. Also be sure to check the type of local access that is provided. You'll want fast access that is compatible with your modem. In some areas you can use 56K modems or even ISDN connections, but you'll need to check to see if this service is available in your area. In reality, fewer than half of the phone lines in the country support 56K connections.

TAKE NOTE

▶ IF THE CONNECT TO THE INTERNET ICON IS MISSING

If your desktop has no Connect to the Internet icon, do not worry. You can access the Internet in other ways. One way is to click the Internet Explorer icon. If you do not already have Internet access, any attempt to gain Internet access starts the Internet Connection Wizard. Another way is to select the Connection Wizard command from the Start ⇨ Programs ⇨ Internet Explorer selection.

▶ YOU'LL PROBABLY NEED A CREDIT CARD

Most large ISPs require that you provide a valid credit card account number to sign up for service. If you prefer to pay for your Internet access directly, you'll probably have to contact and set up an account with a local ISP. You may want to look in the Yellow Pages under Internet to find the options that are available locally.

CROSS-REFERENCE

See "Adding New Hardware" in Chapter 5.

FIND IT ONLINE

You may also wish to check out the ISP services available through **http://www.earthlink.net**.

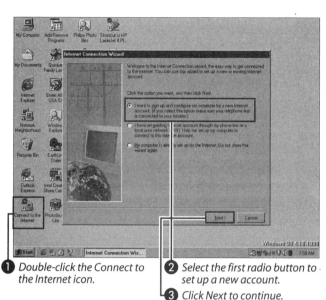

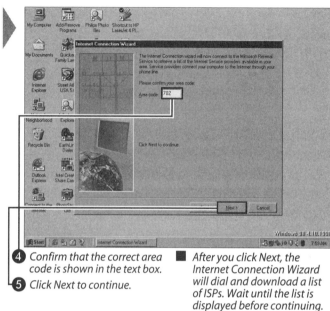

1 Double-click the Connect to the Internet icon.

2 Select the first radio button to set up a new account.

3 Click Next to continue.

4 Confirm that the correct area code is shown in the text box.

5 Click Next to continue.

■ After you click Next, the Internet Connection Wizard will dial and download a list of ISPs. Wait until the list is displayed before continuing.

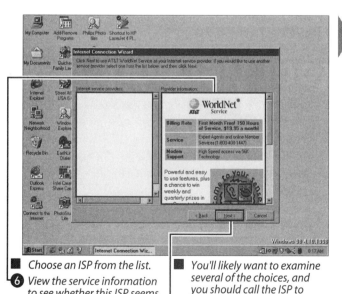

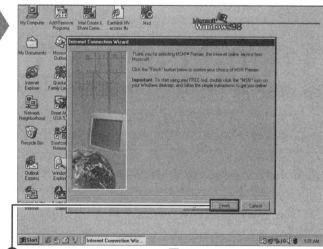

■ Choose an ISP from the list.

6 View the service information to see whether this ISP seems to fit your needs.

■ You'll likely want to examine several of the choices, and you should call the ISP to verify rates and ask questions.

7 Click Next to continue.

8 Click Finish to complete the task.

■ After you've selected an ISP, follow the directions for signing up when you go online.

■ No matter which ISP you select you should now be ready to begin using the Internet.

Starting Internet Explorer

indows 98 provides you with plenty of ways to start Internet Explorer. In this section you learn about a few of them and see why you may sometimes prefer to use one of the alternatives instead of simply clicking the Internet Explorer icon.

If you click one of the Internet Explorer icons — either on your desktop or on the Quick Launch toolbar — Internet Explorer opens to the page that is configured to be the default home page for your computer. Initially, that page is the page found by the location address http://www.home.microsoft.com (see the Take Note titled "Understanding Uniform Resource Locators"). (You can change your default home page under the View ⇨ Internet Options command in Internet Explorer.)

You can also access the Web through the Start button. Windows 98 lists Web sites you designate as Favorites under Start. Choosing one of them from the list opens Internet Explorer to that exact Web page.

Later in this chapter you learn how to add Web pages to your list of favorites.

Another useful way to start Internet Explorer is to type a Web page address in the Address toolbar and press Enter. If you type the address correctly and the link is active, you'll be connected to the Internet and the exact page you want.

TAKE NOTE

► UNDERSTANDING UNIFORM RESOURCE LOCATORS

Each page on the Web has an address by which the browser finds the page. That address is called the Uniform Resource Locator (URL). The Internet Explorer Address Bar contains the address that is the URL for a Web page. A URL typically consists of a protocol identifier — such as http:// www, which tells the browser that the page can be found on the Web, the domain name where the page can be found, and sometimes directory and filenames. Not all Web servers include the www portion of the address. When the address includes filenames, they identify the text file on the server that represents the page's informational display. When the browser provides no filenames to the server, the server assumes that the browser is requesting a page in a file named index.html, default.htm, or mypage.htm. Links on the page are internally associated with URLs. When you click a link, the browser requests that URL from the server.

► YOU MAY NEED TO CONFIRM THE CONNECTION

Depending on the configuration settings on your system, you may need to confirm the connection to the Internet by clicking a Connect button when you start Internet Explorer. You may also need to confirm your calling location as shown in the lower-right figure on the facing page.

CROSS-REFERENCE
See "Saving Your Favorite Web Sites" later in this chapter.

FIND IT ONLINE
You can find out more about URLs at http://www.w3.org/.

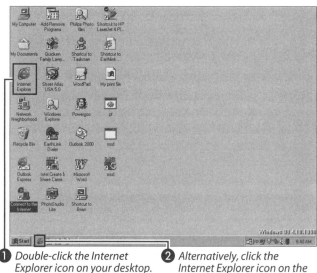

1 Double-click the Internet Explorer icon on your desktop.

2 Alternatively, click the Internet Explorer icon on the Quick Launch toolbar.

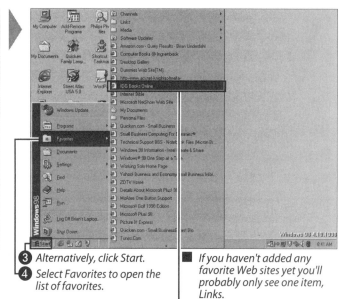

3 Alternatively, click Start.

4 Select Favorites to open the list of favorites.

■ If you haven't added any favorite Web sites yet you'll probably only see one item, Links.

5 Click a Web site you wish to see.

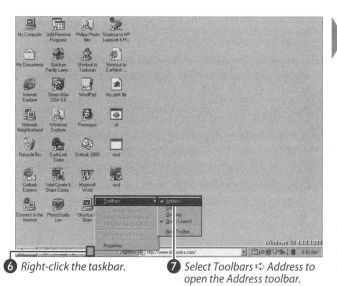

6 Right-click the taskbar.

7 Select Toolbars ⇨ Address to open the Address toolbar.

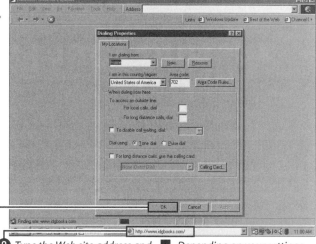

8 Type the Web site address and press Enter.

9 If the Dialing Properties dialog box appears, click OK to continue.

■ Depending on your settings, you may need to confirm your location in the Dialing Properties dialog box.

■ You may also have to click a Connect button.

241

Visiting Web Sites

When you *browse* the Web, you select and display different pages of information. Starting from your home page you can find your way to the millions of pages of information available on the Web.

A *link* is text or a graphic on a page that, when you click it, causes the browser to request the new page from the server. Links can be underlined text fields, graphical representations of buttons, banners, or anything else the page designer chooses. When you move the mouse cursor across a link, the cursor changes to a pointing finger, and the URL associated with the link displays in Internet Explorer's status bar in the leftmost panel.

Internet Explorer includes Back and Forward tool buttons. When you first open Internet Explorer, those buttons are dimmed, indicating that they are not active. After you have taken the first step away from your home page, the Back button becomes active. The Back button navigates to the page that you viewed just before the current one. After you've used the Back button, the Forward button becomes active, indicating that you can move forward to the page from which you just came.

Loading a page into your browser may take a long time, for a variety of reasons. The server may be busy serving many users. The Internet itself may be busy. The page you wish to view may consist of a huge volume of text or many high-resolution graphics. While Internet Explorer is waiting for a page to complete loading, it displays a progress bar control in the status bar. To stop the server from trying any further to load a slow page and to tell the browser to stop waiting for the server, click the Stop button.

It is possible to be viewing a page with Internet Explorer that has changed since you first loaded it. For example, some pages are generated by the server in real time in response to the actions of users who are currently logged on. Some pages are updated frequently by their designers. If you suspect that your view of a page is not current, click the Refresh button.

TAKE NOTE

▶ FOLLOWING LINKS

Most Web pages include links you can click to view related pages. Often, you'll find that those links will take you to interesting sites you probably would not have found on your own. Some Web sites have entire pages devoted to useful links.

▶ GO BACK SEVERAL PAGES

After you've visited several Web pages you may find yourself wanting to return to a page that is several pages before the current page. Click the down-arrow next to the Back button to display a list of recently visited pages. Choose the page you want from the list, and you'll skip the pages in between.

CROSS-REFERENCE
See "Searching for Web Sites" later in this chapter.

FIND IT ONLINE
See **http://www.w3.org/WWW/** for more information on the origins of the Web.

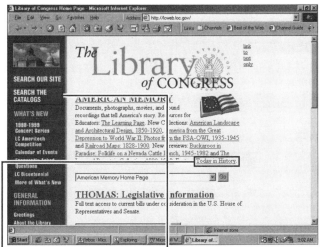

1 With a Web page already open, click an underlined link to jump to that page.

2 Alternatively, click a button to visit the link.

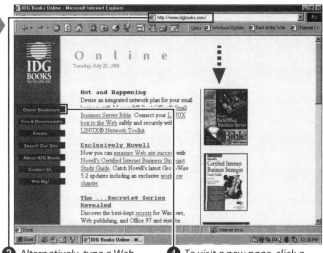

3 Alternatively, type a Web page address and press Enter.

4 To visit a new page, click a graphic that is a link.

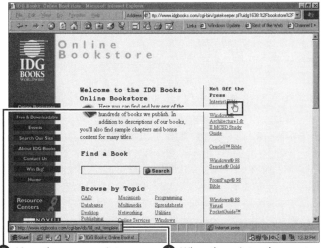

5 Move the mouse pointer over a link to view the link's address.

6 When the pointer changes to a hand, view the link address here.

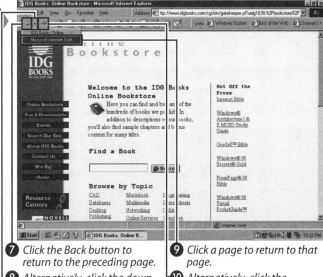

7 Click the Back button to return to the preceding page.

8 Alternatively, click the down-arrow to view the list of recently visited pages.

9 Click a page to return to that page.

10 Alternatively, click the Forward button to move forward one previously visited page.

Searching for Web Sites

There are millions of Web sites you can visit on the Internet. Finding sites that have the information you're looking for would be impossible if there weren't a way to search for them. Fortunately, dozens of ways are available to find what you want on the Internet.

You can use special services — called *search engines* — on the Internet to search for Web sites. Using many of the search engines is free, although you will see advertisements on most of them. Search engines often use *keywords* to find sites of interest. A few search engines examine the complete text on each Web page to find those sites that match your search goals.

You enter a *search string:* one or more words you think will define the Web sites you'd like to see. Some search engines treat each word in a search string as a separate phrase, so a search for **boat books** would find sites that relate to boats and sites that relate to books. One way around this is to enclose the search phrase in quotation marks, as in **"boat books"**. Most search engines will then find only sites where the two words appear together.

Placing your search string in quotation marks may not always produce the desired results. If you wanted to find Web sites that mentioned both boats and books but didn't necessarily have the two words directly together, you would need to use a different technique. Most search engines allow some type of

Boolean search technique so that you can search for sites that include both words somewhere on the page. In this case you might specify your search string as **boats AND books** — with the word *AND* in all capital letters. Read the "Take Note" section for more information about using advanced search techniques.

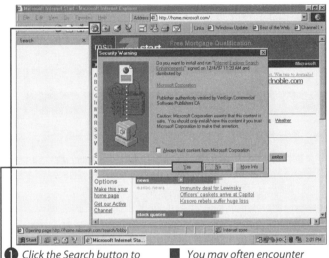

1 Click the Search button to load the Search bar.

2 If necessary, click Yes to install enhancements to your Internet Explorer search capabilities.

■ You may often encounter such messages as you visit sites on the Internet. This one indicates Microsoft has an enhancement for Internet Explorer.

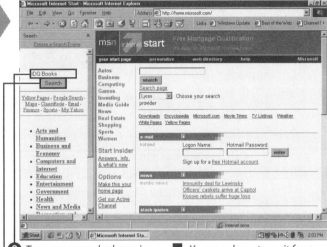

3 Type your search phrase in the text box.

4 Click Search to begin the search.

■ You may have to wait for a few minutes while the search is completed.

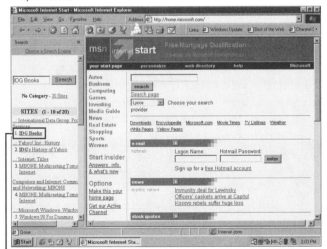

5 Click a link that appears to meet your needs.

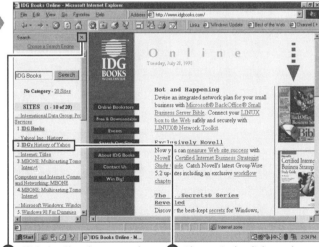

6 Click the Close button to close the Search bar and maximize the browser window.

7 Alternatively, click another link to see if the site has the information you are looking for.

Saving Your Favorite Web Sites

Finding Web sites isn't very difficult, but after you've found your favorite sites it would be nice to be able to return to them quickly.

Fortunately, Internet Explorer makes it easy for you to save a hierarchical list of your favorite Web pages. In that way you'll be able to return to any of those pages with a few quick clicks.

The list of favorite Web sites you see when you click the Favorites menu in Internet Explorer is the same list you see when you select Favorites from the Start menu. In addition, the favorites list includes a shortcut to your My Documents folder and may include a number of other shortcuts.

The upper-right figure on the facing page shows the Add Favorite dialog box you use to add links to your list of favorites. In most cases you'll simply want to save the link so that you can visit the page whenever it is convenient. For example, add the local weather page to your list of Favorites.

If it is important for you to know when a page is changed, select either the second or the third option as appropriate. It's probably not a good idea to automatically download pages that are changed several times each day — you'll never be able to get anything else done! *Subscribing* to a page simply means that Internet Explorer will keep track of when the page changes. Depending on the option you select, Internet Explorer may then download the new page or just tell you that it has changed.

TAKE NOTE

▶ WEB PAGES SOMETIMES DISAPPEAR

It's a fact of life on the Internet that change is the one constant. Your favorite Web pages can disappear as quickly as they appeared in the first place. If you attempt to visit one of the Web sites you saved in your favorites list but you see only a message that the page cannot be found, it's likely that it has moved or no longer exists. Before you decide to delete the link, however, you may want to try the link later to see whether the problem was only temporary.

▶ ORGANIZE YOUR FAVORITES

Just as you can organize your documents by creating extra folders under the My Documents folder, you can also organize your favorite Web sites by creating new folders. The lower-right figure on the facing page shows the Organize Favorites dialog box, which you can use to move, rename, or delete favorite links. But you don't have to use the Organize Favorites dialog box to modify the favorites list; instead, you can drag and drop items to move them in the same way you can change the items on the Windows 98 Start menu.

SHORTCUT
Click the Details button to see when you last visited a Web site.

FIND IT ONLINE
Add **http://www.idgbooks.com** to your favorites list to learn about the latest in computer books.

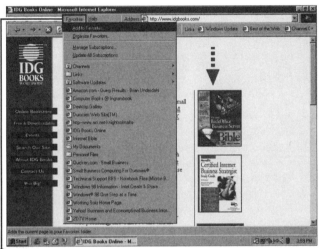

1 Select Favorites ⇨ Add to Favorites to display the Add Favorite dialog box.

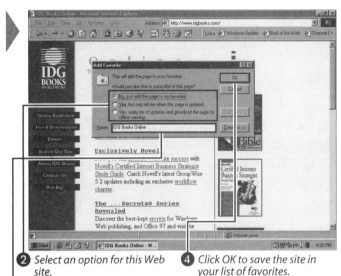

2 Select an option for this Web site.

3 Optionally, enter a name for the site.

4 Click OK to save the site in your list of favorites.

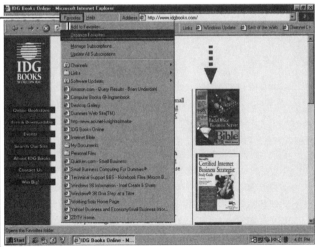

5 Select Favorites ⇨ Organize Favorites to display the Organize Favorites dialog box.

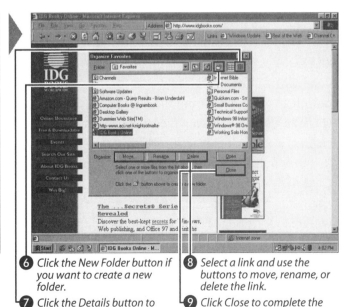

6 Click the New Folder button if you want to create a new folder.

7 Click the Details button to view the details on each link.

8 Select a link and use the buttons to move, rename, or delete the link.

9 Click Close to complete the task.

Viewing Channels

*C*hannels are Web sites that contain up-to-date information and entertainment content to which you can subscribe. The content includes TV cable news channels, stock market services, sports information, and so on. The Internet Explorer Channel Bar lists a number of Internet channels.

In most cases subscriptions to channels are free because the channels are supported largely by advertisements or are provided by services that hope you'll also subscribe to their on-air or print version. Subscribing really means that you're establishing a schedule for having the information updated on your PC.

When you first choose to subscribe to a channel, Windows 98 may inform you that a copy of the channel can be found on the Internet Explorer 4.0 CD-ROM and may offer to load the channel from the CD-ROM. You can insert your Windows 98 CD-ROM in place of the Internet Explorer 4.0 CD-ROM, but it's probably a better idea to simply download the content from the Internet. In that way you'll be assured of having the latest version of the channel and won't end up subscribing to a channel that may have been canceled since your Windows 98 CD-ROM was issued.

After you've subscribed to one or more channels, be sure to leave your PC on and connected to your phone line. Channels can be updated only while your system is connected to the Internet.

TAKE NOTE

TAKE THE CHANNEL TOUR

The first time you click on one of the channel buttons, Windows 98 will offer to give you a brief introduction to the channels. This tour will take only a few minutes, and it will provide you with a nice orientation to using the channels.

RESIZE OR MOVE THE INTERNET EXPLORER CHANNEL BAR

You can resize or move the Internet Explorer Channel Bar if you cannot see all the channel buttons or if the Channel Bar is covering up icons on your desktop. As you slide the mouse pointer over the edge of the Internet Explorer Channel Bar, a gray border will appear. You can drag the edges of this border to resize the bar. To move the bar, slide the mouse pointer just past the top of the bar, and, when the title bar appears, drag the title bar to move the entire bar.

ALLOWING FOR ACTIVEX CONTROLS

You may encounter a specific message during the subscription process. *ActiveX controls* are small programs included on Web pages to enhance the content. To adjust the Internet Explorer security settings to allow ActiveX controls, select the View ⇨ Internet Options command and click the Security tab. Select "Trusted sites" zone from the drop-down Zone list box and add the sites to which you've subscribed. After you've added a site to the "Trusted sites" zone you will no longer see the ActiveX warning message for that site.

CROSS-REFERENCE

See "Adding Active Desktop Content" in Chapter 4.

FIND IT ONLINE

See **http://www.windowsmedia.com/guide/en/ en_us.asp** to access the channel guide.

Receiving Updates to Channel Subscriptions

To update channel subscriptions, your PC must be connected to the Internet. In most cases you can accept the default schedule for these updates. Many channels provide up-to-the-minute information by way of a screen saver. To create an update schedule, select the service you want, select the update option you prefer, and click the Customize button to customize the update schedule. Next, follow the directions in the few remaining dialog boxes to receive the latest information at the time you want it.

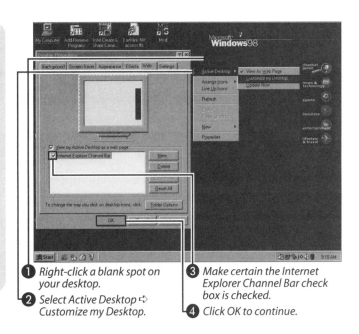

❶ *Right-click a blank spot on your desktop.*

❷ *Select Active Desktop ⇨ Customize my Desktop.*

❸ *Make certain the Internet Explorer Channel Bar check box is checked.*

❹ *Click OK to continue.*

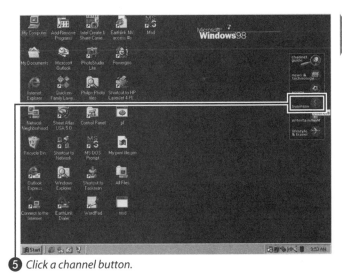

❺ *Click a channel button.*

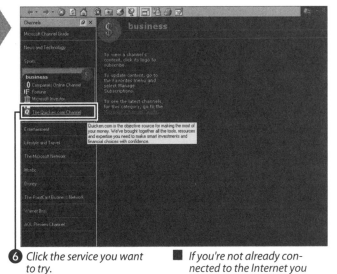

❻ *Click the service you want to try.*

■ *If you're not already connected to the Internet you may need to confirm that you wish to connect.*

Using Windows Update

There's almost always room for improvement in software. Maybe a new feature needs to be added, or a new piece of hardware needs to be supported. Or perhaps there's a bug that needs to be fixed. Whatever the reason, keeping your computer software up-to-date has never been as easy as most people would like, but Windows 98 makes it much easier.

Windows 98 includes a new feature called Windows Update that uses the Internet to make certain your copy of Windows 98 is up-to-date. If newer video drivers are available to make your display adapter work a little better, Windows Update can download and install them. Similarly, if a newer modem driver or a security update is available, Windows Update can handle this task, too.

Windows Update may offer several classes of system updates. Critical updates are important fixes that you should download because they may address security issues that could have serious consequences if not corrected. Many of the other types of updates are optional but often are a good idea, especially the items listed as recommended updates. Some of the updates are samples that Microsoft provides to show you a new piece of software, such as a trial version of a new game or one of the desktop themes from the Windows 98 Plus package. It's up to you to decide which of these updates are worth the time it takes to download them.

Continued

TAKE NOTE

YOU MUST REGISTER TO USE WINDOWS UPDATE

Windows Update is free, but you must register your copy of Windows 98 to access the service. When you register your copy of Windows 98, it's likely that Microsoft makes note of the 25-character CD-Key that you were required to enter when you installed Windows 98. If several different people attempt to register copies of Windows 98 that all use the same CD-Key, there's a good chance that the Microsoft user database will recognize that each of them is using the same copy of Windows 98. Because most copies of Windows 98 are licensed for use on a single PC, this is another good reason for buying your own copy of Windows 98 rather than "borrowing" a copy from a friend.

CLOSE APPLICATIONS BEFORE RUNNING WINDOWS UPDATE

After Windows Update downloads a system update, it often must restart your PC to complete the installation process. To protect yourself from data loss and to ensure the updates are properly applied, always close all other applications before you start Windows Update. Be sure to disable antivirus software before running Windows Update, too, because many updates must modify system files, and they won't be able to do so while antivirus software is running.

CROSS-REFERENCE

See "Adding New Hardware" in Chapter 5.

FIND IT ONLINE

See **http://windowsupdate.microsoft.com**.

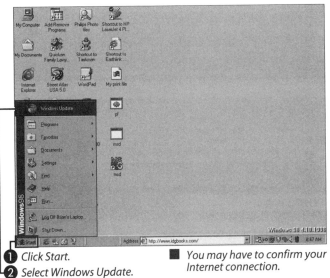

1 Click Start.

2 Select Windows Update.

■ You may have to confirm your Internet connection.

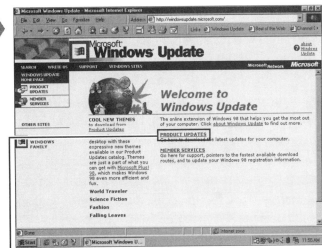

3 Click the Product Updates link to continue.

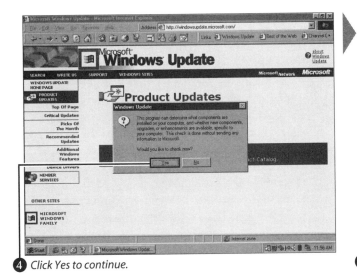

4 Click Yes to continue.

5 Select the updates you wish to download and install.

6 Click Download to continue.

After you've selected the updates you wish to download and install, Windows Update displays a list of your selections so that you can verify the list is correct. In addition, you are given the opportunity to view the instructions for the software that you've selected. It's a good idea to take the opportunity because you may not be able to easily find those instructions later. It may also be a good idea to print a copy of the instructions, especially if you're not completely sure you understand the entire download and update process.

In most cases you won't have to do anything special to install the software updates. After the file has been downloaded it will generally complete the installation process automatically. It's usually necessary to restart your PC after the update has been installed, especially if the update changed critical system files. Most system files cannot be changed while they are in use, so the restart is required before the update will be completed.

After you click the Start Download button you'll see a dialog box that reports on both the download and the installation progress. You don't need to do anything while this dialog box is being displayed. Depending on the size of the updates you selected, the download could take several minutes to several hours, and it's best not to try to do anything else on your PC during this process. If you're downloading a very large update you may want to schedule it for a time when you won't need to use your system. Don't forget, though, that after the download is complete you may need to confirm that it's okay to restart your system. After your PC restarts, the update process will continue for a few minutes while the menus and shortcuts are updated.

TAKE NOTE

▶ CHECK FOR SYSTEM UPDATES OFTEN

It's a good idea to make regular visits to the Windows Update Web site. This will ensure that your PC always has the latest upgrades to Windows 98 and may solve some issues you weren't even aware existed. Because many system updates are actually bug fixes, you could have a problem and not know about it until it's too late.

▶ USE WINDOWS UPDATE WHEN YOU INSTALL HARDWARE

Be sure to visit the Windows Update Web site whenever you install new hardware on your PC. It's very common for manufacturers to release newer versions of the driver software that they include with new hardware, so even though you just purchased a new piece of hardware, a newer version of the software may exist. You may also need to visit the manufacturer's Web site if no updates appear on the Windows Update Web site.

CROSS-REFERENCE

See "Searching for Web Sites" earlier in this chapter.

FIND IT ONLINE

You'll find more downloads at
http://www.microsoft.com/msdownload/.

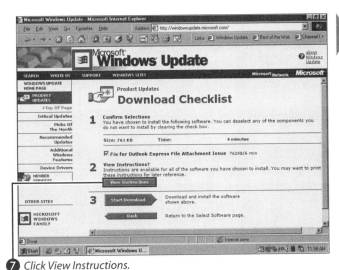

⑦ *Click View Instructions.*

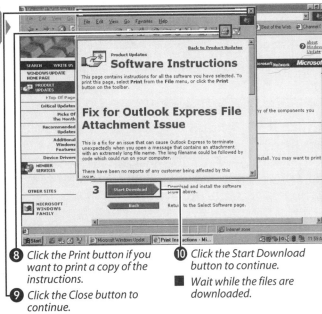

⑧ *Click the Print button if you want to print a copy of the instructions.*

⑨ *Click the Close button to continue.*

⑩ *Click the Start Download button to continue.*

■ *Wait while the files are downloaded.*

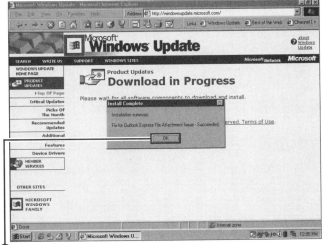

⑪ *Click OK to continue.*

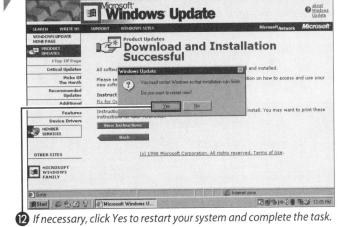

⑫ *If necessary, click Yes to restart your system and complete the task.*

Personal Workbook

Q&A

1 What does underlined text on a Web page usually represent?

_____

_____

2 How can you tell when you are pointing to a link on a Web page?

_____

_____

_____

3 What is a URL?

_____

_____

_____

4 How can you make certain that a search engine looks for two words that are together?

_____

_____

_____

5 What is the term Internet Explorer uses for Web pages you save so that you can easily return to them?

_____

_____

6 What are channels?

_____

_____

_____

7 What must you do before you can use Windows Update?

_____

_____

_____

8 What type of update should you always download and install?

_____

_____

_____

ANSWERS: PAGE 363

EXTRA PRACTICE

1 Visit http://www.idgbooks.com.

2 Search for books about boats.

3 Open the advanced search page in the search engine and see how you can narrow your search for more focused results.

4 Visit the Windows Update Web site and see what updates are available.

5 Subscribe to the Quicken.com Small Business Web site.

6 Save your favorite Web site in your list of favorites.

REAL-WORLD APPLICATIONS

✔ Your neighbor claims that Microsoft founder Bill Gates is the nephew of Howard Hughes. You want to do research on the Internet to find out whether that's true. You use what you've learned in this chapter to find sites that cover your topic.

✔ You're an investor, and you want to learn about news items that may affect the market. You subscribe to a news channel available on the Internet.

✔ You depend on your PC to keep all the records for the flower shop you own and operate. To make certain your PC is always running at its best, you use Windows Update to ensure your system files are up-to-date.

Visual Quiz

How can you display this dialog box? What do you need to do to display the detailed list that is shown? How can you use this dialog box to find out the last time you visited a Web page?

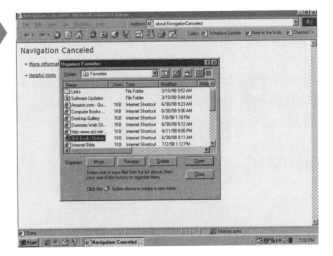

_____

_____

_____

_____

_____

CHAPTER **15**

Using Outlook Express

Outlook Express is a Windows 98 applet that lets you exchange e-mail with other Internet users and join, read, and post messages to Internet newsgroups. This chapter explains these concepts.

Electronic mail, or *e-mail,* is the technology with which Internet users exchange mail messages. These messages can consist of text and files that you attach. You can send messages to individuals or groups; reply to and forward messages; and save messages for later review or delete them when you have read them.

E-mail is known for its convenience. Unlike a telephone call, which requires your immediate attention, your e-mail messages are received and saved by a mail server, a computer provided by your ISP. When you are ready to receive your e-mail, Outlook Express reads all incoming messages from the mail server and moves them into a local inbox in your computer. You can then read, reply to, forward, and file your messages at your convenience.

When you compose messages or reply to messages that you receive, Outlook Express saves them in your outbox until you are ready to send them. If you are connected to the Internet and running Outlook Express, your outbox messages are transmitted right away and incoming messages are placed in your inbox right away.

Newsgroups are gatherings of people on the Internet who discuss topics that interest them. There are thousands of such groups with millions of users. You subscribe to newsgroups and log in to them at your convenience. Newsgroups are organized according to areas of interest, and each group contains so-called threads, which are topical sequences of messages. You can initiate a thread on a newsgroup, and you can add your own messages to the threads.

To use Internet mail, you must have an account with a mail server, which your ISP usually provides. To use Internet news, you must have an account with a news server, which your ISP also usually provides. Be sure to set up these accounts before you begin the exercises in this chapter. Your ISP should be able to provide any necessary information.

Even if you use another e-mail program, use Outlook Express for the exercises.

Creating E-mail Messages

As you learned in the chapter introduction, *e-mail* stands for electronic mail. You can send and receive e-mail messages that include text, pictures, and other attachments. You can reply to messages that you receive, and you can forward your messages to other Internet users. To read and manage e-mail, you must launch Outlook Express, and you must be connected to the Internet so messages can be sent and received.

The left pane of Outlook Express displays a list of folders that contain mail messages. The topmost folder is always your Inbox, which contains messages that Outlook Express has downloaded into your computer from the mail server. The Outbox folder contains messages that you have composed and sent but that Outlook Express has not yet sent to the mail server. The Sent Items folder contains copies of the e-mail messages that Outlook Express has transmitted from the Outbox to the mail server. The Deleted Items folder contains messages that you have deleted from other folders. If you delete messages from the Deleted Items folder, they are gone forever. The Drafts folder is for storing messages that are in progress and that you are not ready to send. The bottom folder is a news server. You will learn what to do with it later in this chapter.

When a folder's name is displayed in a bold font, the folder contains messages that you have not viewed. The number in parentheses specifies how many unviewed messages are in the folder. Outlook Express does not know whether you actually read the messages, only whether you opened them into the message viewer.

TAKE NOTE

► YOU CAN ADD NEW FOLDERS

If you like, you can add message folders of your own in which you can organize e-mail messages. Folders can contain subfolders. To create a new folder, choose the File ⇨ Folder ⇨ New Folder command to open the Create Folder dialog box. Type a name for the new folder. Select where to put the folder from the tree control. If you select Outlook Express, the new folder will be at the highest level in the hierarchy. You can, however, create a hierarchical structure of folders by selecting a folder or a subfolder in which to put the new folder. Click OK.

► MESSAGE FORMATTING MAY NOT TRAVEL WELL

Although Outlook Express enables you to format your message just as you would in a word processor document, it may not always be safe to assume that the message recipient will see the formatting you've applied. Many people use e-mail software that shows only the text of a message without any formatting. If you must include formatting in your message, you may wish to create your message in your favorite word processor and send the message as a file attachment.

CROSS-REFERENCE

See "Sending Files" later in this chapter.

FIND IT ONLINE

For more on Outlook Express, see **http://www.zdnet. com/pcmag/features/e-mail/mail22.html**.

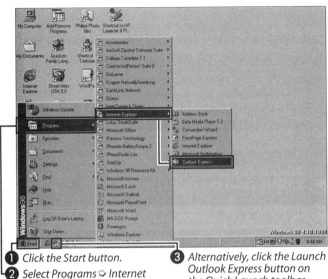

1 Click the Start button.

2 Select Programs ➪ Internet Explorer ➪ Outlook Express.

3 Alternatively, click the Launch Outlook Express button on the Quick Launch toolbar.

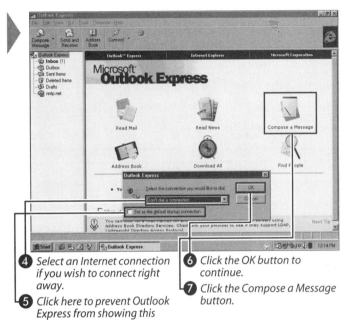

4 Select an Internet connection if you wish to connect right away.

5 Click here to prevent Outlook Express from showing this dialog again.

6 Click the OK button to continue.

7 Click the Compose a Message button.

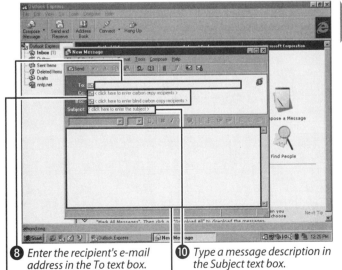

8 Enter the recipient's e-mail address in the To text box.

9 Enter any additional e-mail addresses in the Cc and Bcc text boxes.

10 Type a message description in the Subject text box.

11 Type your message here.

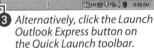

12 Use the format toolbar if you wish to format your message.

■ Remember, some mail recipients won't be able to receive formatting.

13 Click the Send button to complete the task.

■ Depending on your configuration, Outlook Express may send the message immediately or wait.

Sending and Receiving E-mail

E-mail accomplishes its purpose only when it's sent to the recipients and received by them. Outlook Express makes this process a simple one. If Outlook Express is configured to check for e-mail automatically, you may not need to initiate the connection yourself.

To send and receive e-mail Outlook Express must be able to connect to your mail server on the Internet. Usually, this means your PC must have access to a phone line, although in some cases you may make the connection through your network. If you share a telephone line between voice and modem calls, remember that Outlook Express will not be able to access the mail server while you're using your telephone for voice calls. If you're connected to a network, consult with the network administrator before you start sending e-mail. Your administrator may need to make some adjustments to your system, or inform you of things specific to your network setup.

After you've created a new e-mail message and clicked the Send button, Outlook Express moves the message to the Outbox folder. Clicking the Send button may also cause Outlook Express to establish a connection with the mail server. If you'd prefer to hold messages rather than have them sent as soon as you've composed them, select Tools ➪ Options and click the Send tab. Clear the "Send messages immediately" check box and click OK. You'll need to either send your messages manually or wait until the next scheduled connect time. Holding messages in the

Outbox for a few minutes may be a good idea, especially for messages you may wish to reconsider. Once a message has been sent there's no way to retrieve it — there's no "Unsend" button.

TAKE NOTE

BE SURE TO SEND AND RECEIVE

The Tools menu includes a Send and Receive command as well as a Send command. If you choose Tools ➪ Send, you won't receive any new messages that have been sent. To make certain that all messages are sent and received, always use Tools ➪ Send and Receive.

TROUBLESHOOTING MAIL SERVER PROBLEMS

If Outlook Express seems to be having trouble connecting to your mail server reliably, you may need to do a little troubleshooting. If the program can connect sometimes but not other times, you may be experiencing excessive noise on your phone lines. But if you can pick up the telephone handset and not hear a lot of static or other noise, the problem may be in the mail server itself. Some mail servers are slow to realize that a previous connection was terminated, and they may not allow you to reconnect for several minutes following your last connection. You may want to try increasing the time slightly between connection attempts to see whether it solves the problem.

CROSS-REFERENCE
See "Opening and Saving File Attachments" later in this chapter.

FIND IT ONLINE
See http://www.webfoot.com/advice/email.top.html for tips on sending e-mail.

Control the Message Schedule

By default, Outlook Express checks for e-mail every 30 minutes — assuming that Outlook Express is running. You can change this interval or even disable the automatic e-mail checking if you like. Select Tools ⇨ Options to display the Options dialog box. Remove the check from the "Check for new messages every xx minute(s)" check box to disable automatic checking. To change the schedule, leave the check box selected and use the spin box to set the new interval.

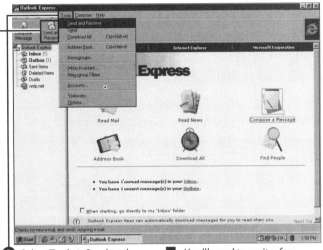

1 *Select Tools ⇨ Send and Receive.*

2 *Alternatively, click the Send and Receive button.*

■ *You'll need to wait a few minutes while Outlook Express connects to the mail server and sends and receives the messages.*

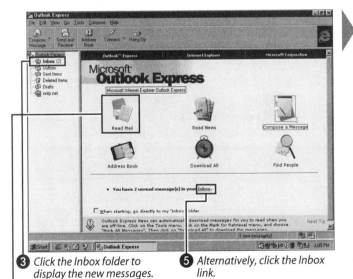

3 *Click the Inbox folder to display the new messages.*

4 *Alternatively, click the Read Mail button.*

5 *Alternatively, click the Inbox link.*

6 *Click a message to read the message.*

■ *You can also double-click a message to open it in a new window.*

7 *Click a column header if you wish to sort the messages by the values in that column.*

Sending Files

I n addition to text messages you can send *file attachments* with your e-mail messages. For example, you may want to send a word processor document file, a spreadsheet file, or a graphics image as part of your message. In each case the attachment can include far more information capability than would be possible in a simple text message.

The figures on the facing page show you how to insert a file attachment into a message. You can send any type of file as an attachment, although if the file is too large your mail server may refuse to send it, or the recipient's mail server may not accept it. Mail systems often limit the size of messages, and many of them reject messages more than 2MB in total size. You may be able to reduce the size of the message by using a program such as WinZip—a shareware program you can find on the Internet—to compress the file before you attach it to the message.

You can send a file attachment without including any message, but it's usually best to include both a descriptive subject line and a brief message. Otherwise, the recipient may not know what type of file you've sent. This is especially true if the recipient receives the attachment as Winmail.dat, as mentioned in the "Take Note" section. Be sure to mention that you've attached a file and include the filename.

CROSS-REFERENCE

See "Creating E-mail Messages" earlier in this chapter.

FIND IT ONLINE

See **http://www.winzip.com** for information about a popular file compression program.

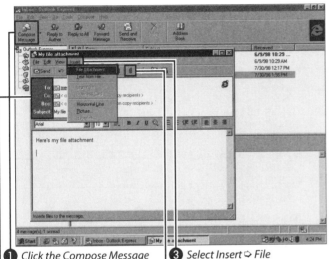

1 Click the Compose Message button.

2 Address the message, add a subject line, and type a brief message.

3 Select Insert ⇨ File Attachment.

4 Alternatively, click the Insert File button.

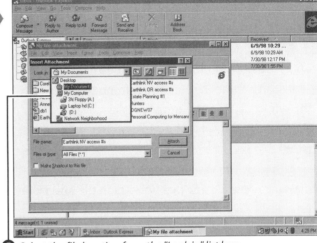

5 Select the file location from the "Look in" list box.

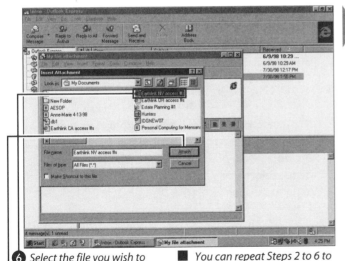

6 Select the file you wish to attach.

7 Click the Attach button to insert the file into the message.

■ You can repeat Steps 2 to 6 to attach additional files.

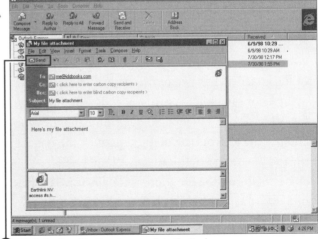

8 Click the Send button to complete the task.

Opening and Saving File Attachments

As the upper-left figure on the facing page shows, Outlook Express uses a small paper clip icon to let you know when e-mail messages include an attachment. This icon appears both in the column to the left of the sender's name and in the message header when the message is displayed in the message preview pane.

Although you can view the text of a message in the message preview pane that appears in the lower portion of the Outlook Express window, you cannot access file attachments without opening the message. When you open a message that includes a file attachment, the message window includes an upper pane for the message text and a lower pane for any file attachments. Each file attachment has its own icon in the file attachment pane.

After you've opened a message that contains file attachments, you can choose what to do with the attachments. The options vary according to the type of file attached, but two options are always available: opening or saving the file. If you choose to open the file, Windows 98 attempts to determine the file type and use the appropriate method to open the file. If the file is a program, this means Windows 98 attempts to run the program. If the file is a data file or a document, Windows 98 tries to open it in the associated application. If you choose to save the file, Windows 98 displays the Save Attachment As dialog box shown in the lower-left figure. Note the location where the file is saved so that you can find it later.

TAKE NOTE

UNDERSTANDING E-MAIL AND VIRUSES

You've probably heard plenty of scary stories about computer viruses. You've probably even received a few messages warning you about so-called e-mail viruses that can affect your PC simply because you open a message. Most of these scares have no basis in fact, and it's extremely unlikely that any e-mail message will do much more than simply waste your time. Computer viruses are actually programs, and just opening an e-mail message won't activate a virus program. File attachments that accompany e-mail messages can be another story. If you run a file attachment that contains a virus, your PC is in danger. The best way to protect yourself against this threat is never to save or open file attachments unless you're certain you can trust the source.

ADD THE SIZE COLUMN TO OUTLOOK EXPRESS

File attachments can greatly increase the amount of space necessary to store messages in your Inbox. To see how much space is being used by your messages, select View ⇨ Columns and add the Size column to the Inbox view.

CROSS-REFERENCE

See "Sending Files" earlier in this chapter.

FIND IT ONLINE

See http://www.idg.net/idg-frames/english/content.cgi?vc=docid_0-71699.html for file attachment tips.

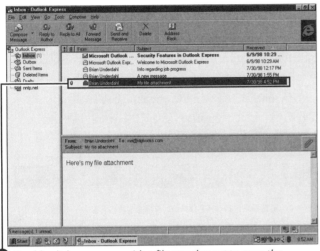

1 *Double-click a message with a file attachment to open the message.*

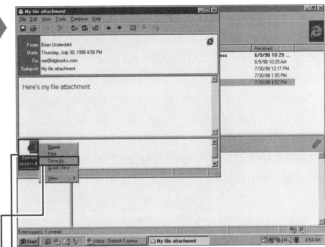

2 *Right-click the attached file to open the shortcut menu.*

3 *Select Save As to display the Save Attachment As dialog box.*

■ *You can also opt to choose one of the other selections on the shortcut menu.*

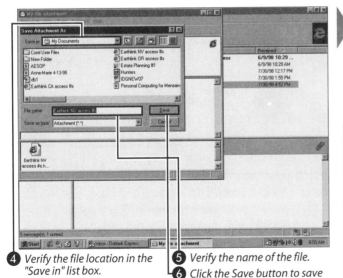

4 *Verify the file location in the "Save in" list box.*

5 *Verify the name of the file.*

6 *Click the Save button to save the file.*

7 *An alternative way to open an attachment is to double-click it.*

8 *Select this check box to require verification for this type of file.*

9 *Select Save it to disk or Open it.*

10 *Click OK to complete the task. If you selected "Save it to disk," you will need to complete the file saving steps.*

Using the Newsreader

If you've used Internet Explorer to explore the Internet (see Chapter 14), you've probably seen one part of the Internet: the Web. Outlook Express includes a tool that you can use to explore another part of the Internet: Usenet newsgroups. These newsgroups are giant discussion groups in which people from all around the world come together to discuss, argue, and dissect all manner of topics.

Newsgroups can provide fascinating glimpses at the broadest range of personalities you may possibly imagine. You may find true experts who are willing to share insight and information you cannot find elsewhere. But you're also likely to run into many characters dispensing incredibly bogus stories and negativity. In other words, newsgroups can be useful and fun, but you need to take what you find there with a large grain of salt.

The first time you open the Outlook Express newsreader you'll need to download the list of newsgroups that are available on your news server. You need do this only once; in the future, Outlook Express will download only new newsgroup names. Depending on your news server, this initial list may have tens of thousands of entries and will take several minutes if you connect to the Internet using a modem.

After you've downloaded the list of newsgroups, you can view the messages in a newsgroup by double-clicking the newsgroup name or by selecting the newsgroup and clicking the Go To button. To view a different newsgroup, click the "News groups" button that appears on the Outlook Express toolbar whenever the news server folder is open. View a message by double-clicking the message. Usually, messages that have responses show the responses as folders under the original message.

TAKE NOTE

▶ IGNORE OFF-TOPIC MESSAGES

As you browse through the available newsgroups you'll soon notice that most newsgroups contain a large number of messages unrelated to the newsgroup topic. Many of these off-topic messages fall into two categories: get-rich-quick schemes and advertisements for pornographic Web sites. Unfortunately, there isn't much you can do to avoid seeing these types of messages. As a rule, the best defense is to simply ignore them. The worst thing you can do is to respond. After the message originator has your e-mail address you're likely to be buried in unwanted junk e-mail.

▶ SUBSCRIBING TO NEWSGROUPS

If you like, you have the option to *subscribe* to newsgroups. Subscribing to a newsgroup isn't the same as subscribing to a magazine; you don't pay for a subscription, and you aren't obligated to participate. Subscribing to a newsgroup simply tells Outlook Express that you want the newsgroup to appear in the folder list and that you always want the latest messages from that newsgroup available.

CROSS-REFERENCE
See "Finding Newsgroups" later in this chapter.

SHORTCUT
To find the latest newsgroups fast, click the New tab.

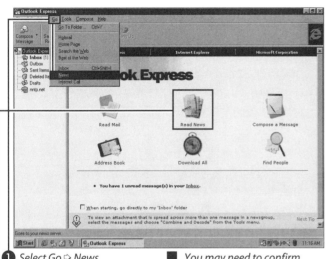

❶ Select Go ➪ News.

❷ Alternatively, click the Read News button.

■ You may need to confirm whether you'd like to designate Outlook Express as your default newsreader.

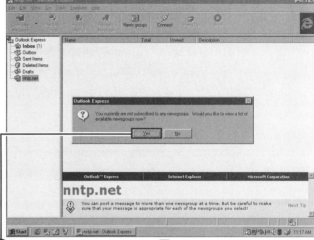

❸ Click the Yes button to view the list of newsgroups.

■ If you've subscribed to any newsgroups you'll need to click the "News groups" button to view the entire list.

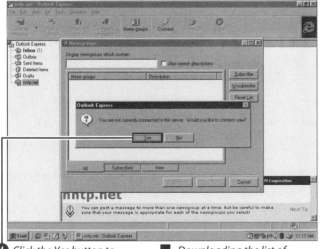

❹ Click the Yes button to connect to the server and download the list of newsgroups.

■ Downloading the list of newsgroups will take several minutes the first time you access the news server.

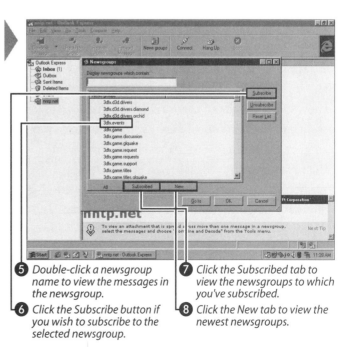

❺ Double-click a newsgroup name to view the messages in the newsgroup.

❻ Click the Subscribe button if you wish to subscribe to the selected newsgroup.

❼ Click the Subscribed tab to view the newsgroups to which you've subscribed.

❽ Click the New tab to view the newest newsgroups.

Finding Newsgroups

What's worse than trying to find a needle in a haystack? How about trying to find newsgroups that deal with a subject that interests you? Depending on your news server, the list of available newsgroups may contain 60,000 to 100,000 newsgroups. Just looking at all the newsgroup names would take you days. By the time you finished your search you'd be so confused you probably wouldn't remember more than a small fraction of the interesting-looking newsgroups.

Outlook Express enables you to look for specific words in newsgroup names. If you want to search for newsgroups that include the term *jobs* in their title, Outlook Express will whittle down the list so that you may have only a few hundred newsgroups to search rather than thousands.

Even after you narrow the list of newsgroups by entering a search phrase, you can make your search still more precise. The figures on the facing page show two methods of narrowing the search. As shown in the first three figures, you can search for a single term, subscribe to the resulting groups, and then search for the second term within the subscribed groups. The lower-right figure shows another alternative: Specify more than one term in a single search by separating the terms with spaces. All the terms must be found in each newsgroup name that qualifies.

TAKE NOTE

USE THE RIGHT TOOL FOR THE JOB

The Outlook Express newsreader is handy if you are a casual newsgroup browser, but if you want to find interesting and important items in the newsgroups, Outlook Express may not be the right tool for the job. Outlook Express finds newsgroup names, but suppose you don't know where to begin looking? By some estimates there are more than 200,000 items posted to newsgroups daily. Can you imagine trying to figure out which of those postings might cover a topic of interest to you? If it sounds as if finding the right newsgroup articles is almost impossible, don't worry — there is a solution.

TechSmith Corporation has a program on its Web site that you can download and try for free. Called NewsMonger, this program does the work for you by searching newsgroup posts automatically and informing you when the topics you specify appear in a message posted to a newsgroup. NewsMonger does far more than simply look at the newsgroup names; it looks inside all the messages to find what you want.

CONSIDER ALTERNATIVES

If you don't find newsgroups that seem to cover topics of interest, consider alternative ways of specifying the topic. For example, you may find topics relating to radio stations under radio, stations, broadcasting, FM, AM, or any of a number of additional titles.

SHORTCUT

To fine-tune your searches, use as few characters in the search phrase as possible.

FIND IT ONLINE

See http://www.techsmith.com/ for more information about NewsMonger.

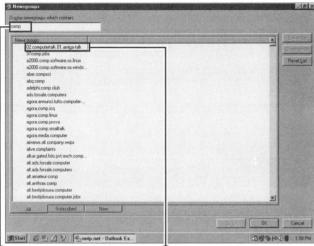

1 Enter the first search phrase in the text box.

2 Click the first newsgroup in the list.

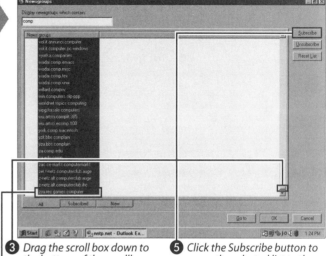

3 Drag the scroll box down to the bottom of the scrollbar.

4 Press and hold Shift as you click the last listed newsgroup.

5 Click the Subscribe button to move the selected list to the Subscribed tab.

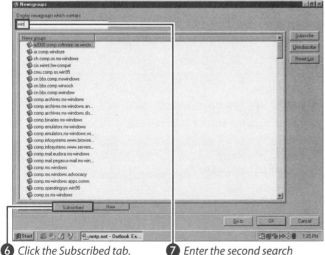

6 Click the Subscribed tab.

7 Enter the second search phrase in the text box to further narrow the list.

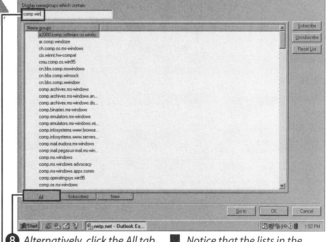

8 Alternatively, click the All tab to begin a new search using both phrases at once.

9 Enter both search phrases in the text box separated by spaces.

■ Notice that the lists in the lower-left and lower-right figures show the same results.

Personal Workbook

Q&A

1 What is the meaning of the number in parentheses following an Outlook Express folder name?

_____

_____

2 Why do folder names sometimes appear in boldface?

_____

_____

_____

3 Where do messages you've created reside until they're sent to the mail server?

_____

_____

_____

4 What do you call files that you send along with an e-mail message?

_____

_____

5 What do you need to do before you can save a file that came along with an e-mail message?

_____

_____

6 What can you do to make certain you see the latest messages in a particular newsgroup?

_____

_____

_____

7 How can you find newsgroups that pertain to a specific subject?

_____

_____

_____

8 What must Outlook Express connect to in order to send and receive e-mail?

_____

_____

ANSWERS: PAGE 364

EXTRA PRACTICE

1 Create and send an e-mail message to a friend.

2 Attach several files to a message.

3 Open a file attachment.

4 Change the Outlook Express e-mail schedule to check for mail every 15 minutes.

5 Locate newsgroups that discuss computers and jobs.

6 Subscribe to a newsgroup that relates to your favorite hobby.

7 Create a new folder to store messages from family members.

REAL-WORLD APPLICATIONS

✔ You and five of your cousins are organizing a family reunion. Your cousins live in four different states, and the other extended family members live in ten states and two foreign countries. To save time and money, you use e-mail to communicate about the reunion.

✔ You want to find out about a tourist spot halfway around the world. You send an e-mail message to a local tourist authority to find out about events scheduled during the time you're thinking of visiting.

✔ You want to boost the power of the three-year-old PC you're passing down to your niece, but you're having trouble working with the motherboard you bought locally. You search the Internet for newsgroups where you can find experienced users who can help you.

Visual Quiz

How can you display this dialog box? If you want to place your outbound messages in the Outbox rather than sending them as soon as you've created them, what setting do you need to adjust?

_____

_____

_____

_____

_____

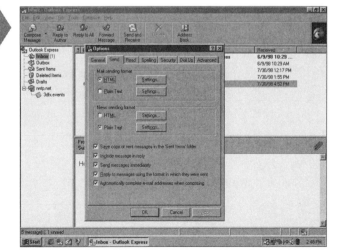

CHAPTER 16

MASTER THESE SKILLS

Using Networks and Mobile Computing

A local network consists of computers that are connected so that they can share resources: files, CD-ROM drives, printers, faxes, and e-mail. Windows 98 incorporates several layers of network support. You can connect Windows 98 machines to one another and to machines running Windows for Workgroups, Windows 95, Windows NT, and Novell NetWare. This chapter explains how to use Windows 98 in a network in which all the machines run Windows 98.

This chapter also introduces you to using dial-up networking to access your network remotely. You can connect to your network through your laptop computer's modem and access network resources as if you were in your office. Even if your home office consists of a single, stand-alone computer, you can still use the dial-up networking features to access your system remotely. You don't need a real network that connects several computers.

You should make certain your network is properly installed and functioning. Windows 98 has all the basic networking software you need, so installation is primarily a matter of installing the proper network adapters and cabling. Many types of network hardware are available, so make certain your network vendor understands your needs. Your network package should include all the adapters, cables, connectors, and so on that you need. Follow the installation instructions precisely, and don't be afraid to ask the vendor if something is unclear. Installing the network isn't difficult, but it must be done correctly.

If you have more than one computer but don't yet have a network, you'll probably want to browse through this chapter. Seeing the examples may make it easier for you to determine whether a network would offer you enough benefits to make it worthwhile.

Installing a network makes several changes on your Windows 98–based PC. These changes enable you to find other computers on the network, share files and printers, and log on to the network. If you haven't installed a network, some of the things you'll see in this chapter won't exist or won't work in quite the same way. For example, the Network Neighborhood icon won't appear on your desktop, and you won't see Sharing in the Windows Explorer shortcut menus until you install a network.

Finding Computers on Your Network

If you want to use any of the resources on your network, a good place to start is by knowing how to find the computers that are on the network. In this section you'll learn how to find out which computers are available on the network.

After you install a network, a new icon — Network Neighborhood — appears on your desktop and in the Windows Explorer folder tree. This new icon enables you to browse the shared resources on the network. *Shared* resources are files, folders, drives, or printers that have been made available for use on the network. As discussed later in this chapter, resources must be shared explicitly before they'll appear on the network. If no one is willing to share anything that is a part of his or her computer, no resources will be available. You'll probably still be able to see the computers in the Network Neighborhood, but you won't be able to see any of the files or folders on those computers.

Windows 98 displays the Network Neighborhood as a folder, just as it displays My Computer as a folder. Each computer on the network, including your own, appears as a folder in the Network Neighborhood folder. You can open those folders just as you'd open folders on your own computer, but the only things you'll see are the shared files and folders.

If you find it a little difficult to use the folder view that's displayed when you open the Network Neighborhood icon on your desktop, open Windows Explorer instead. When you open the Network Neighborhood folder in Windows Explorer, you'll see the more intuitive folder tree view.

TAKE NOTE

▶ UNDERSTANDING WORKGROUPS

Depending on the size of the network and the structure of the organization, you may have several workgroups. A *workgroup* is a set of computers configured to work together. Workgroups are typically organized along functional lines within a company — accounting, marketing, shipping and receiving, management, and so on. Each workgroup shares resources common to the functional entity that the workgroup supports. The network shares resources common to everyone.

▶ TROUBLESHOOTING NETWORK NEIGHBORHOOD

One of the most frustrating Windows 98 networking problems is usually also fairly easy to correct. If you can't see any computers in Network Neighborhood or if the other computers can't see your system, the most common cause is that the NetBEUI protocol is not installed. Double-click the Network icon in Control Panel and look for NetBEUI on the Configuration tab. If this protocol is missing on any of the network's computers, click the Add button and install NetBEUI. After you restart your system, the problem will probably disappear. If not, you may need to ask your network vendor for assistance.

CROSS-REFERENCE

See "Sharing Your Files" later in this chapter.

FIND IT ONLINE

See **http://ourworld.compuserve.com/homepages/ j_helmig/faq.htm** for more on Win98 networking.

1 *Double-click Network Neighborhood on your desktop to open the Network Neighborhood folder.*

■ *You can also access Network Neighborhood through Windows Explorer by clicking the Network Neighborhood folder in the Windows Explorer folder tree.*

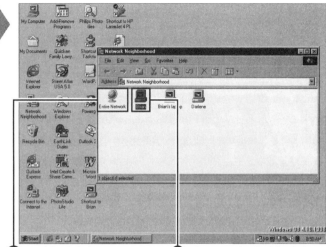

2 *Double-click the Entire Network icon to view the workgroups on the network.*

3 *Alternatively, double-click a computer icon to view the shared resources on that computer.*

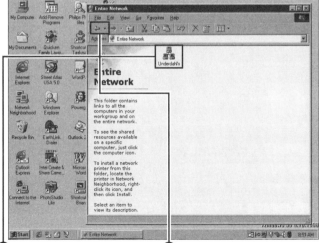

4 *Double-click a workgroup icon to view the computers in the workgroup.*

5 *Alternatively, click Back to return to the previous folder.*

6 *Double-click a computer icon to view the shared resources on that computer.*

7 *Click the Close button to close Network Neighborhood and complete the task.*

Sharing Your Files

Some people have a hard time working on a computer network, because if no one wants to share, there isn't anything available for use on the network. *Sharing* is the process of allowing other people access to files, folders, and printers. Initially, nothing on the network is shared — you must initiate sharing explicitly for each resource that you want to be available on the network.

Windows 98 file sharing is done at the folder level. If you want to share a set of files you do so by sharing the folder containing those files. Windows 98 itself has no file-level sharing controls, but the application programs you use to create your document files generally enable you to specify passwords to control access from within the program. Depending on your security needs, this procedure may be all you need, but see the "Take Note" section for more information about Windows 98 security and sharing.

As the figures on the facing page show, several access settings are available for you to use. You can allow *read-only* access so that visitors can open or copy a file but cannot delete, modify, or create a file. *Full* access allows a visitor to do anything that you can do. You can specify passwords that enable either read-only or full access.

Users who access your network through a dial-up server have the same access rights as users who are connected locally. If you're concerned about the resources that people can access through your network, make certain you fully understand what you are sharing.

TAKE NOTE

▶ ADDRESSING NETWORK SECURITY CONCERNS

If all the computers on your network are running Windows 98 or Windows 95, your network may not be as secure as you might like. On a Windows 9x–based network you can specify passwords that enable access to shared folders, but you cannot restrict access to specific users. Everyone who knows the access passwords has the same level of access. If you need more control over which users can access network resources, you'll need at least one Windows NT–based (or Novell NetWare) server on the network. A Windows 98 PC on a Windows NT network can take advantage of the stricter security measures available on the Windows NT system.

▶ BE CAREFUL WHAT YOU SHARE

When you share a drive or a folder, everything contained in it is also shared. You cannot restrict access to a folder on a shared drive or to a folder contained within a shared folder. So, for example, if your \My Documents folder contains a folder named Resume and you share \My Documents, anyone on the network can access \My Documents\Resume. If you need to keep certain folders private, be sure they are not contained in shared drives or folders.

CROSS-REFERENCE

See "Running Dial-Up Server" later in this chapter.

FIND IT ONLINE

For more on network security, check the links at http://www.testra.com.au/info/security.html.

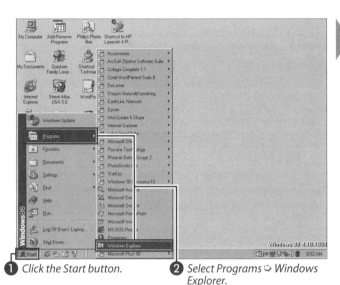

1 Click the Start button.

2 Select Programs ➪ Windows Explorer.

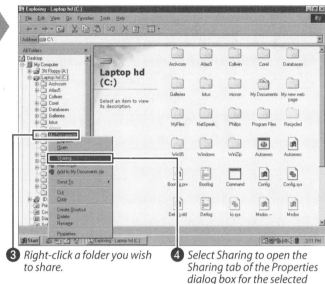

3 Right-click a folder you wish to share.

4 Select Sharing to open the Sharing tab of the Properties dialog box for the selected folder.

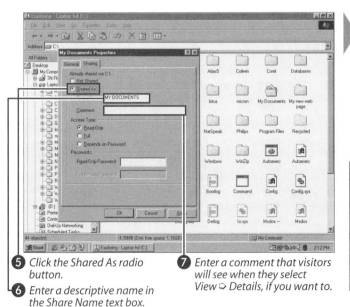

5 Click the Shared As radio button.

6 Enter a descriptive name in the Share Name text box.

7 Enter a comment that visitors will see when they select View ➪ Details, if you want to.

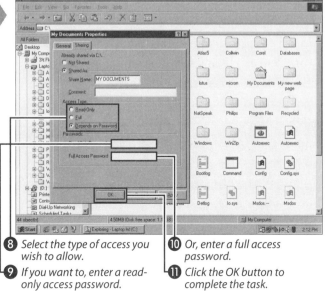

8 Select the type of access you wish to allow.

9 If you want to, enter a read-only access password.

10 Or, enter a full access password.

11 Click the OK button to complete the task.

Finding Files on Your Network

Files are of no use if you can't find them. Having a network doesn't mean that finding files will be any easier. In fact, although you use almost the same techniques to locate files on your network as you do to find files on your stand-alone PC, there are a few tricks to finding what you need on a network.

One of the differences you may encounter on a network is that computers may come and go without warning. A computer may not always be available, either because someone turned it off or because it was physically removed from the network connection. Even if the computer remains available on the network, the files it contains may not always be accessible. The owner may decide to stop sharing a folder or may delete a file that you expected to access.

Before you can search for files on the network, Windows 98 must open Network Neighborhood to find out which computers are available on the network. You can then select the computer you wish to search, as the lower-left figure on the facing page shows. You cannot do a general search that includes all the computers on the network in one step, but, unless your network is very large, you should be able to locate the files quickly in a few steps.

Just as when you're searching your PC, you can narrow the search by specifying the starting folder rather than searching the entire drive. This is often a good idea because it reduces network traffic and speeds the search.

TAKE NOTE

UNDERSTANDING NETWORK COMPUTER NAMES

Windows 98 needs a means of identifying the computers on a network so it can specify the exact location of files on the network. On your computer Windows 98 uses the drive letter, a colon, and a backslash to identify the drive where files can be found. This approach isn't practical on the network because there would be no way to discern whether C:\ referred to drive C on your local PC or to drive C on one of the other computers on the network. To remedy this problem, Windows 98 uses *Universal Naming Conventions* (UNC) to designate computers that are on the network. For example, if a computer is named Brian, on the network that computer would be referred to as \\Brian.

NETWORK CONNECTIONS REMAIN OPEN

If you open a shared network folder during a session, you don't need to browse the Network Neighborhood to access that folder during the same session. The folder will remain visible in the "Look in" list box. After you restart your system, it is necessary to again browse Network Neighborhood to verify the folder is still available.

CROSS-REFERENCE

See "Finding Computers on Your Network" earlier in this chapter.

FIND IT ONLINE

More Windows 98 tips can be found at
http://www.chami.com/tips/.

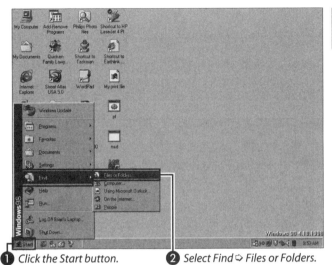

1 Click the Start button.

2 Select Find ➪ Files or Folders.

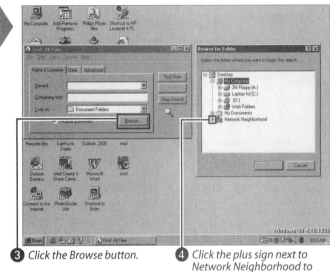

3 Click the Browse button.

4 Click the plus sign next to Network Neighborhood to view the computers on the network.

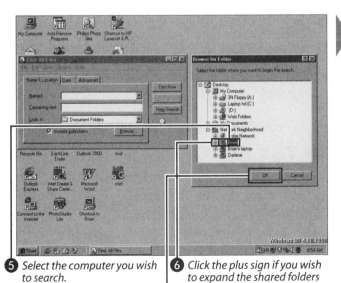

5 Select the computer you wish to search.

6 Click the plus sign if you wish to expand the shared folders tree so you can select a specific folder to narrow the search.

7 Click OK to continue.

8 Enter the name of the file you'd like to find.

■ You can also enter any additional search conditions as necessary.

9 Click the Find Now button to complete the task.

Sharing a Printer

For many people, sharing a printer is at least as important a reason to have a network as is the capability to easily share files. Although few of us would argue with the convenience of having a printer connected directly to our PC, it's also hard to ignore the advantages of sharing printers on a network. For example, if several people are sharing a printer, it's much easier to justify the expense of a premium printer that has additional capabilities.

There are two sides to sharing a printer on your network. The PC that connects directly to the printer must make the printer available for sharing, and the other computers must connect to the shared printer. Each computer that will use the printer must have the correct drivers. Be sure to first install the printer on the computer it is connected to and then share the printer before you attempt to install it on the other computers. Otherwise, you may see error messages when the printer cannot be found on the network.

The first three figures on the facing page show how to share your printer with others on your network. The lower-right figure shows how to connect to a shared printer on the network. As the lower-right figure shows, connecting to a shared printer is no more difficult than selecting which port a printer might use to connect directly to your PC. The Sharing tab appears only if you've told Windows 98 that the printer is connected directly to your PC, because only the printer's owner can control sharing.

TAKE NOTE

SHARE PRINTERS TO SPARE PORTS

Although it is possible to add more than one printer to a single PC by adding an additional parallel printer port, it isn't always the easiest thing to do. In addition to requiring an open expansion slot in the PC, adding a printer port may cause conflicts with system resources such as IRQs. One way to eliminate these types of problems is to share printers that are connected to separate PCs on the network. In that way, you won't have to add anything extra, and you won't have to worry about creating extra conflicts.

NAMING NETWORK COMPUTERS AND PRINTERS

When you connect to a network printer, you select the printer port by choosing the computer name and shared printer name, as shown in the lower-right figure on the facing page. If you are sharing several printers on your network, it helps if both the computer names and the shared printer names are descriptive enough so that users can easily determine the correct names. If you have more than one shared printer of similar types, be sure the names are different enough to prevent confusion.

CROSS-REFERENCE

See "Adding New Hardware" in Chapter 5.

SHORTCUT

Select Properties from the shortcut menu to configure a network printer.

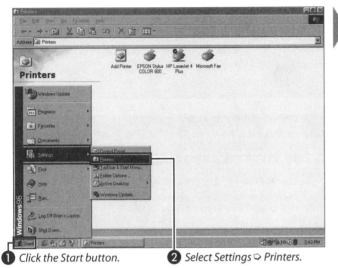

❶ *Click the Start button.*

❷ *Select Settings ➪ Printers.*

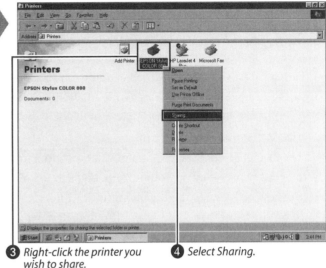

❸ *Right-click the printer you wish to share.*

❹ *Select Sharing.*

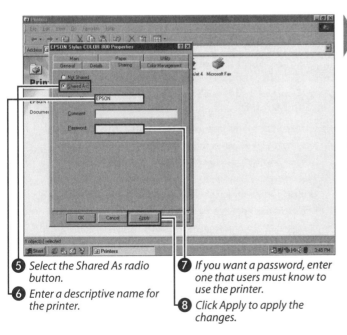

❺ *Select the Shared As radio button.*

❻ *Enter a descriptive name for the printer.*

❼ *If you want a password, enter one that users must know to use the printer.*

❽ *Click Apply to apply the changes.*

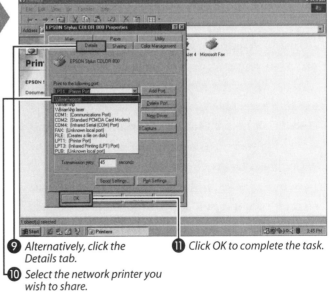

❾ *Alternatively, click the Details tab.*

❿ *Select the network printer you wish to share.*

⓫ *Click OK to complete the task.*

Running Dial-Up Server

You don't have to be in your office to connect to your network. Windows 98 includes an optional component, called Dial-Up Server, which enables you to set up a PC as a gateway to your network. Dial-Up Server doesn't require that you have a network—it works on a stand-alone PC, too.

Because Dial-Up Server is an optional component, it may not be installed on your system. You can install it if necessary by selecting the Communications category on the Windows Setup tab of the Add/Remove Programs dialog box. You'll need to do this if the Connections menu in Dial-Up Networking doesn't include the Dial-Up Server option as shown in the upper-right figure on the facing page.

After you enable caller access in Dial-Up Server, anyone with the correct password can call in and access your system until you specifically disable caller access. To determine when an outside user is connected to your system, you monitor the Status box on the Dial-Up Server window. If necessary, you can instantly disconnect a caller by clicking the Disconnect User button. Unless you want your system to always be available for dial-up access, be sure to disable caller access when it is no longer needed.

In most cases you should not have to modify the server type settings. If a user simply cannot connect, you may need to experiment with these settings. The one that is most likely to cause problems is the

"Require encrypted password" setting. If Dial-Up Server disconnects callers as soon as they enter a password, deselect this option.

TAKE NOTE

▶ BE SURE TO USE AN ACCESS PASSWORD

Anyone who connects to your PC through Dial-Up Server has the same access rights as all other users on your network. If you don't set an access password, anyone can dial in to your system and access all shared resources just as if they were physically connected to your network. If you allow full access to shared folders, dial-up users can create, delete, modify, or rename any of the files or folders in those shared folders. So if you've shared your entire hard disk, dial-up users will essentially have complete control of your PC. To make sure that the dial-up password cannot be easily guessed, include both numbers and letters in the password.

▶ USE DIAL-UP NETWORKING TO CONNECT

The easiest way to connect to a Dial-Up Server is to click the New Connection icon in the Dial-Up Networking folder. Follow through the Make New Connection dialog boxes, entering the correct phone number for your Dial-Up Server. After you've completed setting up your new connection, you may want to create a shortcut to the connection on your desktop so that you can dial in easily.

CROSS-REFERENCE
Don't forget that Dial-Up Server remains active whenever caller access is enabled.

FIND IT ONLINE
Download Windows 98 networking software at **www.microsoft.com/windows/downloads/ default.asp.**

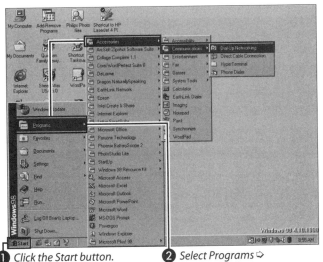

❶ *Click the Start button.*

❷ *Select Programs ➪ Accessories ➪ Communications ➪ Dial-Up Networking.*

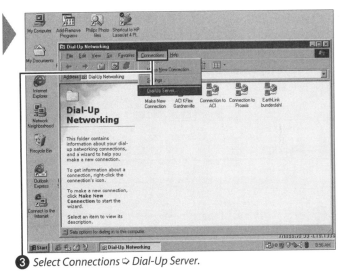

❸ *Select Connections ➪ Dial-Up Server.*

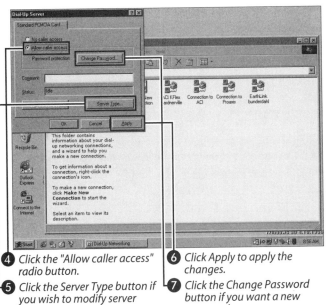

❹ *Click the "Allow caller access" radio button.*

❺ *Click the Server Type button if you wish to modify server settings.*

❻ *Click Apply to apply the changes.*

❼ *Click the Change Password button if you want a new password.*

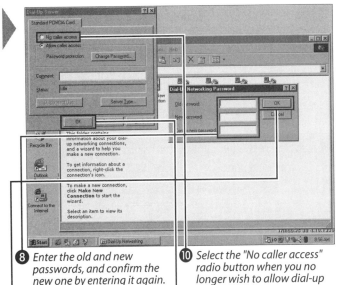

❽ *Enter the old and new passwords, and confirm the new one by entering it again.*

❾ *Click OK to continue.*

❿ *Select the "No caller access" radio button when you no longer wish to allow dial-up access.*

⓫ *Click OK to complete the task.*

Personal Workbook

Q&A

1 What is the most important thing people must do to make files available on a network?

_____

_____

_____

2 How can you tell that you're seeing the name of a computer that is on the network?

_____

_____

3 What icon do you use to find other workgroups on the network?

_____

_____

4 What are the two types of access you can allow to a folder on a Windows 98 network?

_____

_____

_____

5 How many passwords can you use to control access on a Windows 98 network?

_____

_____

6 When you're trying to find a file, how much of the network can you search at any one time?

_____

_____

_____

7 What happens to folders that are contained in a folder you share on the network?

_____

_____

_____

8 Who has control over whether folders and printers are shared on the network?

_____

_____

_____

ANSWERS: 365

EXTRA PRACTICE

1 Open Network Neighborhood and determine how many computers you can find on the network.

2 Look in your Printers folder and see which printers are shared on the network.

3 Find all the files with a DOC extension that are available in one of the shared folders on your network.

4 Open Dial-Up Server and enable dial-up access.

5 Change the dial-up password and watch the status monitor while someone dials in to your system.

6 Figure out a method of allowing access to some of your document files without making all the files available on the network.

REAL-WORLD APPLICATIONS

✔ You run a small insurance office where various people handle client files. To help everyone work more efficiently together, you analyze the workflow and determine that it's a good idea to network your computers.

✔ One of the printers you use in your five-person office is on its last legs. You really need a color laser printer but can't justify the expense. You discover that sharing the new printer on your network would make the cost more reasonable.

✔ You're about to order a newer, faster computer, and you wonder what to do with your old machine, which contains thousands of files you still want to use. You network your new and old systems rather than copy all the files to the new system, giving you a backup system in the event of problems with the new computer.

Visual Quiz

How can you display a dialog box such as this one? Why does it show three computers but no Entire Network icon?

_____

_____

_____

_____

_____

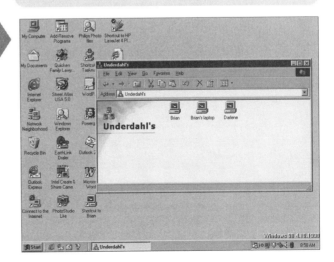

CHAPTER **17**

Using HyperTerminal

You can connect two computers with a local area network or the Internet. This chapter describes how to use HyperTerminal to connect to another computer, exchange files, and even keep a printed log of your online session.

HyperTerminal is a *terminal* program— meaning a program that you use for general communications between computers. Essentially, HyperTerminal turns your PC into a computer terminal.

Chapter 14 showed how to use Internet Explorer to connect to the Internet and communicate with other computers on the Internet. Internet Explorer is a specialized program that interprets and displays HTML documents, usually Web pages. Unless you set up your computer as a Web server, no one would be able to use Internet Explorer to connect and communicate directly with your system. For that, you need a more general communications program such as HyperTerminal.

HyperTerminal displays the text it receives from another computer without attempting to interpret the text, which makes HyperTerminal

a poor choice for displaying Web pages, but perfect for communicating directly between two PCs. In fact, if you wish to transfer files between two PCs, you'll appreciate another of HyperTerminal's benefits: HyperTerminal can transfer files much faster than the Internet.

Anything you send across the Internet travels through many different computers along its way. If you're concerned about privacy and security, you probably realize messages and files that travel through so many different computers are easy prey for snoops. If you use HyperTerminal and connect directly to another computer, you eliminate this potential problem.

Aside from security issues, using HyperTerminal to communicate directly from PC to PC is fun. Unlike browsing the Web, an online session with HyperTerminal is highly interactive. What you type appears on both computer screens, and you interact with the person or computer at the other end of the connection. Things happen almost immediately without any of the long delays you've become used to when you're browsing the Internet.

Opening a New HyperTerminal Connection

Because HyperTerminal is intended for communications directly between two computers, you create *connections*— groups of settings specific to a single computer—when you use HyperTerminal. After you've created a connection for a specific computer, you simply click the icon for that connection to start a new session with the remote computer. HyperTerminal includes several sample connections you can try, but you may not find the samples useful unless you have an account with the specific online service named in the connection. If you have an account with one of these services, you may not want to use the samples because they are set up to dial an 800 number.

The figures on the facing page show the process of setting up a new HyperTerminal connection. As the lower-right figure shows, HyperTerminal assumes that you want to connect immediately when you have completed the setup. This may be OK if you're dialing in to a computer that is waiting for your call, but if you need to make arrangements with another computer user to set up the receiving system to answer, do so before you click the Dial button.

If you need to do anything special to dial an outside line, to dial a long distance call, or to disable call waiting, click the Dialing Properties button shown in the lower-right figure. You can also use the Dialing Properties dialog box to specify that a call be dialed as a long distance call even if it is in your area code. If you are traveling and need to use a calling card to place a long distance call, you also have the option to specify the calling card information. The settings you select also apply to calls you make when using other communications programs such as Internet Explorer.

TAKE NOTE

COPYING THE CONNECTION ICON TO YOUR DESKTOP

After you've created and tested your HyperTerminal connection, create a copy of the connection icon on your desktop for easier access. Point to the connection icon in the HyperTerminal folder, hold down the right mouse button, drag the icon onto your desktop, and select Create Shortcut(s) Here.

TROUBLESHOOTING A HYPERTERMINAL CONNECTION

Although the default HyperTerminal connection settings should work in most cases, you may encounter a few problems. If you don't see anything you type, if everything appears on one line, if the lines are double-spaced, or if all you see is garbage, select File ➪ Properties and then click the ASCII Setup button on the Settings tab. The seven options on the ASCII Setup dialog box can solve many problems. Use the question mark help button to view pop-up help on these options.

CROSS-REFERENCE
See "Capturing a Session Record" later in this chapter.

FIND IT ONLINE
See **http://www.hilgraeve.com** for information on upgrading HyperTerminal.

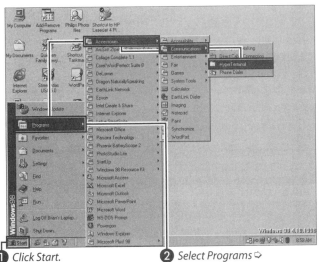

1 Click Start.

2 Select Programs ➪
Accessories ➪
Communications ➪
HyperTerminal.

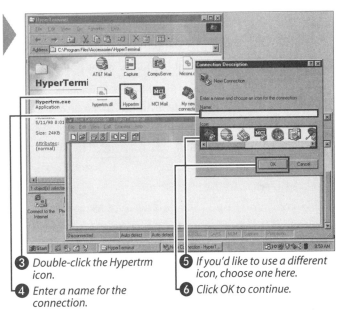

3 Double-click the Hypertrm
icon.

4 Enter a name for the
connection.

5 If you'd like to use a different
icon, choose one here.

6 Click OK to continue.

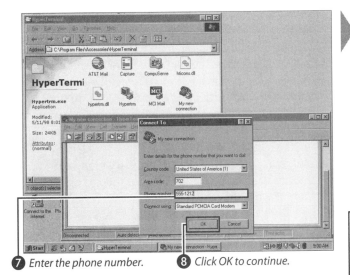

7 Enter the phone number.

8 Click OK to continue.

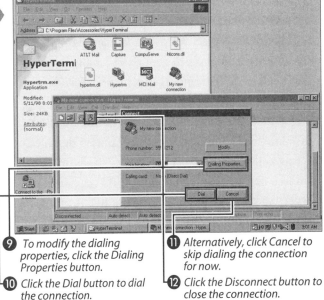

9 To modify the dialing
properties, click the Dialing
Properties button.

10 Click the Dial button to dial
the connection.

11 Alternatively, click Cancel to
skip dialing the connection
for now.

12 Click the Disconnect button to
close the connection.

Answering a Call with HyperTerminal

Making a call with HyperTerminal is similar to making a regular phone call in that someone must place a call and someone else must answer. If you wish to communicate with another PC user who is also using HyperTerminal, one of you must place the call and the other must answer. The version of HyperTerminal that comes with Windows 98 makes this easy to do.

There is one important difference between connecting to another PC and connecting to a computer configured as a dial-in host. Unless you make a change in the HyperTerminal connection configuration, you won't be able to see anything you type when you connect to another PC. The reason is that the remote PC won't "echo" your characters back to you. The two upper figures on the facing page show you how to correct the problem by making your PC display the characters you type. You simply make certain that the "Echo typed characters locally" check box is selected. This option should be checked on both PCs.

You may also need to select the "Send line ends with line feeds" check box or the "Append line feeds to line ends" check box. These two settings are used to force new lines of text to appear on new lines (wrap) instead of overwriting the same line. In most cases, you either make both of these settings on just one of the PCs or make one of the settings — the same one in each case — on and the other one off on both PCs.

TAKE NOTE

AVOID CONFLICTS WITH OTHER SOFTWARE

If you set up HyperTerminal to answer incoming calls, you should first disable other software that may attempt to answer calls. For example, if you use fax software to receive incoming faxes, you can create a conflict if both HyperTerminal and the fax software are configured for answering. To avoid this, make certain that the fax software is disabled before you tell HyperTerminal to wait for calls.

SWITCHING FROM VOICE TO MODEM

If you use a single phone line for both voice and modem calls, you may be able to switch from a voice call to a modem call by typing the proper commands in the HyperTerminal window. Not all modems recognize the complete set of available modem commands, but if you want to give switching from a voice to a modem call a try, enter **ATO** on one PC and **ATA** on the other while your voice call is still connected. If the modems connect, hang up the receivers and proceed with your modem call. If the modems don't connect, you'll probably have to hang up and let one of the modems make the call while the other is placed in wait mode.

CROSS-REFERENCE

See "Opening a New HyperTerminal Connection" earlier in this chapter.

FIND IT ONLINE

See **http://www.hilgraeve.com/hawin32. html#download** for a trial version of HyperACCESS.

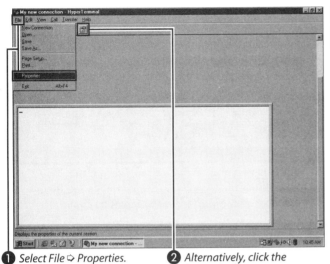

① *Select File ▷ Properties.*

② *Alternatively, click the Properties button.*

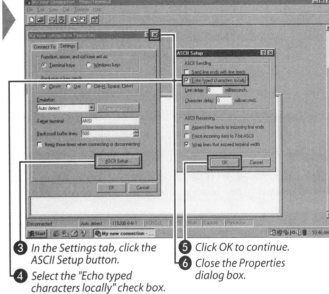

③ *In the Settings tab, click the ASCII Setup button.*

④ *Select the "Echo typed characters locally" check box.*

⑤ *Click OK to continue.*

⑥ *Close the Properties dialog box.*

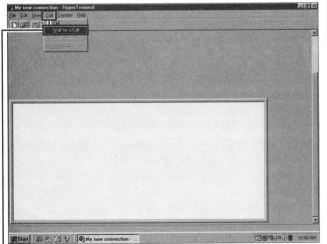

⑦ *Select Call ▷ Wait for a Call to begin waiting for incoming calls.*

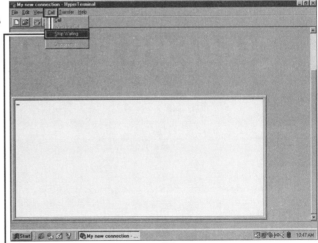

⑧ *Select Call ▷ Stop Waiting to stop answering calls.*

■ *If you've made a connection, click the Disconnect button to terminate the call.*

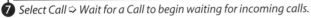

Sending and Receiving Files with HyperTerminal

After you've made a HyperTerminal connection between your PC and someone else's PC, you and your colleague will probably play around for a while, typing messages back and forth. Eventually, though, you'll probably want to exchange files between the two systems. File transfers using HyperTerminal are generally quite fast, usually much faster than sending the files over the Internet.

Standard telephone lines were never intended for the transmission of computer data. Some people consider it almost miraculous that any data, much less complete files, can be sent. Noisy phone lines mean that random errors are likely. Computers, of course, don't look kindly on having files changed randomly. A single change in a file could result in its becoming completely unusable. Or, such a change could leave the file *looking* perfect — but with a hidden error in the data that is almost impossible to catch.

To prevent errors from creeping into files that you transfer over phone lines between computers, you use a *file transfer protocol* — a method of checking for and correcting errors in the transmission. Protocols are like languages. Both parties must be speaking the same language or using the same protocol if they're going to understand each other and accomplish anything. HyperTerminal supports several different protocols, so even if the remote computer isn't using HyperTerminal you will likely still be able to find at least one protocol supported by both computers. Be

sure to see the "Take Note" section for more information on protocols.

Continued

TAKE NOTE

▶ DEALING WITH PROTOCOL INCOMPATIBILITIES

If you have a problem transferring files, even though it appears that the same protocol has been selected on both systems, you may be encountering a case of protocol incompatibilities. Not all implementations of a particular protocol are necessarily equal. If the file transfer won't start or it encounters so many errors that the transfer stalls, you may want to try a different protocol. Be sure to make the change on both systems before you attempt to restart the file transfer.

▶ USE ZMODEM IF POSSIBLE

Zmodem, the best file transfer protocol for use with HyperTerminal, also happens to be the default selection. This protocol offers one significant advantage over any of the other protocols supported by HyperTerminal. As soon as you begin a Zmodem file transfer to a PC running HyperTerminal, the receiving system automatically starts the transfer without requiring you to do anything on the receiving end. Zmodem also has the ability to restart a file transfer that has been interrupted. This capability means you won't have to start back at the beginning of the file, a fact you'll appreciate if something causes a large file transfer to crash partway through.

CROSS-REFERENCE

See "Capturing a Session Record" later in this chapter.

FIND IT ONLINE

See **http://www.hilgraeve.com/** for more advanced file transfer software.

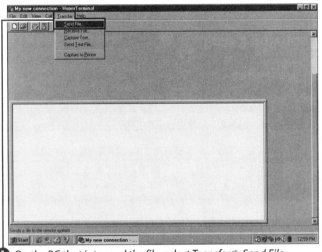

1 On the PC that is to send the file, select Transfer ➪ Send File.

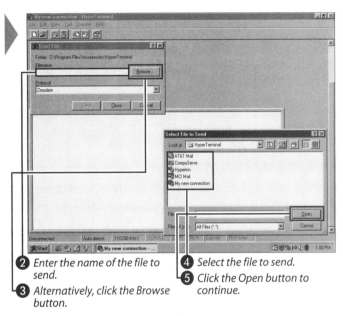

2 Enter the name of the file to send.

3 Alternatively, click the Browse button.

4 Select the file to send.

5 Click the Open button to continue.

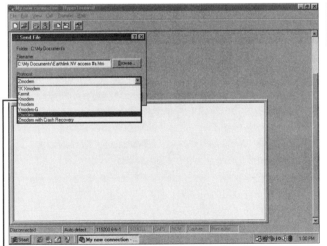

6 Select the file transfer protocol.

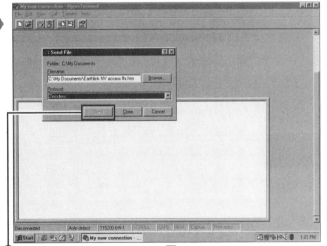

7 Click the Send button to begin the transfer.

■ You must be connected to the remote system to activate the Send button.

If both PCs use HyperTerminal and you select the Zmodem file transfer protocol, the file begins transferring when the Send button is clicked on the sending system. If you select a different protocol or if the remote system isn't using HyperTerminal, you may need to initiate the process for receiving files.

Depending on the size of the file you're transferring, the transfer may take several minutes. During this time, HyperTerminal displays a file transfer status box that shows you the transfer progress. Don't do anything as long as this dialog box is displayed.

In addition, you can send the contents of a text file to the remote computer. This capability may be handy if you need to transmit a complicated login command or some other type of text that is cumbersome to retype each time it is needed.

Although you can send a complete text file to the remote system, you may not want to send the whole file at once. For example, if you were going to interview someone online, you might want to prepare a list of questions in advance. You wouldn't want to send all the questions at once, so sending the complete file wouldn't work very well. A better way to handle this type of situation would be to open the questions document and copy each question to the Clipboard just before you needed it. Then select

Edit ⇨ Paste to Host in HyperTerminal to quickly send the question. Copy the next question while the guest is preparing the answer and you'll be ready to paste the question as soon as the guest is ready.

TAKE NOTE

CHANGE FONT SIZE TO IMPROVE READABILITY

If the HyperTerminal session window seems hard to read, change to a different font or a larger font to improve the readability. Select View ⇨ Font to display the Font dialog box. Select the font, font style, and size. Your selections are displayed in a preview window. Click OK to confirm your changes. Any text in the HyperTerminal window appears in the font you selected. If you choose a larger font, be careful that you don't choose one that is so large that you must scroll the window to see a complete line of text. Any changes you make to the font settings will have no effect on what is sent to the remote system.

Although TrueType fonts — those fonts shown in the list of fonts with a TT symbol — generally have a better appearance than non-TrueType fonts, you may wish to avoid using TrueType fonts in the HyperTerminal window. TrueType fonts don't work very well for displaying online sessions.

CROSS-REFERENCE
See "Opening and Saving File Attachments" in Chapter 15.

SHORTCUT
Use Ctrl+V to paste Clipboard text to the remote computer.

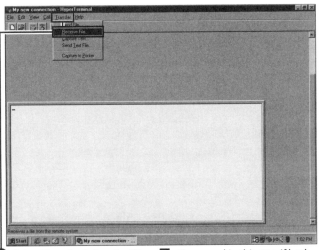

8 *Select Transfer ⇨ Receive File on the PC that is to receive the file.*

■ *You can skip this step if both PCs are using HyperTerminal and the Zmodem protocol.*

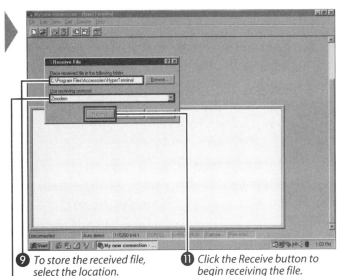

9 *To store the received file, select the location.*

10 *You select the protocol here.*

11 *Click the Receive button to begin receiving the file.*

■ *To activate the Receive button, you must be connected to the remote system.*

12 *Select Transfer ⇨ Send Text File to display the Send Text File dialog box.*

13 *Select the text file you wish to send.*

■ *Make certain you don't send anything other than a plain text file.*

14 *Click the Open button to immediately begin sending the contents of the text file.*

Capturing a Session Record

How many times have you seen something on your computer screen and later wished you had a record of the information? It can be frustrating to realize that the information was right there and now it's gone. Fortunately, HyperTerminal provides you with the tools to capture onscreen text to a file or directly to your printer.

The figures on the facing page show how to capture text during an online session. It's important to understand that HyperTerminal doesn't capture any text that is already on the screen when you issue the command to begin the capture. To learn how you can save existing text if you started capturing text a bit too late, be sure to see the "Take Note" section.

Although you can capture text both to a file and to the default printer at the same time, it's usually better to capture text to a file first. You can then open the text file, do any necessary editing, and print the text file as needed. If you decide to capture text directly to a printer, remember that many printers — especially laser printers — print one page at a time. The final page may not print until you press a button on the printer. This button is usually labeled "Form Feed" or something similar. The Transfer ⇨ Capture to Printer setting is a toggle. When a check appears, text is being captured to the printer.

CROSS-REFERENCE
See "Opening Documents" in Chapter 7.

FIND IT ONLINE
See **http://www.hilgraeve.com/** for information on HyperTerminal Private Edition.

① *Select Transfer ➪ Capture Text to display the Capture Text dialog box.*

■ *You can also select Transfer ➪ Capture to Printer to create a printed copy of the session.*

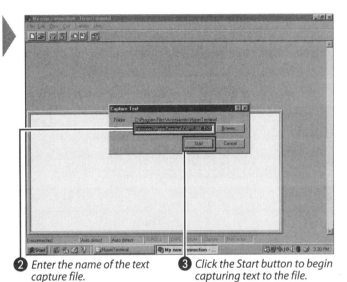

② *Enter the name of the text capture file.*

③ *Click the Start button to begin capturing text to the file.*

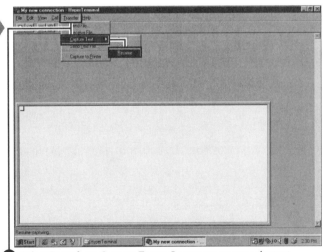

④ *Select Transfer ➪ Capture Text ➪ Pause to pause the text capture while leaving the file open for later captures.*

⑤ *Select Transfer ➪ Capture Text ➪ Resume to resume the text capture into the existing capture file.*

Personal Workbook

Q&A

1 How many computers can you connect using HyperTerminal?

_____

2 What should you do if you can't see anything you type in the HyperTerminal window?

_____

_____

_____

3 What should you do if lines of text overwrite the same line?

_____

_____

_____

4 How can you temporarily suspend capturing text to a file?

_____

_____

_____

5 What can you do if the text you need to keep is already on your screen?

_____

_____

6 What setting must be the same on both the sending and the receiving computer before you can transfer a file?

_____

_____

_____

7 Why is Zmodem the best choice for sending files between two PCs running HyperTerminal?

_____

_____

_____

8 What command can you use to send text from the Clipboard during a HyperTerminal session?

_____

_____

ANSWERS: 366

EXTRA PRACTICE

1 Set up a new connection that you can use to connect to a friend's PC.

2 Transfer several files to another PC.

3 Try some of the available file transfer protocols and determine which of the protocols won't work between two PCs.

4 Send a complete text file.

5 Send lines of text one at a time from a text file.

6 Capture the text of a session and figure out how you can resend the text to the other computer.

REAL-WORLD APPLICATIONS

✔ You're planning a trip to a remote outpost in the Himalayas. You'll have phone capabilities but no Internet access. To transfer the text files of your adventure diary, you find that HyperTerminal is an invaluable tool.

✔ You're scheduled to participate in an online job interview. You use HyperTerminal to keep a complete log of the session for future reference.

✔ You often need to access a remote computer that makes you enter a number of answers to obtain admittance. To save time you capture a session and then later use the Edit ➪ Paste to Host command.

✔ You need to transfer some sensitive files. To send them directly you use HyperTerminal on both PCs.

Visual Quiz

How can you display this ASCII Setup dialog box? Which three settings will solve most problems you may have viewing text in the HyperTerminal window?

_____

_____

_____

_____

_____

_____

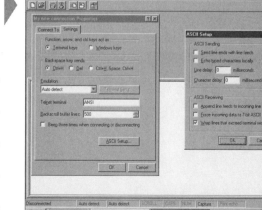

PART

VI

Maintaining Windows 98

This part teaches you how to keep your Windows 98 system running at its best. No computer can maintain its performance without a little help now and then, and here you learn how to use the powerful tools provided in Windows 98 to make certain your PC stays in tip-top shape.

Your disk drives store the most valuable resource on your computer: your important files. Your disk drives are also the most mechanical of the critical components and the most prone to develop problems. By learning how to cope with, correct, or even prevent problems before they occur, you'll gain confidence in using your system. In addition, you learn how you can make your PC last longer by making more space available on your hard disk without even opening the box.

The final chapter in this part shows you what to do when your computer gets sick. By knowing what to do to prevent some common problems that can stop your PC from functioning, you'll be able to keep your system running and even get it going again faster if problems crop up.

CHAPTER **18**

MASTER THESE SKILLS

▶ **Checking for Errors with ScanDisk**

▶ **Improving Performance with Disk Defragmenter**

▶ **Using the Disk Cleanup Tool**

▶ **Making Space with Disk Compression**

▶ **Backing Up Files**

Managing Your Disks

The disk drives connected to your PC probably affect the overall system performance more than almost any other part of your computer. Every document you create, every program you run, and any data files you use are stored on your disk drives. If they aren't working up to their potential, you may waste a lot of time and may risk losing important files.

Windows 98 provides a number of tools to help you manage and maintain your disk drives. In this chapter you learn how to use ScanDisk to make certain that your system has no physical or file system errors to prevent Windows 98 from properly reading and storing files. You learn how to use Disk Defragmenter to rearrange your files so that you don't lose performance through file space fragmentation. You see how to use the Disk Cleanup tool to remove files that are hogging space. In addition, you learn how to use disk compression to create additional space. Finally, you see how to protect yourself from disk problems by using the Backup program.

One other disk maintenance tool — the FAT 32 converter — isn't covered in this chapter.

Although it is an important tool for users who have a large hard disk and who are upgrading from an earlier version of Windows, there are several reasons I've chosen not to cover it. This tool cannot be used along with disk compression, and your hard disks must be larger than 512MB to use it. If your PC is fairly new, the hard disk may already use FAT 32. The FAT 32 converter can be used only once on a disk drive, and there's no method for undoing the conversion. What's more, there's little useful information that I can show you about using the FAT 32 converter because it runs in a special, noninteractive operating mode.

As you work through the tasks in this chapter, it's a good idea to use floppy disks for practice. Not only will you be able to try out the steps much faster, but also you won't run the risk of doing any permanent damage to your hard disk if you make a mistake. In addition, you can practice using disk compression on a floppy disk even if your hard disk is already using the FAT 32 file system. Just make certain that any disks you use don't contain important files you can't afford to lose.

Checking for Errors with ScanDisk

Disk drives are mechanical marvels. The disk itself spins at speeds as fast as 10,000 RPM. The head reads and writes data files so close to the disk that a human hair or a speck of dust would seem like a boulder. The clearances and tolerances within the drive are so fine that an ordinary piece of paper is many times as thick as the difference between a perfect part and one that is out of spec.

Disk errors are of two basic kinds. *Physical* errors are places where the disk is physically unable to read or write reliably. All hard disks have some physical errors, but in most cases you won't be aware of them because most modern hard drives have a small amount of extra capacity used to compensate for a certain number of physical errors. When the drive is initially prepared for use, any existing physical errors are mapped out and the drive skips the bad spots automatically. After the drive has been prepared, any new physical errors are called *bad sectors,* and they, too, are avoided if they have been added to the bad sector list by ScanDisk.

File system errors are much more common than physical errors. Disk space is allocated using special information tables stored on the disk. Errors in these tables can result in space being marked as in use when in fact it should be free. Other, more serious file system errors can cause two or more files to be allocated the same disk space.

Any of these errors can cause serious problems. You can lose important files, or your entire system could lock up and refuse to function. ScanDisk looks for disk errors of various types and attempts to correct them. Advanced features include a summary report and a variety of ways to log results.

TAKE NOTE

► TO AVOID DISK ERRORS, SHUT DOWN PROPERLY

Many disk errors can be traced to a simple cause: PC users who don't bother to properly shut down their systems. Unless you close your programs correctly and then use the Shut Down option on the Start menu, you may still have important files open when you turn off your PC. These open files can be corrupted, and the file system can easily lose track of the space allocated to the files. When this happens several times, your disk drives become a mess.

► TO FIND PHYSICAL ERRORS, USE THE THOROUGH TEST

ScanDisk can perform two types of tests. The *standard* test looks only for file system errors. The *thorough* test also checks for physical errors. You can save quite a bit of time by using the standard test, but it's a good idea to use the thorough test at least once a month or whenever you suspect physical problems.

CROSS-REFERENCE

See "Adding a Scheduled Task" in Chapter 10.

FIND IT ONLINE

See http://webopedia.internet.com/TERM/S/ScanDiak.html for more information on ScanDisk.

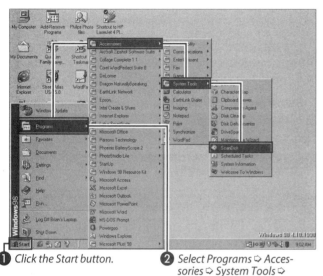

① *Click the Start button.*

② *Select Programs ➪ Accessories ➪ System Tools ➪ ScanDisk.*

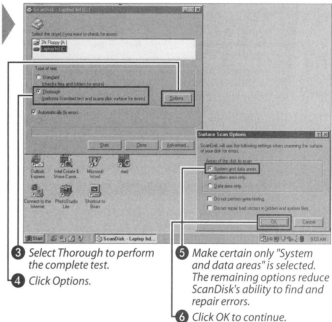

③ *Select Thorough to perform the complete test.*

④ *Click Options.*

⑤ *Make certain only "System and data areas" is selected. The remaining options reduce ScanDisk's ability to find and repair errors.*

⑥ *Click OK to continue.*

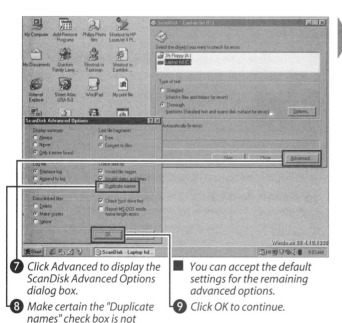

⑦ *Click Advanced to display the ScanDisk Advanced Options dialog box.*

⑧ *Make certain the "Duplicate names" check box is not selected.*

■ *You can accept the default settings for the remaining advanced options.*

⑨ *Click OK to continue.*

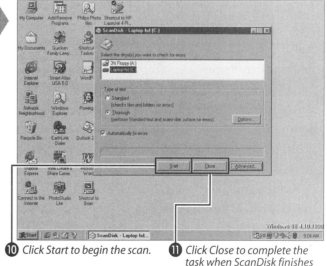

⑩ *Click Start to begin the scan.*

⑪ *Click Close to complete the task when ScanDisk finishes the scan.*

Improving Performance with Disk Defragmenter

The longer you use your PC, the more likely it is that accessing files on your disks will become slower. It's not that your hard disks are getting worn out; it's only that they become *fragmented*. Disks become fragmented in use in the same way that parking spaces in a shopping mall parking lot become fragmented. When the parking lot is first opened in the morning, it's easy to find a number of adjacent spaces where you and a group of your friends can park next to one another. As the day goes on, the spaces fill up with other cars, and you're more likely to find one space here, two spaces over there, and so on. As more of your friends arrive, the only parking spaces they can find are ones that fragment the group into several different locations.

Disk space is allocated in much the same way as are the parking spaces in the mall parking lot. Files that are created and saved first get the first available spaces. Later files use the spaces further out on the disk. But when a file is deleted from the disk, an open space is available for new files. If the next new file can fit into the opening, it is stored *contiguously*. But if the file is too large to fit into one space, it is fragmented into two or more pieces.

Reading and writing fragmented files takes longer, and this has an adverse effect on system performance. Your disk drives are much slower than most of the components in your computer simply because the disk drives are mechanical components. As a result, the effects of disk fragmentation are somewhat exaggerated in their overall impact on system performance.

TAKE NOTE

▶ USE THE REARRANGE PROGRAMS OPTION

As the lower-left figure on the facing page shows, the Windows 98 Disk Defragmenter has an option that you can use to rearrange your program files so that programs will start more quickly. This option can cut quite a bit of time from the launch of your favorite programs. Although the actual difference may be only a few seconds, the perceived difference may seem like more. Your PC will seem livelier because your programs will load faster.

▶ USE DISK DEFRAGMENTER ALONE

Disk Defragmenter can work efficiently only if nothing attempts to write to your hard disk while Disk Defragmenter is working. Anything that writes to your hard disk will either delay Disk Defragmenter or make it restart the process. Be sure to stop your e-mail program and any other applications before you start the disk defragmentation. Constant restarting of Disk Defragmenter is a sure sign that something is writing to your hard disk.

CROSS-REFERENCE

See "Using the Disk Cleanup Tool" later in this chapter.

FIND IT ONLINE

See http://webopedia.internet.com/TERM/D/ Defrag.html for more information on disk defragmenting.

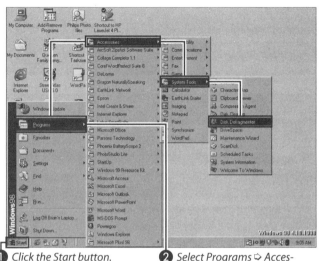

1 Click the Start button.

2 Select Programs ➪ Accessories ➪ System Tools ➪ Disk Defragmenter.

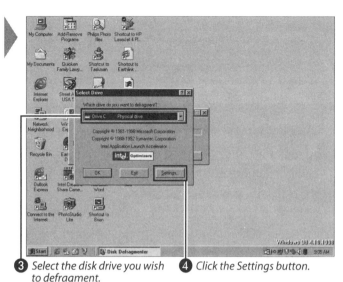

3 Select the disk drive you wish to defragment.

4 Click the Settings button.

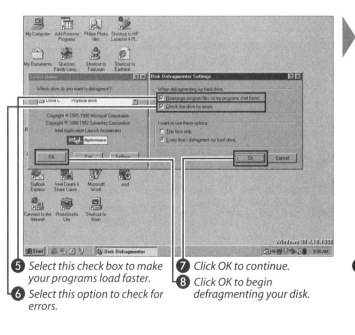

5 Select this check box to make your programs load faster.

6 Select this option to check for errors.

7 Click OK to continue.

8 Click OK to begin defragmenting your disk.

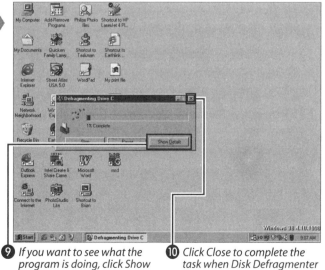

9 If you want to see what the program is doing, click Show Details.

10 Click Close to complete the task when Disk Defragmenter finishes.

Using the Disk Cleanup Tool

The Disk Cleanup tool operates on a simple principle: Files that are simply wasting disk space should be deleted to free up the space. This concept may not be original, but you may be surprised at how much space is being wasted on your hard disk.

For many reasons, your hard disk contains files that are wasting space. Whenever you browse the Internet, temporary files are stored on your hard disk so that Internet Explorer can later load those same Web pages more quickly. When you install new software, the installation program may not remove all the temporary files that were used in the installation. Even creating a document may leave temporary files on the hard disk, especially if you don't close your programs or Windows 98 properly. The Disk Cleanup tool also allows you to delete files stored in the Recycle Bin. All of these file types can be safely removed to reclaim the wasted disk space.

You can view a description of each file type by selecting its type in the "Files to delete" list box. Depending on the type of file that you've selected, you may see a View Files button near the bottom of the dialog box. View Files allows you to see the contents of the folder currently selected in the Files to delete box. In most cases, viewing the files won't serve much purpose. Do you really know whether a particular temporary Internet file is worth saving?

TAKE NOTE

OTHER DISK CLEANUP OPTIONS

The More Options tab of the Disk Cleanup dialog box is not covered in the figures on the facing page. The More Options tab offers three additional ways to free disk space. You can remove Windows 98 components that you aren't using. For example, if you've installed Web TV for Windows, removing it will free more than 40MB of disk space. You can also uninstall programs that you no longer need. You may find that you can free several hundred megabytes by junking old programs. Finally, if you aren't using disk compression you may be able to convert your hard disk to the FAT 32 file system, a much more efficient way to store files that often frees hundreds of megabytes.

USE THE SETTINGS TAB TO AUTOMATE DISK CLEANUP

The Settings tab includes one option. If the check box on the Settings tab is selected, the Disk Cleanup tool will automatically run if the selected drive runs low on disk space. Although this option sounds handy, you probably don't want to rely on it to ensure that you won't run out of disk space. If your disk space is so low that the Disk Cleanup tool automatically runs, you'll likely run out of space very soon regardless of the efforts of this tool. Use the More Options tab options to free significant amounts of disk space.

CROSS-REFERENCE
See "Making Space with Disk Compression" later in this chapter.

FIND IT ONLINE
See http://www.cybermedia.com/products/uninstaller/plus98.html for a powerful disk cleanup tool.

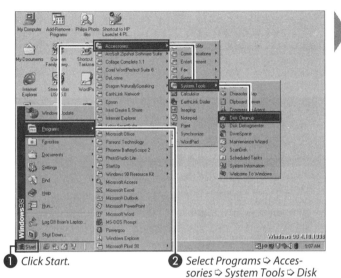

1 Click Start.

2 Select Programs ➪ Accessories ➪ System Tools ➪ Disk Cleanup.

3 Select the disk drive you wish to clean up.

4 Click OK.

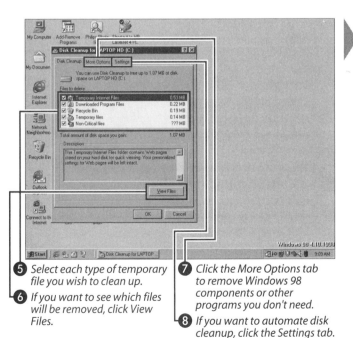

5 Select each type of temporary file you wish to clean up.

6 If you want to see which files will be removed, click View Files.

7 Click the More Options tab to remove Windows 98 components or other programs you don't need.

8 If you want to automate disk cleanup, click the Settings tab.

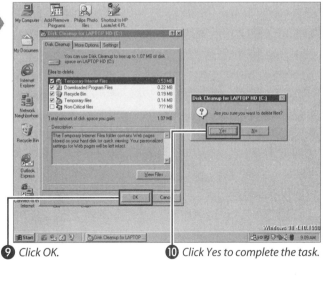

9 Click OK.

10 Click Yes to complete the task.

Making Space with Disk Compression

isk compression is a method of packing more data into a given amount of space. If you've ever ridden on a large city subway system at rush hour, you can understand the concept. Rather than allow each data file to waste disk space, disk compression cuts down on unused space and also packs redundant data into smaller packets. The Windows 98 disk compression tool is called DriveSpace.

On an uncompressed disk, data is stored in *allocation units* (also called *clusters*). These units represent the smallest amount of space that can be used by any file, even one that is only one byte. The size of the allocation units varies according to several factors. You can get a rough idea of how much disk space can be wasted by considering that on a 2GB hard disk that uses the FAT 16 file system, the minimum space that can be allocated is 32K, or 32,768 bytes. Your one-byte file would be wasting 32,767 of those bytes.

Disk compression reduces the wasted space in two ways: by using a different method of allocating space and by packing files into less space. In the figures on the facing page, the effects of disk compression are clear. After compression, the disk has 2MB of apparent free disk space, even though the disk is actually a 1.4MB disk.

Whenever you compress a disk, DriveSpace creates a *host* drive for the compressed drive. You can

generally ignore any host drives on your system because the only purpose they serve is to assist DriveSpace. You must not delete any of the files on the host drive because this can cause major problems and may even result in your losing all the files on the compressed drive.

TAKE NOTE

▶ DISK COMPRESSION AND FAT 32

You cannot use disk compression and the FAT 32 file system on the same disk, although this does not prevent you from combining disk compression and FAT 32 on the same computer. FAT 32 is the best choice for hard disks that are larger than 512MB. Use disk compression on smaller disks. For example, you may want to use disk compression to save more data on a floppy disk or on a Zip drive.

▶ TAKE DISK SPACE ESTIMATES WITH A GRAIN OF SALT

When you compress a disk, DriveSpace makes an estimate of the available free space. This estimate is based on how well DriveSpace was able to compress the existing files as well as a rough guess of future compression ratios. Unfortunately, some files do not compress as well as others, and any estimate of free space is nothing more than a guess until the actual files are added to the disk.

CROSS-REFERENCE
See "Backing Up Files" later in this chapter.

FIND IT ONLINE
See **http://www.webopedia.com/disk_compression. htm** for more on disk compression.

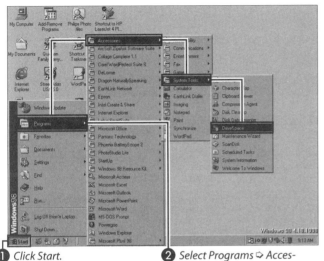

1 Click Start.

2 Select Programs ➪ Accessories ➪ System Tools ➪ DriveSpace.

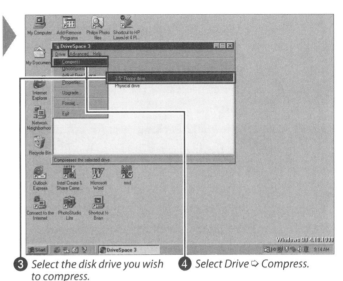

3 Select the disk drive you wish to compress.

4 Select Drive ➪ Compress.

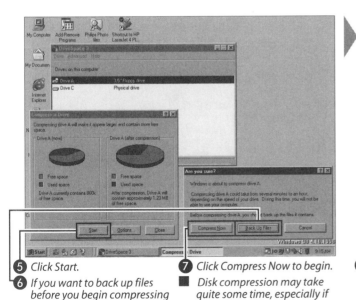

5 Click Start.

6 If you want to back up files before you begin compressing the disk, click Back Up Files.

7 Click Compress Now to begin.

■ Disk compression may take quite some time, especially if the disk contains a large number of files.

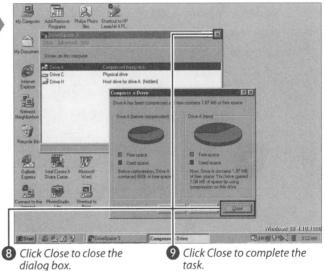

8 Click Close to close the dialog box.

9 Click Close to complete the task.

311

Backing Up Files

acking up your files is the best way to protect yourself against losing important data. In spite of the importance of backups, few computer users take the time to protect themselves against this type of loss. In this section you'll learn how to make backing up both fast and easy and increase the likelihood that you'll follow this important precaution.

The figures on the facing page and the second following page provide an overview of the backup process using floppy disks as the backup medium. If you have another type of backup medium or if your backup requires a different amount of disk space, you'll probably see a slightly different set of screens. You may also see some differences depending on whether you've used Backup in the past. In addition, we've skipped showing a few of the simpler steps so that you can see the important points.

Using the Backup program offers several advantages compared with simply copying your data to floppy disks. Backup automatically spans disks, so if you have files that are too large for a single disk, Backup will prompt you for an additional floppy disk. Backup also uses compression on the backup media so that you'll need fewer disks than if you simply copied the files.

Backup uses *backup jobs* to keep track of what you want to back up. You can name your backup job and then open the same backup job later when you want to back up the same set of files. By doing this, you avoid going through most of the steps shown in the figures and the backup process is even easier. One good way to use backup jobs is to first create and test them. If everything works as planned, you can then show a less experienced PC user how to back up his or her files using the backup job.

Continued

TAKE NOTE

▶ KEEP YOUR BACKUPS SMALL

One of the best ways to ensure you'll actually back up your files is to keep your backups small so that they take less time to complete. If you store your document files in the My Documents folder, you can concentrate on backing up that folder and your backups will take only a few minutes. In addition, you may want to limit your backups to new and changed files so that you're not backing up the same old files each time.

▶ MAKE SURE YOUR BACKUP DISKS ARE EMPTY

If you are backing up to floppy disks, make certain the disks are empty before you begin the backups. Although Backup won't overwrite any existing files, it also won't erase them. As a result, your backup could require many more disks than it would if you erased the existing files before you began.

CROSS-REFERENCE
See "Opening the My Documents Folder" in Chapter 1.

SHORTCUT
Use the Quick Format option of the Format command to erase all the files on a floppy disk before backups.

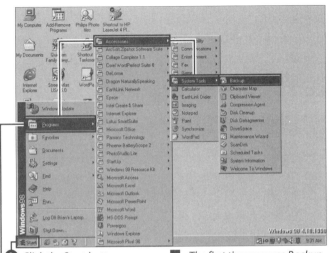

1 Click the Start button.

2 Select Programs ➪ Accessories ➪ System Tools ➪ Backup.

■ *The first time you use Backup you may need to confirm whether you have any backup devices installed. Click No to back up to disks or to your network.*

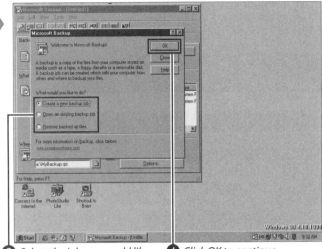

3 Select the job you would like to perform.

4 Click OK to continue.

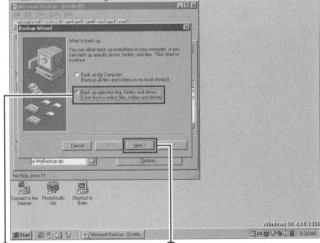

5 *Select the second radio button to limit your backup to selected files.*

6 Click Next to continue.

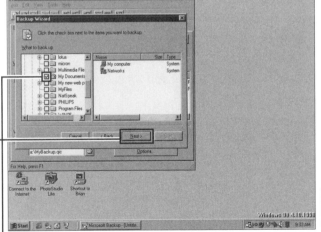

7 Click the check box next to any files or folders you wish to back up.

8 Click Next to continue.

■ *Next, click the "New and changed files" radio button and click Next to continue.*

313

Backing Up Files

Continued

On the preceding pages you learned how to specify what you want to back up. The figures on the facing page take the task to the next step — specifying how to perform the backup.

If your PC has a tape drive you'll probably want to use the tape drive for your backups. Magnetic tape is a good choice because it's usually one of the easiest ways to back up: You plug in a tape and off you go. If you don't have a tape drive but are on a network, you may want to back up to a folder on one of the other computers on the network. Network folders are also a good backup choice because it's unlikely that you'll lose files that are stored on two different systems, and backing up across the network is fast and easy. The next choice for the backup destination is to use a removable drive on your computer. This may be a floppy disk drive or a drive with higher capacity, such as a Zip drive. Backups to floppy disks can involve a lot of disk swapping. The poorest choice is to create the backup on your hard disk. Not only does this provide little protection, but it also eats valuable disk space.

You can choose to compare the backed-up files with the originals and to compress the backups. Both of these options are good choices. Comparing the backups to the originals takes extra time, but if you can't trust your backups, why bother doing them?

Compressing the backup data usually saves on backup media. There's no advantage, however, to compressing your floppy disks before using them as backup media.

You may be prompted to insert additional backup media during the backup. This is especially likely if you're backing up to floppy disks.

TAKE NOTE

▶ KEEP TRACK OF THE BACKUP MEDIA

If you're using backup media such as floppy disks and require more than one disk for a backup, be sure to label each one with a sequence number and the backup date. If you restore files from a backup set, you'll need to place the disks in the drive in the correct order, and this is much easier if you've labeled the disks properly.

▶ CONSIDER STORING BACKUPS ELSEWHERE

After you've gone to the trouble of backing up your important files, you may want to consider storing the backups someplace away from your computer. Backups are meant to protect you in the event of a disaster, and they can't do it if the same disaster destroys your backups. If you are backing up files from your office, consider taking the backups home. At the very least, use a fireproof storage location such as the office safe.

CROSS-REFERENCE
See "Checking for Errors with ScanDisk" earlier in this chapter.

FIND IT ONLINE
See **http://www.seagatesoftware.com** for information on upgrades to Backup.

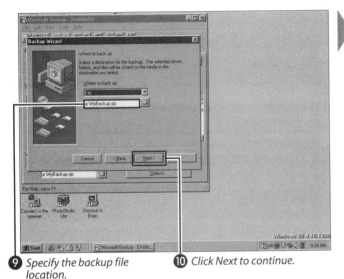

9 Specify the backup file location.

10 Click Next to continue.

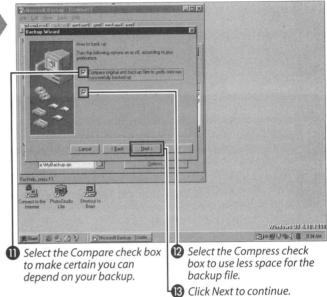

11 Select the Compare check box to make certain you can depend on your backup.

12 Select the Compress check box to use less space for the backup file.

13 Click Next to continue.

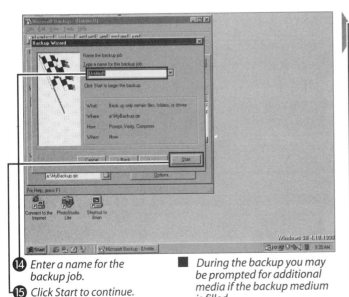

14 Enter a name for the backup job.

15 Click Start to continue.

■ During the backup you may be prompted for additional media if the backup medium is filled.

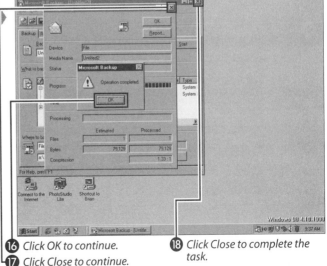

16 Click OK to continue.

17 Click Close to continue.

18 Click Close to complete the task.

315

Personal Workbook

Q&A

1 What type of errors will ScanDisk look for if you use the standard disk test?

_____

_____

_____

2 What additional type of errors will ScanDisk look for if you use the thorough disk test?

_____

_____

_____

3 What is the difference between contiguous and fragmented files?

_____

_____

4 What is the name of the extra drive that is created when you compress a drive?

_____

_____

5 What selection can you make to ensure your backups don't include old files that haven't changed since the last backup?

_____

_____

6 Where should you store your document files to make backups easier?

_____

_____

7 What tool can you use to remove old files that are no longer needed on your PC?

_____

_____

8 Why should you check any floppy disks before you use them for backups?

_____

_____

ANSWERS: 366

EXTRA PRACTICE

1 Run the thorough disk test to make certain there are no physical errors on your hard disk.

2 Run Disk Defragmenter and check to see which options are selected.

3 Use the More Options tab on the Disk Cleanup dialog box to see how much additional disk space you can free.

4 Compress a floppy disk and then use the advanced options to adjust the apparent free space.

5 Back up your My Documents folder.

6 Add or change a few document files and then run the backup job again, making certain that only new or changed files are backed up.

REAL-WORLD APPLICATIONS

✔ You often take your laptop PC with you when you travel. To make certain that your system didn't sustain any damage during transit, you run the thorough disk test after you return.

✔ As the school term nears its end, you use your PC for many hours to complete term papers. To bring back the disk performance that is slowly lost the longer you use your computer, you run the Disk Defragmenter tool.

✔ You are working on a complex project that will make or break your fledgling ad agency. To prevent the loss of work that would be hard to re-create, you perform frequent backups.

Visual Quiz

How can you display this dialog box? Which setting on the displayed tab will have the greatest effect on the number of disks you'll need to use for backups?

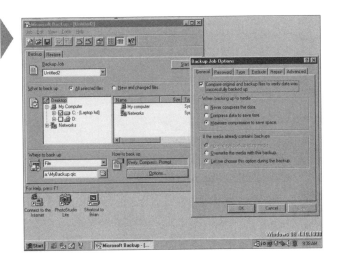

CHAPTER 19

Managing Your System

Chapter 18 detailed some of the tools Windows 98 provides to help you maintain and manage your disks. This chapter covers additional system tools that you use to maintain the other parts of your PC. You won't use these tools daily for routine maintenance, but they can be important in helping you keep your computer running in top condition.

Before you try the exercises in this chapter, it's vital to realize the importance of the Windows 98 system files. If these files are damaged, you may not be able to start your computer, and you could potentially lose access to your data files. If you are careless or don't think you need to read the warnings that Windows 98 displays when you're about to do something that presents a danger to your system, this chapter isn't for you. This chapter requires you to think about what you're doing.

Computers are complex systems. For your PC to operate properly, all the pieces of hardware and software must cooperate. If you add a new piece of hardware or install new software, you may be creating a unique combination of pieces, or at least one that may not have been tested by the hardware or software manufacturer. It's unrealistic to expect everything to work under those conditions without some effort on your part. But no one expects you to buy a PC and just leave it alone. Adding on is part of the fun of owning a PC.

One common problem is that either the new piece doesn't work or something that was working before has stopped working. In most cases these types of problems are caused by the software or hardware manufacturers, who can't resist bending the rules to "improve" things. The various programs you run on your PC share many of the components that make up Windows 98. If a manufacturer can't resist the urge to "tweak" one of these shared components, the results are easy to predict — the product may work fine, but other hardware or software that shares the component may fail. That's why you need many of the tools discussed in this chapter. With these tools you can discover what has changed, and you'll have a chance to undo any damage that was done to your system.

Tuning Up with the Maintenance Wizard

The Maintenance Wizard schedules important system maintenance tasks that you should do on a regular basis but that you probably don't do as often as you should. Essentially, the Maintenance Wizard provides an easy way to add tasks to the Scheduled Tasks folder.

If you followed along in Chapter 18, you're familiar with the tasks that the Maintenance Wizard schedules. First, the Maintenance Wizard schedules the Disk Defragmenter tool using the option to optimize the loading of your program files. You may forget to do this manually after you've added or removed programs from your system, so having this as a scheduled task helps keep your PC's performance at its peak. Next, the Maintenance Wizard schedules ScanDisk to check for and repair any disk errors. Because you may not always realize when an event has caused disk errors, scheduling this check on a regular basis helps prevent more serious problems. Finally, the Maintenance Wizard schedules the Disk Cleanup tool to remove unnecessary files that clog your hard disk.

You may not have to run the Maintenance Wizard yourself to get these benefits. If you upgraded your PC to Windows 98, the Maintenance Wizard may have been a part of the upgrade process. Still, it won't hurt to run the Maintenance Wizard again — you'll simply modify the existing maintenance schedule to something that better suits your needs.

TAKE NOTE

DON'T FORGET TO LEAVE YOUR SYSTEM TURNED ON

After the Maintenance Wizard schedules the system maintenance events, be sure you leave your system running at the scheduled time. If you prefer not to leave your computer on all the time, choose a maintenance schedule that allows the tasks to be performed at a time when you are comfortable leaving the system on, such as during lunch. If you select the custom setup rather than the express setup shown in the upper-right figure on the facing page, you'll also be able to more closely control the task schedule. For even more control over the schedule, you can open the Scheduled Tasks folder after the Maintenance Wizard has created a schedule.

FOR MORE CONTROL, USE THE CUSTOM OPTION

If you select the Custom radio button, you'll see additional options not shown in the figures on the facing page. One of these options enables you to disable programs that load automatically when Windows 98 starts. Be careful when selecting this option, especially if you rely on having the services of the program that loads automatically. You'll also have the option of selecting the settings for each of the three routine maintenance items that the Maintenance Wizard schedules, and you can choose to eliminate one or more of them from the schedule.

CROSS-REFERENCE

See "Modifying a Scheduled Task" in Chapter 10.

FIND IT ONLINE

For more on the Maintenance Wizard, see
http://www.microsoft.com/windows/info/maintwiz.htm.

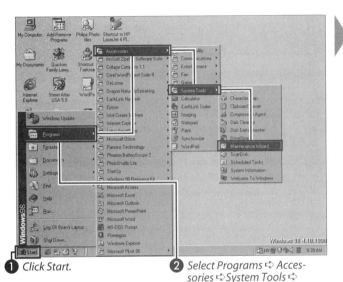

1 Click Start.

2 Select Programs ➪ Accessories ➪ System Tools ➪ Maintenance Wizard.

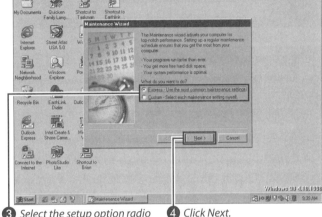

3 Select the setup option radio button you prefer.

■ Use the Express option for the quickest setup.

4 Click Next.

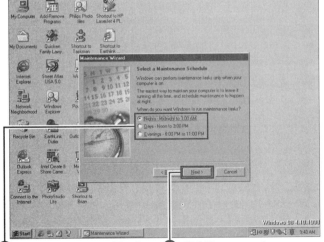

5 Select the time period for the routine maintenance items.

6 Click Next to continue.

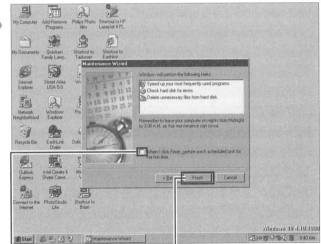

7 To run the maintenance items when you complete the task, select this check box.

8 Click Finish to complete the task.

Using Device Manager to Look for Problems

Adding new hardware to your PC can be a real adventure. A limited number of system resources are available, and most hardware that you add requires the use of at least some of them. In this section, you learn how to discover whether you have a system resource problem that is causing parts of your computer to refuse to work properly.

Device Manager is a tool that enables you to examine the devices installed in your system. When you open Device Manager, as shown in the figures on the facing page, you'll be able to see a lot of technical information, most of which you can safely ignore. If some of the devices installed in your PC are experiencing a problem, Device Manager will use either a yellow exclamation point or a red X to indicate the problem.

Device Manager primarily looks for conflicts in which two or more devices are trying to use the same resources at the same time. These resources include *interrupt requests* (IRQs), *input/output* (I/O) addresses, *direct memory access* (DMA), and *memory* addresses. Most problems you'll encounter will be with IRQs. In some cases, you can choose new, nonconflicting resource settings on the Resources tab of the device's Properties dialog box. Deselect the "Use automatic settings" check box and choose one of the optional configurations. If you cannot resolve the problems by choosing new settings, be sure to see the "Take Note" section for additional hints about what to do to solve resource conflicts.

CROSS-REFERENCE
See "Adding New Hardware" in Chapter 5.

FIND IT ONLINE
Search the IDG site at http://www.idg.net/ for more troubleshooting tips.

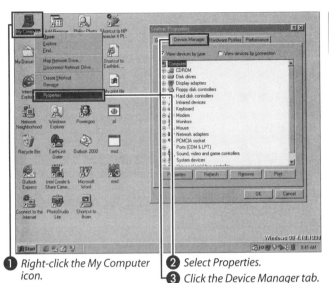

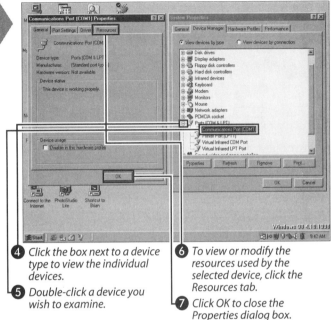

❶ *Right-click the My Computer icon.*

❷ *Select Properties.*

❸ *Click the Device Manager tab.*

❹ *Click the box next to a device type to view the individual devices.*

❺ *Double-click a device you wish to examine.*

❻ *To view or modify the resources used by the selected device, click the Resources tab.*

❼ *Click OK to close the Properties dialog box.*

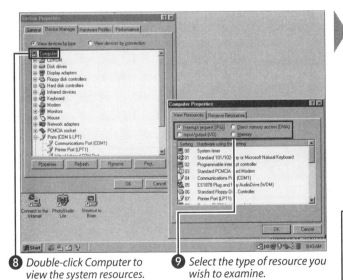

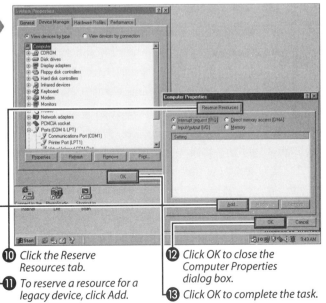

❽ *Double-click Computer to view the system resources.*

❾ *Select the type of resource you wish to examine.*

❿ *Click the Reserve Resources tab.*

⓫ *To reserve a resource for a legacy device, click Add.*

⓬ *Click OK to close the Computer Properties dialog box.*

⓭ *Click OK to complete the task.*

Checking for Version Conflicts

Because many common files are shared among various Windows 98 programs, it's inevitable that there will be conflicts between those programs. The reasons are simple. The shared files, like any other program files on your PC, may go through several revisions as bugs are found or new features are added. These revised versions may include a number of subtle and not-so-subtle changes, even though the expectation is that they're fully compatible with the older versions.

Naturally, application programmers who use these shared files use the latest versions that are available to them, and they generally assume that there won't be a problem. It isn't a problem in most cases because the shared files are often distributed along with the programs. So if the programmer used a common file such as MFC42.DLL to create a program, a copy of it is usually included in the setup for the program.

Unfortunately, the copy of the shared file that is distributed along with a new program may not work correctly with all other programs that use the shared file. For example, suppose you already have MFC42.DLL revision 4.21.7325 on your PC. Now imagine that the programmer used revision 4.21.7320 to create the program. Ideally, the setup program would recognize that you already had a later version and wouldn't touch the existing copy on your system. In the real world, though, that's not always the case. Sometimes an installation program doesn't check, or perhaps the version numbers are incorrect.

In other cases, programmers replace your version simply because that way they can be sure their application won't have a problem.

Microsoft has collected a number of important system tools under the heading System Information. The figures on the facing page show you how to open the System Information utility and then the Version Conflict Manager. Be sure to leave the System Information utility open because you'll need to use it for the tasks on the following pages.

CROSS-REFERENCE
See "Installing and Uninstalling Programs" in Chapter 6.

FIND IT ONLINE
For more on Windows 98 troubleshooting, see
http://www.zdnet.com/sr/issues/980720/337564.html.

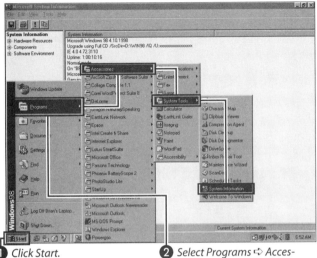

1 *Click Start.*

2 *Select Programs ➪ Accessories ➪ System Tools ➪ System Information.*

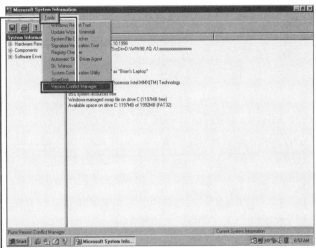

3 *Select Tools ➪ Version Conflict Manager.*

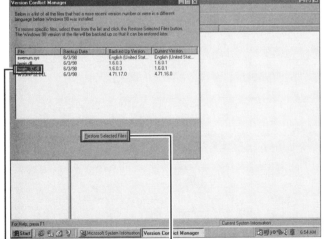

4 *Select a system file you think may be causing a problem.*

■ *Look for files backed up on the date you installed a new program.*

5 *Click Restore Selected Files to revert to the backed-up version.*

■ *Restart your system to test the changes.*

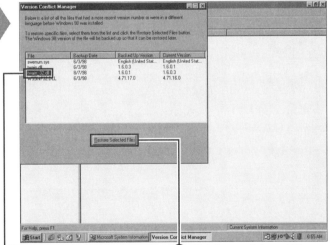

■ *If problems aren't corrected, try reopening the Version Conflict Manager and restore the files.*

6 *You can select the files that you restored earlier.*

7 *Click Restore Selected Files to reverse your earlier changes and complete the task.*

Checking System Files

indows 98 includes another, more comprehensive tool for checking system files: the System File Checker. Whereas the Version Conflict Manager looks for differences in the reported versions of system files, the System File Checker digs deeper, looking for system files that are corrupt, that have been changed, or that have been deleted. Any of these types of changes can cause serious problems, so fixing them is an important part of keeping your Windows 98 system functioning properly.

The System File Checker is another of the tools on the Tools menu of the System Information utility program. This powerful set of tools must be used with care because they can affect the very heart of Windows 98. If you don't understand what one of these tools is telling you, the safest course of action is to cancel without making any changes.

The System File Checker normally looks only for corrupted system files, but you can select options to have it check for changed or deleted system files, too. These two options are not selected by default because interpreting them can be confusing. It's better to use the Version Conflict Manager to check for system files that have been changed because you can easily switch between two versions for testing. Similarly, system files that have been deleted are not usually a problem you need worry about. If Windows 98 or an application program cannot find a system file that was deleted, you'll probably see an error message telling you the name of the missing file. If Windows 98 displayed the message, you'll be given the option to restore the file. If an application program displays the message, you can usually correct the problem by reinstalling the application program.

TAKE NOTE

THE LOG FILE CAN ASSIST TECH SUPPORT

System File Checker keeps a log file — SFCLOG.TXT — in the \Windows folder. If you are experiencing problems making your system or a particular program function properly, you can offer to send a copy of the log file to the tech support person who is assisting you. Because this log file lists the current version numbers and dates of your system files, it may provide the clue that is needed to resolve the problems.

SAVE TIME WITH FILE BACKUPS

Make certain you select the "Always back up before restoring" radio button on the System File Checker Settings dialog box shown in the upper-right figure on the facing page. Otherwise, the existing files either won't be backed up or you'll have to confirm each one that is replaced. Making the backup automatic can save you time because you probably wouldn't know which files to back up anyway.

CROSS-REFERENCE
See "Checking for Version Conflicts" earlier in this chapter.

SHORTCUT
Make certain the default "Prompt for backup" button is not selected to save time when replacing files.

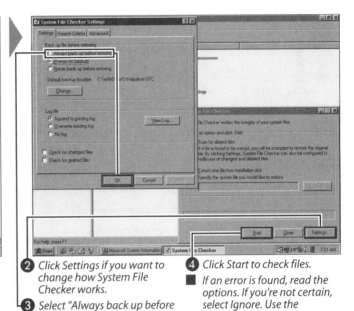

1 Select Tools ➪ System File Checker.

2 Click Settings if you want to change how System File Checker works.

3 Select "Always back up before restoring", and click OK to continue.

4 Click Start to check files.

■ If an error is found, read the options. If you're not certain, select Ignore. Use the resulting SFCLOG.TXT to get advice before replacing file.

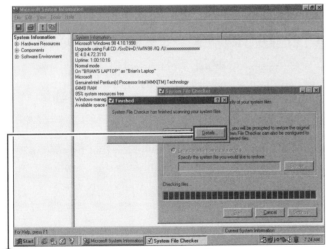

5 If you want to view the results, click Details.

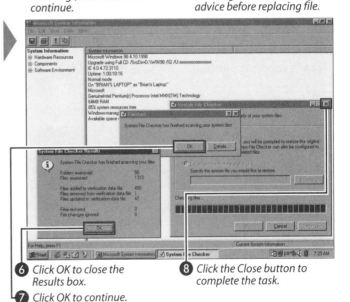

6 Click OK to close the Results box.

7 Click OK to continue.

8 Click the Close button to complete the task.

327

Checking the Registry for Errors

The Windows 98 Registry is an important part of your system. The Registry is a database that contains information about the hardware, software, drivers, preferences, and a multitude of other pieces of data that enable your PC to run correctly. If the Registry is damaged, your computer may not be able to start Windows 98, or it may not be able to use some pieces of the system properly. Maintaining the integrity of the Registry is vital if you want to use your computer for anything other than as a paperweight.

The final Windows 98 system tool examined here is the Registry Checker. This tool does two things: It checks for Registry errors and backs up the Registry. If an error occurs in the Registry, your system can often start successfully by reverting to a saved version of the Registry. If you have a recent good backup you won't lose very many updates, so it's important to have a recent backup.

Whenever you install new hardware or software, changes are made to the Registry. If you later uninstall a piece of hardware or software, other changes occur. Although these changes shouldn't cause problems, errors can occur. If your system crashes or loses power suddenly in a power failure, the Registry can be corrupted. No matter what the cause, Registry errors can ruin more than your day. If you're lucky, Windows 98 will restore a corrupt Registry from a backup and all will be fine. If you're not so lucky,

Windows 98 may start in *Safe Mode* so that you can try to fix the problems. Otherwise, you may need to use your startup disk and your Windows 98 CD-ROM to reinstall Windows 98.

TAKE NOTE

DON'T MESS WITH THE REGISTRY

The Registry is one of the most complex structures imaginable. Understanding all the keys, subkeys, and values is extremely difficult. Even experienced systems programmers have been known to make mistakes modifying the Registry, and these errors can easily result in an unusable computer. Avoid making changes to the Registry unless there is no other option. If a tech support person asks you to modify the Registry, use the Registry Checker to make a backup of the Registry before you make any changes.

CLEAN UP YOUR REGISTRY

Although you should avoid making changes to the Registry manually, Microsoft has a tool you can use to automatically clean up your Registry. This tool is called REGCLEAN, and you can download it from the Internet. REGCLEAN checks for unused or obsolete entries in the Registry and safely removes them. Removing these old entries may make your system start faster and may also eliminate errors that can be caused by attempting to load files and services that aren't needed.

CROSS-REFERENCE
See "Using Windows Update" in Chapter 14.

FIND IT ONLINE
See ftp://ftp.microsoft.com/softlib/MSLFILES/REGCLEAN.EXE for a copy of REGCLEAN.

Regedit Modifies the Registry

If you have no choice except to manually modify the Registry, look for a file called Regedit in the \Windows folder. This application is designed specifically for editing the Registry. Make certain you use extreme caution when using Regedit. Don't change any values unless you are absolutely certain you are changing the correct value. Many Registry keys look very similar but unless you find exactly the correct one you're likely to do very serious damage that may be impossible to repair without formatting your hard disk and starting over from scratch.

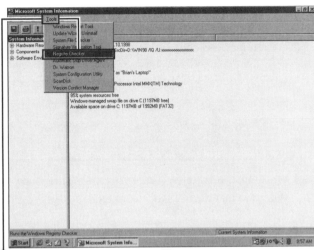

① *Select Tools ⇨ Registry Checker.*

■ *The Registry Checker will start automatically and run without waiting for any input.*

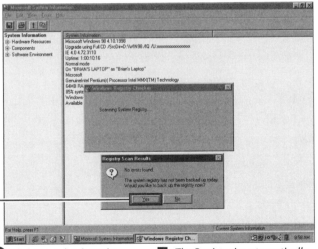

② *Click Yes to back up the Registry.*

■ *The Registry is automatically backed up when you start your system, but if you don't shut down your PC very often you'll want a recent backup.*

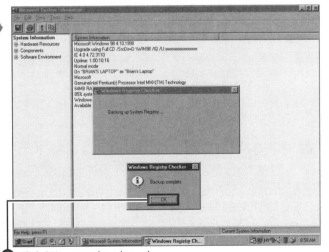

③ *Click OK to complete the task.*

Personal Workbook

Q&A

1 What three tasks does the Maintenance Wizard schedule?

_____

_____

2 What must you do after you've used the Maintenance Wizard so that the tasks will run as scheduled?

_____

_____

_____

3 What do you call older devices that do not support plug and play?

_____

_____

4 How does Device Manager indicate that a device has a problem?

_____

_____

5 What system resources does Device Manager track?

_____

_____

_____

6 What tool can you use to try out a backed-up version of a system file?

_____

_____

7 What tool can you use to check for corrupted system files?

_____

_____

8 Why is it important to have a recent backup of the Registry?

_____

_____

_____

ANSWERS: PAGE 367

330

EXTRA PRACTICE

1. Use the Maintenance Wizard to adjust the schedule for the maintenance tasks.

2. Open Device Manager and see what device is using IRQ 7.

3. Copy the Version Conflict Manager list to the Clipboard and then print a copy of the list for future reference.

4. Change the System File Checker settings so that changed files are shown and then run the check. Don't replace any of the files.

5. Make a backup of the Registry.

6. Download REGCLEAN and use the program to clean up your Registry.

REAL-WORLD APPLICATIONS

✔ You install a new printer and then find that your desktop publishing program won't let you print to a file. To determine whether any resource conflicts exist, you use Device Manager.

✔ You install a photo retouching program recommended by your best friend, an artist. The software works fine on her system, but every time you try to use the zoom feature, your PC crashes. You use the Version Conflict Manager to see what changes were made by installing the new software.

✔ You usually leave your computer running all the time, so you can't take advantage of the fact that your PC makes a copy of the Registry every time you fire it up. You use the Registry Checker to make Registry backups at least once a week.

Visual Quiz

How can you display this dialog box? Which setting on the displayed tab will cause a new log file to replace the old log file?

_____

_____

_____

_____

_____

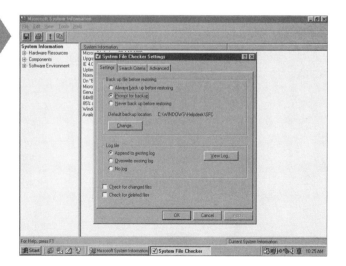

PART

VII

CHAPTER **20**   Using Plus! 98

Using Microsoft Plus! for Windows 98

This part of the book provides an overview at Plus! 98, an extra set of enhancements for Windows 98 that you can purchase at a store or from Microsoft online.

The chapter starts with some installation instructions, and then individual components of the software are covered.

Plus! 98 provides some fun, and some very useful utilities. You learn about a tool to work with images you've scanned or downloaded from your digital camera, a top-notch virus software, and a deluxe CD Player. Plus! 98 also includes an improved disk cleanup tool, an improved wizard to help you keep your system running at peak performance levels, and compressed folders to help you make the most of your disk space.

Also covered in this part are the fun utilities in Microsoft Plus! 98. These include creative desktop themes, a screensaver, and three games that are bound to keep you entertained on rainy days.

CHAPTER 20

Using Plus! 98

Plus! 98 is a set of optional enhancements you can buy for Windows 98. None of these enhancements are necessary to run Windows 98, but many of them are very useful and others are simply a lot of fun. Plus! 98 includes such important tools as McAfee VirusScan and fun games such as Lose Your Marbles. The components of Plus! 98 include the following:

▶ Golf 1998 Lite, Lose Your Marbles, and Spider Solitaire, three games that are almost guaranteed to keep you occupied for more hours than you can imagine

▶ McAfee VirusScan to protect your computer from viruses you may accidentally download from the Internet or that you may encounter if you share files with other computer users

▶ Deluxe CD Player, a replacement for the Windows 98 CD Player that can download information about your audio CDs from the Internet so that you no longer have to type out song lists manually

▶ New desktop themes and an Organic Art Screensaver that can make your PC a lot more interesting and fun to use

▶ An improved Disk Cleanup tool that can recover additional space on your hard drives by removing many more types of files than the standard Windows 98 Disk Cleanup tool

▶ An improved Maintenance Wizard to help you keep your system running at peak performance levels

▶ Compressed Folders to help you make the most of your disk space

▶ Picture It! Express, a "lite" version of Microsoft Picture It! that you can use to clean up and modify images you've scanned or downloaded from your digital camera

If you've already bought Plus! 98, this chapter provides you with a quick start at using some of the more popular features of Plus! 98. If you don't already have Plus! 98, this chapter gives you a quick preview so you can decide if it's really worth spending the extra money to buy Plus! 98. Either way you'll have fun learning about Plus! 98, and we won't spoil your fun by showing you how to win the games!

Installing Plus! 98

Before you can install Microsoft Plus! 98, you must first install Windows 98 itself. Plus! 98 only runs on Windows 98 — you cannot use Plus! 98 with any other version of Windows. Also, the version of Plus! that was designed for Windows 95 should not be installed on a system that is running Windows 98.

Installing Plus! 98 isn't an all or nothing affair. If you're short of disk space or if you simply don't care about a particular Plus! 98 component, you can pick and choose just what will be installed. For example, if you aren't interested in the Plus! 98 desktop themes, you can save over 57MB of disk space by choosing to skip them. Or you can be selective about which themes are installed and only install those that interest you.

A complete Plus! 98 installation can require up to 150MB of disk space — although the figure will likely be closer to 130MB if your hard disk uses the FAT 32 file system. Plus! 98 also requires at least a 90 MHz Pentium processor, 16MB of memory, and a CD-ROM drive. A number of the components of Plus! 98 also depend on an Internet connection.

Don't store your Plus! 98 CD-ROM away once you've installed Plus! 98. You'll need the CD-ROM in your CD-ROM drive in order to access some of the features of Plus! 98. Golf 1998 Lite, for example, must be able to load scenes from the CD-ROM. Well over 130MB of additional content that is not installed on your hard drive is available when the Plus! 98 CD-ROM is in the drive.

TAKE NOTE

► SUPER VGA RECOMMENDED

Although Plus! 98 will run on systems that use VGA (640 by 480) resolution, it's recommended that you use a higher resolution setting for most Plus! 98 components. Golf 1998 Lite, for example, uses Super VGA (800 by 600) resolution and 16-bit (high) color mode. Many of the screen savers have both 800 by 600 and 1024 by 768 modes and display very poor video quality at lower resolution settings.

► CHANGE PLUS! 98 INSTALLATION OPTIONS LATER

It's usually best to install Plus! 98 completely as shown in the figures on the facing page, and then remove components you don't want later. Once you've installed Plus! 98, you'll find Microsoft Plus! 98 in the list on the lower half of the Install/Uninstall tab of the Add/Remove Programs dialog box. Doing a complete install of Plus! 98 will enable you to sample each of the Plus! 98 components, and you may discover that some of them are more useful or interesting than you thought they might be.

SHORTCUT

Double-click Setup.exe on the Plus! 98 CD-ROM to install Plus! 98 if AutoPlay is not enabled.

FIND IT ONLINE

See **http://www.microsoft.com/Windows98/Basics/plus/default.asp** for more on Plus! 98.

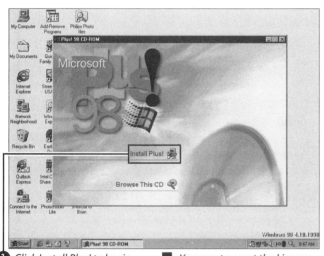

1 *Click Install Plus! to begin installing Plus! 98.*

■ *Click Next at each of the screens that follow after you've made any necessary selections.*

■ *You must accept the License Agreement by selecting the I accept the Agreement radio button.*

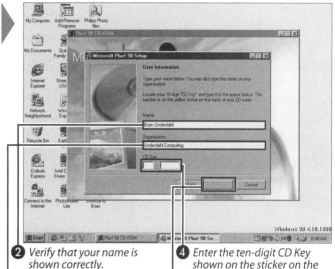

2 *Verify that your name is shown correctly.*

3 *You can enter your company or organization name here.*

4 *Enter the ten-digit CD Key shown on the sticker on the back of the CD-ROM case.*

5 *Click Next to continue. You can then choose whether you'd like to scan for viruses.*

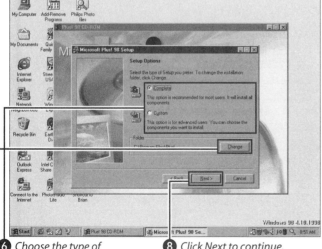

6 *Choose the type of installation you prefer.*

7 *Click Change if you want to choose an alternate location to install Plus! 98.*

8 *Click Next to continue.*

■ *As the installation proceeds you may need to make a few additional choices depending on your selections.*

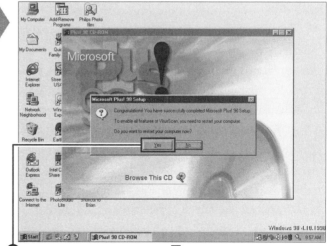

9 *Click Yes to restart your computer.*

■ *It's always a good idea to restart your system after installing new software.*

Using McAfee VirusScan

Computer viruses can be a real threat to the health and well-being of your computer and any work that you've stored on your computer's disk drives. Viruses can destroy your files, reformat your hard disk, or do any number of other less severe yet very annoying types of damage to your computer. Using a PC without protection against virus attack — especially if you download files from the Internet — is simply asking for trouble!

Plus! 98 includes one of the most highly respected antivirus programs — McAfee VirusScan. This program actually consists of two main components that provide different types of protection to your computer, VirusScan and VShield. VShield is a *memory-resident* program, which means it watches for virus activity constantly as you use your computer. VirusScan (which is also referred to simply as Scan) is a virus scanner that you run to check for viruses in the files on your disk drives. Unlike VShield, VirusScan looks for viruses before they get a chance to run.

Whereas VShield guards against known viruses when you launch applications, VirusScan searches for viruses on disks *before* you launch an application. You may encounter several different types of computer viruses. *Boot sector* viruses are programs that attach themselves to the critical area of a disk that must be read whenever a computer is started from the disk. *File* viruses are programs that infect files — generally program files — and do their damage when

the infected file is run. *Macro* viruses are programs written in the macro language of an application program such as Word or Excel. These macro viruses run when the infected document is opened. *Stealth* and *encrypted* viruses attempt to hide their existence from antivirus programs.

TAKE NOTE

MAKE AN EMERGENCY DISK

If a virus infects your computer, you may discover that you have an even worse problem than you imagine. Once your hard disk is infected, it can be extremely difficult to remove the infection because the virus may make itself memory-resident. This means that your system could be reinfected as soon as your antivirus program removes the virus. To prevent this you need an emergency disk that you can use to start your system without loading the virus. Use the Programs ➪ Microsoft Plus! 98 ➪ McAfee VirusScan ➪ Create VirusScan Emergency Disk command on the Windows 98 Start menu to create this disk before your system is infected.

DISABLE VSHIELD BEFORE INSTALLING PROGRAMS

Before you install a new program or update Windows 98, be sure to temporarily disable VShield by right-clicking the VShield icon on the system tray and choosing Disable. Reenable VShield once you complete the software installation.

CROSS-REFERENCE

See "Installing Plus! 98" earlier in this chapter for more on scanning for viruses before installing Plus! 98.

FIND IT ONLINE

See **http://www.nai.com/products/securecast/obs/ 1button.asp** for more on McAfee antivirus programs.

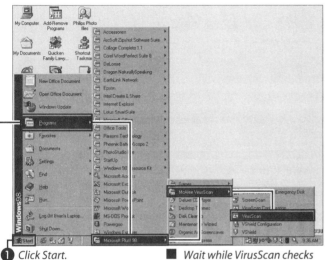

① *Click Start.*

② *Select Programs ⇨ Microsoft Plus! 98 ⇨ McAfee VirusScan ⇨ VirusScan to load the program.*

■ *Wait while VirusScan checks to make certain no viruses are currently in memory.*

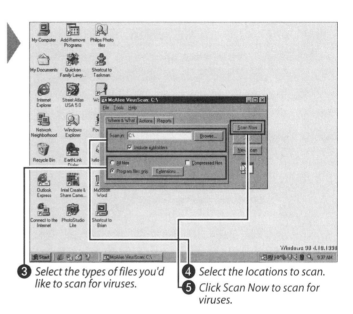

③ *Select the types of files you'd like to scan for viruses.*

④ *Select the locations to scan.*

⑤ *Click Scan Now to scan for viruses.*

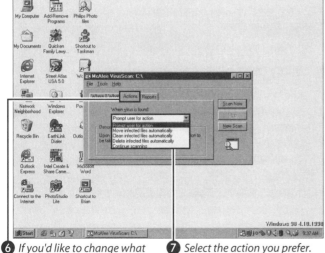

⑥ *If you'd like to change what VirusScan does when it finds a virus, click the Actions tab.*

⑦ *Select the action you prefer.*

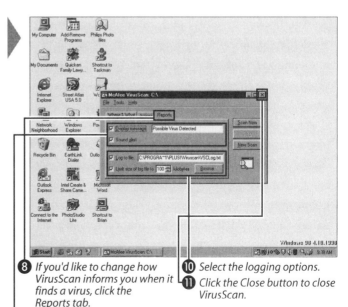

⑧ *If you'd like to change how VirusScan informs you when it finds a virus, click the Reports tab.*

⑨ *Select the display and sound options.*

⑩ *Select the logging options.*

⑪ *Click the Close button to close VirusScan.*

Using the Deluxe CD Player

Virtually all Windows 98–based PCs have considerable multimedia capabilities built into the system. The CD-ROM drive in your computer does a perfectly good job of playing audio CDs, and because the CD-ROM drive is probably just sitting there idle most of the time, you can easily use it to add some enjoyment in the form of music to your workspace.

The standard CD Player that's provided with Windows 98 is pretty well equipped. You can insert an audio CD into the CD-ROM drive and then enter the name of the CD, the artist, the track names, and even choose a play list of your favorite songs from the CD. The next time you insert the same audio CD, the CD Player remembers all of the information you entered so you don't have to go through the whole process all over again. What more could you want?

Well, how about not having to enter all of that information in the first place? Wouldn't it be nice to simply insert an audio CD and have the CD, Player automatically know everything there is to know about it? That's just what the Plus! 98 Deluxe CD Player does — with a little help from the Internet, that is. When you insert a new audio CD the Deluxe CD Player has the ability to download all of the pertinent information from sites on the Internet that maintain huge databases of information about audio CDs. With just a few quick clicks of your mouse, the song titles, the album title, and the artist are all stored right on your computer, and you don't have to worry about typing errors. You can sit back and listen to your favorite music!

TAKE NOTE

▶ NOT ALL MUSIC SITES ARE EQUAL

The Deluxe CD Player can use a play list you already entered using the standard CD Player. But if Deluxe CD Player recognizes a new audio CD that has not already been entered in the Windows 98 audio CD database, it will offer to download the information from the Internet. Several music information sites exist on the Internet, but you may discover that some sites don't include information on some of the more esoteric CDs. If your musical tastes run a bit astray from the mainstream, you may need to select a different music information site to enable Deluxe CD Player to find the information on your favorite CDs.

▶ EXERCISE FINER CONTROL

Deluxe CD Player has a large number of options you can use to fine-tune the way the player works. Click the Options button and select Preferences to display the Preferences dialog box. The Playlists tab of this dialog box enables you to view and modify the information for any audio CD that is stored in the Windows 98 audio CD database.

CROSS-REFERENCE

See "Using CD Player" in Chapter 11 for more information on play lists.

FIND IT ONLINE

See **http://www.tunes.com/tunes-cgi2/tunes/ home_page_aff/0/203** for more on audio CDs.

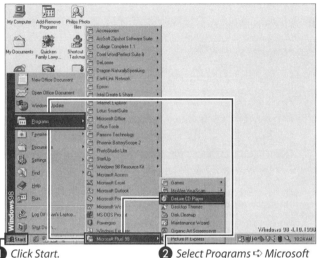

1 Click Start.

2 Select Programs ➪ Microsoft Plus! 98 ➪ Deluxe CD Player.

■ Insert an audio CD.

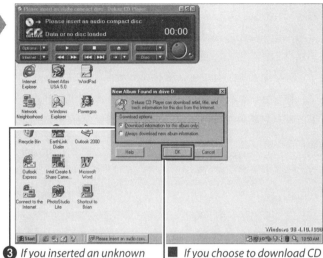

3 If you inserted an unknown audio CD, choose an option for downloading the information.

■ If you choose to download CD information, make certain you are connected to the Internet before you continue.

4 Click OK to continue.

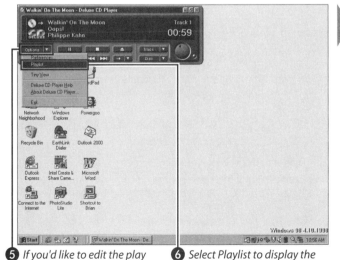

5 If you'd like to edit the play list, click Options.

6 Select Playlist to display the Preferences dialog box Playlists tab.

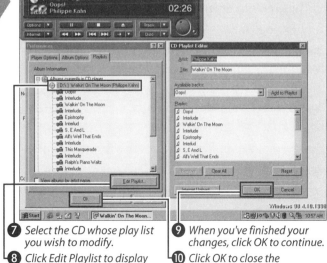

7 Select the CD whose play list you wish to modify.

8 Click Edit Playlist to display the CD Playlist Editor dialog box.

9 When you've finished your changes, click OK to continue.

10 Click OK to close the Preferences dialog box.

341

Using Plus! 98 Desktop Themes

Just in case you haven't found just the right look and feel for your Windows 98 desktop, Plus! 98 has 18 more desktop themes to help you find what you're looking for. Desktop themes can include a broad range of options from different mouse pointers, colorful wallpaper, unusual sounds, screen savers, different screen fonts, new color schemes, and so on. Some of the Plus! 98 desktop themes include 3-D effects that will make your monitor appear to be a window on a strange universe rather than a flat piece of glass!

The Plus! 98 desktop themes are versatile, meaning you don't have to use all the components from a theme if you'd prefer to use something else. For example, you may discover that you like the icons, screen saver, and sounds from the Science Fiction theme but that you don't care for the colors or fonts included in that theme. If so, you can simply choose to use the elements you want and skip the rest when you're selecting a theme. If you've already applied a desktop theme, you can still make any changes you like primarily using the Display Properties dialog box that appears when you right-click the desktop and choose Properties. You'll need to use the Sounds Properties dialog box that appears when you double-click the Sounds icon in Control Panel to change sounds.

TAKE NOTE

WATCH YOUR DISK SPACE

The complete set of Plus! 98 desktop themes uses over 57MB of disk space. If you find that you like certain desktop themes, you can recover quite a bit of space by uninstalling those themes that you don't use. To see just how much space a desktop theme folder uses, open Windows Explorer and navigate to the \Program Files\Plus!\Themes folder. Right-click one of the desktop theme folders and select Properties from the shortcut menu. The Properties dialog box will show the amount of space that the folder and its contents are using. You can remove unwanted desktop themes using the Add/Remove Programs dialog box.

BE CAREFUL OF POWER MANAGEMENT

A number of the Plus! 98 desktop themes include 3-D screen savers, and these screen savers are generally incompatible with the Windows 98 monitor power management features. On most computers, monitor power management is automatically turned off if you choose a 3-D screen saver, but that doesn't prevent you from manually turning this feature back on. If you do so, you may discover that your computer locks up if the monitor is set to go off at the same time the screen saver starts. Double-click the Power Management icon in Control Panel to adjust the power management settings.

CROSS-REFERENCE

See "Using a Screen Saver" in Chapter 4 for more on setting up a screen saver.

FIND IT ONLINE

See **http://www.microsoft.com/Windows98/Basics/Plus/PlusDetails.asp** for more desktop themes.

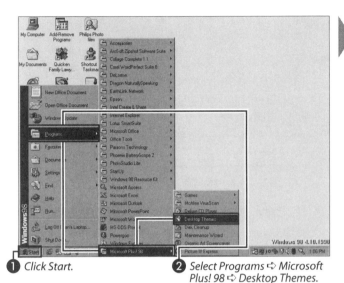

1 Click Start.

2 Select Programs ➪ Microsoft Plus! 98 ➪ Desktop Themes.

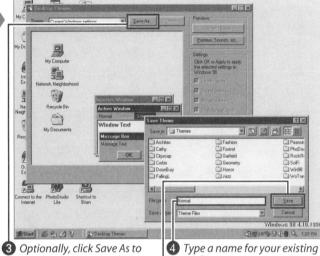

3 Optionally, click Save As to save your current settings so that you can easily return to them later.

4 Type a name for your existing settings.

5 Click Save to save your current settings.

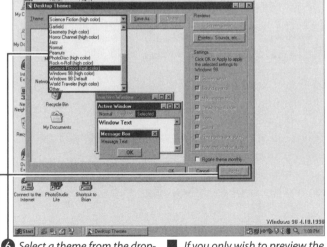

6 Select a theme from the drop-down list box.

7 If you wish, click Apply to view the theme on your desktop.

■ If you only wish to preview the theme in the Desktop Themes preview pane, don't click Apply.

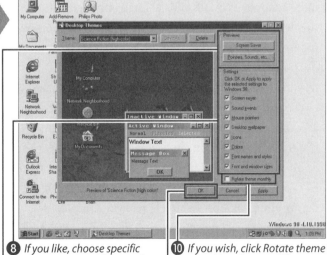

8 If you like, choose specific elements you wish to apply.

9 If you want to preview additional theme elements, click one of these buttons.

10 If you wish, click Rotate theme monthly to have a different theme applied automatically each month.

11 Click OK to close the dialog box and apply any changes.

Using the Plus! 98 Utilities

Plus! 98 adds several new utility features to Windows 98. The Plus! 98 box shows these as File Cleaner, Start Menu Cleaner, and Compressed Folders. File Cleaner has been renamed as Disk Cleanup and Start Menu Cleaner is now part of Maintenance Wizard. Compressed Folders simply show up as an option on the shortcut menu when you right-click in Windows Explorer.

In Chapter 18 you learned how to use the standard Windows 98 Disk Cleanup tool to remove unneeded files from your hard drive. Plus! 98 enhances this tool by giving you the ability to remove additional files you aren't likely to need. The figures on the facing page show you how to use this feature.

Chapter 19 showed you how to use the Maintenance Wizard to schedule routine maintenance chores. Plus! 98 adds a small enhancement to this wizard that cleans up your Start menu by removing broken links and empty folders that serve no purpose. Because you don't have to do anything differently to use the new capabilities, there's no need to cover the Maintenance Wizard again here.

Compressed folders work almost the same as programs such as WinZip to enable you to store additional data on your disks. When you right-click in Windows Explorer, you can choose to create a compressed folder — which is really a ZIP file. You can store files in the compressed folder just as you would in any other folder, but those files will use far less room because they are compressed.

TAKE NOTE

▶ WATCH WHAT YOU REMOVE

The enhancements to the Disk Cleanup tool in Plus! 98 enable you to regain much more disk space than is possible with the standard Windows 98 Disk Cleanup tool, but you must use caution in choosing what to delete. Unlike the standard tool, the Plus! 98 version presents you with several large lists of files that you can delete. These lists are broken down into three groups. Files that are marked with a green triangle are probably safe to remove. Files marked with a yellow box are possible candidates for removal, but could cause problems if they are deleted. Files that are marked with a red stop sign really aren't safe to remove.

▶ BE SAFE NOT SORRY

Because you must remove the extra files shown by the Plus! 98 Disk Cleanup tool manually, you have the option of taking a few simple steps to protect yourself from problems. First, use the File ⇨ Print List command to print a copy of the file listing so that you can see the original location of the files if you need to restore them later. Second, use the Move To command on the shortcut menu to move the files to floppy disks or to other removable media such as a Zip drive rather than simply deleting those files. Moving files to another place means you can restore them if necessary. Quick View lets you view selected files to determine if they are safe to delete.

CROSS-REFERENCE

See Chapter 19 for more on setting up an automatic maintenance schedule.

FIND IT ONLINE

See **http://www.winzip.com/** for information on WinZip.

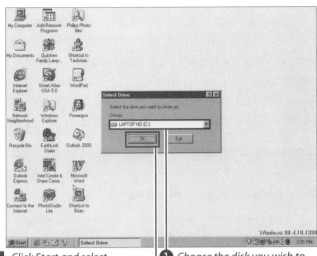

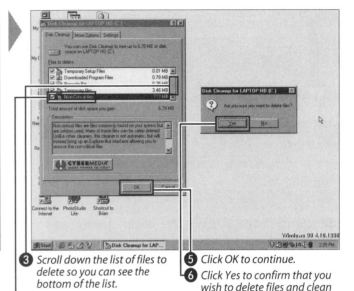

■ *Click Start and select Programs* ➪ *Microsoft Plus! 98* ➪ *Disk Cleanup.*

① *Choose the disk you wish to clean up.*

② *Click OK to continue.*

③ *Scroll down the list of files to delete so you can see the bottom of the list.*

④ *Place a check in the Non-Critical Files check box.*

⑤ *Click OK to continue.*

⑥ *Click Yes to confirm that you wish to delete files and clean up your hard disk.*

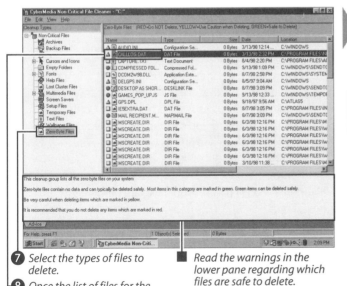

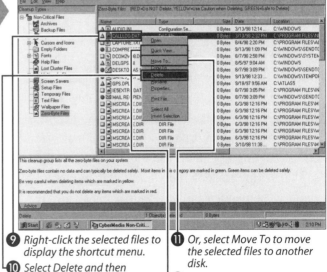

⑦ *Select the types of files to delete.*

⑧ *Once the list of files for the selected type is displayed, select the files you wish to delete.*

■ *Read the warnings in the lower pane regarding which files are safe to delete.*

■ *Hold down Ctrl while clicking files to select several files at once.*

⑨ *Right-click the selected files to display the shortcut menu.*

⑩ *Select Delete and then confirm the deletion if you're sure you want to delete the files.*

⑪ *Or, select Move To to move the selected files to another disk.*

⑫ *Or, select Quick View to view the contents of the selected files.*

Modifying Images with Picture It! Express

If you have a digital camera, a scanner, or even some digital images that someone has given you on your PC, Picture It! Express will be of great interest to you. Picture It! Express is a "lite" version of Microsoft's Picture It! 2.0 image editing software. With this software you can prepare digital images for printing, for use on your Web site, or for sending to someone as an attachment in an e-mail message.

Picture It! Express handles the basic photo editing functions such as acquiring an image; moving and cropping the image; removing "red eye" — the red spots that often show up in flash photos; modifying brightness, contrast, and tint; adding a softer edge; saving images in different file formats; and printing your photos. You'll probably find that this program does just about everything you really need and that it's very easy to use.

You'll probably use the options on the Paint & Color Effects menu more than most of the other features of the program. For example, if you have a picture that you took on a cloudy, overcast day, you may want to slightly enhance the brightness and contrast to improve the picture's appearance. You may want to adjust the tint of a photo you took in artificial light so that skin tones look more natural. If you took a photo of someone when you were using a flash, you may want to use the touchup option to remove the red spots from the eyes.

Because Picture It! Express is a "lite" version, you'll find some of the options don't really have much purpose. Because the lite version doesn't give you the option to combine several images, for example, the move, flip, and rotate options on the Size & Position menu don't serve a useful purpose.

TAKE NOTE

▶ USING REGULAR PHOTOS

If you don't have a digital camera or a scanner, you can still use Picture It! Express to modify your pictures. Many photo finishers offer the Kodak Photo CD service that places a copy of your photos on a CD-ROM. Picture It! Express understands how to open at least 17 different types of image files including Kodak Photo CD, so this is a good way to ease yourself into the world of digital image editing without investing a lot of time and money.

▶ PROTECT YOUR ORIGINAL IMAGE

When you modify images in Picture It! Express it's a good idea to use the Save As option on the Save, Print, & Send menu to save the file under a different name. That way you can experiment with the different touchup and effects options without affecting your original image. This is especially important since Picture It! Express lacks an undo option — any changes you make are permanent!

CROSS-REFERENCE

See "Configuring the Desktop Background" in Chapter 4 for more on using images as wallpaper.

FIND IT ONLINE

See **http://www.microsoft.com/pictureit/ express.htm** for more on Picture It!

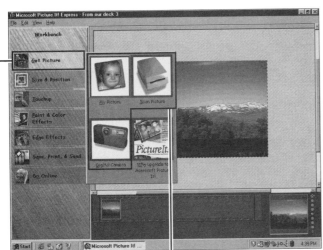

■ Click Start and select
Programs ⇨ Microsoft Plus!
98 ⇨ Picture It! Express.

❶ Click the Get Picture menu
button to display the menu
options.

❷ Choose a method to load a
photo into Picture It! Express.

■ Each method varies, so
continue on to the next step
once the picture is finished
loading.

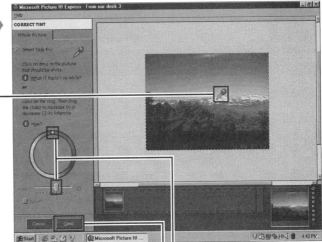

■ Select Paint & Color Effects ⇨
Correct Tint from the
Workbench to display the tint
correcting tools.

❸ Click an area of the image
that should be white.

❹ Alternatively, drag the ball
and slider to manually adjust
the tint.

❺ Click Done to continue.

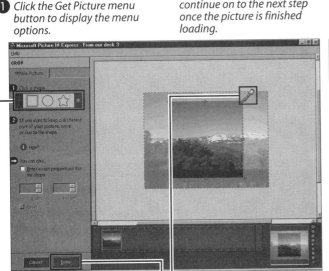

■ From the Workbench, select
Size & Position ⇨ Crop to
display the cropping tools in
place of the menu bar.

❻ If you wish, select a cropping
shape from this list.

❼ If you want to resize the
cropping area, drag one of
the handles.

❽ Click Done to continue. If you
cropped the image, click OK
to accept the changes.

❾ Click the Save, Print, & Send
menu button to display the
menu options.

❿ Select Save to save your
modified image.

⓫ Alternatively, select Print This
Picture to print the image.

■ Use Save As to change the file
name or type or Close This
Picture to cancel your
changes.

Playing Games

All work and no play makes for a dull day (or something like that). Plus! 98 includes three games to help you waste hours of your time playing with your computer. If you're a busy person and never seem to have enough time, don't even start playing. If you do, you'll soon find that you've wasted hours and haven't gotten any work done.

Spider Solitaire is a two-deck solitaire card game that starts with ten stacks of cards across the screen. Like any other solitaire game, the objective of Spider Solitaire is to build same-suit stacks of cards that are complete starting with the King and ending with the Ace. There are a couple of very tricky elements to this game. First, you have to open up a spot for the same-suit stack by moving other cards, and second, the rules for moving the cards are probably quite different from any solitaire game you've ever played. Without revealing too much, I'll just tell you that you can only move a group of cards if they're all the same suit. You can only stack a card on another card that has a value just above the card you're moving. That is, you can place a five on top of a six, but not directly on top of any other card. The suit of the card you're stacking on top of doesn't matter.

Lose Your Marbles is a fast-paced game of marbles. You play against the computer and each player has a box with two lines drawn across near the middle.

Your side is on the left side of the screen. Your goal is to line up three or more similar colored marbles in a row between those two lines. Every time you line up three or more of the marbles correctly, that group of marbles disappears. You use the mouse to move the stacks of marbles up or down, and click within the lines to move the marbles one position to the right. As you play, additional marbles will drop in from the top or come up from the bottom of the box. The first player whose box is filled with marbles loses the game.

Golf 1998 Lite is a nine-hole version of Microsoft Golf 1998. You can select the conditions before you begin a round, and then you're ready to slice, wiff, or hit a hole-in-one with the masters. Golf 1998 Lite may not improve your swing, but at least you'll get to tour a real golf course in the digitized images on the screen. Because your computer keeps score, there's no cheating on your log book, either!

TAKE NOTE

COMPETE ONLINE

Microsoft offers an online gaming site at http://www/zone.com that allows you to compete with friends and strangers in a variety of games, if you have the right hardware and software.

CROSS-REFERENCE

See "Installing Plus! 98" earlier in this chapter for more information on installing all of Plus! 98.

FIND IT ONLINE

See **http://www.microsoft.com/sports/golf/** for more on Microsoft Golf 1998.

Keep Your Plus! 98 CD-ROM Handy

If you want to play Golf 1998 Lite, be sure to keep your Plus! 98 CD-ROM handy. Much of the scenery for this game is stored on the CD-ROM, so you won't be able to play unless the CD-ROM is in your CD-ROM drive. Also, you may need to connect to the Internet to access some of the game's features — especially if you select the Preview.

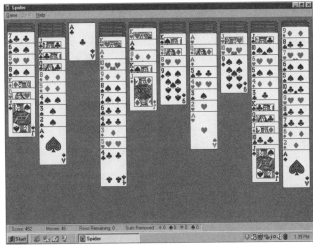

You'll waste hours of time playing Spider Solitaire. This is a two-deck solitaire game that is fiendishly difficult to win.

Lose Your Marbles is a simple game guaranteed to have your heart pounding as you try to keep up with the marbles that drop in from the top and pop up from the bottom.

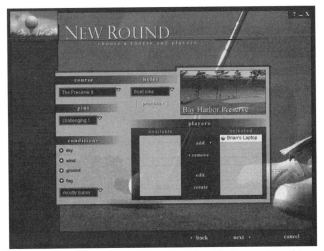

Golf 1998 Lite can't supply the fresh air, but it's the next best thing to being right out there on the links.

Personal Workbook

Q&A

1 What McAfee VirusScan option should you use to make certain you'll be able to start your system safely if a virus hits?

_____

_____

2 What part of McAfee VirusScan should you disable before installing new programs?

_____

_____

3 What kind of a virus could you get in a word processing or spreadsheet document file?

_____

_____

_____

4 What is the major advantage of the Deluxe CD Player compared to the standard Windows 98 CD Player?

_____

_____

_____

5 What problem might you encounter if you choose one of the Plus! 98 3-D screen savers?

_____

_____

_____

6 Which items shown by the Plus! 98 Disk Cleanup tool are considered safe to delete?

_____

_____

_____

7 What feature of Plus! 98 will require you to have the CD-ROM in your drive?

_____

_____

8 What common defect in flash photos can Picture It! Express automatically remove?

_____

_____

ANSWERS: 368

EXTRA PRACTICE

1. Use the Disk Cleanup tool to see if you have fonts that can safely be removed.

2. Move some of the unneeded files found by the Disk Cleanup tool from your hard drive to floppy disks or to another type of disk.

3. Open a picture in Picture It! Express and change the brightness and contrast.

4. Check your hard drive for virus infections.

5. Try out the Science Fiction desktop theme.

6. Get the gang together for a round of indoor Golf.

REAL-WORLD APPLICATIONS

✔ If you often share files with other PC users, you run the risk of having your system infected by a virus. Use McAfee VirusScan to check files before you open them.

✔ If you use a digital camera or a scanner to get photos into your system, you may discover that the colors don't seem quite right. You can use Picture It! Express to adjust the tint to correct for poor lighting conditions.

✔ If you install and try out a lot of different programs, you may find that your hard disk is becoming filled up even though you removed the programs you didn't need. Use Disk Cleanup to find and remove the leftover files cluttering your hard disk.

Visual Quiz

The image at the right shows a dialog box. How can you display the dialog box? What should you do before you select a new theme? How can you preview the screen saver for the theme?

_____

_____

_____

_____

_____

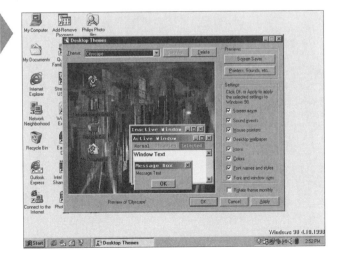

Appendix A: Personal Workbook
Answers

Chapter 1

see page 4

1 **In addition to clicking the Start button, what else can you do to display the Start menu?**

A: In addition to clicking the Start button, you can press the Windows key or press Ctrl+Esc to display the Start menu.

2 **What does a small arrow next to an item on the Start menu mean?**

A: A small arrow next to an item on the Start menu means that selecting the item will display a cascading menu.

3 **What do three periods following a menu item mean?**

A: Three periods following a menu item tell you that choosing this item will display a dialog box.

4 **What does an arrow on a desktop icon mean?**

A: An arrow on a desktop icon tells you that the icon is a shortcut.

5 **What does it mean if the icons on your desktop are underlined?**

A: If the icons on your desktop are underlined, you can activate them with a single-click rather than with a double-click.

6 **What can you do if you add icons to the Quick Launch toolbar but can't see them?**

A: If you add icons to the Quick Launch toolbar but can't see them, drag the edge of the toolbar to make the toolbar larger.

7 **How can you find out what a system tray icon does?**

A: To find out what a system tray icon does, hold the mouse pointer over the icon for a few seconds.

8 **How can you quickly switch between two programs without using your mouse?**

A: You can quickly switch between two programs without using your mouse by pressing Alt+Tab.

9 **What is the purpose of the Entire Network icon?**

A: The Entire Network icon can be used to show you workgroups in addition to the one you're logged into.

10 **How can you print a help topic?**

A: You can print a help topic by selecting Options ⇨ Print in the help window.

Visual Quiz

Q: How can you display this folder? What must you do to make the folder display the message shown here?

A: Double-click the My Computer icon to open the folder. Click the Printers folder to display the message.

353

Appendix A: Personal Workbook Answers

Chapter 2

see page 26

1 How do you display a specific folder when you open Windows Explorer?

A: To display a specific folder when you open Windows Explorer, use the Windows Explorer command line options in the Run dialog box or create a shortcut that specifies the correct command line options.

2 How do you run programs that don't appear on your Start menu?

A: To run programs that don't appear on your Start menu you can double-click their icon in the Windows Explorer window or use the Run dialog box.

3 What will happen if you try to place a second copy of the same file in a folder?

A: If you try to place a second copy of the same file in a folder, Windows 98 will either ask if you want to replace the existing file or add "Copy of" to the filename.

4 What type of Windows Explorer view should you select if you want to sort the file listing according to the file attributes?

A: If you want to sort the file listing according to the file attributes, select the details view.

5 What two groups are Windows Explorer file listings always divided into?

A: Windows Explorer file listings are always divided into groups of folders and groups of files.

6 How can you add a background image to a folder's Windows Explorer display?

A: To add a background image to a folder's Windows Explorer display you must display the folder as a Web page and customize the folder.

7 How can you keep the standard button toolbar and still maximize the space for the Windows Explorer file listing?

A: You can keep the standard button toolbar and still maximize the space for the Windows Explorer file listing by hiding the text labels and by dragging the toolbar to the menu bar row.

Visual Quiz

Q: How does this view differ from the standard Windows Explorer view, and how can you make Windows Explorer display image previews like this?

A: The image shows the folder displayed as a Web page. Select View ⇨ as Web Page to display this view.

Chapter 3

see page 44

1 How can you bypass the Recycle Bin, and delete a file permanently?

A: You can skip the Recycle Bin by holding down the Shift key when you delete a file.

2 Why is it more dangerous to delete files from floppy disks than from hard disks?

A: It is more dangerous to delete files from floppy disks than from hard disks because there is no Recycle Bin for floppy disks.

3 What two methods can you use to determine the original location of files in the Recycle Bin?

A: To determine the original location of files in the Recycle Bin you can select the file or you can change the Recycle Bin view to the details view.

Appendix A: Personal Workbook Answers

④ How much space will the default size Recycle Bin take on a 2GB hard disk?

A: The default size Recycle Bin on a 2GB hard disk will require 200MB of disk space.

⑤ How do the Delete and Cut toolbar buttons differ?

A: The Delete button moves all currently selected objects to the Recycle Bin, whereas the Cut button moves the objects to the Windows 98 Clipboard.

⑥ How can two objects in the Recycle Bin appear to have the same name?

A: Two objects in the Recycle Bin can appear to have the same name if they originated in different locations on your hard disk.

⑦ How can you change the Recycle Bin sort order?

A: You change the Recycle Bin sort order by selecting View ⇨ Arrange Icons and choosing a sort order, or by clicking a column heading in details view.

Visual Quiz

Q: How do you display this dialog box? Which part of the dialog box do you use to control how much disk space the Recycle Bin uses? Where would you place a check mark if you didn't want deleted items to go to the Recycle Bin?

A: Right-click the Recycle Bin icon and select Properties to display the dialog box. Use the slider to control how much disk space is used. Use the Do not move file to the Recycle Bin check box to skip the Recycle Bin.

Chapter 4

see page 58

① What do you need to activate before you can use a JPEG image as your desktop wallpaper?

A: You need to activate the Active Desktop before you can use a JPEG image as your desktop wallpaper.

② What is the fastest way to choose a desktop element on the Appearance tab of the Display Properties dialog box so you can change the element's color?

A: The fastest way to choose a desktop element on the Appearance tab of the Display Properties dialog box so you can change the element's color is to click the element in the preview window.

③ How can someone bypass your screen saver password?

A: Someone can bypass your screen saver password by restarting your computer.

④ What is the name of the process that automatically updates Active Desktop content?

A: The process that automatically updates Active Desktop content is called subscribing.

⑤ What will happen if you change the screen resolution setting but don't click the Yes button?

A: If you change the screen resolution setting but don't click the Yes button within 15 seconds, Windows 98 will restore your previous settings.

⑥ How can you make a hidden taskbar pop up without moving the mouse?

A: You can make a hidden taskbar pop up without moving the mouse by pressing Ctrl+Esc or by pressing the Windows key.

APPENDIX A: PERSONAL WORKBOOK ANSWERS

❼ How can you find a hidden taskbar using the mouse?

A: You can find a hidden taskbar using the mouse by sliding the mouse off the edge of the screen where the taskbar is hidden.

❽ What setting will make the taskbar hide even from the mouse?

A: Removing the check from the Always on top check box will make the taskbar hide even from the mouse.

❾ What will Windows 98 do when you double-click on a document on the desktop?

A: When you double-click on a document, Windows 98 will open the document in the application that produced the document.

Visual Quiz

Q: This image shows the 3D FlowerBox Setup dialog box. How can you display this dialog box? What purpose does it serve?

A: Display the dialog box by selecting 3D FlowerBox as the screen saver and then clicking the Settings button. This enables you to control how the screen saver functions.

Chapter 5

see page 78

❶ How can you tell, by looking at your desktop, whether your mouse is configured for single-clicking?

A: You can tell if your mouse is configured for single-clicking by looking at your desktop to see if the icons are underlined. If they are underlined, single-clicking will open objects.

❷ What can you do to make your mouse pointer easier to follow?

A: To make your mouse pointer easier to follow, you can activate pointer trails.

❸ How can you change your keyboard layout without actually moving any keys?

A: You can change your keyboard layout without moving any keys by using the Properties button on the Language tab of the Keyboard Properties dialog box.

❹ Where do you need to go to assign sounds to Windows 98 events?

A: To assign sounds to Windows 98 events you need to open the Sounds object in Control Panel.

❺ What option do you activate to allow the Shift, Ctrl, or Alt keys to be pressed once and act as if they were being held down while the next key is pressed?

A: You need to activate the StickyKeys option to allow the Shift, Ctrl, or Alt keys to be pressed once and act as if they were being held down while the next key is pressed.

❻ How can you cause Windows 98 to make a sound when the Caps Lock key is pressed?

A: You can cause Windows 98 to make a sound when the Caps Lock key is pressed by activating the ToggleKeys option.

❼ What type of peripheral installs automatically when you plug in its cable?

A: USB peripherals install automatically when you plug in the USB cable.

❽ What are animated mouse pointers called?

A: Animated mouse pointers are called animated cursors.

Appendix A: Personal Workbook Answers

❾ Where do you find the options that enable you to configure Windows 98?

A: You find the options that enable you to configure Windows 98 in the Control Panel.

Visual Quiz

Q: How can you display this dialog box? What purpose does it serve?

A: Display this dialog box by clicking the Browse button while you are choosing a mouse pointer. Use this dialog box to select different mouse pointers.

Chapter 6

see page 98

❶ Why should you avoid installing Windows 3.*x* programs on your Windows 98 system?

A: You avoid installing Windows 3.*x* programs on your Windows 98 system because those older programs often are prone to crashing because they were not designed for Windows 98.

❷ Where should you place items you want to start automatically whenever you start Windows 98?

A: You place items you want to start automatically whenever you start Windows 98 in the C:\Windows\Start Menu\StartUp folder.

❸ Why is it best to place shortcuts rather than actual programs on your desktop?

A: It is best to place shortcuts rather than actual programs on your desktop because if you accidentally delete a shortcut you won't remove the program itself.

❹ How does setting your mouse for single or double-click affect menu selections?

A: Your mouse single- or double-click setting has no affect on menu selections.

❺ What is a hotkey?

A: A hotkey is a keystroke combination that acts as a shortcut for executing a command.

❻ What does the size of the scroll box indicate?

A: The size of the scroll box indicates the percentage of the document that is visible in the workspace.

❼ How many options can you select at the same time from a group of radio buttons?

A: You can select one radio button in a group of radio buttons.

❽ How many options can you select at the same time from a group of check boxes?

A: You can select as many check boxes in a group as necessary.

❾ Why is it important to close programs correctly?

A: It is important to close programs properly to prevent data loss.

Visual Quiz

Q: How can you display this dialog box? What purpose does it serve? What are the items in the list box?

A: Display this dialog box by clicking the Add/Remove Programs icon in the Control Panel. Use this dialog box to install or uninstall programs and Windows 98 components. The items at the bottom of the dialog box are installed programs.

Appendix A: Personal Workbook Answers

Chapter 7

see page 118

❶ Why must you be careful about changing file extensions on your document files?

A: You must be careful about changing file extensions on your document files because Windows 98 uses the file extension to determine which application to use to open the file.

❷ Where can you quickly find a list of the documents that were most recently opened on your PC?

A: You can quickly find a list of the documents that were most recently opened on your PC by opening the Documents list on the Start menu.

❸ What happens to data that you've copied to the Clipboard when you copy additional data to the Clipboard?

A: When you copy additional data to the Clipboard any existing data is replaced.

❹ How can you copy data using drag and drop within a single document?

A: You can copy data using drag and drop within a single document by holding down Ctrl while you drag and drop.

❺ What happens when you drag and drop data between two different documents without holding down any keys?

A: When you drag and drop data between two different documents without holding down any keys you make a copy of the data.

❻ What is the fastest method of selecting an entire paragraph?

A: The fastest method of selecting an entire paragraph is to triple-click within the paragraph.

❼ What shortcut can you use to copy selected text to the Clipboard?

A: To copy selected text to the Clipboard, you can press Ctrl+C.

❽ What shortcut can you use to paste text from the Clipboard?

A: To paste text from the Clipboard, you can press Ctrl+V.

❾ How can you control the format of data you paste from the Clipboard?

A: To control the format of data you paste from the Clipboard, select Edit ➪ Paste Special.

❿ If you are unable to open a document that appears on the Documents list, what might be the cause?

A: You may be unable to open a document that appears on the Documents list because the Documents list contains shortcuts, and the shortcuts aren't updated if you delete or move the file without opening it.

Visual Quiz

Q: How can you display the active folder? What purpose does it serve? How can you learn more about the items in the folder?

A: Double-click the My Computer icon on your desktop to display the folder. This folder holds your documents and you can learn more about each document by selecting it.

Appendix A: Personal Workbook Answers

Chapter 8

see page 134

1 **How can you save paper while still seeing how your printed output will appear?**

A: You can save paper while still seeing how your printed output will appear by using the File ⇨ Print Preview command.

2 **What must you do before someone on your network can use your printer?**

A: Before someone on your network can use your printer you must share the printer using the Shared as radio button on the Sharing tab of the printer Properties dialog box.

3 **How can you print using a printer that isn't connected to your PC or your network?**

A: You can print using a printer that isn't connected to your PC or your network by printing to a file and then copying that print file to the printer.

4 **What is the best way to print multiple copies of the same document?**

A: The best way to print multiple copies of the same document is to select the number of copies in the Print dialog box.

5 **What do the terms portrait and landscape refer to?**

A: The terms portrait and landscape refer to the orientation of printing on the page.

6 **How can you make certain your documents will print on your preferred printer?**

A: You can make certain your documents will print on your preferred printer by selecting the Set as Default option for the printer.

7 **Why do you have to specify the correct printer before printing to a file?**

A: You have to specify the correct printer before printing to a file because a print file contains commands specific to the selected printer, and the file likely won't print correctly on other types of printers.

8 **What type of command do you need to use to print a print file?**

A: You need to use an MS-DOS COPY command to print a print file.

9 **Why would you want to place a printer icon on your desktop?**

A: You might want to place a printer icon on your desktop so you could drag and drop document files for printing, or so you could access the status box for the printer.

Visual Quiz

Q: **How can you display this dialog box? What purpose does it serve? How can you change the type of paper?**

A: Display the dialog box by clicking the Properties button in the Print dialog box. Use the settings in this dialog box to control how your printer works. Click a choice in the Paper size box to change paper types.

Chapter 9

see page 146

1 **How can long filenames complicate the search for files?**

A: Long filenames can complicate searching for files because if you use spaces in a filename, Windows 98 may try to search for each word in the filename as a separate search phrase.

Appendix A: Personal Workbook Answers

② **How can you avoid problems with searching for filenames that include spaces?**

A: You can avoid problems with searching for filenames that include spaces by enclosing the complete filename in quotation marks or by replacing the spaces with question marks.

③ **What Windows 98 accessory enables you to quickly look at the contents of most of the files you find?**

A: The Windows 98 Quick View accessory will enable you to quickly look at the contents of most of the files you find.

④ **What will happen if you don't click the New Search button between searches?**

A: If you don't click the New Search button between searches, Windows 98 will continue to use the criteria you've already specified in addition to the new criteria you add.

⑤ **What usually happens to the search location when you click the New Search button?**

A: When you click the New Search button, the search location is usually changed to your documents folders.

⑥ **How can you specify that you want to limit your search to files larger than a certain size?**

A: You can specify that you want to limit your search to files larger than a certain size by using the file size options on the Advanced tab.

⑦ **What step must you take before saving a search for future use?**

A: Before saving a search for future use, be sure to first perform the search — otherwise some of the search criteria may not be saved.

⑧ **How can you reuse a search you've saved?**

A: You can reuse a search you've saved by double-clicking the desktop icon for the search and clicking Find Now.

⑨ **How can you find a file if all you know is two words that occur together somewhere in the filename?**

A: You can find a file where two words occur together somewhere in the filename by specifying those two words separated by a question mark in the Named text box.

Visual Quiz

Q: How can you display this dialog box? What purpose does it serve? How can you change the search location to your CD-ROM drive?

A: Click the Browse button to display the dialog box which you can use to set the starting location for your search. Click the CD-ROM drive icon to select that drive.

Chapter 10

see page 162

① **To be a good candidate for a scheduled task, what capability does a program need?**

A: A program needs the capability to perform a task without intervention in order to be a good candidate for a scheduled task.

② **What is the quickest method of opening the Scheduled Tasks folder?**

A: The quickest method of opening the Scheduled Tasks folder is to double-click the Task Scheduler icon on the Taskbar.

Appendix A: Personal Workbook Answers

③ **Why might you want to enter a descriptive name for a task?**

A: You may want to enter a descriptive name if you schedule several different versions of the task.

④ **What is the shortest interval you can specify for repeating a scheduled task?**

A: The shortest interval you can specify for repeating a scheduled task is one day.

⑤ **What do the Idle Time options do?**

A: The Idle Time options specify how a scheduled task should delay if you are using your PC at the task schedule time.

⑥ **How can you get an onscreen notification that advises you when a scheduled task did not run?**

A: If you'd like an onscreen notification that advises you when a scheduled task did not run, select Advanced ➪ Notify Me of Missed Tasks.

⑦ **How can you suspend a task?**

A: You can suspend a task by unchecking the Enabled check box.

⑧ **If you receive a notice that a task did not run, how can you find the problem?**

A: If you receive a notice that a task did not run, you can find the problem by selecting Advanced ➪ View Log to view the events log.

⑨ **How can you set a date range for scheduled tasks?**

A: You can set a date range for scheduled tasks by clicking the Advanced button on the Schedule tab for the task.

Visual Quiz

Q: How can you display the dialog box at the right side of the figure? What purpose does this dialog box serve? How can you limit the task to run only during a specified month?

A: Click the Advanced button on the Schedule tab of the Disk Defragmenter dialog box to display the Advanced Schedule Options dialog box so you can set the times when Disk Defragmenter will run. Click the End Date check box and specify a Start and End date in the same month to limit the task to one month.

Chapter 11

see page 174

① **What are the two types of sounds the Windows 98 multimedia accessories can play?**

A: The two types of sounds the Windows 98 multimedia accessories can play are wave sounds and MIDI sequences.

② **Why are most video files shown in a small window?**

A: Most video files are shown in a small window rather than full screen because otherwise the data file would be too large.

③ **Which Windows 98 tool would you use to record a voice message?**

A: The Windows 98 tool you would use to record a voice message is called Sound Recorder.

④ **How can you make CD Player skip the same song on an audio CD every time you play the CD?**

A: You can make CD Player skip the same song on an audio CD every time you play the CD by entering a play list for the CD and leaving that song off the play list.

Appendix A: Personal Workbook Answers

⑤ **What is the quickest method of displaying the full volume control?**

A: The quickest method of displaying the full volume control is to double-click the speaker icon in the system tray.

⑥ **How does doubling the selected sample rate affect sound files you record?**

A: Doubling the selected sample rate for sound files you record doubles the size of the files.

⑦ **What should you do if you don't see the speaker icon in the system tray?**

A: If you don't see the speaker icon in the system tray, ensure that "Show volume control on the taskbar" is checked on the Audio tab of the Multimedia Properties dialog box.

⑧ **What type of files does the Sound Recorder produce?**

A: The Sound Recorder produces wave sound files.

Visual Quiz

Q: **This is a slightly different control than the one you're probably used to seeing. How can you display this window? What purpose does it serve?**

A: Select Options ⇨ Properties in the Volume Control and choose the Recording radio button to display this control. You can then use the displayed controls to adjust recording levels.

Chapter 12

see page 198

❶ **Where should you go to install missing Windows 98 accessories?**

A: If some of your Windows 98 accessories are missing from your Start menu, open the Add/Remove Programs item in Control Panel, and then click the Windows Setup tab. You may need your Windows 98 CD-ROM.

② **How can you transfer data between the calculator and other applications?**

A: The easiest way to transfer data between the calculator and other applications is to use copy and paste.

③ **How can you save Clipboard contents for future use?**

A: To save Clipboard contents for future use, open the Clipboard Viewer and select File ⇨ Save. You can later reload the saved contents using File ⇨ Open.

④ **When is Notepad the best choice for editing files?**

A: Notepad is the best choice for editing files that must be plain text files, such as MS-DOS batch files.

⑤ **What can you do if the lines of text in a Notepad document extend past the right edge of the window?**

A: If the lines of text in a Notepad document extend past the right edge of the window, select Edit ⇨ Word Wrap.

⑥ **How can you add a picture to a WordPad document?**

A: You can add a picture to a WordPad document by selecting Insert ⇨ Object and then choosing Windows Bitmap. You can also use drag and drop or paste an image you've copied to the Clipboard.

⑦ **What must you do if you want to edit an image from Imaging in Paint?**

A: If you want to edit an image from Imaging in Paint, be sure to save the image in Windows Bitmap format.

Visual Quiz

Q: **What is the purpose of this dialog box? How do you display it? Why isn't the Format Bar option checked?**

A: Display the dialog box by selecting View ⇨ Option for the WordPad menu. Use the dialog box to control what is displayed when different types of documents are open. Text documents don't use formatting, so displaying the Format Bar would serve no purpose.

APPENDIX A: PERSONAL WORKBOOK ANSWERS

Chapter 13

see page 222

1 How can you switch a program that is running in an MS-DOS window to full-screen view?

A: You can switch a program that is running in an MS-DOS window to full-screen by pressing Alt+Enter.

2 What should you do if the MS-DOS window says "finished" in the title bar?

A: If the MS-DOS window says "finished" in the title bar, click the Close button to close the window.

3 What types of files does MS-DOS recognize as programs?

A: MS-DOS recognizes files with BAT, COM, or EXE extensions as programs.

4 What does the message "Bad command or file name" mean?

A: The message "Bad command or file name" means that MS-DOS could not find an internal command or program file with the name you typed at the command prompt.

5 What happens to your Windows 98 programs when you enter MS-DOS mode?

A: When you enter MS-DOS mode your Windows 98 programs shut down.

6 How many programs can you run at one time in MS-DOS mode?

A: You can only run one program at a time in MS-DOS mode.

7 What do you type to close the MS-DOS window?

A: You type **EXIT** to close the MS-DOS window.

8 What type of drivers do you need to load to run things such as your mouse in MS-DOS mode?

A: You need to load real-mode drivers to run things like your mouse in MS-DOS mode.

Visual Quiz

Q: Why does this dialog box show the message rather than enable you to set the properties? How can you change these properties?

A: The dialog box shows the message because the program is set to run in MS-DOS mode. To make changes to these settings you must change the settings on the Program tab so the program does not require MS-DOS mode.

Chapter 14

see page 236

1 What does underlined text on a Web page usually represent?

A: Underlined text on a Web page usually represents a link that you can click to view another Web page.

2 How can you tell when you are pointing to a link on a Web page?

A: You can tell when you are pointing to a link on a Web page when the mouse pointer changes to a hand.

3 What is a URL?

A: A URL (Uniform Resource Locator) is the address of a Web page.

4 How can you make certain that a search engine looks for two words that are together?

A: You can make certain that a search engine looks for two words that are together by enclosing them in quotes.

Appendix A: Personal Workbook Answers

⑤ What is the term Internet Explorer uses for Web pages you save so you can easily return to them?

A: Internet Explorer uses the term *Favorites* for Web pages you save so you can easily return to them.

⑥ What are channels?

A: Channels are Web sites you subscribe to in order to automatically obtain content.

⑦ What do you need to do before you can use Windows Update?

A: Before you can use Windows Update, you need to register your copy of Windows 98.

⑧ What type of update should you always download and install?

A: You should always download and install critical updates.

Visual Quiz

Q: How can you display this dialog box? What do you need to do to display the detailed list that is shown? How can you use this dialog box to find out the last time you visited a Web page?

A: Select Favorites ⇨ Organize Favorites from the Internet Explorer menu to display the dialog box. Click the Details button to display the detailed list so that you can view the details such as the date modified and the last visit date.

Chapter 15

see page 256

① What does the number in parenthesis following an Outlook Express folder name mean?

A: The number in parenthesis following an Outlook Express folder name is the number of unviewed messages in the folder.

② Why do folder names sometimes appear in boldface?

A: Folder names appear in boldface when the folder contains messages you haven't viewed.

③ Where do messages you've created reside until they're sent to the mail server?

A: Messages you've created reside in the Outbox folder until they're sent to the mail server.

④ What do you call files that you send along with an e-mail message?

A: Files that you send along with an e-mail message are called attachments.

⑤ What do you need to do before you can save a file that came along with an e-mail message?

A: Before you can save a file that came along with an e-mail message you must open the message — you cannot save the file attachment from the message preview pane.

⑥ What can you do to make certain you see the latest messages in a particular newsgroup?

A: To make certain you see the latest messages in a particular newsgroup, you subscribe to the newsgroup.

Appendix A: Personal Workbook Answers

7 **How can you find newsgroups that pertain to a specific subject?**

A: You can find newsgroups that pertain to a specific subject by entering a search phrase in the Display newsgroups which contain text box.

8 **What must Outlook Express connect to in order to send and receive e-mail?**

A: Outlook Express must connect to a mail server on the Internet in order to send and receive e-mail.

Visual Quiz

Q: How can you display this dialog box? If you want to place your outbound messages in the Outbox rather than sending them as soon as you've created them, what setting do you need to adjust?

A: Select Tools ⇨ Options from the Outlook Express menu to display the dialog box. Remove the check from Send messages immediately to save outgoing messages in the Outbox.

Chapter 16

see page 272

1 **What is the most important thing people must do to make files available on a network?**

A: In order for files to be available on a network, users must share folders that are on their computer.

2 **How can you tell that you're seeing the name of a computer that is on the network?**

A: The names of computers on the network are preceded by two backslashes when they are used in filenames.

3 **What icon do you use to find other workgroups on the network?**

A: You use the Entire Network icon to locate other workgroups on your network.

4 **What are the two types of access you can allow to a folder on a Windows 98 network?**

A: The two types of access you can allow to a folder on a Windows 98 network are read-only and full access.

5 **How many passwords can you use to control access on a Windows 98 network?**

A: You can use two passwords per shared folder and one password for the Dial-Up Server on a Windows 98 network.

6 **How much of the network can you search at any one time when you're trying to find a file?**

A: You can search one computer on the network at a time when you're trying to find a file.

7 **What happens to folders that are contained in a folder you share on the network?**

A: Folders that are contained in a folder that you share on the network are also shared.

8 **Who has control over whether folders and printers are shared on the network?**

A: The person whose PC contains the folders or is connected to the printer has control over whether folders and printers are shared on the network.

Visual Quiz

Q: How can you display a dialog box such as this one? Why does it show three computers but no Entire Network icon?

A: Click the Network Neighborhood icon on your desktop to display this dialog box. Then click the workgroup icon to display only the computers within the workgroup.

Appendix A: Personal Workbook Answers

Chapter 17

see page 286

1 How many computers can you connect using HyperTerminal?

A: You can connect two computers at a time using HyperTerminal.

2 What can you do if you can't see anything you type in the HyperTerminal window?

A: If you can't see anything you type in the HyperTerminal window make certain the "Echo typed characters locally" check box is selected.

3 What can you do if lines of text overwrite the same line?

A: If lines of text overwrite the same line, select the "Send line ends with line feeds" check box or the Append line feeds to line ends check box.

4 How can you temporarily suspend capturing text to a file?

A: To temporarily suspend capturing text to a file, select Transfer ➪ Capture Text ➪ Pause.

5 What can you do if the text you need to keep is already on your screen?

A: If the text you need to keep is already on your screen, highlight the text and then select Edit ➪ Copy to place the text on the Clipboard.

6 What setting must be the same on both the sending and receiving computers before you can transfer a file?

A: In order to transfer a file both the sending and receiving computers must use the same file transfer protocol.

7 Why is Zmodem the best choice for sending files between two PCs running HyperTerminal?

A: Zmodem is the best choice for sending files between two PCs running HyperTerminal because only the sending PC needs to begin the transfer.

8 What command can you use to send text from the Clipboard during a HyperTerminal session?

A: To send text from the Clipboard during a HyperTerminal session, select the Edit ➪ Paste to Host command.

Visual Quiz

Q: How can you display this ASCII Setup dialog box? Which three settings will solve most problems you may have viewing text in the HyperTerminal window?

A: Click the ASCII Setup button in the Properties dialog box to display the ASCII Setup dialog box. The first three check boxes are very useful in solving most text viewing problems.

Chapter 18

see page 302

1 What type of errors will ScanDisk look for if you use the standard disk test?

A: ScanDisk will look for file system errors if you use the standard disk test.

2 What additional type of errors will ScanDisk look for if you use the thorough disk test?

A: ScanDisk will look for physical errors on the disk in addition to file system errors if you use the thorough disk test.

Appendix A: Personal Workbook Answers

❸ What is the difference between contiguous and fragmented files?

A: The difference between contiguous and fragmented files is that contiguous files are stored in one piece, whereas fragmented files are stored in multiple pieces.

❹ What is the name of the extra drive that is created when you compress a drive?

A: The extra drive that is created when you compress a drive is called a host drive.

❺ What selection can you make to ensure your backups don't include old files that haven't changed since the last backup?

A: To make certain your backups don't include old files that haven't changed since the last backup, select the New and changed files radio button.

❻ Where should you store your document files to make backups easier?

A: Store your document files in the My Documents folder to make backups easier.

❼ What tool can you use to remove old files that are no longer needed on your PC?

A: You can use the Disk Cleanup tool to remove old files that are no longer needed on your PC.

❽ Why should you check any floppy disks before you use them for backups?

A: You should check any floppy disks before you use them for backups because Backup won't delete existing files, and this may limit the amount of data you can backup on a floppy disk.

Visual Quiz

Q: How can you display this dialog box? Which setting on the displayed tab will have the greatest effect on the number of disks you'll need to use for backups?

A: Click the Options button in the Backup window to display the Backup Job Options dialog box. Select the Maximize compression to save space to reduce the number of floppy disks you'll need.

Chapter 19

see page 318

❶ What three tasks does the Maintenance Wizard schedule?

A: The Maintenance Wizard schedules Disk Defragmenter, ScanDisk, and Disk Cleanup.

❷ What must you do once you've used the Maintenance Wizard so that the tasks will run as scheduled?

A: Once you've used the Maintenance Wizard to schedule tasks, you must make certain your PC is on at the scheduled time so that the tasks will run as scheduled.

❸ What do you call older devices that do not support plug and play?

A: You call older, non–plug and play devices *legacy* devices.

❹ How does Device Manager indicate that a device has a problem?

A: Device Manager indicates that a device has a problem by using a yellow exclamation point or a red X.

❺ What system resources does Device Manager track?

A: Device Manager tracks *interrupt requests* (IRQs), *input/output* addresses (I/O), *direct memory access* (DMA), and *memory* addresses.

6 What tool can you use to try out a backed up version of a system file?

A: You use Version Conflict Manager to try out a backed up version of a system file.

7 What tool can you use to check for corrupted system files?

A: You use System File Checker to check for corrupted system files.

8 Why is it important to have a recent backup of the Registry?

A: It is important to have a recent backup of the Registry so that Windows 98 can attempt to use the backup if the Registry is corrupted.

Visual Quiz

Q: How can you display this dialog box? Which setting on the displayed tab will cause a new log file to replace the old log file?

A: Select Tools ⇨ System File Checker from the Microsoft System Information menu to display the dialog box. Select the Overwrite existing log radio button to always create a new log file.

Chapter 20

see page 334

1 What McAfee VirusScan option should you use to make certain you'll be able to start your system safely if a virus hits?

A: Use the McAfee VirusScan Create VirusScan Emergency Disk option to make certain you'll be able to start your system safely if a virus hits.

2 What part of McAfee VirusScan should you disable before installing new programs?

A: Before installing new programs you should disable VShield.

3 What kind of a virus could you get in a word processing or spreadsheet document file?

A: A word processing or spreadsheet document file could contain a macro virus.

4 What is the major advantage of the Deluxe CD Player compared to the standard Windows 98 CD Player?

A: The major advantage of the Deluxe CD Player compared to the standard Windows 98 CD Player is that the Deluxe CD Player can download information on your CDs from the Internet.

5 What problem might you encounter if you choose one of the Plus! 98 3-D screen savers?

A: You might encounter a problem with your monitor's energy saving features if you choose one of the Plus! 98 3-D screen savers.

6 Which items shown by the Plus! 98 Disk Cleanup tool are considered safe to delete?

A: Items shown with a green triangle by the Plus! 98 Disk Cleanup tool are considered safe to delete.

7 What feature of Plus! 98 will require you to have the CD-ROM in your drive?

A: Golf 1998 Lite requires the Plus! 98 CD-ROM to be in the drive.

8 What common defect in flash photos can Picture It! Express automatically remove?

A: Picture It! Express can automatically remove red eye from your flash photos.

Visual Quiz

Q: The image at the right shows a dialog box. How can you display the dialog box? What should you do before you select a new theme? How can you preview the screen saver for the theme?

A: Click the Start button and choose Programs ⇨ Microsoft Plus! 98 ⇨ Desktop Themes to display the dialog box. Be sure to click the Save As button to save your current settings before choosing a new theme. Click the Screen Saver button to preview the screen saver.

Appendix B:
Installing Windows 98

Installing Windows 98 is really pretty simple and straight-forward. Mostly you'll just have to answer a few easy questions and then sit back and wait while Windows 98 installs. In this appendix, you learn what you need to do to prepare for installing Windows 98.

If you buy a new PC today, it's likely your PC will come with Windows 98 already installed. If you're upgrading to Windows 98 from an older operating system, you'll find that it's easy to install Windows 98 yourself.

Getting Ready to Install Windows 98

Here are a few steps you need to follow before you install Windows 98:

1. Make sure your computer is compatible with Windows 98. It must have an 80486, Pentium, Pentium Pro, Pentium II, or compatible processor, 8MB of memory, and 50MB or more of free disk space. You'll be happier if you don't try to run Windows 98 on a 486, because most 486 systems will be pretty slow. You're also better off with at least 16MB of memory, and 100MB+ of free disk space.
2. Make sure you don't have any unresolved hardware problems or conflicts. If something isn't working right before you install Windows 98, it won't be working afterwards, either. The only exception to this is if you take the radical step of completely formatting your hard drive and starting from scratch.

In that case, you would be starting with a clean slate, but you may need to ask a computer expert to help you so you don't create an even bigger mess.
3. Back up any of your critical files. Installing Windows 98 shouldn't cause any data to be lost, but why take the chance? If you do decide to format your hard drive first, all of your files will be lost so making a backup will be critical.
4. Make sure you have a blank, high-density floppy disk available. Windows 98 can be installed without creating a startup floppy disk, but you should create one to protect yourself in the event problems occur.
5. If you're connected to a network, make certain you have a list of your user names and passwords. Otherwise you may not be able to log onto the network when you're finished installing Windows 98.

Installing Windows 98

You need about an hour to install Windows 98 — maybe longer if you encounter problems or have a slow system. You'll need a couple of hours if you decide to allow Windows 98 to convert your hard disk to the FAT32 file system during the installation of Windows 98 (it may be better to delay any such conversion until after you make certain Windows 98 runs properly on your PC). When you're ready to begin installing Windows 98, follow these steps:

1. Place the Windows 98 CD-ROM in your CD-ROM drive. If you're running Windows 95, you'll probably

see a message informing you that the CD-ROM contains a newer version of Windows and asking if you want to install it now. If so, choose to install Windows 98 and skip to Step 4.

2. If you're running Windows 3.*x*, select File ⇨ Run.

3. Type the following text (if your CD-ROM drive is not drive D, use the correct drive letter): **d:\setup**

4. Follow the prompts and click the Next button when necessary. Most of the questions will appear in the first few minutes of the installation process, and prompts will tell you when the rest of the process will proceed automatically.

5. If the setup program prompts you to choose a directory, choose the option to install Windows 98 in the same directory as your existing version of Windows — otherwise you'll have to reinstall all of your programs.

6. At one point the Setup program will direct you to make a startup disk. This will create a floppy disk that you can use to start your PC in case there's a problem with your hard disk. You can skip this if necessary — for example, if you are installing Windows 98 on a laptop PC that cannot have both the CD-ROM and floppy disk drives installed at the same time. Be sure to open the Add/Remove Programs dialog box later and make a startup disk if you skip this now.

7. Continue to follow the prompts and finish the installation. Be sure to remove any floppy disks before allowing the system to restart. Your computer may restart several times during the installation process.

If Windows 98 has any problems restarting, wait a few minutes before you do anything. Remember that it may take an hour or so to complete the installation. If problems do occur and your system seems to be locked up for ten minutes or more, turn off your computer, wait a minute, and turn the power back on. Windows 98 should be able to continue from the point it stopped.

Appendix C:
A Brief History of Windows

It seems hard to believe now, but Windows wasn't always everywhere. In November 1983, Microsoft announced the first version of an as-yet undesigned and unspecified operating environment with the seemingly uninspired name of Windows. This operating environment would add to the IBM PC a graphical user interface (GUI) and device independence for applications. The announcement was a preemptive marketing ploy to offset in-place and impending announcements from other vendors of similar GUI environments for personal computers, most prominently the Macintosh. The announcement promised shipment by April 1984, but Windows was not ready until November 1985.

Windows

The first version of Windows was premature at best and underpowered at worst. There were no applications of any consequence to run on it, and its GUI used a tiled window presentation instead of the overlapped window model that the Macintosh had introduced nearly two years earlier. Windows 1 was ugly and ineffective. The marketplace of users and applications developers mostly ignored it.

Windows 2.0

In October 1987, Microsoft announced Windows 2.0 and a companion product named Windows 386, which ran only on 386 machines and which took advantage of the newer CPU's advanced architecture. Both products used overlapping windows. Windows 2.0 was shipped with Microsoft Excel, the company's spreadsheet application, which ran under the Windows GUI. Windows 2.03, a retail version of the operating environment alone, shipped in January 1988. Application developers began to warm up to this environment, but its poor performance on mainstream PCs of the day postponed its widespread acceptance by users, and applications developers, seeing no demand for Windows applications, didn't create many.

Windows 3

Windows 3 was announced in May 1990 in a Manhattan media-blitz extravaganza. The new version offered minimum workstation support for networks (assuming that the workstation software was already installed in the host MS-DOS environment) and an improved user interface. Windows 286 and 386 were merged into a single product with Windows 3. PCs with sufficient speed and memory had become widely available to support this platform, and

Appendix C: A Brief History of Windows

Windows software development finally took off, fueled by a new demand for Windows versions of popular applications.

Windows 3.1 and Windows NT

In April 1992, Microsoft announced Windows 3.1 and Windows NT at the Windows World Conference in Chicago. Version 3.1 added TrueType fonts, more improvements to the user interface, and object linking and embedding (OLE), a technique for sharing data between complying applications.

Windows NT is a portable operating system with roots in OS/2, which Microsoft originally developed through an agreement with IBM. When IBM and Microsoft severed their association, Microsoft proceeded with NT, developing it to run on other hardware platforms in addition to the PC. Windows NT does not run on top of MS-DOS; it is its own operating system and integrates the file system and the GUI. NT also integrates networking software with the operating system. A network installation does not need to run a separate network operating system, such as NetWare, to connect NT machines in a network. Windows NT is a 32-bit, protected mode, preemptive multitasking, threaded operating system with a GUI shell that is virtually the same as the Windows 98 GUI. You can run MS-DOS programs, Windows 3.1 programs, Windows 98 programs, Windows NT programs, and even some OS/2 and POSIX programs under Windows NT. Windows NT, through Version 3.51, operates with the same user interface as Windows 3.1.

Windows for Workgroups Joins the Team

In 1993, Microsoft introduced Windows for Workgroups. This product is Windows 3.1 with peer-to-peer networking support added, which means that PCs running Windows for Workgroups and connected in a network can share resources such as files and printers. No third-party network software is required.

A 1994 upgrade of Windows 3.1 and Windows for Workgroups to Version 3.11 added 32-bit file support and other advanced features that Microsoft was testing for Windows 95, which was still under development.

Windows 95 and NT 4.0

Windows 95, released in August 1995, represented a major change in the desktop user interface metaphor, and featured 32 bit, protected-mode execution, which provides a more reliable and almost crash-proof operating environment.

In 1996, Microsoft released Windows NT 4.0, which featured the Windows 95 desktop user interface.

Microsoft Focuses on Web Browsing

In 1997, Microsoft released Internet Explorer 4.0, a Web browser that Microsoft distributed at no cost. The browser was designed to be integrated with the Windows 95 and NT 4.0 user interfaces to enable access of the Web and to enhance the local computing environment with browser-like characteristics.

Internet Explorer 4.0 became a controversial issue when purveyors of other browsers, primarily Netscape, complained that Microsoft was taking unfair advantage of the competition. As a result of these complaints, the Department of Justice issued an order in December 1997 compelling Microsoft to cease the practice wherein they required computer vendors to bundle Internet Explorer with all computers that shipped with Windows 95, and to support versions of Windows 95 that do not depend on Internet Explorer. Naturally, Microsoft opposed the ruling, arguing that removing Internet Explorer would cripple Windows 95, an apparent attempt to obscure the issue for the technically challenged judicial system. They interpreted the judge's orders literally and built a version of Windows 95 with the browser code completely removed, a version that would not work. Microsoft opponents countered this demonstration by showing how to remove Internet

Appendix C: A Brief History of Windows

Explorer from Windows 95 by simply uninstalling it. This attempt on the part of Microsoft to obfuscate the issue angered the judge, and he threatened to fine Microsoft one million dollars a day until they complied with his order. In January 1998, Microsoft capitulated and agreed to permit OEMs to ship at their option a version of Windows 95 that did not include the Internet Explorer icon on the desktop and did have the capability to install other Web browsers. Windows 98 is fully integrated with the Internet Explorer technology. The actions of competitors, the Justice Department, and the legislatures of several states failed to prevent Microsoft from releasing an integrated operating environment and Web browser.

Windows 98

Windows 98, the subject of this book, was released in a beta configuration to software developers in early 1997 and to users in mid-1997. It employs most of the user interface features of Windows 95 but integrates them, at the option of the user, with Internet Explorer 4.0 Web browser technology. Microsoft's Internet Explorer Web browser is now an integral part of the Windows 98 user interface. Windows 98 employs an optional new disk file storage mechanism called FAT32 that improves storage and retrieval performance and disk drive efficiency.

Windows 98 adds many new features to the Windows operating environment, but you lose some things, too. For example, Windows 95 included Microsoft Fax, which supported sending and receiving faxes through your fax modem. That feature was an integral part of Microsoft Exchange, which managed local e-mail and faxing. Microsoft Exchange has been replaced by Outlook Express, which does not include fax support. If you upgrade from a Windows 95 system that had Microsoft Fax installed, the feature remains in the new installation. If you upgrade from Windows 3.1 or install from MS-DOS, no fax support is included in the installation.

Glossary

A

accelerator key A Ctrl+ key combination that, when pressed from anywhere within an application, executes the corresponding menu command even when the menu is not open.

active window The one into which user inputs are read. The active window has its title bar highlighted. *See also* focus.

address book A database of electronic mail recipients.

applet A Windows 98 application included with the operating system. Examples are the accessory applications Notepad, WordPad, and Paint. The Control Panel's icons launch applets to configure the system. The term applet is also used to identify small applications loaded from the Internet.

application window The first window that displays for an application. An application has only one application window. *See also* document window.

arrow keys The up, down, right, and left arrow keys on the keyboard. They are typically used to move a text cursor.

ASCII American Standard Code for Information Interchange. The eight-bit coding system that encodes letters, digits, and punctuation characters. Text-only files consist of ASCII characters. Applets such as NotePad work with ASCII text files. HTML files are ASCII text files.

Authenticode A security feature that enables users to verify that files have not been tampered with.

AutoPlay A feature that enables Windows 98 to automatically execute a program on a CD-ROM disk when Windows 98 senses that you have loaded the disk in the CD-ROM drive.

auto-resume A feature usually found on laptop computers. When auto-resume is enabled, you can turn off the computer's power while the operating system and applications are still running. When you turn the power on again, the computer resumes processing in the same configuration of applications and operating system.

B

back up To save a designated set of disk files on a backup storage medium, such as tape, floppy disks, or the shared hard drive of another computer in a network.

beta test A test of a software product before release as a commercial product. Beta testers are volunteers who do not work for the vendor. They test the product and report problems in exchange for the privilege of using the product before its availability for general consumption.

bit A data storage unit that stores an atomic unit of data that has one of two states: zero and one.

GLOSSARY

bitmap The internal representation of a graphics image. Wallpaper is stored in bitmap format. The Paint accessory application reads and writes bitmap files, which use the filename extension .BMP.

boot To load the operating system into the computer and start a new session.

browse To search the drives and folders on your computer and others in the network to find resources — files, printers, applications, and so on.

byte An eight-bit unit of data storage that contains one alphabetic character or one numeric integer value in the range –127 to 128.

C

cascaded menu A menu that opens when you select a command from a higher-level menu.

cascading windows An arrangement of document windows that display in an overlapping cascade. *See also* tiled windows.

CD-ROM Compact Disc Read Only Memory. A compact disc configured to contain data. A CD-ROM is a read-only removable mass-storage medium capable of storing up to 650 megabytes of data.

check box A square box in a dialog box that you can set to on or off. When on, it contains an X. When off, it is blank.

choose To execute a command from a menu or dialog box.

click To press and release the left mouse button once with the mouse cursor pointed at the screen item you wish to select. *See also* double-click.

client A network computer that uses the shared resources of other computers in the network. *See also* server.

clip A file of streaming multimedia data, typically sound, video, or MIDI data.

Clipboard The Windows 98 repository into which you cut and copy text and graphics from applications and from which you paste text and graphics to applications. The method by which many Windows 98 applications share information.

Clipboard viewer A utility available in Windows 98 that lets you see the contents of the Clipboard.

cluster A group of contiguous disk sectors allocated to a file by the File Allocation Table. Files are constructed of chains of sectors.

COM port *See* communications port.

combo box A data entry control on a dialog box that consists of a text box for typing and a list box from which you can select predefined text selections.

command An instruction from the user to the computer to do something. Commands are implemented by one or more user interface controls. Menus contain command labels. When you click a menu command label, you execute the associated command. Toolbars contain tool buttons that, when clicked, execute the associated command. Dialog boxes contain command buttons. Some commands are associated with key strokes on the keyboard. For example, F1 executes the Help command. Many applications implement commands by using combinations of these user interface controls, often implementing commands with multiple controls so the user can choose from a selection of command idioms to use one that is preferred, convenient, or familiar.

command button A rectangular box in a dialog box that contains a command label. When you click the command button, you execute the command.

command-line The text-mode single-line user interface of nongraphical operating systems.

communications port A hardware device to which you can connect a modem, a terminal, a plotter, or a serial printer.

compressed drive A disk drive in which the data storage is compressed so that the effective byte capacity of the drive is increased. *See also* host drive.

Compression Agent A utility program that allows you to schedule when the System Agent automatically recompresses your hard drive, compressing files you've expanded or added since the last compression.

control A data entry or command field in a dialog box. Controls are buttons, text boxes, tabs, list boxes, and so on.

control menu The menu that accompanies most windows. It allows you to restore, close, move, size, minimize, and maximize the window.

copy Write text or graphics from an application to the Clipboard.

cursor A pointing icon associated with the keyboard or mouse. The cursor takes different forms depending on its current purpose.

cut To write text or graphics from an application to the Clipboard and delete the text or graphics from the application.

default The initial setting for a parameter, usually established by the system. You can change the default setting for many parameters. *See also* parameter.

defragmentation The process by which the files on a disk drive are reorganized so that every file is constructed from a contiguous chain of clusters, all files are together toward the beginning of the drive, and the free chain of clusters follows the last file.

desktop The Windows 98 user interface. The desktop contains the Start button, taskbar, and a user-customized collection of folder and application icons.

dialog box A window with various kinds of fields, called controls, into which the computer user enters commands and data values.

Dial-Up Networking A Windows 98 feature that helps you access your computer and data files from a remote site.

directory A group of files organized together in a structure of a root directory and subdirectories.

directory tree The Explorer's display of a disk drive's root directory and the subdirectories under it and each other.

disk A mass storage medium. *See also* CD-ROM, floppy disk, and hard disk.

Disk Defragmenter A Windows 98 utility that cleans up and consolidates file fragments on your disk.

DMA Direct Memory Access. A hardware architecture that transfers blocks of data between a device and the computer's memory without consuming microprocessor cycles. A PC has seven DMA channels. Devices that use DMA must be configured to use one of the seven. No two devices can use the same DMA channel at the same time.

dockable toolbar An application toolbar that can be dragged from its current position to a side, the top, or the bottom of the application window frame. The dockable toolbar attaches itself to the new edge, and the window's workspace adjusts to the new position of the toolbar.

Glossary

document A unit of work for the computer user. A word processing document, spreadsheet, illustration, sound effect file, database record, and so on.

document-centric A view of one's work that emphasizes the document rather than the application that processes it.

document window A window in which an application displays documents. An application can have multiple document windows. Some applications use the workspace of the application window for documents and do not have individual document windows.

DOS box A session in which you run MS-DOS as an application within Windows 98. The DOS box can occupy the full screen, or it can run in a window. The DOS box window emulates the full-screen text mode in which MS-DOS operates. *See also* MS-DOS, MS-DOS application, and MS-DOS mode.

double-click Click the left mouse button twice rapidly to choose an item on the screen. *See also* click.

drag and drop To press and hold the left mouse button while you move the mouse cursor across the screen. The object under the mouse cursor follows the cursor if the object is subject to being dragged. When the object is at its destination, drop it by releasing the mouse button.

driver An operating system program that manages control, input, and output of a specific hardware device.

DriveSpace 3 The disk compression utility.

drop-down list box A list box that has only one visible entry, which displays the current setting. When you click its down arrow, the box opens to reveal a list of settings from which you can choose.

dual boot A PC configuration that permits the selection of alternate operating systems when the computer is booted. Typical dual boots run combinations of OS/2, Windows 98, Windows NT, and earlier versions of

MS-DOS. Often, one or both options in a dual boot configuration are another dual boot selection, making multiple boot configurations possible.

E-mail An electronic message system in which remote computer users exchange mail messages and attached files.

Emergency Startup Disk *See* Startup Disk.

extension The one-to-three-character extension to a filename. The filename and its extension are separated by a period. *See also* filename.

FAT File Allocation Table. A table stored on every disk medium. The FAT records the allocation of disk clusters to files.

fax/modem A modem capable of sending and receiving faxes.

file A collection of information stored into one logical group on a disk. A file can be a document, an application, or a data file.

filename The 1-to-256-character name of a file. *See also* extension.

fixed disk *See* hard disk.

floating toolbar A toolbar that can be disconnected from its application window's frame and moved anywhere on the screen, inside or outside the application window.

floppy disk Removable disk medium. Also called diskette.

focus The condition by which a window receives user input. Only one window has the focus at a time, and that window accepts data input. You change the focus by clicking a different window, tabbing to the next control, or pressing an accelerator or shortcut key.

folder A logical collection of documents and applications organized by the user. Folders are implemented as subdirectories in the file system.

font A character set characterized by the shape and design of its characters. *See also* point size.

footer A body of text printed at the bottom of every page in a document. *See also* header.

format To prepare a floppy disk for use by writing formatting data bytes onto its tracks.

fragmentation The condition in which a disk medium's files and its free chain are constructed from many noncontiguous clusters.

free chain The chain of clusters on a disk that are not in use and are available to be assigned to files.

ftp An acronym for *file transfer protocol*, ftp is a method of sending and retrieving files to and from various sites around the world.

Gopher A powerful text-based search tool used on the Internet that enables you to locate and download files on the subjects you specify.

GUI Graphical user interface. An interface between the user and the computer that uses graphical elements — icons, windows, controls — rather than text messages and responses.

H

hard disk A high-capacity, nonremovable mass storage medium.

header A body of text that is printed at the top of every page in a document. *See also* footer.

hidden file A file with the hidden attribute set. Such files do not display in an Explorer file tree or a folder window unless you change the Explorer's or window's properties to display them.

highlighted An item is highlighted when you have selected it and it is ready to be activated or acted upon by a command.

home page The first page of an individual, company, or organization on the World Wide Web.

host drive The uncompressed component of a compressed drive. The host contains uncompressed data space and one large hidden file that represents the compressed drive's contents.

HTML Hypertext Markup Language, the ASCII text language that describes the content and appearance of Web pages. HTML comprises tags that enable Web page designers to specify fonts, backgrounds, graphics placements, text alignment, and more on the pages they create for the World Wide Web.

icon A small picture that represents an object on the desktop, in a folder, or in a document.

inactive window An application window that is displayed while another window is active. The inactive window's title bar is displayed without highlighting.

Glossary

Internet A worldwide and ever-changing network of interconnected computer systems.

Internet Explorer Microsoft's Web browser.

IRQ Interrupt request line. Fifteen hardware lines that devices use to signal the microprocessor that a device needs attention.

J

Java A programming language extremely popular for applications developed for the World Wide Web.

K

kernel The innermost part of an operating system.

L

LAN *See* local area network.

legacy application An application developed to run under an earlier operating system, typically MS-DOS or Windows 3.1.

links Users move among pages of information on the World Wide Web by clicking links on the page. A link can be text, graphics, a button, or a sound object — the user is taken to the page to which the item is linked when he or she clicks the link.

list box A text box in a dialog box that contains a list of selections. You can select and choose one of the items. If the list is longer than the box, the box has a vertical scroll bar.

local area network A network of computers locally connected at a site.

local printer A printer that is connected directly to your computer.

M

mark Select a block of text or part of a picture to delete or to cut or copy to the Clipboard. *See also* select.

maximize Cause a window to occupy the entire screen.

MDI Multiple Document Interface. A type of application that displays more than one document in its workspace. Each document occupies its own document window.

menu A vertical list of commands from which you choose. A menu displays in its own window, which pops down from a menu bar or pops up in the area in which you press the right mouse button.

menu bar A horizontal display of menu names. The menu bar appears at the top of an application window under the title bar. When you select a menu name, its menu pops down.

Microsoft Outlook Express An e-mail and news-reading utility.

MIDI Musical Instrument Digital Interface. A serial protocol and message format that encodes musical instrument events.

minimize Reduce an application window to an icon.

modal dialog box A dialog box that captures the focus until it closes.

modeless dialog box A dialog box that permits other windows to take the focus before the dialog box closes.

modem Modulator-demodulator. A device that connects the serial port of a computer to a telephone line. The modem dials the number of another computer that has a compatible modem. Each computer's modem translates the computer's transmitted serial digital data stream into modulated tones suitable for transmission on telephone voice-quality lines. The receiving computer's modem demodulates the tones into an input serial digital data stream.

MS-DOS The operating system under which the PC operates. Windows 98 integrates a graphical user interface with MS-DOS.

MS-DOS application A DOS program that Windows 98 runs in a DOS box.

MS-DOS mode A Windows 98 operating mode that uses a command-line user interface only.

multimedia A type of application that uses combinations of several computer media — sound effects, music, graphics, video, and so on. The operating system components that support multimedia applications.

multiple document *See* MDI.

N

NetMeeting A conferencing feature that enables you to have online meetings and view and share files, chat, and send and receive data.

NetShow 2.0 A feature that lets users listen to or watch broadcasts online.

network A configuration of computers connected by cables or telephone lines. The computers share resources among themselves.

network adapter The circuit board that connects a computer to a network. Cabling from the circuit board is strung to the circuit boards on other computers in the network.

network drive A logical drive letter in a local computer that is mapped to a shared drive or subdirectory in another computer in the network.

network printer A printer on a computer in a network; the network printer is shared by other computers.

OEM Original Equipment Manufacturer. A manufacturer who assembles a product (typically a computer) from hardware and software components obtained from other manufacturers.

OLE Object Linking and Embedding. A technique for sharing data between applications.

operating system The program that manages two interfaces — the interface between the user and the applications and the interface between the applications and the computer's devices and files.

option buttons *See* radio buttons.

original equipment manufacturer *See* OEM.

parameter A value that controls or affects the operation of an application and that appears on the application's command line following the application's executable filename.

paste To write a block of text or a picture from the Clipboard into an application.

Glossary

path The DOS path that leads from the root directory to the filename. Expressed as a string such as c:\windows\system\filename.

peer-to-peer network A network wherein the users share resources with one another rather than all sharing only the common resources of a server. *See also* server network.

Personal Web Server A Windows 98 feature that lets users publish personal Web sites.

picture element *See* pixel.

pixel Picture element. The smallest item of information in a graphics picture. A picture is made up of rows and columns of pixels, each one being a single dot of color.

Plug and Play A specification for hardware and drivers that enables the operating system to automatically recognize the presence or absence of devices and to configure its drivers accordingly without user intervention beyond the changing of the physical device.

point size The size assigned to the characters in a font.

preemptive multitasking An application operating mode wherein the operating system preempts the execution of applications to service the needs of other applications.

print queue A queue of jobs waiting to be printed.

properties The parameter settings assigned to a device, application, or Windows 98 component. The Control Panel manages most of the Windows 98 properties. Applications manage their own properties.

protected mode An operating mode for operating systems such as Windows 95, Windows 98, and Windows NT wherein the internal memory that a program owns is protected from inadvertent violation by other programs that are concurrently loaded and executing. *See also* real mode.

protocol The method by which the two ends of a network connection or communications link coordinate the connection. Protocols exist at several levels, from the hardware protocols that physically connect the two computers to the data protocols that the two computers use to synchronize the transfer of data files and perform error detection and correction.

radio buttons A set of two or more selections in a dialog box. Only one of the set may be selected at one time. The buttons are represented by small round circles. The selected radio button has a dark circle inside the button; the others are empty. Also called option buttons.

read-only file A disk file that has the read-only attribute set. Users can read the file, but they cannot modify or delete it.

real mode An operating mode for operating systems such as MS-DOS and Windows 3.1 wherein the internal memory that a program owns is unprotected from inadvertent violation by other programs that are concurrently loaded and executing. *See also* protected mode.

reboot To boot the computer from a running condition as opposed to a power-down condition.

Recycle Bin The repository for deleted objects. You can recover deleted objects by taking them out of the recycle bin.

Registry A set of initialization and configuration files Windows 98 uses to keep track of important system information.

right-click To press the mouse's right button. Windows 98 uses the right button to open context-sensitive menus. The context is based on the position of the mouse pointer.

right-click menu The menu that opens when you press the right mouse button. A right-click menu is not attached to the Start menu or to an application's menu bar.

root directory The top directory in the directory structure of a disk device.

S

safe mode A mode in which you boot Windows 98 so that it does not try to load any of its device drivers. You use safe mode to remove drivers that you suspect are crashing or otherwise compromising the system.

scroll bars Horizontal and vertical bars that appear on the bottom and right side of a window when its contents do not fit in the visible workspace.

sector A section of a disk track.

select To point to an item before choosing it for an action. Mark a block of text to move, copy, or delete, or for Clipboard activity.

serial port *See* communications port.

server A network computer that shares resources for other computers in the network to use. *See also* client.

server network A network organized into a file server and workstations. The workstations support users. The file server is often unattended. The users share files in and printers connected to the file server. *See also* peer-to-peer network.

shared resource A resource — printer, fax/modem, disk, post office — that a server computer shares with client computers.

shell The user interface command processor of an operating system.

shortcut An icon that represents an application, printer, or fax/modem. The shortcut is located somewhere other than the resource's residence.

shortcut key A designated keystroke to select a menu command or dialog control while the menu or dialog box has the focus. Shortcut keys are assigned from the label that identifies the command or control. The shortcut key is an underlined letter or digit in the label. Example: File.

sound card An adapter card that the computer uses to produce sound effects and music. You attach speakers or earphones to the sound card.

spin button A control consisting of a numeric text field and two opposite arrow buttons. Clicking and holding an arrow button increments or decrements the text field depending on which button you click.

Start button The button at the left end of the taskbar. Clicking the Start button opens the Start menu.

Start menu The top-level menu in Windows 98. It pops up when you click the Start button or press Ctrl+Esc.

Startup Disk A floppy disk that you can use to boot Windows 98 in MS-DOS mode from the A drive. Also called Emergency Startup Disk.

status bar A bar at the bottom of an application window. The status bar typically displays one-line help notes about menus and menu selections. The status bar often contains buttons that display the current settings of the CapsLock and NumLock keys.

system file A file that has the system attribute set.

T

tab control A control that looks like the tabs in a notebook. Each tab is labeled and opens an associated page on the dialog box.

Task Scheduler A utility that monitors your system and runs system-maintenance utilities at the times you specify.

Glossary

taskbar The bar at the bottom of the Windows 98 desktop that contains the Start button, buttons for each of the desktop's open windows, and a button that displays the time of day and has icons that control some system resources.

tech support An organization within a software or hardware company that takes calls from users who have questions about or problems with the vendor's products.

text box A box in a dialog box into which you enter text data.

tiled windows Windows arranged so that each one is fully visible, their borders abutting each other. The windows are all the same size and shape. *See also* cascading windows.

title bar The top bar of a window where its title appears. When the window is active, the title bar is highlighted.

toggle command A menu command with two states: on and off. When the state is on, the menu command label displays a check mark. Toggle commands alter the application's behavior.

tool button A command button on a toolbar. A tool button usually has a tiny icon to represent its purpose and a corresponding menu selection.

tool tip A small yellow window that pops up when you place the mouse cursor over a tool button and leave it there for a moment. The tool tip contains a word or two to explain the purpose of the tool button. The tool tip window closes when you move the mouse cursor away from the tool button.

toolbar A collection of tool buttons for an application's commands.

track A ring of data storage on a disk medium. Disks are organized into concentric tracks.

U

uninstall Remove all traces of an operating system or application from the operating environment, retreating to the previous configuration.

UPS Uninterruptible power supply. A device that stores sufficient electrical energy to keep your PC running for 10 to 15 minutes following a power failure. The UPS sounds an alarm to alert you that it is now the PC's main A/C power source. The short time period reflects the UPS's battery capacity, and it is designed to supply enough emergency power to enable you to save your work and shut down the system.

URL An acronym for Universal Resource Locator, a URL is the Web name for the Web site's address. Microsoft's URL is http://www.microsoft.com/.

user interface The method by which the operating system and applications interact with the computer operator to receive and process commands and data entry.

W

wallpaper The bitmap pattern that displays on the desktop. People select wallpaper patterns to personalize their Windows 98 operating environment.

Web *See* World Wide Web.

Web browser A program that enables you to move among and view pages of information on the World Wide Web. Internet Explorer is the Web browser that is built into Windows 98.

wildcard A component in a filename to make it ambiguous so that a file selection function will find multiple matching files. Wildcards are asterisks and question marks.

window The basic unit of display for Windows 98 and all its applications. A rectangular area of the screen with a border and other common window elements. A window contains documents, icons, or other information meaningful to the computer user in the context in which the window is being displayed.

wizard A process that uses dialog boxes to lead you through a series of questions and answers. Wizards install things and gather complex but necessary information in order to complete tasks.

word wrap The ability of a text editor or word processor to automatically move the word and the cursor to the next line when the word you are typing goes past the right margin.

workgroup An organization of computers and computer users dedicated to a common mission. Workgroups are subsets of networks.

workspace The area in a document window where the application displays the document data and where the user makes changes.

World Wide Web A graphical means of displaying and navigating through information on the Internet. Web pages provide pages of data that can include multimedia effects like music, animation, photos, and more. Clicking a link on a Web page takes you to some other page.

Index

Index

INDEX

D

Index

encrypted viruses, 338
End Task button, 20
Entire Network icon, 18
Eraser tool, 218
errors. *See also* troubleshooting
    file transfers and, 292
    on disks, detection of, 303, 304–305
events log, for scheduled events, 170, 171
.EXE filename extension, 226
Exit command, 114, 224, 225

F

FAT 32 converter, 303
FAT 32 file system, disk compression with, 310–311
Favorites list, of Web sites, 246–247
fax software
    HyperTerminal conflict with, 290
    Imaging accessory, 214
    Windows 98 utility, 200, 214
file attachments, 262–265
    opening, 264, 265
    saving, 264, 265
    sending, 262–263
File Cleaner, 344, 345
file compression, for e-mail messages, 262
file formats
    for Imaging, 219
    for Paint, 218, 219
    sound quality and, 184
file maintenance, advanced, 50
File menu, 108, 114, 140
file size
    checking, 36
    of file attachments to e-mail messages, 264
file system errors, 304
file transfer protocol, 292

file transfers
    downloadable advanced software for, 290
    with HyperTerminal, 292–295
file utilities, online source for, 150
file viruses, 338
filename extensions
    .AVI, 175, 178
    .awd, 214
    .BAT, 226
    .bmp, 214, 218
    .CLP, 204
    .COM, 226
    .EXE, 226
    .FND, 156
    .gif, 218
    meanings of, 120, 156
    .MID, 175
    MS-DOS, 226
    .RMI, 176
    .tif, 214
    .TXT, 206
    .WAV, 86, 176, 184
filenames, long, problems with finding files due to, 148–150, 151
files
    back up, comparing to originals, 314
    backing up. *See* backing up
    caution in deleting, 344
    checking sizes and dates of, 36
    copying, 32–33
    deleting, 46, 48, 52. *See also* Recycle Bin
    duplicate, 32
    finding. *See* finding files
    fragmented, rearranging, 303, 306–307
    Imaging, size of, 214
    moving, 32–33, 344
    multimedia. *See* multimedia
    on floppy disks, deleting, 48, 312
    printing list of, 344
    printing to, 142–143

Index

H

hard disk, for backups, 314
hardware. *See also* specific hardware
    adding, 92–93
    detecting problems with, 322–323
    drivers for. *See* drivers
    legacy, 322
    multimedia, list of, 182
    plug and play method for, 322
    removing, 322
    troubleshooting, 322–323
    uninstalling, Registry and, 328
hearing restrictions, accessibility options for. *See* accessibility options
Help button, 112
Help menu, 108
help system, 22–23
    context-sensitive help and, 22
    for earlier versions of Windows, 22
    in MS-DOS, 226, 227
    online support information and, 22
hidden files, Windows Explorer display of, 34, 35
hiding
    of annotations in images, 216
    of taskbar, 72, 73
    of Windows Explorer toolbar, 40
high-contrast color schemes, 62, 90, 91
home pages, 237
    default, for your computer, 240
horizontal scroll bar, 110
host drive, for compressed drive, 310
hotkey combinations, for menus, 108
HyperACCESS, trial version of, 290
HyperTerminal, 286–297
    answering calls with, 290–291
    capturing session records and, 296–297
    downloadable upgrade for, 288
    opening new connections with, 288–289
    sending and receiving files with, 292–295
Hypertext Markup Language (HTML), 38
    for e-mail messages including pictures, 262

I

icons, 5, 8–9. *See also* specific icons
    adding to Quick Launch toolbar, 14, 15
    adding to system tray, 16
    aligning, 8, 9, 74
    creating, 102
    for file attachments, 264
    in My Computer, 10, 11
    moving, 9
    removing from Quick Launch toolbar, 14, 15
    restoring, 102
    saving searches and, 156
    shortcut, 8
    viewing descriptions of, 11, 13
    with arrows, 8
IDG Web site, 122
Idle Time section, 168
images. *See* graphics; Imaging accessory; Paint
Imaging accessory, 214–217
    annotating images using, 216, 217
    file formats for, 214
    printing using, 217
    scanning images into, 214, 215
    sharing images with paint and, 219
Inbox folder, in Outlook Express, 258
Index tab, in help system, 23
input, alternative options for, 90
input/output (I/O) addresses, 322
insertion point, moving in WordPad, 208

Index

M

Mac OS, problems with programs ported from, 124
macro viruses, 338
Magnifier tool, 218
mail servers, 256
    troubleshooting problems with, 260
main button toolbar, 40
Maintenance Wizard, 320–321, 335, 344
margin settings
    in Notepad, 206
    in WordPad, 208
McAfee VirusScan, 335, 338–339
measurement unit, default, for WordPad, 212, 213
Media Player, 182–183
    default playback device for, 192
memory. *See also* disk space
    for playing sound files, 182
    in MS-DOS mode, 228, 229
memory addresses, 322
memory-resident programs, 338
menus, 108–109. *See also* specific menus
    backing out of, 108
    cascaded, 6, 7
    context (right-click), 5
    for Active Desktop items, 68
    shortcut, 9
    submenus, 6
messages. *See* e-mail; newsgroups
Microsoft, controversy regarding Internet Explorer and, 374–375
Microsoft Fax, 200, 214
The Microsoft Sound, 86
.MID filename extension, 175
MIDI Sequencer selection, 182
MIDI sounds, 175, 176, 182

MIDI tab, of Multimedia Properties dialog box, 194, 195
minus (-) icons, 30, 31
mobility restrictions, accessibility options for. *See* accessibility options
modal dialog boxes, 112
modeless dialog boxes, 112
modem status icon, 16
monitors. *See also* screen entries
    accessibility options for, 90, 91
    energy-saving features of, 64
    refreshing screen and, 18, 38
    resolution of, 70–71
More Options tab, in Disk Cleanup dialog box, 308
mouse
    accessibility options for, 90, 91
    clicking on icons and, 8
    configuring, 82–83
    in MS-DOS mode, 230
    left-handed use of, 6
    pointer trails with, 82, 83
    selecting text using, 126–127
    single-click, changing to, 80–81
    three-button, 80
Mouse properties dialog box, 82, 83
mouse speed, 83
mouse techniques, 5. *See also* drag-and-drop technique
mouse wheel, 110
MouseKeys, 90, 91
moving. *See also* navigating
    of data between documents, 128–131
    of files, 32–33, 344
    of insertion point in WordPad, 208
    of Internet Explorer Channel Bar, 248
    of Start button, 6
    of taskbar, 72, 73
Msd.exe, 228, 229
MS-DOS, 222–231

N

Index

O

objects, inserting into WordPad documents, 210, 211
online support information, 22
opening
    of documents, 120–123
    of file attachments, 264, 265
    of folders, 30, 31
    of items in applications in which they were
        created, 13
    of MS-DOS window, 224, 225
    of programs, 30, 31
    of two document windows at same time, 130
Organic Art Screensaver, 335
Organize Favorites dialog box, 246, 247
Outbox folder, in Outlook Express, 258
Outlook Express, 256–269. *See also* e-mail; newsgroups
Outlook Express button, 14
Outlook Express icon, 8
overall preferences, for WordPad documents, 212, 213

P

Page Setup command, 140
Page Setup dialog box, 140, 141
pages, moving between, 110, 111
Paint, 199, 218–219
    sharing images with Imaging and, 219
Paint & Color Effects menu, 346, 347
paper orientation, 137, 141
paper size, 137, 141
passwords, 65
    network security and, 276
    with Dial-Up Server, 282
Paste command, 128, 129
path, 226

Pattern Editor dialog box, 61
Pause command, in HyperTerminal, 296, 297
pausing Task Scheduler, 170, 171
Pencil tool, 218
PF.bat file, for printing to file, 142, 143
phone lines
    for e-mail, 260
    for Internet connections, 238
    noise on, 260
photos
    copying to CD-ROMs, 346
    editing, 346–347
physical errors, on disks, 304
Pick Color tool, 218
Picture It! Express, 335, 346–347
Pixel to pixel option, in Print dialog box, 217
pixels, 60, 70
plain text format, 210
Play button, in Sound Recorder, 187
Plug and Play standard, 92, 322
Plus! 98, 334–349
    Deluxe CD Player and, 335, 340–341
    desktop themes of, 335, 342–343
    games included in, 335, 348–349
    installing, 336–337
    McAfee VirusScan and, 335, 338–339
    Picture It! Express and, 335, 346–347
    utilities features of, 335, 344–345
plus (+) icons, 30, 31
Plus! upgrade, CD Player and, 180
pointer trails, 82, 83
ported programs, problems with, 124
ports
    printer, adding, 280
    USB, 92
Power Management Properties dialog box, 64, 65
Power Management settings, 168
powering down, 114
Print dialog box, 136, 140, 141, 143, 217
Print Preview command, 140

INDEX

INDEX

Index